MORTAL SINS

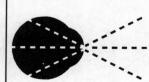

This Large Print Book carries the
Seal of Approval of N.A.V.H.

MORTAL SINS

SEX, CRIME, AND THE
ERA OF CATHOLIC SCANDAL

MICHAEL D'ANTONIO

THORNDIKE PRESS
A part of Gale, Cengage Learning

GALE
CENGAGE Learning®

Detroit • New York • San Francisco • New Haven, Conn • Waterville, Maine • London

GALE
CENGAGE Learning·

LIBRARY OF CONGRESS CATALOGING-IN-PUBLICATION DATA

D'Antonio, Michael.
  Mortal sins : sex, crime, and the era of Catholic scandal / by Michael
D'Antonio. — Large Print edition.
    pages cm. — (Thorndike Press large print nonfiction)
  Includes bibliographical references.
  ISBN-13: 978-1-4104-6154-4 (hardcover)
  ISBN-10: 1-4104-6154-8 (hardcover)
  1. Child sexual abuse by clergy. 2. Catholic Church—Clergy—Sexual
behavior. 3. Catholic Church—Discipline. 4. Catholic Church—United States.
5. Large type books. I. Title.
  BX1912.9.D365 2013b
  261.8'327208828273—dc23   2013016097

Published in 2013 by arrangement with St. Martin's Press, LLC

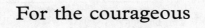

For the courageous

CONTENTS

7

8

INTRODUCTION

On the morning of September 20, 1870, fifty thousand troops massed outside Rome to engage the Pope's army and complete the unification of modern Italy. The defeat of the Vatican's force was inevitable, but Pope Pius IX had rejected negotiations. Preferring to be conquered, and thereby retain some small claim to sovereignty, he had ordered his officers to mount a defense. The Italians, who had moved slowly in order to give Pius a graceful way out, began firing at sunrise. Cannon shots whistled over buildings and rattled windows as they hit mortar and brick. Smoke and dust filled the air. Debris fell on city streets and red tile rooftops.

Three hours after the bombardment began, shells breached the wall near Porta Pia gate and elite fighters from the Bersaglieri corps raced through. Dressed in dark blue blouses and broad-brimmed hats, these foot soldiers from Piedmont were followed by a small contingent of cavalry. Inside the wall, the

9

invaders broke past a line of pine trees and came under fire. After a few intense skirmishes, white flags of surrender were raised atop the basilica of St. Peter and other church buildings. When the bodies were counted, officials determined that the Pope's symbolic gesture had cost the lives of sixty-eight men. Nineteen of the dead were his own guards.

After the Vatican's surrender, celebrating Romans poured out of their shuttered homes. The American flag, chosen as a symbol of democracy, fluttered from windows across the city. Dozens of them hung in the Piazza di Spagna alone. People in the streets held small paper signs printed with the word "Si" to show their support for an upcoming vote on a new system of government.

For nationalists, September 20 would forever mark Rome's liberation. For the Church it ended more than a thousand years of rule over a territory that once encompassed a third of the Italian peninsula. During this time the Roman Catholic Church had exercised governmental power in every imaginable form. Popes had fielded armies, levied taxes, negotiated treaties, and formed alliances. With Victor Emmanuel II's conquest of Rome, these tools of state evaporated.

Pius, who was the last pope born in the 1700s, had been preparing for this day ever since his elevation in 1846. For more than a decade he had supported a conservative "ultramontanist" movement that had consolidated religious power in the papacy, quashed theological debate, and punished liberals. Months before the bombardment at Porta Pia, the First Vatican Council of bishops formally granted Pius a new form of authority: infallibility. This doctrine holds that under certain circumstances the Pope may define the dogma of the Church in a way that must be obeyed by all members and cannot be changed. These declarations need not be ratified and they establish irrevocable positions on matters of faith and morality.

Nearly sixty years would pass before the Vatican's civil status would be resolved by a concordat signed by Italian prime minister Benito Mussolini and Cardinal Pietro Gasparri, Vatican secretary of state. Under the terms, the Vatican would be required to maintain political neutrality and could not develop a true military force. It would, however, gain legal independence and the right to practice diplomacy around the world through a governing authority called the Holy See. Thus, Catholicism became the only religion in the world with the status of a country, ruled by a churchman who was also a monarch.

Combined with infallibility, the special position of the Catholic state allowed the Pope to become a unique player on the world stage. For generations the influence of the

Church grew as it presented steadfast absolutes as an alternative to secular turmoil and change. It was a state based not on the power of its industry or military but on its claim to moral superiority. The Pope defined good and evil and his preferences, whether they pertained to world affairs or the most intimate and vulnerable aspects of human life — sexuality, childrearing, faith — were promoted by a legion of priests operating in the most far-flung and responsive network on the face of the Earth.

In much of Western Europe the Church also functioned as an adjunct to government, supplying education, health care, and social services, often in exchange for tax dollars. In America it helped waves of immigrants adjust to life in a new land. Tightly controlled, the institution presented itself as a disciplined army in clerical fatigues. Its tough-mindedness found popular expression in the movie priests of the postwar era who were played by Spencer Tracy, Pat O'Brien, and other men with strong chins and confident strides.

Individually, clergy were assumed to be either humble role models or dynamic leaders who moved in the world without needing romantic love, sex, or family life. Collectively, ordination established them as a class above regular human beings. Within this class, the hierarchy enjoyed escalating status with the

12

Pope, at the very top, ruling with the authority granted by the Almighty. The main price paid for admission to this society was the vow of celibacy. This promise deprived the clergy of many of the deepest rewards of life, including sexual relationships and parenthood. But since they shared this sacrifice, clergymen were bound together by it in a way that made them more devoted to each other.

In the early 1960s the Church almost turned away from its rigid class structure and toward a more democratic model. The historic Second Vatican Council, called by Pope John XXIII, elevated the role of laypeople. Rituals were demystified as Latin was replaced by local languages. For a moment it appeared that bishops were going to be given a collegial role in the high-level affairs of the Church. At the height of Vatican II excitement, liberals hoped that the institution would recognize its lay members as equals of the clergy. However, John XXIII died before the end of the council and an antireform backlash quickly developed. His successor, Paul VI, disappointed reformers by publishing an encyclical letter called *Humanae Vitae,* which upheld an all-out ban on birth control in 1968. The document dashed the hopes of those who expected that laypeople might have more to say about church teachings, especially those on sex and morality.

After *Humanae Vitae,* conservatives defeated the democratic impulses expressed in the Second Vatican Council to guarantee the one-man rule of the Pope and assure that the priesthood continued to exclude women. At the same time, the political power of the Church reached its modern height under Pope John Paul II. The former cardinal of Krakow, Karol Józef Wojtyla was elevated in October 1978 and immediately showed the charisma and political savvy that would make him the model of modern authority. In his native Poland his operatives worked with the American government to funnel equipment, cash, and strategic advice to the banned Solidarity movement. This aid, and several wildly successful papal visits, led to the end of the communist state and the election of Solidarity's leader Lech Walesa as the country's first democratically chosen president. Solidarity's success was followed by the fall of all of Soviet-bloc communism.

During the battle against communism, all that the Church accomplished in geopolitics was based on its claim to moral power and its alliances with Western governments, especially the United States. But when victory came, with the end of European Communism, the common cause that superseded every other issue disappeared. In the vacuum, the Vatican and Washington disagreed on everything from family planning to affairs in the Middle East. And in the American public mind, accusations of sexual abuse of minors by clergy gradually became the worldly issue most associated with the Church and its hierarchy. The institution entered the most severe crisis since the Reformation, one that would burn for thirty years and still remain unresolved.

The shift from victory to scandal began with seemingly isolated charges of child rape and sexual molestation lodged against individual priests. Then, as media accounts prompted more victims to come forward, investigations by civil authorities showed that Church higher-ups had been aware of the problem, enabled criminal priests, and covered up thousands of rapes and sexual assaults. Scattered outbreaks of accusation became a firestorm that consumed huge portions of the Church's resources and reputation. The Vatican's claim to moral supremacy, the basis for all of its influence after the fall of Rome, became the standard by which it was judged and found wanting.

In the course of the continuous scandal, more than 6,100 priests were deemed by the Church itself to be "not implausibly" or "credibly" accused of sexual crimes against more than 16,000 underage victims in the United States alone. More than five hundred American priests were arrested and prosecuted. Of these, more than four hundred were convicted and imprisoned. As of 2012, the worldwide church had paid about $3 billion to settle civil suits, but countless claims remained unresolved. The financial burden, coupled with the flight of disillusioned members, forced the shutdown of nearly 1,400 parishes in the United States. Similar abuse crises erupted around the world, beginning first in Ireland, then spreading to the European continent and beyond. No agency within the Church or outside of it kept track of the number of cases, or the burden they imposed on Catholic institutions, but the public outrage and sense of betrayal were the same, everywhere.

The leaders of the institutional Church reacted to these crises with denial, defensiveness, dismay, and concern for both the victims and the future of Catholicism. The most assertive defenders of the hierarchy saw anti-Catholic bigotry at work in the press coverage of the crisis. Marginal figures within the institutional Church saw something worse. In 2010 retired bishop Giacomo Babini publicly blamed "the freemasons and the Jews" for the scandal and added that the Holocaust was actually "provoked by the Jews."

Days after Babini sparked outrage with his anti-Semitic rant, the Vatican issued a protocol for bishops to follow when handling sex abuse claims. John Paul II's successor, Pope

16

Benedict XVI, promised to take "effective measures" to protect children and described the crisis as "the greatest threat" to the Church in modern times. It was also a threat to the campaign begun by those who hoped John Paul II would be declared a saint. Cries of *santo subito*" — Italian for "saint now" — had echoed in St. Peter's Square when he died in 2005. The odds turned against John Paul II's immediate elevation as the world learned that he had promoted bishops accused of abuse and blocked an investigation of Austrian cardinal Hans Hermann Groer, who had been accused of sexually violating seminarians.

Before Benedict spoke, pollsters found that more than half of all Americans and 30 percent of practicing Catholics had an unfavorable opinion of the Church. In Germany, where the pope was born, less than a quarter of the people surveyed said they trusted him. In Austria, where Catholics can earmark tax dollars for the Church, more than 100,000 had cancelled such payments. In Ireland, that most Catholic of countries, 8,500 baptized members of the Church publicly renounced their religion in the first eight months of a campaign called Count Me Out. By 2011 the standing of the hierarchy was so low that the Republican leader of the New Hampshire House of Representatives publicly dismissed Bishop John J. McCormack of Manchester as a "pedophile pimp" who had "absolutely no moral credibility to lecture anyone."

Although Rep. D. J. Bettencourt's words were extreme, they highlighted a decline in the hierarchy's status that has been so broad and complete that one could almost imagine that it was caused by a highly organized, well-funded, and intentional campaign. Certainly many inside the institution saw things this way. At one time or another layman activists, bishops, cardinals, and even the popes have blamed the crisis on greedy lawyers, vindictive clergy abuse victims, power-mad advocate groups, and ego-driven journalists working in concert and motivated by hatred.

In fact the siege of the Church had been mainly an organic phenomenon, with individuals taking action when crimes were discovered and continuing to act as Church leaders failed to resolve their problems. This activity had been encouraged by attorneys and leaders of organizations that serve victims of pedophile priests. They acknowledged as much by referring to their efforts as a "movement," by sharing strategy and tactics, and by occasionally pooling their resources. To this extent, victims of pedophile priests and their supporters did create an organized and concerted attack on Rome. However, the emotion that energized the fighters was not hatred. They were, rather, inspired by anger over the crimes that had been committed, by empathy for victims, and by a fierce commitment to exposing the truth.

Truth-telling was the main tool employed by victims who feared their physical and psychological suffering were obscured by Church secrecy, confidentiality agreements, and euphemisms. Typical was a twenty-one-year-old rape victim named Megan Peterson, who demanded that the Church begin a sexual abuse safety campaign before she would settle her legal claim. She then spent much of 2011 and 2012 telling anyone who would listen about the priest who had raped her and how his repeated assaults had ruined her faith, burdened her with shame, and driven her to attempt suicide, all before she graduated high school.

In 2004 Peterson was a fourteen-year-old ninth-grader who was so devout she thought she might become a nun. She spent more time in church activities than any kid in her home town and made the parish the main focus of her life. She often stopped at Blessed Sacrament church to pray alone, in the quiet light that came through the stained glass windows. She counted the people she met there, especially the priests, as family. When the pastor offered to lend her a religious book she thought nothing of stopping at his office before going home from school. She trusted him so thoroughly that she didn't even flinch when he locked the door and joined her on a sofa. Then he began grabbing at her body and mumbling about how God wanted him and Megan to be together. This was okay, he said. It was alright.

Pressing his weight on her, Father forced Megan onto the floor, and began to pull off her clothes. Megan struggled against him, too shocked to speak. She thought about Father's pledge of celibacy and how wrong he was to push himself on her. She wondered if she had done something to provoke this. Then he had his pants open and was on top of her. His smell made her feel sick to her stomach and she found it hard to breathe. The speed and force he used to rape her shocked Megan into a dissociated state of mind. Now her body was there, but she wasn't truly present. Her consciousness drifted away from that room, floating into a state of detachment until he was finished. Then she scrambled away from him, pulled her clothes on, and fled.

Highly religious and socially isolated, Megan couldn't trust any adult with the truth of what happened to her. She was orally and vaginally raped several more times by the same pastor, who insisted he was acting out God's will. Although Megan surely felt anger, it was buried by shame and the childlike belief that somehow, *she was responsible* for the sin and violence Father had committed. Terrified that she would be blamed, she was afraid to tell anyone what had happened. To add to her fear, he threatened to kill members of her family if she reported his crimes.

Brutalized by a man she had once trusted, Megan Peterson fell into periods of deep depression that others interpreted as teenage moods. She tried to kill herself with pills and almost succeeded. She was admitted several times to a psychiatric clinic. Shamed, humiliated, and frightened, she struggled to attend school and barely received a high school diploma. When she finally revealed what had happened to her, many of her friends and members of her family abandoned her. She moved away from her rural home to a small city where she lived alone and tried to create an adult existence. The psychological injury she suffered continued to cause her anxiety, loneliness, and terror. Sometimes the pain was so intense that she could feel it, physically, as a hollow ache that filled her body and made it difficult for her to think, or act, or feel anything else. Days and weeks were lost to immobilizing depression.

"It cost me everything," she said of the violence she suffered as a child. "It has even put me in the position where I feel like I have to put parts of my life on hold so I can participate in this movement to get the truth out. I don't really have a choice about this. In all the time this has been going on, the Church has been unable to deal with it

21

honestly. That means it's up to me to do the right thing. I don't like it, but that's what it is."

As a victim/survivor, Peterson joined thousands who made their suffering public and used the courts and the power of shame to confront the Church. Almost thirty years had passed since the first abuse case gained widespread attention. In that time, Catholicism's all-male leadership caste responded erratically and inconsistently. At times priests, bishops, cardinals, and popes showed compassion for victims, but throughout the crisis they also resisted telling the whole truth about the crimes priests had committed against children and adolescents. Their failure caused the widespread decline of public respect for the Church, especially in developed industrial countries where popes have visited with great pomp and ceremony but did not act decisively. Those who support benevolent Catholic institutions such as hospitals, schools, and social programs, where the good works are done mainly by laypeople and nuns, fear that their practice of Christian faith through service to others is threatened by the legalism and defensiveness of a hierarchy more concerned with power and authority than morality and justice.

This book is the story of the tragedy caused by the sexual crimes of priests, the movement that coalesced around the pursuit of justice for victims, and the scandal of denial, cover-up, and indifference that continues to afflict Church leaders. As one priest observed during a public appearance of Pope Benedict in Austria, he is like a man who comes upon a burning house and focuses his attention on the pretty flowers in the front garden. The moral structure of the institutional Church has been burning for almost three decades. The question now is whether anything of value can still be saved.

1.
CLERICAL CULTURE

On a hot summer morning in 1984, the Vatican's ambassador to Washington arrived at his daily staff meeting — he called it "la congressa" — with an armful of files and letters. A trim, broad-shouldered sixty-two-year-old who played tennis several times a week, Cardinal Pio Laghi understood the importance of La Bella Figura (the beautiful figure). His tanned face practically glowed against his black jacket and white Roman collar, and he rarely showed signs of wilting in the Potomac swelter. His aides, who also dressed in priestly black, sometimes joked that the man had been born without sweat glands.

As Laghi took his place at the conference table he deftly separated the items he had brought and began distributing them like a card dealer working through a deck. With each envelope or folder the ambassador, who was born in Emiglia-Romagna, offered a bit of direction in slightly accented English. Let-

25

ters from American bishops, archbishops, and cardinals were to be given immediate attention. The same priority applied to communiqués from Rome, which came each day via sealed, diplomatic pouch. But staffers were free to handle other matters, like requests from laypeople and ordinary priests, as they saw fit.

Pope John Paul II's envoy, or *nuncio,* in America leaned on his aides to help him with a heavy portfolio. Besides minding the Holy See's relations with the most powerful nation in the world, Laghi had to keep an eye on Catholics in America, who were by far Rome's greatest source of both donations and headaches. On this morning the workload included a letter from Monsignor Henri Larroque of Lafayette, Louisiana, which noted a multimillion-dollar payment he had approved to settle lawsuits filed by the parents of several boys who had been sexually assaulted by a local priest named Gilbert Gauthe.

At la congressa, Laghi held the letter from Lafayette and fixed his gaze on his church law specialist, a thirty-nine-year-old American named Fr. Thomas Doyle. Laghi said that he had a sensitive problem that needed special attention. He explained the issue in brief and handed Doyle the letter from Frey with instructions to draft a reply and start a file on the case. No one said much about the crimes, the priest, or his victims. Everyone, including Doyle, just assumed he would handle the matter with efficiency and discretion. They then turned their attention to the next item on Laghi's agenda.

The calm and deliberate way that Laghi dealt with something as disturbing as the case of a pedophile priest reflected the self-confidence of a man who had risen to the top of a profession that required equanimity above all else. Tapped to be the Vatican's first full-fledged ambassador to America in 1984, when Washington normalized relations with the Holy See, Laghi had previously served in the Middle East and in Argentina at a time when the military terrorized civilians with kidnappings and murders. As thousands were "disappeared," to use the local term, the Pope's man in Buenos Aires played tennis with the generals. He didn't speak against them publicly until he was about to leave for America. Critics would see cowardice in Laghi's silence. Supporters would say he had kept open important channels of communication.

When Laghi arrived in Washington, the Reagan administration greeted him as a wise practitioner of realpolitik and a reliable ally, even if the Church occasionally edged toward Marx in its critique of capitalism and its concern for the world's poor. Among diplomats, his dual role as a religious figure and emissary of a foreign state made Laghi a

27

unique presence. Officials who saw his clerical collar automatically gave him the benefit of the doubt. Everyday Catholics considered his status as the Pope's man in America and assumed, correctly, he had a direct line to the Holy Father.

Insiders at the nunciature, which occupied an imposing and austere building on Washington's Embassy Row, marveled at how Laghi used his special status to advance Pope John Paul II's conservative agenda for the Church and to give the Vatican an outsized role in world affairs. This was especially true when William Casey, director of the Central Intelligence Agency, visited to sip cappuccino and exchange secret information. Special access to Casey and other top officials helped the tiny Vatican state punch well above its weight class in world affairs. In Latin America, for example, the institutional Church was widely viewed as a conduit to American power even where individual priests and bishops opposed U.S. policies.

With America as an ally, John Paul II — the skiing, hiking survivor of war and state repression — would become the most powerful political force in the history of the modern papacy. His popularity increased after he was nearly killed in an attempted assassination in 1981. (The gunman, Mehmet Ali Agca, was a Turk who may have been backed by the Soviet Union.) The Pope's popularity could be seen in the huge throngs that turned out for his many public appearances around the world. Wherever he went, he attracted record crowds.

Global politics, conducted by secret cable and during visits from the director of the CIA, made the Vatican embassy a plum posting for American priests with designs on power. When he was chosen to serve at the embassy Thomas Doyle moved onto the career fast track. Just thirty-seven at the time, Doyle held a bushel full of advanced degrees in everything from political science to administration. Doyle's appointment to the embassy staff signaled that he had both the right background and the proper conservative religious views (at least as far as he stated any) to eventually be named a bishop, archbishop, or even a cardinal.

Athletically built with dark hair and blue eyes, Doyle was also the kind of masculine and energetic fellow who represented the ideal priest as traditionalists imagined him. An amateur pilot, he thought nothing of renting a plane for an afternoon so he could track migrating whales in the Atlantic. His other hobbies revolved around firearms. A lifelong member of the National Rifle Association, Doyle collected all sorts of guns and enjoyed keeping them in proper condition with regular cleaning and oiling. Whenever he got the chance, he went out and shot targets for fun and relaxation.

Of course the aggressive streak that made Doyle a fan of the right to bear arms also made him skeptical in ways that could have given the hierarchy pause. Though a company man, he sometimes cringed at the royalist fervor shown by Catholics who treated the Pope as a kind of god-king and he was put off by the hypocrisy he saw in bishops who called on others for charity but lived in mansions and rode in limousines. Inside the nunciature, Doyle liked to joke about the dreary "Soviet-style furnishings" and the matching mood of lockstep obedience. However, he had made his peace with the institution because it was committed to saving individual souls from hell and the world from communism and he couldn't think of two more worthy missions.

The elements of service that came with a priest's life felt natural to Doyle and so far he had fit into it fairly well. After he was ordained in 1970 he worked in a parish in a Chicago suburb where he spent a lot of time trying to calm the anxieties of people who feared they "were going to get zapped by God" because they used birth control or harbored "impure" thoughts. Doyle quietly counseled them to follow their own consciences. This impulse to privately encourage people to think for themselves clashed with Doyle's respect of papal power and authority, but he didn't give this contradiction much thought. He believed — no, he *knew* — that almost every priest harbored inconsistent and even irreconcilable beliefs and they all just lived with the discomfort.

After his posting in Chicago and further education, Doyle landed at the embassy where he shared the serious sense of purpose everyone brought to work that seemed vastly more important than the duties of mere parish priests. His main job was vetting men who were being considered for promotion to bishop or archbishop. The Pope controlled this process and, like a president who can extend his influence by packing the Supreme Court, John Paul II was packing the American church with conservatives. In the process, he bypassed the favorites of the national bishops' conference and relied instead on references from personal allies, including Archbishops Bernard Law of Boston and John O'Connor of New York, and Bishop Anthony Bevilacqua of Pittsburgh. To the frustration of the more diverse conference of bishops, these bulldog traditionalists told Doyle whom to advance and whom to hold back.

The politicking that accompanied promotions made Doyle's everyday job a bit of a strain. He welcomed the occasional break from routine, like the letter from the bishop of Lafayette. Doyle wasn't entirely shocked by the case. In his years as a priest Doyle had learned that ordination didn't make anyone perfect. Clergy still got into all sorts of trouble. Alcoholism was common among priests, and many fell short of their vows to remain celibate. He had even heard rumors about priests and bishops with girlfriends, boyfriends, and children. In trusting him to handle such a sensitive matter, Laghi acknowledged that Doyle was a team player who would protect the Church. Doyle promptly wrote a reply to Frey confirming that the embassy had received his report. He then created a file for the case and waited to see what would happen next.

The world might never have heard much about Bishop Frey, Gilbert Gauthe, or Tom Doyle if all of the parents who complained about the priest's crimes had accepted payment and agreed to stay silent. But one couple did not go along. Glenn and Faye Gastal wanted the world to know that Fr. Gauthe had sexually assaulted their son and used threats to keep him quiet about it. The attacks, which took place in a church, a parish house, and other settings, included rape and began when the boy was just seven. He was so frightened and confused that he kept it secret.

The truth came out when Gauthe suddenly left town and parents of other victims began to talk about how the priest had manipulated dozens of boys into close relationships that quickly became violently abusive. (As one attorney would later describe it, Gauthe had engaged boys in "every sexual act you can imagine two males doing.") With his parents' reassurances and encouragement, Glenn and Faye Gastal's then nine-year-old son Scott spoke in detail about what had been done to him. A small boy with a soft voice, Scott described how Gauthe befriended him and made him feel appreciated as an altar boy. Like others, Scott often stayed overnight in the priest's house on weekends. It was there that Gauthe engaged him in play and then manipulated and coerced him into oral and anal sex. More rapes occurred in the ensuing year. Scott was most affected by the memory of Gauthe ejaculating in his mouth and forcing his erect penis into his rectum. Once he was injured so severely that he reported the bleeding to his parents, hours after the assault, and had to be treated at a hospital.

Scott was seven when he was first raped by Gauthe and the assaults continued for about a year as he remained one of the priest's altar boys. In this time he became a withdrawn and depressed boy who no longer liked to be hugged or kissed by his parents. Indeed, with every crime committed against his body, he suffered the profound psychological trauma that comes with being painfully and violently

33

sexualized by a grown man who was supposed to take care of him. The humiliation,
terror, and confusion Scott suffered wounded
him much more deeply than the physical assaults. They would also have more lasting effects, influencing how he felt about himself
and others. Sex, relationships, faith, and family would all become layered with pain for
many years to come.

As parents, the Gastals understood the
shame, guilt, and fear Gauthe had instilled in
their child and worried that other boys might
be harmed in the future if the public didn't
know about what had happened. They chose
a Cajun lawyer named J. Minos Simon to
raise the alarm.

Theatrically gifted and relentlessly aggressive, sixty-two-year-old Simon fancied white
suits and broad-brimmed hats and enjoyed
hunting alligators with a handgun. As a child
he had lived on the edge of a Louisiana
swamp in a house without indoor plumbing,
and he didn't speak much English outside of
school. Simon went to college after serving in
the U.S. Marine Corps and then graduated
from the law school at Louisiana State University.

After he passed the Louisiana bar, Simon
found he was shut out of a local legal establishment that was inclined toward quiet deals
that benefited the powerful and preserved the
status quo. Left to practice on his own, he

became famous with a suit against the governor that went all the way to the United States Supreme Court. There he won a ruling that limited the state's power to investigate labor unions. Confident in the extreme, Simon was a hero to fellow Cajuns like the Gastals and a nightmare for opposing counsel. He was so uncompromising and unpredictable that his letterhead was enough to jangle the nerves of anyone he targeted with a lawsuit. When Bishop Frey received notice that the Gastals wouldn't accept a settlement and Simon was suing the diocese on their behalf, he immediately dashed off another report to Washington.

On the day when Frey's update arrived at the embassy, Tom Doyle took it to Pio Laghi but saw that his boss didn't quite grasp the seriousness of the matter. In the ambassador's experience, *no one actually sued the Catholic Church* and problems like Gauthe's crimes were resolved in private. Doyle, who understood the limits of Catholic power in America, tried to explain how the case could become a big scandal.

"You don't understand," he said. "In America this can happen." Laghi still didn't seem to catch on. Too busy for a civics lesson, he told Doyle to contact the Lafayette Diocese, learn what he could, and report back.

Doyle's first call to Lafayette was answered

by a monsignor named Henri Alexandre Larroque, who was so matter-of-fact about the ghastly facts that Doyle wondered if there was something wrong with the man. In the days that followed he noted, with some shock, that besides the Gastal civil suit the Lafayette Diocese was implicated in a criminal case that would be brought against Fr. Gauthe by local prosecutors who believed he had assaulted several boys. (Among them were some who had settled unlitigated complaints against the diocese.) Neither Doyle nor anyone he consulted could recall a case in which a Catholic priest had been charged in criminal court with abusing many different children. For the Church the big danger in all this lay in the scandal that might emerge as lawyers used the legal process called "discovery" to pry documents out of diocesan files and to compel testimony, under oath, from priests, even bishops.

In late summer the press in Louisiana began reporting on the Gauthe cases. Doyle found himself dumbfounded by the way that Frey and Larroque handled things. Every time he spoke with them they minimized the extent of the problem and downplayed the risk faced by the Church. Worse was the almost flippant way Larroque spoke about the kids.

"By the way, what are you doing for the boys?" asked Doyle before ending one of his chats with Larroque. As Doyle would recall it, Larroque's response was succinct, if disappointing.

"As far as I know, nothing."

If Tom Doyle was taken aback by Larroque's casual attitude and his lack of interest in Gauthe's victims, he was alarmed by what he learned from Michael Peterson about the overall problem of pedophilia and the priesthood. Fr. Peterson, who ran a small mental health treatment center for clergy, was both a priest and a psychiatrist. These roles made him the obvious man for Doyle to consult about Gauthe. Conveniently, his clinic was located in a Washington suburb ten miles away from the Vatican embassy. Named the St. Luke Institute, Peterson's clergy treatment center was one of several that operated quietly across the country. By offering care only to ordained men, these clinics assured patients of their privacy and helped the Church to keep secret the extent of its problems with troubled priests. Few outside the circle of clergy and therapists even knew such institutions existed.

During their very first conversation Peterson told Doyle that in the past, priests and bishops with sexual problems were routinely diagnosed with depression, alcoholism, or some other, less stigmatizing problem. In therapy some of these men would eventually refer to sexual misconduct, but Peterson suspected that far more kept these behaviors secret. They preferred to say they were alcoholics, or even drug addicts. Anything to avoid being labeled a sexual deviant. Nevertheless he was seeing an increasing number of priests referred by their bishops after they had been directly accused of some sort of sexual impropriety or crime that could not be readily denied. As a priest, Peterson believed these men had betrayed their victims in profound ways. As a physician he was compelled by the challenge of finding a way to bring their behavior under control.

Peterson had first become interested in the persistent quality of sexual compulsions during a psychiatry residency when he met an exhibitionist who just couldn't stop exposing himself in public. To Peterson, the man's compulsion seemed to mirror many aspects of alcohol and drug addiction, which also seemed to overwhelm the human will. With this realization, he began to treat patients with sexual compulsions with many of the same techniques therapists used with clients who were dependent on drink or drugs. He adapted the "steps" of Alcoholics Anonymous, which begin with an individual's acknowledgment of his powerlessness, gathered patients for group meetings, and offered them intensive psychotherapy.

In the six years since Peterson had founded

St. Luke, addiction had become the subject of intense public and professional interest. A host of problems that had once been considered character flaws or simply bad habits were being redefined as disorders and people were addressing them with the same regimen that had long been deployed against drug and alcohol abuse. Food addiction, sex addiction, and even shopping addiction were creeping into the vernacular and turning up in popular magazines and on television shows.

At the St. Luke center, Peterson encouraged sex offenders to accept responsibility for what they had done but he couldn't help but notice that the atmosphere inside the closed world of priests — he called it the "clerical culture" — contributed significantly to their problems. With elevation a man gained a superior spiritual and practical status. Among the ordained this status created an all-for-one, one-for-all attitude similar to the code that is found among the officers in many police departments. Outside this subculture the Constitutional separation of church and state, as well as a general deference granted by everyone from cops to kindergarten teachers, protected priests from suspicion and accountability. In short, a priest could get away with a lot more than the average man.

Not surprisingly, the culture of sexual secrecy and the almost unattainable requirement of total celibacy made the priesthood attractive to some men who already had psychological or sexual difficulties and considered it a kind of shelter. Church officials knew this for certain long before the modern abuse crisis began. In 1969 Pope Paul VI consulted directly with Dutch psychiatrist Anna Terruwe, who had found a high rate of immaturity among Catholic priests and estimated that as many as 25 percent suffered from serious psychiatric illness. Terruwe and her American colleague Conrad Baars subsequently reported that "Priests in general — and some to an extreme degree — possess an insufficiently developed or distorted emotional life." Addressing America's bishops in 1971, Baars warned that some men joined the priesthood to "make amends for past sexual sins."

Baars, who emigrated to America after being freed from a Nazi concentration camp, was a pioneer in the study of emotional deprivation. In America, he found that many Catholics were emotionally deprived because they believed that feelings "were potentially harmful to one's life in and with Christ." Clergy were especially susceptible to this belief, according to Baars. "More often than not, a priest comes from a 'fine Catholic home,' a strict one with little emotional love." In seminary these men, who already suffered from a "maturity gap," were trained to function without an emotional life. "The consequences of this system," he concluded, "have been largely disastrous."

As he explained what he had learned from working with more than a thousand priests, Baars opened up a topic that was rarely considered in a direct way. Talk of alcoholism or loneliness among priests was common, but here was an expert who said that institutional Catholic culture, and the process for selecting and training clergy, produced a corps of men who were ill equipped to care for themselves, let alone serve others. The picture was bleak, especially since it was drawn by a specialist who was a committed Catholic who supported celibacy.

After Baars made his report the American bishops were so concerned about the priesthood that they commissioned their own study, which was completed in 1972. In *The Catholic Priest in the United States: Psychological Investigations* Eugene Kennedy and Victor Heckler noted that a large proportion of priests "do not relate deeply or closely to other people" and use the institution and their status as "cover-ups for psychological inadequacy." Their report described priests whose "growth had been arrested" and who "function at a pre-adolescent or adolescent level of psychosexual growth."

The phrasing used by Kennedy and Heckler echoed the terms used by experts who tried to explain why any adult man would seek sex with children. As Peterson explained to Doyle, many pedophile priests seemed, to him, to be like children themselves, except they enjoyed an adult status that gave them power and influence. Laypeople, who believed that men were called to priesthood by God, gave clergy the benefit of the doubt and generally assumed that they were extremely good and trustworthy people. Children who were victimized by priests stayed silent out of fear, respect for the collar, or because they had absorbed the shame-bound Catholic sexual sensibility.

The informal conspiracy of silence that protected pedophile priests was reinforced by more widespread ignorance and denial about sexual abuse. As recently as 1965, an authoritative medical guide suggested that most incidents of sexual abuse were extraordinary events for the perpetrators who rarely committed another offense. Among mental health professionals it was generally assumed that people who reported being abused as kids had confused dreams or fantasies with reality.

The modern notion that pedophilia was a rare occurrence was first challenged in 1953 when Alfred Kinsey reported that 25 percent of the women he surveyed said they had experienced sexual abuse in childhood. At first Kinsey's report didn't do much to change public perceptions. In the ensuing decades, however, feminist writers drew attention to the sexual abuse of children as they also addressed violence against women. In the same time new laws required doctors, teachers, and others to report signs of abuse and authorities saw a surge in referrals to police and child welfare agencies. In 1971 the American Humane Association noted 9,000 cases of sexual abuse of children in New York City. This report helped move professional opinion toward the gradual realization that the problem was far more common than previously believed.

Although experts, activists, and lawmakers began to change the ways the professions and public officials regarded child sexual abuse, the mass media played the lead role in shaping public perception about its traumatic effects. In 1976 the TV movie *Sybil* introduced millions of viewers to a character whose sexual trauma broke her psyche into a host of personalities. With Sally Field in the title role and Joanne Woodward cast as her psychiatrist, *Sybil* was a "based-on-a-true-story" work that would provoke enormous controversy and charges that it was a fabrication. However, the subject matter and Field's performance opened a national dialogue on the effects of child abuse. Similar themes subsequently appeared in a flurry of books and films, including *The Color Purple,* by Alice Walker, which won the 1983 Pulitzer Prize. A year later the

ABC network broadcast the film *Something About Amelia,* which revolved around incest.

While the media prompted public discussions, the academic study of abuse became a kind of growth industry as psychologists, psychiatrists, social workers, and others sought to gauge the size of the problem and understand its effect on individuals. University of New Hampshire sociologist David Finkelhor surveyed more than eight hundred students and found that 19 percent of females and 9 percent of males had experienced sexual abuse before age eighteen. Finkelhor's work was confirmed by others and by 1984 a subject that had once been taboo — sexual abuse — had become such a prominent issue that President Reagan noted it in his state of the union speech. "This year," he said, "we will intensify our drive against . . . horrible crimes like sexual abuse and family violence."

Just weeks after Reagan's speech, the press reported the shocking news that the staff at the McMartin preschool in Manhattan Beach, California, had been charged with more than two hundred counts of sexual abuse. Years of furor would pass before trials that produced no convictions. (Jurors who said they believed that some sort of abuse had occurred couldn't separate truthful statements made by children from fabrications created as adults coached them to reconstruct events.) But in the short term the case contributed to a sudden spike in public concern about child sex abuse. Between 1980 and 1990 officials would note a 300 percent rise in allegations. The overwhelming majority of these claims were judged to be well-founded.

No one who worked with children or in the mental health field failed to see the implications in changing attitudes about child abuse. At schools, day care centers, and other facilities staff rushed to create policies and procedures that would prevent a McMartin-like crisis. At St. Luke, Michael Peterson considered the number of pedophile priests he had begun to treat and the changing social landscape and knew that the Catholic Church faced almost certain disaster. Bishops were still handling complaints with apologies, promises that offenders would be disciplined, and transfers. Parishes receiving an accused priest weren't told why he had been reassigned, and feelings of shame typically guaranteed that victims and their families wouldn't tell. On occasions when parents hired lawyers, payments were made in exchange for secrecy agreements. Sometimes these pacts also required that the offending priest be kept away from parish duties, but often they returned to ministry.

Troubled clergy who wound up at St. Luke received round-the-clock attention in a private setting. Peterson once believed that pedophiles might be cured, or at least brought under control. This belief was consistent with the Christian concepts of forgiveness and redemption and conformed to the code that governed how ordained men — priests, bishops, cardinals, and even the popes — related to each other. As a matter of belief and practice, clergy expected extra privileges and consideration and protected the Church by closing ranks and keeping secrets. Indeed, upon their elevation bishops and cardinals usually took an oath to keep secret any information that might cause scandal.

An isolated set of problems in a small diocese like Lafayette would bring scandal to the Church, but as Doyle and Peterson considered the issue they realized that a much bigger crisis would arise if Catholic Church leaders didn't face the larger problem of sexually abusive priests squarely, and immediately.

In the fall of 1984 Doyle invited Peterson to visit the Vatican embassy for lunch so that he might spell things out for Laghi. He hoped that a little expert advice might move the ambassador to seek a shake-up in Lafayette and conduct a real review of the problem throughout the Church. When the moment arrived, however, Laghi was hosting some bishop friends from Latin America who drew almost all of his attention. As Doyle would recall, Peterson tried to get the ambassador's attention but with little success. Instead Laghi and his buddies gossiped in Spanish, English, and Italian about an endless number of topics, including how hard it was to find Latin American priests who would make good bishops. Too many of them had children.

Frustrated by Laghi's inattention, Doyle and Peterson were left to pray that bishops elsewhere handled things better than the crew in Lafayette, where Bishop Frey and his aides had covered up charges of abuse against a number of priests for many years and quietly placed known abusers into jobs where they would continue to have access to kids. As a clinician, Fr. Peterson believed that priests who were pedophiles would inevitably find and exploit new victims. Fr. Doyle, the canon lawyer and loyal church bureaucrat, worried about the potential for future scandal, lawsuits, and suffering. Of course neither of them could be at all certain of the true shape and size of the hidden crisis. Up to this point hardly anyone inside the Church bureaucracy would speak to them about the problem. Most of what they knew came from their own experience, scattered articles in the press, and confidential conversations with a most unexpected source: Gilbert Gauthe's lawyer.

2.
THE CHURCH KNOWS

When F. Raymond Mouton agreed to represent Fr. Gilbert Gauthe he had never dealt with any sort of sex crime. He was repulsed by the idea that adult men might rape children, and appalled by the effects such abuse could have on a youngster's development. However, he had defended people accused of murder and other serious offenses and he believed that everyone, even a priest who victimized little boys, deserved a vigorous defense. Also, he knew that the Catholic Church, which had agreed to receive his bills, would, as he said, "pay like a damn slot machine."

Mouton needed the cash flow to support a lifestyle that included a fleet of expensive cars and a lavishly furnished mansion — complete with pool, horses, maids and a guest house — on a large and lush estate. The property was a comfortable fit for Mouton, who came from Cajun aristocracy. His ancestors had founded Lafayette in the early nineteenth century. They had donated the land for the local cathedral and then built it. In his youth, Raymond played quarterback for Our Lady of Fatima High School. A scrambling, creative playmaker, he was so good that he scored every one of his team's points in one key game and kicked field goals to clinch several others. By the time he graduated he was the league's most valuable player and a legend in football-mad Louisiana. When he returned and hung his attorney's shingle, his football fame and the Mouton name brought clients to his door.

Although he could have immediately claimed a spot inside the clubby legal community that served local corporations and dealmakers, Mouton preferred to jostle and jab as a defense counsel and a plaintiff's lawyer. Thriving on controversy, he challenged the mayor of Lafayette on a host of political issues and tangled with the all-powerful local sheriff on behalf of a group of deputies. He represented an oil driller who had an affair with his boss's wife (the boss had shot him when he found out) and he had forced the state legislature to pay millions for a car crash that occurred at a highway construction site. Mouton even sued a judge to have him evicted from an office in a courthouse that was short on space for the public defender. The judge gave up without a fight.

In his love of legal combat Mouton was a

younger version of J. Minos Simon. And like
the old alligator hunter, Mouton lived a life
of considerable excess. He smoked and drank
enough for three ordinary men. He spent lavishly on himself and on others. And when a
big case was headed for trial, he poured
himself into the work as if the fate of the
world depended on the outcome. As the trial
date neared, he became obsessive and so
focused that everything else, including his
family, receded from his mind. Facts, arguments and strategies whirled in his head and
sometimes he worked around-the-clock for
days on end with little or no sleep.

Mouton deployed his full-court press early
in the Gauthe case, burying himself in the
sordid reports on his client's crimes and flying to Massachusetts, where the priest had
been hidden in a treatment center. There he
met a slightly built thirty-nine-year-old who
was so bland and well mannered that he
would have gone unnoticed in any crowd,
anywhere. Indeed, Fr. Gauthe was a man
distinguished only by his crimes, and these
were grotesque. In each case he began by
selecting a boy to victimize as he faced his
congregation on Sunday mornings. Once he
chose his targets he lavished them with attention and gradually talked them into a variety
of sex acts inside the Church sanctuary, in
his residence, and on outdoor outings. He
photographed them and in some cases per-

suaded boys to have sex with each other while he watched.

Fr. Gauthe didn't deny what he had done because he wanted the chance to explain that he too was a victim. He claimed to be under the influence of a dark psychological impulse — he called it a "sex monster" — which he was unable to control.

The sex monster offered Ray Mouton the glimmer of an insanity defense and leverage to seek a plea bargain. The attorney's goal became a deal that would spare the victims from testifying in court, and give his client some hope of freedom in his old age. As summer turned to fall Mouton grew confident about his strategy because Fr. Gauthe assured him he would say and do anything he asked to help him reach his objective. However, Mouton wasn't sure the Church would do the same.

From the very start of the case, Mouton found himself stonewalled by the people who were paying his bills. Fr. Gauthe's guilt might be mitigated if he could show that his superiors in the diocese failed to supervise him and other troubled priests. However, diocesan officials were fighting the civil suit brought by the Gastal family, and weren't eager to share any information with Mouton for fear that it might then wind up in Minos Simon's hands. Time and again Fr. Gauthe's lawyer requested documents or interviews with church officials, and time and again he was refused.

The frustration Mouton felt as he dealt with the diocese built up inside him until his wife Janis could no longer ignore it. Janis had been Mouton's best friend and closest adviser ever since they met in college and ran away to Mexico to get married. She thought about what her husband told her about the case and instinctively decided that the diocese must have a much bigger problem than her husband imagined.

"It's the only thing that makes sense," she told him. "The Church knows there's a nest of pedophiles."

Fortunately for Mouton, information flows in many directions, and from many sources. Even as the Church was stonewalling Fr. Gauthe's lawyer, Minos Simon received sensitive information from a source inside the diocese, about a secret archive, one separate from the regular records, that was kept under lock and key and could be accessed only by the highest officials in a diocese. He told Simon to ask for access to the "secret archive dossiers" on twenty-seven priests. In Fr. Gauthe's file was proof that his sexual interest in children was first known to the Church during his time in the seminary more than a decade before the Gastals came forward with their complaint. One church official had even opposed Fr. Gauthe's ordination, to no avail, on the basis of his "affinity" for young boys.

Simon used the files, which included reports on priests who had been picked up by police while soliciting sex from men, to link the abuse of minor boys to homosexuality in the priesthood. Since at least 1961, the Vatican had made a point of discouraging bishops from ordaining men who might be homosexual, because this orientation was considered sinful. However, over time the Church adjusted its theology to say that being gay is not sinful, but every homosexual act is an offense against God. This apparent softening was accompanied by a steady rise in the proportion of gay men in the priesthood. As church officials knew, the percentage of homosexuals in the priesthood was higher — by a factor of four or more — than that of the general population.

No study had ever found that homosexuals were more likely to abuse minors, but by the early 1980s several researchers, including Richard Sipe, were investigating the ways an exclusively male institution that discouraged all forms of sex actually attracted many men with psychological problems and then steered them toward secret, sometimes criminal sexual practices. A therapist and social scientist, Sipe was also a part-time lecturer in the department of psychiatry at Johns Hopkins Medical School. In time he would be recognized as a leading scholarly critic of the

Church. However, when he began his research in the 1960s he was still a Benedictine monk and priest, fully immersed in the life of the Church and committed to its culture.

Sipe's change of heart would grow out of thousands of therapy sessions and interviews with ordained men who had violated their vows and revealed to him the hidden realities of the clerical world. As a mental health professional, he was fascinated to discover and document new truths in a corner of humanity that was previously closed. But as a man who had committed his life to the Church, he experienced a slow-motion personal crisis that left him feeling isolated, and sometimes unmoored. These feelings increased as he realized that almost no one in the priesthood adhered to the rules of celibacy and that a powerful culture of secrecy and discipline allowed priests to get away with serious sexual crimes.

Of course as the sex abuse scandal evolved, traditionalists downplayed the effects of the church culture and returned again and again to the argument that the problem was not pedophilia but a matter of gay clergy seeking out partners who just happened to be legally underage. According to this analysis, the Church didn't have a sex abuse crisis, it had a problem with homosexual priests who preferred young partners.

In Louisiana of the 1980s, Simon's move

to link the Gastal lawsuit to gays in the priesthood — suggesting homosexuality was to blame — served his need to put the Church under greater pressure. To his mind, the presence of gay clergy was yet another sign of criminality in the Church. On the other side of this argument stood experts like Sipe. Noting that heterosexual and homosexual men abused minors at roughly the same rate, Sipe considered the issue of homosexuality a smoke screen. He said it was deployed by Church leaders to distract people from the fact that Catholic priests were using their status — they were, after all, especially close to God — to commit sex crimes, and their superiors were covering for them.

As Fr. Gauthe's attorney, Raymond Mouton didn't need to parse the finer points of what constitutes pedophilia or navigate the issue of homosexuality in the priesthood. He only needed to understand the content and context of Gilbert Gauthe's crimes. Given his client's own statements, the content was clear: he had committed every crime he was charged with, and more. However, the context remained occluded. At every turn Mouton saw signs that the diocese had covered up for Fr. Gauthe and many others. But, no one in the hierarchy would tell him the full story. Their refusal was all the more galling to Mouton because in taking up Fr. Gauthe's defense he had accepted a client he found repugnant and opened himself to ridicule and even death threats from locals. His wife and children had been subjected to similar abuse because, as people said, the head of the household was defending a "pervert," so that made him a pervert too.

Given the fact that an angry father in Baton Rouge had recently shot and killed a man charged with abusing his son — he did this in front of TV cameras, no less — Mouton reasonably feared for his own safety and the safety of his family. This kind of risk was not what he signed up for when he agreed to take on the case. Neither did he expect the effects that the case had on his own faith. A closet idealist, Mouton found himself hoping that just as Louisiana stands apart from the rest of the United States, the Lafayette Diocese might be different from the Church across America. Even people who loved Louisiana understood that the state tolerated more corruption and misbehavior than others. Huey Long didn't come from Vermont. This understanding of the state as an especially corrupt place gave Mouton hope that national and international church leaders would do the right thing when properly informed.

Ironically enough, it was one of the stonewalling church officials in Lafayette who put Mouton in touch with the men who would help crush his hopes for the larger church. Monsignor Larroque had urged Mouton to speak with Michael Peterson at the St. Luke Institute so he might learn more about the problems of priests and, presumably, develop a bit more compassion for Gilbert Gauthe. When Mouton called, Peterson invited him to Washington, but he warned Mouton that he wouldn't have much encouragement to offer. As perhaps the leading consultant for the Church on this problem, Peterson knew it was broad and deep and, in his experience, no one in authority was doing much to address it.

On a day in January 1985 when the press back home revealed that church officials had first heard allegations against Fr. Gauthe *ten years before* the Gastals complained, Raymond Mouton flew to Washington, rented a car, and traveled to the Maryland suburbs to begin his crash course in sexual deviance and church politics. At St. Luke's, Michael Peterson couldn't completely explain how sexual abusers came into being, although he noted that some were themselves abused as children, and that some showed signs of hormonal imbalance or neurological abnormalities. When it came to understanding the causes of this behavior, Peterson told Mouton the answer resided in a combination of nature and nurture.

Peterson could be more definitive when it came to the way men like Gilbert Gauthe operated as adults. Unlike the violent rapists many people imagine when they consider sex crimes, repeated studies had found that most pedophiles were charming and generous. They devote considerable time, energy, and even cash to building trust with their victims, and come to believe they are establishing real relationships with them. In this context, they convince themselves that children are equal participants in sexual acts and that they share in the responsibility for whatever occurs.

"They enjoyed it" and "I didn't hurt anyone" are familiar refrains that therapists hear from adults who have had sex with children. In the 1970s the idea that children could enjoy sex with adults fueled the rise of a small but vocal group of activists who sought to decriminalize and even de-stigmatize pedophilia on the grounds that it was harmless and perhaps even beneficial for them. At the extreme edges of this perspective stood groups like Vereniging Martijn in Holland, and the North American Man-Boy Love Association, which began advocating the legalization of pedophilia in 1978. In time the world would learn that Catholic priests were involved in both groups. One, a member of the Selesian order, would join Vereniging Martijn's board of directors.

Because he was in the business of treating them as a psychiatrist, and he felt some priestly empathy for most every sinner, Fr.

Peterson hoped that sexual offenders could be helped. This idea was supported by the occasional paper, published in an academic journal, reporting a therapist's apparent success using talk therapy, or hormones that suppressed the sex drive. It found more currency in interviews that certain experts granted to the popular press and in TV programs like a documentary aired by the Public Broadcasting System in 1984. Titled *The Child Molesters*, the film featured sex offenders at a special rehabilitation facility in New Jersey. *The Child Molesters* portrayed patients and professionals who seemed sincerely engaged in a promising program that would likely produce a cure. This thinking found some support from experts such as criminologist Donald West at the University of Cambridge who appeared in the film citing "practical and humanitarian reasons" for authorities to provide pedophiles with treatment instead rather than imprisoning them.

While films such as *The Child Molesters* and academics like Donald West would suggest pedophiles could be reformed, the best research at the time showed that no specific type or combination of therapies was definitively successful. Indeed, every time experts developed a theory on the causes of pedophilia, evidence arose to contradict the premise. Contrary to popular belief, pedophiles were not more likely to have been abused as children. They weren't disproportionately homosexual (although the vast majority *were* male) nor were they encouraged in their crimes by the use of pornography. Indeed, the most confounding thing about pedophiles was that they were so difficult to distinguish from the general population.

Mouton observed that the Church had taken the "good as new" perspective to heart. One of the chief proponents of this view was a doctor named Fred Berlin, who was Richard Sipe's colleague at Johns Hopkins. Berlin was one of many researchers who argued that with psychological treatment, many if not most sex offenders could get control over their compulsions. As then archbishop of Milwaukee Rembert Weakland would later recall, Berlin attended several national conferences of bishops in the 1980s and suggested that they refrain from dismissing priest offenders and rely on programs akin to the Twelve Steps of Alcoholics Anonymous to treat them.

"He gave us hope for them," said Weakland. "And told us we would do a better job with them than any outsiders. They would be more motivated to change if they stayed in the Church."

Berlin's advice appealed to ordained men who were already inclined to take care of each other. But Mouton couldn't grasp why any organization would tolerate repeated criminal behavior, especially crimes against children. Even if bishops considered only their own welfare and status, they should have thrown out the bad apples. When Mouton's questions about the institutional Church reached a point where Peterson was out of his depth, he suggested a little field trip to the District of Columbia to see Tom Doyle at the Dominican House of Studies. A graduate school of theology, the House of Studies occupied a sprawling, castle-like building set on the south side of Michigan Avenue, across from the Catholic University of America. Since it was run by Doyle's religious order, he was permitted to keep a small office there, safe from the eyes and ears of the staff at the Vatican Embassy.

Doyle met Peterson and Mouton at the front door of the Dominican House of Studies and asked them if they wanted to meet in the chapel or his office.

Mouton chose the office and Doyle brought them down a long corridor and then upstairs to a spare little room. In the course of several hours Doyle explained the way canon law and church practices applied to priests charged with abuse. In his view, bishops had the power to immediately suspend someone who was under suspicion and could bar him from acting as a priest while an investigation was conducted. In practice, however, bishops almost never acted decisively and it was extremely difficult for anyone to defrock — the term "laicize" was also used — a fully credentialed priest.

Considered an almost cruel and unusual punishment, laicization would happen only after investigations and arguments that could take a decade or longer. And even then, a priest found to have abused children could retain his priestly status because of a variety of loopholes. It was much easier, Doyle noted, for a bishop to send an accused priest to another parish, another part of the country, or another part of the world.

How often had abusive priests been shuffled around? Doyle, Mouton, and Peterson knew of more than two dozen instances, but no one was keeping a record of cases around the country. Fr. Gauthe, a lone abuser, had confessed to molesting dozens of boys. With more than 60,000 priests and sixty million Catholics in America alone, the possibilities were frightening.

As the only attorney in the room, Mouton couldn't help but reflect on the financial liability the Church faced if even a small percentage of priests had violated a man, woman, or child. If 2 percent were involved, that would mean 1,200 potential perpetrators and many times that many victims. If victims began bringing lawsuits, the settlements could easily run into the hundreds of millions of dollars or more. This burden would fall almost entirely on local dioceses, which serve as the financial backstop for local parishes. Typically organized as a series of corporations, dioceses manage most Church income while also paying the bills. Although their resources were substantial, with enough abuse settlements many could be pushed into bankruptcy.

However, it wasn't just the financial threat that troubled Mouton. He also worried about the damage done to everyone from child victims to families and the Church itself. He may not have been a frequent attendee at Mass, but he still loved the Church and, like Doyle, believed it could do important work in the world. However, if the institution was to pursue its worthy missions, it would have to be saved from itself.

The two priests agreed with Mouton and they settled on a plan to change the way the Church dealt with sexual abuse by priests. Together they would draft a report outlining the scope of the problem. Peterson would handle the medical issues. Mouton would address liability as well as civil and criminal law. Doyle would write on canon law and the Church's institutional response to the problem.

In the meantime Doyle received input from various members of the American hierarchy, including cardinals Bernard Law of Boston and John Krol of Philadelphia. He also urged Laghi to ask the Pope to appoint an outside bishop to go to Lafayette to look through files because he feared they held evidence of other victims. He suggested Bishop A. J. Quinn of Cleveland and prepared a report for the Pope to back up the recommendation. Cardinal Krol took it to Rome on a Sunday night. Quinn was appointed before the next Sunday.

Doyle chose Quinn because he had been trained as both a canon lawyer and a civil attorney and seemed to have the right temperament for the job. He had been pleased when Laghi made sure the Vatican dispatched the bishop to Louisiana. Perhaps, Doyle thought, the nuncio was waking up to the impending crisis.

With Laghi and Quinn encouraging them, Mouton, Doyle, and Peterson aimed to deliver something to the American bishops when they gathered for a conference at Collegeville, Minnesota, in the middle of June. Knowing church politics, Doyle and Peterson sought and received support from key hierarchs, including Philadelphia's Cardinal John Krol, Bishop William Levada of Los Angeles, and Cardinal Bernard Law of Boston. Law and Levada served on a committee that would likely take up the report. As winter turned to spring, the paper evolved into a primer on the problem of pedophile priests that warned of "a real, present danger." The three authors agreed that the Church should create a formal Crisis Control Team to manage cases as they arose and an official Policy and Planning Group to investigate what was going on and devise a long-term response.

Peterson, Mouton, and Doyle worked with the belief that they were racing against a gathering tidal wave of litigation as publicity about the Louisiana case would make victims and their families in other dioceses more likely to sue. Plaintiffs' lawyers, recognizing the deep pockets of the Church, would line up to take these cases and, even when the law went its way, the Church would pay a heavy price in negative publicity. Mouton had already been contacted by a New Orleans–based journalist named Jason Berry who was investigating the accusations against Fr. Gauthe. A hard-digging reporter with a bushy brown moustache and deceptively casual demeanor, Berry moved comfortably with people as varied as sharecroppers in the Mississippi Delta and political power brokers in Baton Rouge. His recent work had exposed toxic waste dumping and politically motivated audits by the Internal Revenue Service. As Mouton told his clients, a reporter who was willing to take on Gulf Coast chemical companies and the IRS wouldn't be deterred by stonewalling monsignors and bishops.

3.
SEXUAL INTELLECTUALS

A son of the Church, and of Louisiana, Jason Berry was perfectly suited to write the story of the sex abuse scandal in the Diocese of Lafayette. As a young man he had worn the crisp khaki uniform of New Orleans' Jesuit High School and continued his education with the Church's intellectual elite at Georgetown University in Washington, D.C. Berry had left the university with lots of contacts in the priesthood and a truly Jesuitical respect for the pursuit of knowledge. In this case he was able to work his own contacts, lawyers in Lafayette, and Minos Simon's secret inside source, whom he called "Chalice," to piece together a narrative that was a compelling tale, but also a blow to his own faith as a Catholic.

Before he heard about Gilbert Gauthe, Berry knew, in his soul, that the Catholic Church was a force for good in the world. In New Orleans the parochial schools were integrated long before anyone even thought about integrating the public system, and across the South priests and nuns had risked their lives in the wider cause of civil rights. As a youth he was uneasy with the white backlash he witnessed in otherwise genteel New Orleans. He would never forget, for example, the boy he saw bicycling in circles in the street chanting, in an almost hypnotic state:

All we want is
A clean white school
A clean white school
A clean white school
All we want . . .

In contrast with the bigotry in the street, Berry grew up with Catholic parents who taught him to reject racism and he attended peacefully integrated Catholic schools where his teachers talked about the evil of prejudice. Of course he had a few brushes with odd characters in the clergy. One priest at Jesuit High demonstrated what he'd like to do to lazy students by dipping a net into a fish tank, scooping out a guppy, and flushing it down the toilet. But he had dismissed these odd-balls as bit players in the comedy of life. Growing up in a place where adults put on costumes and danced in the streets at carnival, young Berry's outlook was one part irony to three parts optimism. He had to believe that everyone, from demagogue politicians to fish-flushing priests, had inside them more than a little goodness.

Fr. Gauthe became the exception that disproved the rule for Berry. The more he dug into the case, interviewing families of his victims and reviewing files and depositions, the more he realized that the man was devoid of empathy. Gauthe's entire life seemed to be built around winning the trust of parents so he could sexually violate their children. Even after he had been found out and the damage he caused was made clear, he showed little appreciation for the pain he had caused, and little remorse. Worse, he seemed to believe that he shared some sort of love with his victims.

Although he was disturbed by Fr. Gauthe's character and crimes, Berry was outraged by the way the priest's superiors neglected his victims and covered up his offenses. Here the source he named Chalice was indispensable, pointing him toward patterns of bureaucratic denial and secrecy he could not have seen on his own. In many ways the man functioned like the storied figure "Deep Throat" in Robert Woodward and Carl Bernstein's unraveling of the Watergate conspiracy that destroyed Richard Nixon's presidency. With the portrayal of their secret source in both the 1974 book and film about the reporters' work — both were called *All the President's Men* —

the principled individual who reveals important truths became a heroic icon in American culture. Ever since, reporters, lawyers, and others have sought Deep Throats to overcome secrecy, and outraged individuals who fear the consequences of speaking public have known there are ways to share what they know confidentially, and to great effect. Indeed, the model of Deep Throat made every cubicle-dwelling bureaucrat and disgruntled functionary a potential hero.

In Lafayette, Chalice told Berry that Fr. Gauthe wasn't the only credibly accused priest being sheltered by the diocese. And in the case of Fr. Gauthe, others had failed to act on evidence that should have moved them. Afraid their suspicions would be regarded as false accusations, nuns in one parish had kept silent as Fr. Gauthe made a habit of keeping boys overnight. A monsignor who heard parents complain that Fr. Gauthe made advances on their sons sent him for counseling, but then allowed him to take groups of boys on overnight trips. When pressed by superiors to explain how he could restrict the priest's access to boys in one moment and allow it in another he had answered, simply, "I am trained as a priest to forget sins."

Considering what he heard from Chalice and what he learned about pedophiles in general, Berry concluded that Fr. Gauthe had likely abused many more boys than he had said. (A social worker Berry interviewed said the number could easily exceed one hundred.) Because of the special status a priest enjoys — they are addressed as "father," after all — these crimes were as psychologically devastating as incest. However, the same status seemed to prevent the Church leaders from acting on complaints. The clergy considered themselves a type of family. They protected their own and projected to the world an image of perfection. As a comparison, Michael Peterson would eventually offer Berry the example of members of an Irish Catholic family who go to extraordinary lengths to project a public image of perfection and deny problems like alcoholism and domestic violence. Given the number of Irish names found in the ranks of the American Catholic clergy, the analogy fit.

With all that had been laid out for him by Chalice, plaintiffs, lawyers, and experts, Berry made himself into an authority on a subject that, months before, he would have considered beyond the pale. The notion that a Catholic diocese would be shot through with sexual scandals and cover-ups sounded to the reporter like the kind of stuff one might read in a conspiracy theorist's pamphlet. Historically, the worst of hateful attacks on the Church always included something about abusive sex and secrecy. However, Berry also knew that between depraved popes, the Inquisition, and inaction during the Holocaust, the Church had given its harshest critics ample ammunition over the years.

Of course, it's one thing to get the story and another to publish it. As Berry sought an outlet for his investigative article he met a somewhat queasy response. An editor at *The New York Times Magazine,* where some of his previous work had appeared, said she and her colleagues were interested in publishing something about child abuse, but not if it involved the Catholic Church. Editors at *The Nation* and *Rolling Stone,* hardly shy about taking on the powerful, couldn't imagine a way to publish the story and *Vanity Fair* didn't respond at all. Most surprising to Berry, the liberal *Mother Jones* magazine balked at the prospect of calling pedophile priests to account. Finally, Berry found welcome at the *Times of Acadiana,* a scrappy weekly newspaper that served Lafayette and surrounding towns. Editors at the *Times* said they would go all-in, risking the loyalty of readers and advertisers who might resent an exposé about pedophilia in the Church. Berry also struck a deal with the *National Catholic Reporter,* which would use a condensed version of his reports to reach an international audience with a package of more wide-ranging stories, after the paper in Lafayette got its exclusive.

By May 1985 Berry was deep into his research. He had seen much of the evidence gathered in the Gauthe case, and interviewed the Gastal family and officials in the Church. He also sought the most current thinking on pedophilia from experts like John Money of Johns Hopkins University and David Finklehor at the University of New Hampshire. Money, who treated sex offenders, did not dispute the intractability of pedophilia, which can last a lifetime, but he minimized its effects on children. Finklehor was far more concerned about the negative impact of a grown man's sexual advances on boys and girls that, like the pedophile's pathology, could also last a lifetime. These conversations left Berry thinking that church leaders faced a problem that was much tougher than they knew. As he shared some of what he was discovering with Ray Mouton, the lawyer agreed, and predicted that once the dam was broken by the *Times of Acadiana* and, in particular, the *National Catholic Reporter,* major media outlets would find the story irresistible.

"CBS news is going to be landing helicopters on their lawns," said Ray Mouton. "Maybe that'll make them realize they better get ahead of this thing."

Mouton wanted to scare the American

bishops into action and the helicopter warning, or something close to it, was going to be included in the report he was crafting with Peterson and Doyle. Mouton was sure that a cascade of media reports would follow Berry's exposés and the publicity would begin a cycle of lawsuits, scandal, and negative press that might whirl around the country and well into the future, draining the Church of its resources and reputation. As someone still inclined to call himself Catholic, he dreaded this prospect.

Two weeks before Berry's series was to be published, Doyle and Mouton met in a Chicago hotel to finish drafting their report, which would incorporate pages sent to them by Peterson. Before they started, Mouton turned to Doyle and told him that the document they were about to draft would either save the Church or end any hopes he might have for a successful career.

"You've got the most to lose," he told Doyle, who had a bright future in the Church bureaucracy.

"Screw it," said Doyle. "Let's get to work."

The men hired a typist who worked for the Chicago Symphony but freelanced on weekends. She borrowed a typewriter from the symphony office and brought it to the hotel where she pounded on the keyboard to record the final draft of the memo. Doyle and Mouton began by counting up all the cases they had unearthed in one fashion or another, and realized they knew of at least thirty instances where priests had been credibly accused of sexually molesting children. Extrapolating from Lafayette, where more than $4 million had already been paid to hush up complaints, they estimated the American church faced more than $1 billion in liability.

Beyond the monetary damage, bishops were confronted by the prospect of being subjected to depositions, subpoenas for sensitive documents, and even police raids on chancery offices. They could expect this onslaught because they, and ultimately the Pope, were responsible for the priests who served under them. Doyle and Mouton would also warn that victims of priest offenders, their families, and the Church as a whole would be spiritually demoralized by these scandals while the press would "portray the Church as hypocritical, as an organization preaching morality and providing sanctuary to perverts."

The recommendations that flowed from the long list of problems in the report revolved around a few basic principles. The Church should provide counseling and other services to victims and their families. Offenders, who faced possible criminal consequences, should be suspended from their duties immediately. After a psychiatric evaluation the only viable treatment would be at in-patient facilities where they could be safely confined while receiving a range of services. However, the authors could say nothing conclusive about if, and when, an abusing priest might return to work.

Where the Catholic community and wider public were concerned, Mouton and Doyle saw that the Church needed to face the problem of clergy abuse squarely. They wrote:

The Church must remain open and avoid the appearance of being under siege or drawn into battle. All tired and worn policies utilized by bureaucracies must be avoided and cliches such as "no comment" must be cast away. In this sophisticated society a media policy of silence implies either necessary secrecy or cover-up.

Once they had drafted eighty pages of assessment, analysis, and recommendations the men decided to propose a sweeping, national response to the looming crisis. At its core would be a three-person "crisis control team" comprised of a canon law expert, a psychiatrist, and a lawyer — individuals identical to Mouton, Peterson, and Doyle — who would develop a standardized approach to allegations so that every Catholic institution would follow the same procedure. This crisis group could deliver a level of expertise beyond what most smaller dioceses, like Lafayette, might be able to deploy. As outsiders they could claim a higher level of credibility than local officials facing parishioners angered by discovering that priests had committed crimes and/or violated their vows and that they had been enabled and protected by their superiors.

As the typist clacked through the last pages of the report, Fr. Doyle left Chicago for Montreal where he was going to perform a first communion mass for a niece. Mouton stayed behind to copy and send the document to the bishops who had expressed their support and could present it at Collegeville.

The paper, titled *The Problem of Sexual Molestation by Roman Catholic Clergy,* was both a withering evaluation and a cautionary forecast. It also offered the American bishops a way to respond to the sex abuse problem with a Christian spirit. The authors believed they were offering the bishops a lifeline. And at least one agreed. Bishop William Levada of Los Angeles, who was a rising star in the American Church, encouraged them to move forward. Doyle would recall that he also agreed that it should be distributed at an upcoming conference of bishops to be held in Collegeville, Minnesota.

"He admitted it was a big issue," said Doyle, years later. "He also said something like, 'Thank God we don't have any of these problems in Los Angeles.' "

Levada's enthusiasm for the work done by Doyle, Peterson, and Mouton was short-lived. Before the Collegeville meeting he called Doyle to say the report would not be presented. Levada's about-face troubled Doyle, who believed that the Church faced a true emergency. But in an institution defined by intrigue and secrecy he would never get a full explanation of what happened to derail his campaign. Left to guess, he wondered if Monsignor Daniel Hoye, executive director of the bishops' conference, had sabotaged him.

Doyle knew that Hoye had resented his involvement in the selection of bishops candidates. (Hoye had made his displeasure known to others.) However, Doyle also had to consider that bishops coveted the authority they wielded in their dioceses. If the Pope was a king, they were like dukes who enjoyed, in every sense of the word, unassailable authority within their estates. Few would welcome outsiders promising to solve a difficult problem. Finally, it seemed to some, that Doyle was devising an employment project for his little group. They asked why the Catholic Church should pour millions of dollars into an operation that duplicated functions already carried out by local officials and their attorneys.

The Roman Catholic Church had weathered storms in the past and bishops who knew this history couldn't believe that a little bad publicity, even if it related to the sexual crimes of priests, would have much effect. This wasn't Watergate circa 1972, and they weren't elected officials subject to public opinion.

Jason Berry's series on Gilbert Gauthe finally appeared in the *Times of Acadiana* at the end of May 1985. A week later the *National Catholic Reporter* presented his reporting and expanded it with references to fifteen similar cases around the country. The *NCR* special report included an article on a victim who had committed suicide. However, it did not trigger an immediate response by mainstream media. Indeed, even in the cities where *NCR* identified priests who had been charged, such as Bishop Levada's Los Angeles, the local press did not take up the issue.

At Collegeville, the bishops heard a presentation on sexual abuse offered by a psychologist who worked with the Archdiocese of Chicago, a canon lawyer, and the counsel to the National Conference of Catholic Bishops. These three men occupied positions similar to Doyle, Mouton, and Peterson, but they were not equally versed in the nature and scope of the problem. After this private session the bishops focused on a "pastoral letter" that would call on American Catholics to support the poor and work against poverty.

Two years before, a letter supporting nuclear disarmament had succeeded in provoking a national debate and caused many Catholics to reconsider their views. This achievement had made the bishops more visible in the public square and they liked the attention.

The group drafting the letter on poverty was led by Archbishop Weakland. In the complex political landscape of the Catholic Church, Weakland was a liberal who, since the ascension of John Paul II, stood on the losing side of every argument about celibacy, marriage for priests, the status of women, and papal authority. However, he was useful to his more conservative brother bishops when it came to social issues like poverty. Weakland and his letter gave his traditionalist peers a way to appear compassionate and even radical in the pursuit of justice for the poor. For this reason New York's Archbishop John O'Connor, one of the Pope's favorites, seemed to enjoy rebuking pro-business laymen as he claimed for the conference the role of "worrying" the consciences of Catholics. Of course he played this role while living in a mansion, and being attended by paid helpers whenever he needed them.

Although they considered the issue in private, the bishops chose to stay silent on the Gauthe case and the general problem of sexual abuse by priests. When Laghi returned to Washington he bumped into Doyle in the hallway at the embassy and asked, "Why weren't you there, Tom? They needed you." Doyle, who understood that the bishops set their own agenda, agreed.

Two weeks after the bishops finished their work in Collegeville, *Time* magazine suddenly made Gilbert Gauthe and the "painful secrets" revealed by Jason Berry national news. *Time*'s article signaled to the rest of the media that the story was fair game. The year to come would see an uptick in the number of articles published on priest offenders from coast to coast.

In Lafayette, district attorney Nathan Stanbury intended to put Gilbert Gauthe in prison for the rest of his life. He found support among local Catholics as he rebuffed Ray Mouton's efforts to achieve a plea bargain based on the idea that Fr. Gauthe was mentally ill and therefore less than fully responsible for his actions. Mouton couldn't be sure that an expert witness would testify that his client was insane at the time when he abused his victims. Michael Peterson, who had evaluated Fr. Gauthe, considered the man's utter lack of empathy for his victims and concluded he was a sociopath. By definition sociopaths are profoundly disordered, and often dangerous, but not insane.

A week before the trial was to start, Mouton changed his approach. He asked Stanbury if he wouldn't want to spare the victims and their parents the pain of testifying in public. One of the boys was just six years old. "I'll put 'em all on the witness stand," promised Mouton. "It won't be pretty."

Nathan Stanbury could not be sure that a jury would turn away the insanity argument and he had taken note of how one particular boy had trembled as he told his story in a private setting. If he could spare this child and the others from public testimony, and assure them that their tormentor would be locked up for an exceedingly long time, a deal might be the best option. The two lawyers eventually agreed on a twenty-year sentence in a prison, not some comfortable psychiatric center. The victims and their parents assented to the deal and Gilbert Gauthe was locked away in a medium security state penitentiary.

The civil case filed by the Gastal family would not be resolved so readily. Minos Simon and his clients did not seek a settlement with the Church. They wanted a trial, so that Simon could impress upon a jury the damage done to his clients. Gilbert Gauthe had robbed Faye and Glenn Gastal of their faith. He had taken much more from their son, whose psychological suffering could last a lifetime. The jury seemed to agree. They awarded the family $1.2 million. To avoid a long appeals process, the Gastals accepted a bit over $1 million.

Meanwhile, the Lafayette Diocese faced new allegations against a former priest who had transferred to Washington State, and against a local pastor who faced accusations by five sisters who said he had molested them. The reported incidents occurred when the victims were between the ages of four and fourteen. Three of them had been photographed in the nude. The priest, John Engbers, fled to his native Holland before he could be confronted.

As Jason Berry investigated and reported on the new cases, he watched church officials in Lafayette act like corporate officers instead of pastors, complaining about insurers who resisted settling claims and litigants who threatened the solvency of the diocese. He came to accept that deceptions and transgressions he never imagined possible occurred with regularity inside the Church.

Although he continued to believe in the message of Christ and attended Mass, the assumptions he once held about the goodness of ordained men disappeared. When police called because they were investigating complaints of abuse filed against his source codenamed Chalice, Berry was not entirely surprised. (He had sensed something "creepy" about the man.) Chalice would deny the charges even after he was sent to prison. He would eventually die of AIDS.

■ ■ ■ ■

After they were brushed aside by the American bishops, the three experts who thought they might save the Church from a long nightmare related to sexual abuse continued to try to get their message across. Michael Peterson made hundreds of copies of the report and sent them to bishops across America. Doyle spoke to anyone in the Church who would listen, reminding them of their duty to laypeople, especially children. He received some private encouragement, but no public support. At the Vatican embassy where he once joked with colleagues about how American bishops were "sexual intellectuals" — translation, "fucking idiots" — he was now met with silence and cold stares. After he discovered that his desk and file cabinets had been searched when he was away from his office, Doyle began taking sensitive papers home at the end of every day. For the first time in his life, he worried about how much he depended on a couple of glasses of wine to relax in the evening.

As Raymond Mouton followed up on new cases of clergy abuse reported in the press, he became particularly upset about the suffering of victims and their families. Mouton had never been so frustrated by a problem. Nor had he felt so pained. After long days focused on sexual abuse and cover-ups, he would drink until he passed out. His wife and children began to feel neglected. Michael Peterson, who was a psychiatrist, began to talk to him about a condition called manic depression.

Peterson had his own problems. Months of constant travel and consultations with troubled priests seemed to have aged him. As his friend Doyle would recall, Peterson grew weak and exhausted but pushed himself to work harder. In March 1986 he flew to Rome to alert higher officials to the looming sex abuse scandal, but he returned to report he had little impact. At that time the Vatican was focused not on controlling abusive priests, but on disciplining theological liberals. The Pope had summoned the bishops of Brazil to discuss their support of liberation theology and its main proponent, Brazilian friar Leonardo Boff, who had been officially forbidden to speak publicly.

Given his own personality, the monarchical structure of the Church, and its tradition of discipline, John Paul II's crackdown on liberation theology was an inevitability. Boff and his allies offered a searing critique of all hierarchical power systems. The Church was the ultimate hierarchy, and had been equipped with a punishing impulse when Pope Gregory IX established the Inquisition in 1231. From the start, the officers of the

Inquisition built a network of informants who identified those who deviated from the codified rules of the Church and alerted higher authorities so they could move against the offenders. Filled with absolute certainty, the early Inquisitors tortured and killed supposed apostates. They also built an enduring bureaucracy that maintained meticulous records and worked slowly, but relentlessly, to enforce the will of the hierarchy that they, of course, called God's will.

In the modern age, the Inquisition was called the Congregation for the Doctrine of the Faith. Torture and killing were out, but moral certainty still ruled the game and in 1986 investigators were finishing reports that would lead then Cardinal Joseph Ratzinger to strip an American professor of his right to teach Catholic theology. Charles Curran would be cast out for condoning dissent and teaching ideas that were, Ratzinger wrote, "in open contrast with the teaching of the Magisterium." Except for the topic of euthanasia, every item Ratzinger addressed in his criticism of Curran was related to sex, and in every case, from masturbation to homosexuality, he and the Church were against it.

In this period Ratzinger would earn his reputation as the enforcer of papal authority, exponent for traditional theology, and defender of the clerical culture. Ratzinger was in the middle of investigating Seattle archbishop Raymond Hunthausen, who had worked in an open and positive way with a group of gay Catholics. In the fall, Hunthausen would be subjected to a humiliating censure from the Vatican and the assignment of a watchdog who would share the administration of his territory. After Hunthausen pleaded for their support, his American colleagues would instead vote to publicly affirm their loyalty to the Pope.

After he returned to America, Peterson was hospitalized in Washington. He told Mouton and Doyle that he had lymphoma and was dying. Heartbroken, the two men promised to carry on their effort. They flew to New Jersey in a rented plane, piloted by Doyle, for a conference of canon lawyers.

Technically speaking, the canon law system offered ways for Church leaders to investigate abuse allegations and remove priests from ministry. However, church law offered nothing to address real-world crimes. Canon law courts could not put anyone in prison or levy fines. And in practice, the ample rights accorded to ordained priests protected many of them from ever facing a tribunal. A five-year statute of limitations meant most complaints could never be brought to a tribunal because child victims are usually so traumatized that they are unable to disclose what happened to them until they are well into adulthood. Also, offenders who claimed they were drunk or psychologically impaired — and almost all abusers are by definition impaired — were almost automatically immunized from prosecution. Under these conditions, most experts advised bishops against using the system to try to cast out a priest and, as far as Doyle could tell, none tried.

At the meeting, Fr. Doyle stood and argued that "extreme judgmentalism in matters of sex" combined with the fear of scandal threatened to create "the most serious problem the Church has faced in centuries." He advised the Church to inform parishioners when a complaint against a priest has been confirmed and to respond compassionately to victims and their families. "Don't send some imperious cleric out there to show them how bad they should feel about dragging the Church's name through the mud."

As Doyle spoke, Mouton noted that he was sounding more and more liberal and less like a traditionalist. In fact, Doyle had become convinced that his old loyalty to the hierarchy had been misplaced. Although he hadn't found a new basis for his faith, and this made him uneasy, he was certain that the clerics who claimed to be so much closer to God couldn't have been more wrong about themselves, or the deity.

When it was Mouton's turn to address the canon lawyers he offered a few observations as a loyal layperson, including a warning that the Church "cannot credibly exert moral authority in any area where the public perceives it as incapable of maintaining moral authority internally." But Mouton's main focus was on what he could say as an attorney. He told them that liability insurers were cancelling policies held by dioceses around the country and that almost every day new charges were being made somewhere. When he said that the prior Monday had brought two new allegations Doyle held up three fingers and Mouton corrected himself.

The meeting of the canon lawyers turned out to be the high point for Mouton and Doyle's campaign. The two men had become close friends and drinking buddies who enjoyed going to Cajun dancehalls around Lafayette and lolling in Mouton's swimming pool. Doyle had become so close to Mouton's family and friends that he performed the marriage ceremony for the lawyer's secretary.

Friendship and alcohol helped the men cope with their feelings of failure, which grew more intense as the country's Catholic bishops ignored their work. By the summer of 1986 Mouton was convinced that almost every ordained man in America bore some responsibility for the sexual abuse of children because the problem was an open secret. Having concluded that the mission he had undertaken to save his church had failed, he became depressed and even more dependent on alcohol. Michael Peterson, who had recovered enough to leave the hospital, found a doctor in Louisiana who would treat Mouton for bipolar disorder.

Of course the "cure" for Mouton wouldn't come immediately. He would resist treatment for three years, denying his diagnosis and throwing himself into his work. Mouton, Peterson, and Doyle were confident in their assessment of the Church's problems and pushed Catholic leaders to confront them. However, no amount of effort, even by a ferociously assertive and maniacally energetic Mouton, was going to make the Church move quickly enough in the right direction. Increasingly frustrated, Mouton's personal troubles worsened. He lost his marriage, his home, and daily contact with his children. Eventually, Mouton would realize that "from the time I met Fr. Gilbert Gauthe" until he had walked away from the issue of priests and sexual abuse, "I was in a sustained manic episode." His preoccupation with all the issues that arose in the wake of his work for Gilbert Gauthe led to his divorce, and early retirement from the law. In the years to come he would find sobriety and get mental health treatment.

Michael Peterson died on April 9, 1987, after telling friends that he was gay and that he had AIDS. His funeral would mark the first time the Church acknowledged the loss of a priest with AIDS. Thomas Doyle was one of one hundred white-robed priests — white to symbolize the soul's victory over death — who participated in the Mass at St. Matthew's Cathedral in Washington, D.C.

By the time of Peterson's death, Fr. Doyle had begun to feel a bit paranoid. All the things about the Church that rubbed him the wrong way — the spiritual class system, the authoritarian structure, the vestments and incense — seemed more irritating than ever. At the same time, he felt like he was the subject of gossip and scrutiny by his colleagues. A two-glasses-per-night white wine habit became four, and he realized that he couldn't stand working at the embassy. He had to quit immediately.

Pio Laghi didn't seem surprised when Doyle appeared in his office to resign. Although they conducted a face-saving exchange of good wishes, both men knew that Doyle had spoiled his own chance to become a bishop, or perhaps a cardinal, and would be lucky to land any job at all. Doyle didn't mention it, but he planned to enlist in the Air Force and become a chaplain. The service, which might require him to accept postings abroad, would take him out of the mainstream of American Catholic life, but this change appealed to him.

Soon after Doyle enlisted, but before he

reported for training at Andrews Air Force Base, he took a phone call from a television producer in Los Angeles. The producer had read about his work on the issue of priests and sexual abuse and wanted him to appear on a talk show called *Hour Magazine.* After hearing the producer's request, Doyle's only concern was travel expenses. When he learned that the program would cover the cost, he flew to Los Angeles for the broadcast. Although Doyle preferred civilian clothes, he made the choice to show up at the studio wearing clerical black and a Roman collar. The look was not just slimming — they say TV cameras add ten pounds — but it also signaled that he was an authority in good standing with the Church.

In the interview Doyle spoke plainly about priests and criminal sexual behavior and the subculture of privilege that made it difficult for bishops to respond decisively. He was delighted after the program to meet Dr. Ruth Westheimer in the reception area for guests. A psychoanalyst trained at the Sorbonne, Dr. Ruth was at the height of her fame as a sex educator and advocate for sexual pleasure of all types. "When it came to sex," Doyle would recall, "she made more sense in five minutes than a hundred bishops talking for an hour."

Though not the most-watched TV program in America, *Hour Magazine* was seen by enough viewers that word of Doyle's appear-

91

ance spread quickly among the American bishops. Bishop Quinn, who had once encouraged Doyle's work, wrote Laghi to complain that, "The continuing comments attributed to Father Doyle and Mr. Mouton are not serving the image of the Church and the priesthood." He reminded Laghi that "Doyle and Mouton want the Church in the United States to purchase their expensive and controversial leadership" and concluded that "the Church has weathered worse attacks, thanks to the strength and guidance of the Holy Spirit. So, too, will the pedophile annoyance eventually abate." Laghi didn't agree with Quinn's criticism of Doyle, but after he received the letter he called Doyle and asked him to come to the embassy.

On the day Laghi called Doyle, the clerical rumor mill was churning with talk of a bishop from Spokane who had been interrogated by police in Chicago, where he was attending a Knights of Columbus convention. The officers had confronted Bishop Lawrence Welsh with a complaint from a male prostitute who said the bishop had picked him up, engaged him in sex, and then beat him. Though the complaint was dropped, Welsh eventually confirmed much of the prostitute's story for police. Doyle had heard about all of this and was certain Laghi wanted his counsel. He was surprised when, instead, Laghi brought up his TV appearance.

"He warned me that my future would be very negatively affected if I continued to speak out," recalled Doyle. "I told him that when people asked me questions I was going to answer them honestly."

After the two men went back and forth on the matter Doyle interrupted Laghi and said, "Archbishop, what we call this in America is a Mexican standoff. It means you aren't going to back down and neither am I." Laghi looked at Doyle as if he was watching a man throw away his life, and then invited him to lunch at the embassy. Doyle thought about the cold stares that would greet him in the dining room and the amount of alcohol he would have to consume to get through the meal and declined.

With one dead, one retired, and one ruined as a career churchman, the trio of loyal Catholics who set out to save the Church from itself had finished their effort to change it from within. Their report, however, would become a primary text for victims of clergy abuse and their attorneys, as well as writers and TV producers. In the courts and the press it would be cited repeatedly as evidence that church leaders had been informed of the problem and were given options for addressing it, which they rejected.

The power of the Mouton-Doyle-Peterson report was also obvious to the investigative reporter Jason Berry. From the moment he heard about it, Berry recognized that the document could either save or imperil the institution and he recognized that when the bishops rejected it, they were choosing peril over salvation. Berry would stay on the story of the Church for decades to come. Outside this topic, he became known for works of fiction, nonfiction, and film that dwelled on music and politics. But even when he was tending to these other topics, Berry heard regularly from victims of clergy abuse, lawyers, and other journalists who wanted his help. Eventually he would be all but defined, as a writer, by a story that never ceased to make him uncomfortable.

Minos Simon, having earned hundreds of thousands of dollars from the settlement of the Gastal claim, predicted that clergy abuse would open up a huge new market for trial lawyers who would find clients in every diocese. Like Jason Berry, Simon was one of the few members of his profession who had successfully navigated this new territory. However, he would not devote himself to the practice of suing the Church. He had other priorities.

Minnesota lawyer Jeffrey Anderson telephoned Simon for what he had hoped would be a collegial chat about suing the Catholic Church. Among plaintiffs' lawyers, informal consultations are common courtesy, especially when they involve attorneys who practice in different states. These contacts are especially valuable when a new area of law is being developed, and they add important networking links on both sides of the conversation. But instead of warmth and welcome, Simon gave Anderson just a brief review of the facts Anderson had already seen in the press and few words of warning about the intimidating power of the Catholic Church. With a perfunctory "Good luck," he then hurried off the phone.

4.
SPIRITUAL BETRAYAL

Tom Krauel and Jeffrey Anderson would disagree over whether the term "fearless little bastard" had actually been spoken when Krauel referred the Lyman family to him for representation. However, they agreed when it came to Anderson's reputation. In the mid-1980s he was famous around the courthouses of Minneapolis–St. Paul for providing aggressive representation to the kinds of clients many other lawyers would turn away. He was also infamous for parties that would put a rock band to shame.

Anderson's Friday night blowouts began in his office, at around 4 P.M., and continued until the crowd decamped for dancing at local clubs like Tonkin and Oz, where mirror balls scattered light in a thousand pieces and the music was nonstop disco. The attendees included prosecutors, defense lawyers, and the occasional criminal. When a judge was present, the cocaine, acid, and pot were handled discreetly.

Though he was just five foot four and weighed less than a hundred and fifty pounds, Anderson presided over these parties with an energy that made him seem seven feet tall. The first to laugh, or to dance, he consumed whatever was at hand and everything put him in a good mood. Once the drug of the day sent him up onto the windowsill to howl with laughter and piss on the sidewalk below. In fairness it must be said that the hour was late and the sidewalk was empty. And when he sobered up Anderson admitted that using the window as a urinal was a bad idea. If he had slipped, the landing from eight stories up would have killed him.

Much of what Anderson did in his early years involved bad ideas. Most of these arose when he was consuming alcohol, which he began when he was fourteen. Back in high school, in the posh Minneapolis suburb of Edina, Anderson and his best friend Grant Hall formed the core of a group that became known for their drunken wild ways. Drinking caused Anderson to miss so many practices that he was kicked off the wrestling team. On one frozen night he passed out in a stubbly cornfield, where he would have died of exposure if he hadn't been rescued by his friends. He promised moderation, but within a week he was back to getting drunk in the car on the way to a local club called Big Reggie's Danceland. It was there where one night he picked Patti McDonough out of the crowd. A beautiful dark-haired girl from an Irish/Italian family of twelve, she was the most exciting person he had ever met.

Patti announced she was pregnant during Anderson's first semester at college. He did what he had to do, dropping out of school and getting married. Though they attended the wedding, Anderson's mother and father were sorely disappointed. Stoic Lutherans, Eleanor and Robert Anderson never actually spoke about sex and contraception, but he knew what they expected of him. They covered their living room sofa in plastic, for God's sake.

Nineteen and already a family man, Anderson worked three jobs. By day he labored at a warehouse. In the evenings he sold shoes at the department store Montgomery Ward. And when he got home at night he shoveled coal and operated the furnace in the basement of his apartment building. (This job covered the $50 per month rent.) Of the three occupations, salesman fit Anderson best. At Wards he discovered he had a gift for persuasion. Attentive fitting and flirting broke many a woman's resolve and budget. Purses were opened. Boys were summoned to carry out the boxes.

With Patti's encouragement, Anderson enrolled at the University of Minnesota and, in between civil rights marches and protests against the Vietnam War, he finished his undergraduate degree in two years. A magna cum laude diploma helped him win a job at the Leo Burnett advertising agency in Chicago. He arrived as the city was gripped by the conspiracy trial of the famous "Chicago Seven," who were represented by lawyer/celebrity William Kunstler. From his first day at his tiny, all-white office at Burnett, Anderson knew he wouldn't stay long. He soon returned to Minneapolis where, inspired by Kunstler, he enrolled at William Mitchell School of Law. Anderson struggled with attendance, but thrived in the school's legal clinic. After he was admitted to the bar in 1975, Anderson set out to become the Twin Cities' version of the attorney for the damned, representing drug dealers, madams, prostitutes, and gay men arrested on morals charges.

Minneapolis–St. Paul circa 1975 was a rather progressive place when it came to sex and the law. Prostitution was rarely prosecuted and the state legislature had taken up a bill to advance gay rights. During debate over the proposal, an activist named Timothy Campbell was arrested when he commandeered a public restroom for a press conference and announced he would begin a hunger strike on the spot. At the jail his first call was to Jeffrey Anderson, who eventually beat the charges against Campbell and in the process became the go-to lawyer for gay men arrested for civil disobedience or on morals charges. Much of the money to pay for his work came from a defense fund created by Philip Willkie, grandson of Wendell Willkie, the Republican Party's 1940 presidential nominee. Willkie was himself arrested in 1979, while protesting in support of a well-known madam named Rebecca Rand, who was also Anderson's client.

Campbell, Willkie, Rand, and others introduced Anderson to a sexual subculture few outsiders ever know. He learned about the politicians and judges who frequented massage parlors and the clergymen who hung around gay clubs. Many of the people arrested in these places simply had the misfortune of being in the wrong spot when local politicians pressured the police to conduct a raid. Anderson's most memorable case in this era involved a crowd of defendants who were rounded up one snowy night at a sex club called The Locker Room, on First Avenue in Minneapolis. Philip Willkie had been tipped off about the raid and arranged for the press to be outside filming as officers emerged from the building with evidence, including a papier-mâché phallus as big as a canoe. It was transported to the precinct house atop the paddy wagon.

At trial Anderson demanded that the police

display in the courtroom every bit of evidence they had seized. When they reported the penis was unavailable because it had broken in an elevator, Anderson was able to cast doubt on everything the officers did on the night of the arrest. However, his case was truly made when prosecutors wheeled in a grocery cart filled with sex toys. Anderson asked the police officer on the witness stand one question:

"Is it illegal to possess these items?"

After the officer answered, "No," the jury found the defendants not guilty. Anderson, and his clients celebrated long into the night. For Anderson, victories were always an occasion to celebrate with a drinking binge, but then again, so were defeats. More often than not he would be joined by his partner, Mark Reinhardt, who had been his instructor at William Mitchell. In time Reinhardt and Anderson would get into high-stakes class action lawsuits. But in the beginning they both depended on run-of-the-mill clients who walked through the door, and on referrals like the one offered by Tom Krauel in the fall of 1984.

A reserved, by-the-book lawyer, Tom Krauel had listened in shocked silence to a couple named Janet and John Lyman[*] who came to his home to discuss a type of problem he had

[*] a pseudonym

never imagined. The Lymans, who were his neighbors, reported that their son Greg was in the state prison in St. Cloud. He had been jailed for a probation violation. He was on probation for two crimes he had committed when he was a minor. One was a burglary. The other involved exposing himself to two young girls, aged seven and four, and coaxing them to touch his penis. Janet had turned her own son in to the authorities when the girls' parents called to complain.

Janet and John had been shocked by the nature of Greg's crimes, but they were not surprised that he had gotten into serious trouble. Angry much of the time, their son had been in different kinds of trouble for years. Social workers, psychologists, and psychiatrists had failed to reach him and Greg dropped out of high school before graduation. He found company with a crowd of kids who drank to excess and committed petty crimes. When he was jailed after burglarizing a liquor store, Greg revealed that had been molested by a priest named Thomas Adamson.

Father Tom had been a family friend to the Lymans when he worked at St. Thomas Aquinas Church in St. Paul Park. A charming, intelligent, and athletic man — he was both class president and captain of a club basketball team at Catholic University — Adamson had seemed the perfect companion and role model for a troubled boy.

A nervous and awkward sixth grader, Greg was not athletic, or academically gifted. He wasn't funny or talented in any way that made him stand out and he wasn't relaxed enough to fit in. He had blue eyes and almost-white blond hair that swooped down across his forehead, skimming his eyebrows like a sailor's hat. He was self-conscious about his teeth, so he didn't smile very much, and his voice was still soft and high-pitched, like a girl's, so he didn't talk much either.

Greg became an altar boy at Father's suggestion and in this role he found a glimmer of self-esteem. Father became Greg's best friend, role model, confessor, and protector. The boy had never trusted any man as much as he trusted Adamson. He eagerly tagged along when the priest asked him to go to the gym and thought nothing of joining him in a steam room. It was there, behind a tightly closed door and obscured by the white vapor, that Adamson asked Greg if he ever masturbated and if he liked how it felt to be touched "there." Greg did not know how to respond. Unable to say "no" he just silently allowed the priest to masturbate him. Before he left him at his home Adamson said, "Don't tell anybody. You'll get in trouble and so will I."

If Greg had been able to speak when Father touched him, he might have said that this was his first real sexual experience. Instead he allowed himself to be quietly overwhelmed with a toxic mixture of fear, shame, anger, physical pleasure, and profound confusion. Greg couldn't believe that what had happened was right, or good. Father wouldn't have warned him to stay silent if it was okay. But he valued his friendship with Adamson so intensely — he loved him in a way — that he kept all of his feelings inside, and tried to act like nothing had happened. He continued serving as an altar boy, and continued going on outings with Adamson. Father's sexual assaults became routine, and escalated to the point where he was demanding Greg perform oral sex on him. As Greg would remember it, "whenever he got the urge" Adamson would find a locked room where he could use the boy for sex. It happened in a church basement, a gas station men's room, a motel, and a YMCA steam room. Father took to keeping a small bag in his car so that he would always have access to towels and a vibrator that he used on Greg.

Although he couldn't understand, intellectually, the effect of these sexual assaults, Greg felt all the different ways that Adamson hurt him. Sexualized in an abusive and premature fashion, he was tormented by his own sexual obsessions and swamped with worry. The attention and sexual gratification felt good even as they felt shameful. He wondered if he was homosexual, heterosexual, or bisexual and when he tried to stop seeing Adamson he felt so lonely that he couldn't keep his distance. Afterward he would feel angry, guilty, and remorseful. At home he seemed angry and moody, which confused his parents. They thought he should be grateful and happy that a man like Father Adamson gave him so much time and attention.

Janet and John Lyman had thought the priest's interest in their son had been a good thing. When they learned what had actually gone on between Greg and Father Tom they felt rage, remorse, and guilt.

As the couple spilled out their story for Krauel they described how they had confronted Adamson directly over lunch at a Perkins pancake house. The priest had not confessed, but he did not deny what had happened. In parting he said something strange and infuriating as he embraced Janet.

"Just you remember," he said quietly, "that I'm not a wealthy person."

While Greg's parents were confronting Adamson, Greg's prison counselor spoke to Catholic Church officials who admitted that they had long known of the priest's sexual problem. Others had complained and Adamson had been required to seek psychological treatment in 1981. When told this, Janet recalled that Adamson had last approached her son for sex in 1982. Clearly the treatment wasn't working.

Concerned for other boys who could become Adamson's victims, Janet and John met with an official of the St. Paul Archdiocese named Bishop Robert Carlson. Carlson also went out to the prison at St. Cloud to see their son. At these meetings Carlson expressed concern for the family, for the priest, and the Church. In the end he suggested Adamson help pay for Greg's therapy. A few days later the mail brought a check for $1,600. John and Janet didn't know what to do with it.

Nothing in Tom Krauel's legal experience had prepared him to answer all of his neighbors' questions about the check, their son, and the priest who had abused their son. In the near term he knew that Greg needed no criminal representation. In the long term, however, he and his family might have reason to sue for the priest's crimes. As a devout Catholic, Krauel knew he wasn't the person for the job, but he had an idea about who might be. As he gave the Lymans Jeff Anderson's name and phone number, Krauel described him in a way that left no doubt about the kind of representation they should expect.

By the autumn of 1984 Jeffrey Anderson had long lost the beard he once wore around the courthouse as a rookie lawyer. He had had his hair cut shorter and begun wearing more expensive suits. The effort made him seem a bit more mature and seasoned and made potential clients feel confident in Anderson, even when he had no particular expertise, or experience, related to their problem.

Of course, in 1984 hardly anyone in the legal profession would have had any experience at all with sex crimes committed by Catholic priests. Anderson had never heard of such a case, but Janet and John showed up in his office carrying the check the bishop had sent and Tom Krauel had vouched for them. If Anderson had been inclined toward skepticism, any doubt he harbored was swept away by their candor. They had accepted that their son was a sex offender and acknowledged the harm he had done to his victims. But they emphasized that Greg was a minor when he committed his crimes and they believed that things would have been different if Thomas Adamson had left him alone.

As he listened to how the Lymans had been treated by the Church, Anderson heard echoes of the big civil rights cases of the 1960s. They were ordinary people being overwhelmed by a powerful institution and they needed someone to stand up for them. In doing so, Anderson would have to challenge the basic assumptions of a society that preferred to believe the Church was good and that authority figures could be trusted. He had worked on enough discrimination cases to feel comfortable in this role. Indeed, he relished the chance to challenge authority.

However, nothing in Anderson's experience had prepared him to understand the spiritual betrayal felt by Janet and John. Although he was raised to believe in a Protestant God, he was not at all devout and could only imagine what faith meant to lifelong, traditional Catholics. Janet seemed especially shaken by Bishop Carlson's almost casual response to the crimes committed by a priest under his supervision. Sending a sexual offender to psychotherapy and then shifting him to a new parish where he had access to children seemed criminally irresponsible to her. Brushing off parents who complained felt like condescension and rejection.

To a lawyer's mind, Carlson's behavior was an invitation to a lawsuit. How could a senior executive at a corporation with the wealth of an archdiocese admit to such a cavalier response to an underling's criminal activity? However, Anderson was hardly an expert in litigation involving churches. Actually, he had never even considered the issues that would arise with a civil case against a religious institution. But like anyone who knew the Constitution, he understood that religion enjoyed special status under the First Amendment of the Bill of Rights, which begins, "Congress shall make no law respecting an establishment of religion, or prohibiting the free exercise thereof." Courts had generally read the First Amendment to protect religion from state regulations, and religious institutions had frequently avoided lawsuits under its protection.

The power and stature of the Catholic Church had played a major role in Tom Krauel's decision to decline John and Janet's request for representation. Krauel also knew that Jeffrey Anderson wouldn't be intimidated, and he was right. As he considered moving forward, Anderson realized he was dealing with an institution with influence at all levels of society. Much like the government, the Church had almost limitless resources. Suing the Church would require several different weapons, including the threat of public scandal, to pressure bishops to do the right thing.

And what was the right thing? In this case the lawyer and the clients agreed that children should be protected from Adamson and that the police and church could both play a role in making this happen. Beyond this public safety concern, Janet and John Lyman wanted compensation that would pay for the psychological care of their son and recognize the pain and suffering visited on their family by Adamson and his superiors. Finally, they hoped to inflict a bit of financial pain on the institution, enough to make bishops everywhere think twice about covering up for pedophile priests and leaving them in positions where they can continue to commit crimes against children. All this could be accomplished, said Anderson, and he would do the work on a contingency basis, for a percentage of any payments made by Adamson, the Church, or insurance companies.

Before the Lymans left his office, Anderson tried to allay their worries about suing an entity as vast and powerful as the Catholic Church. He reminded them that, at least theoretically speaking, no one in America is above the law. And while he had never heard of anyone filing such an action, there was a first time for everything. Since the check sent by the bishop had no strings attached he told them to go ahead and cash it and use the proceeds to help their son. Summoning up his best bedside manner, he shook hands with the couple and promised to start work immediately, with a call to the police. Greg had been the victim of a crime and it should be reported.

As his new clients departed, Anderson felt a combination of shock, sorrow, and rage. He had never contemplated the idea that a priest might abuse a boy in his congregation, or that the Church hierarchy would hide the crime and protect the perpetrator. At the same time, he had rarely seen a couple as grief-stricken as John and Janet Lyman. Their faith had been destroyed by a priest who had transformed their son from an ordinary thirteen-year-old into a shame-bound sex offender. Greg's parents said their son felt profoundly guilty for what he had done and could barely look at himself in the mirror. Would he ever be able to recover his sense of self-worth? Would he be able to have a trusting relationship? What about having children of his own?

The questions were disturbing but they also compelled Anderson to reflect on his role in this drama, and here he felt a rush of adrenaline. Although he was intimidated by the prospect of challenging the Church, he was also excited. Ever since he considered becoming a lawyer he had preferred the idea of representing the powerless against the powerful. This interest had drawn Anderson to represent victims of police brutality and racial discrimination. In this case, he would take on an institution connected to the elite at every level of society, possessing almost unlimited funds with which they could hire the very best lawyers available. The Church was also wealthy enough to pay significant damages.

Any trial lawyer would wish for a less compromised client, but Anderson believed he could present the unseemly parts of Greg Lyman's background as proof of the damage done to him by a priest who should never have been permitted to work with young people. He also suspected that others had been sexually abused under similar circumstances. The publicity around Lyman's case would inspire others who had been victimized to come forward with their own claims. In a few years' time, the exposure of the depth of deception practiced by bishops would change public attitudes toward church authority.

Of course the law, especially statutes of limitation and the First Amendment to the Constitution, would present obstacles to anyone seeking to develop sex abuse claims against the Church. And in Anderson's case the prospects were complicated by a lifestyle that seemed almost designed to create personal problems. Easily bored and craving excitement, he found it hard to turn down the offer of an after-work drink, which invariably led to six more. A true reckoning could have come on one of those nights when he drove his black Mustang through St. Paul at eighty miles per hour, navigating for home with a mind soaked in alcohol. The cops actually stopped him just once. On that occasion his blood alcohol level was well over the legal limit. But this was a time before society had turned decidedly against drunk drivers. Anderson was steady enough to persuade the officers that he wasn't a danger to himself or others and they let him drive home.

On the nights when he didn't come home at all, Anderson's wife Patti worried and then seethed. When she suspected he was involved with another woman she began voicing her fears and challenging his denials.

"Where were you?" she would shout. "Who *is* she?"

As he deflected Patti's questions, Anderson felt flashes of shame and then anger. More drink and drugs freed him from his conscience and allowed him to take what his ego said he deserved. In the back of his mind he knew what he was doing was wrong, but he stubbornly indulged himself. On the rare occasions when he was caught out he would apologize and promise to change. Sometimes he even cried.

While Anderson's personal life spun wildly from crisis to crisis, his friend Grant Hall had gotten sober. It took a month at the Hazelden clinic, which was fifty miles away, and about a year of occasional slips before the cure set in. During that year he hadn't said much of anything about Hazelden, or his affiliation with Alcoholics Anonymous, but they clearly worked. When he reached a crisis point in his marriage Anderson was willing to give rehab a try but not as an in-patient. He signed up instead for a day program at a place called Twin Town Treatment Center, where thirty days of sobriety earned a patient a clean bill of health.

Like most, the program at Twin Town

leaned on AA and its famous Twelve Steps, which require more sincerity than many addicts can muster the first time around. Anderson had trouble with the very first step, which required him to declare he was powerless over drink and that his life was "unmanageable." He could and did stay sober for days and even weeks, which didn't seem like powerlessness to him. As for his life being "unmanageable," Anderson thought his success at work proved he was managing most things well. Finally there were those steps related to "God as we understand him." He didn't believe in a conventional God and wouldn't pretend that he did.

Anderson made it to the twenty-ninth day and then made a deliberate choice — some would call it a "fuck you" decision — to get high and forthrightly report his condition to the staff at Twin Town. In payment for his honesty he was dismissed without whatever ceremony would have accompanied successful completion of the program. Having blown his shot at redemption, Anderson quickly returned to his self-indulgent ways. In a year's time Patti would leave him and begin the long process of divorce. Most of his friends and colleagues, who preferred the fun-loving, generous, and entertaining Jeff Anderson they knew under the influence, rallied around him. But the few who had gotten sober, like Grant Hall, didn't come around

114

as much as they once did.

At work it did occur to Anderson that more than half the criminal cases he saw involved drugs or alcohol or both, but this knowledge did little to change his behavior. Despite his deep-seated sense of right and wrong, he carved out exceptions in his personal life that allowed for a return to drinking and drugs and women who were not his wife. He did feel guilty, but there was something about taking the risk that made him feel good. It wasn't the sex, but rather the feeling that came with a complex and dangerous challenge. The calm sense of focus that he felt when taking a big risk even led him to carry cocaine, secreted in an empty Chapstick tube, when he left the office for appointments.

In the mid-1980s, cocaine was practically a marker of the legal profession across America. A stimulant, it could have the paradoxical effect of calming hyperactive minds, and many lawyers were hyperactive in the extreme. For some, like Anderson, the illegality of the drug added a bit of excitement to life. He actually felt better when living dangerously. In order to keep feeling good, he justified his behavior with the idea that he was special in a way others wouldn't understand.

It was this seemingly invulnerable ego that moved Jeffrey Anderson from case to case and courthouse to courthouse, certain that he could keep every one of his criminal defendants out of prison or win enough money to keep his civil clients happy and pay his own bills. Most of the time he succeeded and his confidence grew. Julie Aronson heard it in his voice when he called the Minneapolis Trial Lawyers Association, and she felt it when she first met him, in February 1982, at a bar at the airport. As staffer for the MTLA she was shepherding a dozen lawyers to Aspen, Colorado, for a conference.

Although she looked and acted like a far more mature person, Aronson was just twenty-one years old and the poise she showed was mostly an act. Born when her own mother Rosalie was just seventeen, Julie was ten when her parents divorced. As a teen she was a lonely girl who claimed no clique or close friends. At the end of the school day she went home to care for her siblings or to work. She studied *Glamour* and *Seventeen* magazines and noted the ways of women on television. (Farrah Fawcett and Marlo Thomas were favorites.) Her father, who read Norman Vincent Peale and Dale Carnegie, helped with the occasional words of wisdom that went into her mind and stuck. "Hold your shoulders back and be proud," he would say. But more often James Aronson would say he was disappointed in his daughter. She never measured up to his expectations.

On the day after she graduated from high

school, Julie Aronson found an apartment, salvaged a bed frame left outside as trash, and began an independent life. With careful shopping she put together a professional woman's wardrobe to support a personality — part Marlo, part Farrah — that she also constructed herself. In order to get the job at the MTLA she lied and said she could type. Hours of drills, conducted into the night, helped her sustain the bluff until she actually could type well enough. But behind the polish, this seemingly well-bred and confident woman was wary, worried, and naive. Alone on Sundays she thought about families sitting down to dinner together. She remembered a recurring fantasy she had as a girl. In this day-dream she was the mother of one child and pregnant with another and she sat beside her husband at a Christmas Eve church service.

The dream was about convention and security but Julie was also, at twenty-one, eager to see more of the world before she settled down. In Aspen she went out every night with the MTLA group and was all but swept off her feet by Jeff Anderson. She considered his job in the growing field of trial law, his clothes, and his personality and judged him "completely legit." By the time they went back to St. Paul, she and Jeff were a couple. By year's end she would move into his house, a huge, halfway restored Victorian landmark that occupied a hill overlooking St. Mary Catholic Church, downtown Stillwater, and the St. Croix River.

During this time Anderson and his partner Mark Reinhardt were flush with money from their thriving legal practice. Both men started dressing in tailor-made suits. Reinhardt bought a full-length fur coat to wear when they went out on frigid Minnesota nights. The firm moved into new offices in a building called the Conwed Tower on Cedar Street. Although the space was modern/bland, the high-rise address had cachet. The views from the tenth floor took in the Mississippi River and the massive dome of the Catholic Cathedral of St. Paul.

Good friends as well as partners, Anderson and Reinhardt began taking three-day weekends in Las Vegas, accompanied by their women friends. Not yet the family-friendly Vegas of the twenty-first century, the town was nirvana for people who loved risk and flash, and Anderson played it to the hilt. He bought a white suit, and a pair of white leather boots decorated with red flames that started on the heel and rose up the shank. Add the heavy gold chains he took in payment for some legal work for a drug dealer and he was the picture of Vegas style circa 1980.

Like many gamblers, Anderson fell under the spell of the very real, but also unpredictable, payouts at the blackjack tables. Psychologists call the tantalizing ways that games of chance reward players "random reinforcement" and note that it's the best way to turn a lab animal into an addict. In Anderson's case, it turned him into a dazzling showman who could entertain not only himself, but a score of strangers at the Riviera Hotel. Watching him, Julie thought she had never seen anyone so confident.

5.
THE CATHOLIC STATES OF AMERICA

While Minos Simon had leveraged the publicity and facts of the criminal case against Gilbert Gauthe to win $1 million from the Diocese of Lafayette for the Gastal family, Jeffrey Anderson found himself blocked by the criminal law in Minnesota. The police wouldn't accept Greg Lyman's complaint against Fr. Thomas Adamson because the offenses took place beyond a three-year statute of limitations and he was no longer a minor. In the meantime the Church did whatever it could to slow Anderson's efforts to discover the facts and context of his civil case. They responded to his requests for documents only when he was able to name the precise papers he was seeking and explain why they were relevant.

This is the catch-22 in the process called "discovery." Litigants are permitted to ask for information and defendants are required to produce it. However, they may also withhold files if the wording of the request is the least bit off, or if the records can be deemed irrelevant. These exceptions meant that Anderson had to imagine which documents might exist, and guess how they were catalogued. Both sides knew his purpose. He wanted to show that Adamson had abused his client, and wasn't a lone actor but rather an agent of the Church who was supervised by higher authorities. This context was vital to the story Anderson would tell a jury, in order to claim compensation, and perhaps punitive damages, from not one diocese, but two.

Anderson was able to pursue two dioceses because Adamson had been sent to St. Paul, where he abused Gregory Lyman, by the bishop of Winona, who covered the state's twenty-two southern counties. Adamson's employment record showed a pattern of sudden transfers within the Winona district. Then suddenly, in 1975, he enrolled at the University of Minnesota in St. Paul to study, of all things, marriage counseling. In the records Anderson received as part of the discovery process, bishops in both dioceses noted that Adamson needed treatment at a church counseling center, but they never mentioned the specific nature of his problem. Typical was this passage in a memo sent by St. Paul Archbishop John Roach to a member of his staff in January 1976:

For reasons which Bishop Watters was unwilling to discuss on the telephone, but which he is promising to share with me later, he is asking that Father Adamson continue to work in the diocese for another year or year and a half.

Reading between the lines, anyone would surmise that Bishop Loras Watters knew of the "reasons" at the time he sent Adamson to St. Paul. It was also reasonable to guess that at some point Watters and Roach discussed the details, which would lead any responsible supervisor to keep a close eye on him. But no note in the files delivered in discovery showed that the men actually had such a conversation. They do refer to his ongoing treatment by a priest/psychologist named Kenneth Pierre. Two years after he sent Adamson away from Winona, Watters told Pierre that despite the psychologist's positive assessment of the priest's progress, Adamson still failed to grasp the seriousness of his situation. Wrote Watters:

I am convinced that he doesn't even begin to appreciate the numbers of people in at least five different communities across the entire diocese who have finally pieced together incidents across a five-year span and now openly raise questions about the credibility of all priests. Obviously I am writing to you in confidence. You would only have to struggle through the painful sessions I have had with heartbroken and bewildered parents who only now have come to discover the source of the some of the problems of their sons.

Going on to note that he had consulted fellow priests who agreed that Adamson had to be kept out of the Winona Diocese, Watters expressed some sympathy for the man. Adamson had begged to come home to the familiar region where he was born and raised. However, Watters was firm in his refusal. Adamson needed more treatment, he wrote, and he needed to "honestly face the fact that he cannot accept an appointment in the diocese now or even in the immediate future."

As Watters and Roach studiously avoided putting words like "sex crimes" or "misconduct" in writing, they also said nothing about preventing Adamson from abusing young people he would encounter while working as a priest in the St. Paul area. These gaps in the record suggested questions for a lawyer who wanted to prove negligence. What did Watters know of Adamson's specific problems? Did he share what he knew with Roach? Who were the parents who had brought their disturbing questions to the bishop?

Armed with these questions, Anderson lined up a series of depositions. The two big ones, interrogations of Watters and Adamson, were set for consecutive days near the end of March 1986. The first took place in a conference room at a bank building in Winona where six lawyers who represented various Church entities crowded around Watters, who, at seventy years old, had thinning white hair and sloping shoulders. Peering from behind thick black-rimmed glasses, he looked to Anderson like an animal frozen in the beam of a high-powered light.

Working from a yellow legal pad filled with handwritten notes, Anderson posed sordid questions in the most respectful way possible. He addressed the witness as "bishop" and allowed the churchman to use a strained kind of language that made sexual assault sound about as serious as a collision of grocery carts in the supermarket.

Besides filling in the details of the case, these depositions provided Anderson with a crash course in the lines of authority within the Church and the prerogatives of power. Watters informed him that while Archbishop Roach may have some oversight responsibilities as regional "metropolitan," a bishop ultimately answers to no one except for "the Pope, John Paul II." Watters also confirmed that the Church maintained a file on every priest — he called it simply "a priest file" — and assured Anderson that no other pertinent documents were maintained on individual clergy. Other questions established that no matter where he goes and what he does, a priest is always a priest and subject to certain expectations for his behavior. Watters also explained the circumstance that might bring a priest from one diocese into another — for education, medical treatment, a job, or other purpose.

In Adamson's case, Watters explained, the priest was sent to St. Paul after vague rumors and accusations began to swirl around the Diocese of Winona. The bishop recalled telephone calls from teachers at parochial schools who thought Adamson was behaving strangely and others from teachers who thought he was a terrific priest who was being unfairly harassed.

When Anderson asked about the details of the complaints Watters claimed he couldn't supply them because the calls were made anonymously and no one said anything specific. It was "not unusual for priests to be unjustly accused," explained Watters, so his first instinct was to protect Adamson from the kinds of people who might set out to "destroy a priest." But since he had heard from several different sources, he thought it best to send Adamson away and, for good measure, he made sure to have him undergo a psychological evaluation.

Like many witnesses who claim poor memory when questions get tough, Watters often seemed at a loss to recall exactly what he knew and when he knew it. As Anderson reached into his files and offered the few carefully worded documents he had received to refresh his memory, Watters described a way of managing people and problems that seemed designed to help him avoid responsibility. He said he did his duty by sending the priest for evaluation, but didn't inquire about the results because they were a matter of doctor-patient confidentiality. He told Archbishop Roach that Adamson had some sort of psychological difficulty, but refused to speculate about its nature.

The more Anderson pressed, the more convoluted were the answers. In an attempt to clear things up, Anderson brought out the letter the bishop wrote to oppose Dr. Pierre's recommendation that Adamson be returned to Winona. In this letter Watters noted "painful sessions" with "heartbroken and bewildered parents." Who were those parents? Anderson asked. What was the subject of those painful sessions?

They weren't about Adamson, said the bishop. Instead he was recalling an experience "in Dubuque" long before he came to Minnesota, "when one such incident happened." He made this reference not because he was concerned about future victims but because he wanted to make sure "this does not happen in the life of Father Adamson."

Watters's descriptions of his personal encounters with Adamson were filled with a similar logic as he explained how they got together on a regular basis to wring their hands and commiserate over issues they never named. He considered Adamson a friend. They played golf together at least once every summer, and he admired the priest's abilities as an administrator. As Watters recalled it, he kept insisting to Adamson that he was in denial about his wrongdoing, like an addict who refuses to admit that his use of drugs or alcohol has gotten out of control. But how could Watters credibly accuse Adamson of denial when the bishop himself avoided knowing the details of his transgressions?

Tellingly, it was the Lyman family's threat of a lawsuit and the possible financial consequences of such a suit that finally moved Watters to consider the actual truth of the trouble that had shadowed Thomas Adamson for more than a decade. When he learned that the family might sue, Watters wrote a letter to the St. Paul Archdiocese noting that he had made demands of Adamson "where his celibacy is concerned" but to no avail. Considering the potential liability faced by the Church he wrote, "I think it is time that Father Adamson accept that he is personally responsible and that he will have to make some kind of financial settlement."

Before the deposition ended, Anderson had

raised the fact that Kenneth Pierre, Ph.D., the priest/therapist whom two dioceses had trusted to get Adamson under control, had no experience treating sex offenders. For his part, Watters painted a self-portrait of a man who assumed the best of everyone — except for complaining about laypeople who sought to "destroy" priests — and yet refused to allow Adamson to return to his diocese until he accepted responsibility for an offense that was never even defined.

In the last minutes of the deposition, Watters seemed weary, and not fully cognizant of the seriousness of the proceedings. Anderson asked whether the bishop had been required to manage other difficulties caused by Fr. Adamson. "Any other problems that you were aware of?" he asked.

"No," said the bishop, pausing for effect. "The only thing is, he could beat me at golf."

After the bishop's deposition, which took place in Winona, Jeffrey Anderson made the two-and-a-half-hour drive to his home in Stillwater, a small town east of St. Paul. Much of his route followed the Mississippi River north on Rte. 61 to the bridge at Wabasha and Highway 25. The trip along winding two-lane roads gave him a chance to consider the Catholic world Watters had revealed in his deposition.

With its schools, universities, counseling

centers, hospitals, legal system, and other institutions, the Roman Catholic Church was much larger and more complicated than Anderson had ever imagined. In organization, the dioceses that spanned the United States seemed like an alternative nation — the Catholic States of America — superimposed on the landscape, but seen only by those who knew it was there. For every neighborhood or village the Church could claim a parish that might be compared with a town hall. In every big city it operated a chancery that controlled regional affairs like a state government.

As a whole, the Catholic Church in America claimed a population of sixty million, which was equal to about the twentieth-largest country in the world, and revenues greater than IBM, which was then the nation's sixth-largest company. Of course its religious mission and tax-exempt status made the Church far more profitable than a comparable corporation. Corporations paid taxes and were obliged to pay competitive salaries to their workers. The Church had no financial obligation to the state. Instead, it received hundreds of millions of dollars from the government as it provided various social services. It also enjoyed the labor of volunteers and religious who took vows of poverty and employees who accepted meager wages because their work was a calling. The total value of the Church's assets — mainly real estate and investments in stocks and bonds — had never been counted, but surely ran into the tens of billions of dollars.

For an outsider like Anderson, discovering the rules that governed the country-within-a-country that was Catholic America was like stumbling upon the alternate reality of a Lewis Carroll tale. In the rest of their lives, American Catholics expected democracy and equal rights and accountability. In the Church they accepted a strict caste system dominated by self-selected men whose powers were checked only by other individuals of higher rank. In exchange for this power, ordained men were required to reject all of the most important relationships that were part of ordinary life, including parent, partner, grandparent, and even lover. Priests, bishops, cardinals, and the popes lived institutional lives, with all their basic needs met by the Church, independent of their own efforts. At the same time they were excused from the kinds of family responsibilities that define other men.

All of this governance and obedience occurred on a voluntary basis, of course. No one was forced to be a Catholic, just as no one was forced to be a Rotarian or a member of the Daughters of the American Revolution. However, most Catholics were born into the Church and were taught to respect and obey its rule from before the age when they could even understand what they were being told. Through culture, ritual, formal education, and family tradition, Catholic children learned that life on this Earth is a mere moment in the soul's eternal existence and that rebellion today would lead to suffering forever and ever. On the other hand, the Church promised never-ending bliss to anyone who professed the faith, adhered to the rules, and sought favor with God through rituals conducted by priests. It was no wonder, under these circumstances, that a sexual offense committed by a priest might be covered up by everyone, including the victim.

The Church system seemed to Anderson like a perfect environment for the abuse of power at all levels. He suspected that more families like the Lymans were suffering, somewhere, from the trauma, loss of faith, and psychological injury that accompany sexual abuse. He also knew that the leaders of the Catholic Church possessed the means to ease their pain. As pastors they could acknowledge the sins committed by priests, recognize the injuries they caused, reform their culture of secrecy, and honor their victims. As corporate officers they could take responsibility for their employees. But just as in Wonderland, where nonsense rules, the shepherds favored wolves over sheep and tended to themselves while ignoring the flock.

By the time he got to Stillwater and parked outside his half-renovated Victorian house, Anderson was overflowing with ideas about the case. Inside, he poured himself what he called a "brandy/seven" (brandy with 7-Up) while Julie made Reuben sandwiches. When they sat down together he told her about what he had heard and offered his unreserved assessment. Bishop Watters had obviously lied about what he knew of Adamson's behavior but he honestly didn't grasp that the priest had committed serious crimes. The same was true for every other bishop, priest, and counselor who dealt with Adamson. They showed enormous concern for his well-being and too little for the adolescent boys he had assaulted.

Anderson used the plural "boys" because of the Watters letter that referred to "five different communities." This was evidence that like so many sexual offenders, Adamson was compelled to carry out his crimes over and over again. Also, Anderson didn't believe for a second that the bishop's sorrowful encounter with "heartbroken and bewildered" parents had taken place in Dubuque and involved some other errant priest. He was sure that Watters had been confronted more recently in Winona, by parents who believed that Fr. Adamson was a sexual predator and that the experience had shaken him.

As the night wore on and Anderson mixed

a second brandy/seven, he and Julie considered the task immediately ahead — tomorrow's deposition with Adamson — and the longer-term implications of what had come to light. Julie enjoyed these late-night sessions when they worked together, bouncing ideas around and making notes on a legal pad. Having moved from her job at the trial lawyers association to one at a local law firm, Julie was becoming familiar with the language of the law and the strategies and tactics attorneys used. She was delighted to watch Jeff's mind race as he dissected the testimony he had heard during the day and framed the issues raised by it.

Where Adamson was concerned, they decided that the interrogation would begin with soft questions that would cover his training and employment, and establish that he had been under the supervision of superiors who understood why he had been transferred from parish to parish and sent for counseling. Anderson would then press for as much detail as possible, hoping that Adamson might discuss other incidents of abuse. At the very least Anderson hoped that something in what the priest said would open new avenues for discovery, including a path to documents that might be harvested from chancery files and the names of witnesses he might pursue.

Beyond this one case, Jeff and Julie began to imagine that other families would come looking for a lawyer if this lawsuit ever made it into the press. Anderson couldn't judge the extent of the problem of the Church covering for abusive priests; however, he knew that Watters and Roach both followed the same speak-no-evil approach. Between the Diocese of Winona and the Archdiocese of St. Paul, the Church could count almost a million members. If you considered the broader area that Roach oversaw as "metropolitan" his management style could affect roughly 1.5 million Catholics tended by more than 1,500 priests. How many of those clerics were offenders? wondered Anderson. How many of those laypeople had been victimized?

The notion that parishes across two states might harbor sex offenders in white collars was hard for Anderson to accept. What were the odds that that many people would close their eyes so the Church could protect bad priests? The answer would have to wait until others found out that it might be possible to sue the Church. For the time being, the proceedings against Adamson and the two dioceses were still hidden from public view and Anderson's clients would be better served if he held on to the threat of making the family's claim public. The leverage might force the Church to offer a settlement that would satisfy the Lymans' desire for accountability and compensation.

The Lyman case had the potential to be

the biggest of Anderson's career. As a matter of justice, he wanted to hold powerful churchmen accountable and, if possible, expose a cover-up that obscured serious crimes. When it came to the money, he could imagine a settlement or jury verdict that would bring him a substantial fee. Some of that cash could be put into new windows to keep out the cold wind that blew through his house in Stillwater. Some might also be spent on a kitchen door tight enough so that their dog Barney wouldn't find a sheet of ice floating in his water when he went to his bowl on winter mornings.

Tantalizing as it might have been to dwell on fees, Clarence Darrow–style glory, and a flood of new clients, Jeff Anderson set aside these exciting thoughts. He made another brandy/seven and took it upstairs to the drafty bedroom. The empty glass rested on the nightstand as he drifted off to sleep.

6.
A WEEPING PRIEST

Dressed in black with a white clerical collar, Thomas Adamson was six feet tall with thick, wavy black hair that was turning gray. Physically fit and with an unlined face, he looked young for his fifty-two years. If he was nervous when he showed up at the conference room in the First Bank Building in downtown St. Paul he didn't show it. Surrounded by attorneys sent to represent him and the Church, he calmly swore to tell the truth and then sat at a table to face Jeff Anderson and a court reporter named Linda Jacobsen. Outside, a late winter storm pelted the streets with icy rain.

As Adamson answered questions with carefully worded sentences, the priest struck Jeffrey Anderson as bright, engaged, and even charming. When Adamson mentioned the influence his Catholic parents and grandparents had on his decision to become a priest it was easy for anyone in the room to imagine a young man trying his best to please his elders. Adamson was self-deprecating as he explained that his terrible singing voice held him back as a preacher, and a bit wistful as he talked about a brief relationship with a young woman that might have been something more if he had taken another path through life.

The man's openness was disarming. As Anderson watched and listened he could imagine how a lonely adolescent boy, especially one who might be struggling in school and desperate for friendship, might see in him a friend and a role model.

Eager to understand how Catholic clergy thought about sex, Anderson didn't confront Adamson when he deployed euphemisms like "touching" and "contact" to refer to incidents of sexual groping and oral sex with various adult partners and child victims. Instead he let the priest get comfortable, so that in the course of a six-hour interview he would reveal details of his own life, and secrets of the Church, that would shock the average Catholic believer.

But as serious as the subject was, Anderson's struggle to grasp Catholic terms and thinking inevitably produced lighter moments. One arose as Adamson described the instruction he had received on living a chaste and celibate life and mentioned something called "de sexto." The words caught Anderson by surprise.

"There was an actual class called *sex day*?" asked Anderson, sounding a bit startled.

"De," replied Adamson. "It's Latin." (The document Adamson referred to was presented to seminarians in Latin, and formed the core of their instruction of sexual morality.)

To get around Latin words and the sideways terms churchmen used to discuss sex, Anderson had to push Adamson to be specific. Once the priest understood what was expected of him, he willingly shared his sexual history. Adamson said that in seminary he had a series of sexual relationships with young men and boys. He continued this behavior at Catholic University in Washington, D.C., in the mid-1950s, and after he became a diocesan priest in Southern Minnesota. In the years since he was ordained in 1958 many of his assignments and transfers had been required because of complaints or rumors of sexual indiscretions and offenses.

When Adamson was working in the town of Caledonia and parents seemed suspicious of his devotion to a boys' basketball team, the bishop had him swap jobs with a colleague in Rochester. Since the priest in Rochester was reportedly having an affair with a woman in his parish, the switch solved two problems. In other instances Adamson was sent to replace priests who resigned to get married, or fled assignments because of "indiscretion with youth." In these cases the bishop wouldn't actually say, out loud, that a predecessor had molested boys, but the priest knew this was the issue.

"Did you know what he was talking about?" asked Anderson.

"Yes," replied the priest.

Adamson said he was once confronted by a fellow priest named Fr. Jansen who worked in a different parish and was aware of a specific incident that occurred at a pool in the city of Rochester. Jansen, who had since died, was upset because he had heard rumors about what occurred.

"Did you, Father, acknowledge to Fr. Jansen that you had touched a boy inappropriately?" asked Anderson.

"Yes."

This confession, along with Jansen's name and the location of the incident, gave Anderson a new line of evidence to pursue as he sought to establish that the Church was negligent in supervising priests. It was a gift, really, and when no one objected to the line of questioning he pressed for more details. To his surprise, Adamson was forthcoming.

"When did you touch this boy inappropriately?"

"In the fall of 1973."

"And it's your recollection that Fr. Jansen got this information from another priest, whose identity you don't know?"

"That's what I think, yes."

"Without describing the boy, who you choose to not identify, would you describe what happened in terms of the inappropriate touching?"

"Yes. It was that I grabbed him and touched him in the groin at a swimming pool."

As Adamson filled in more details, the only interruption came from an attorney for the Diocese of Winona who asked him to raise his voice because a fan in the room was making it hard for him to hear.

The priest recalled that the swimming pool complaint was among several items he had discussed with Bishop Watters in 1974. Another revolved around a series of sexual crimes he had perpetrated over the course of a decade. Adamson said he had met this particular young man when he was still a student in a school where he worked. He pursued him and began having sex with him when he was a teenager. In 1974 the man's relatives went to Bishop Watters to demand that Adamson be disciplined. "I think one of his brothers may have called or contacted Bishop Watters."

"And did Bishop Watters then contact you?"

"Yes."

"What did Bishop Watters tell you that he had learned?"

"He told me that this man was making threats on me, threats of public exposure, that he was angry; those types of things."

"Did Bishop Watters make it clear to you in that conversation that the information that he received was that you had engaged in inappropriate sexual contact?"

"Yes."

"And there is no doubt in your mind that he was talking about inappropriate sexual contact and not chemical dependency or something else?"

"Yes."

The family who had come to Watters to complain was from Adrian, a town of 1,200 in the corner of Minnesota where the state bumps up against Iowa and South Dakota. Adamson said he didn't deny the accusation. Like the others, it was true.

Watching the priest answer as directly as he could, while confessing to behavior that was both criminal and, in the eyes of the Church, profoundly sinful, Jeffrey Anderson couldn't help but feel a twinge of pity. For the record, he asked how Adamson had felt when Watters confronted him.

"It was just a feeling of embarrassment and guilt and sadness."

"Did you cry at that point?"

"I don't know if — during — I don't know if during the conversation I did, but many times I did."

A moment later, Anderson sought the same information, in a different way. "When you had that initial discussion with Bishop Watters did you weep at that point or cry in his presence, do you remember?"

"Probably."

A weeping priest who confesses to seducing a tenth grader is not something anyone would likely forget, which is precisely the point Adamson helped to make. This memory would help attorney Anderson challenge Bishop Watters's testimony and in offering it, Adamson seemed to make common cause with the lawyer who was suing him.

The priest's intent was clear. By recalling what the bishop knew and when, Adamson shifted blame away from himself. Indeed, much of what Adamson said on that stormy day in St. Paul described a bureaucracy that was more concerned with preventing a scandal than protecting children, and wholly inadequate when it came to dealing with a priest who was a sexual predator. Time and again Adamson's behavior would lead to complaints, admonitions, a promise to stop, and a transfer to a new parish where he was free to manipulate and exploit a new batch of boys.

The psychological treatment, as Adamson described it, was haphazard and ill focused. One therapist asked him to interpret ink blots and gave him the Minnesota Multiphasic Personality Inventory, which is supposed to identify various pathologies. However, he was never told that he suffered from a specific syndrome or mental illness and the treatment that followed was not on any consistent schedule. He might attend a session or two and then take several weeks off. And when he did work with his therapist, they didn't focus on his attraction to boys. The same was true for his in-patient treatment at a clinic in Hartford, Connecticut, where all the other patients seemed to be receiving care for drug or alcohol addiction. Adamson said that sex wasn't ever discussed in the group therapy sessions there, and he departed feeling like he had made little or no progress toward controlling his compulsion.

Compulsion was the word that came to Jeff Anderson's mind as Adamson spilled out his sexual history. No matter how often he pledged to be celibate and resolved to stay away from adolescent boys, he couldn't stop. Since he couldn't stop, he began to justify it to himself in various ways. Eventually he came to regard his practice of pursuing, grooming, and then raping adolescents as no more serious than any other priest's struggle with chastity, even though his transgressions involved minors and an obvious imbalance of power. According to this logic, since all sex was sinful, the particular kind of sex a priest enjoyed — from masturbation to adult affairs to violating boys — didn't matter. Sex was sex was sex.

As he listened to the testimony, Jeffrey Anderson refused to make in-the-moment judgments about Adamson. Shock, disgust, or disapproval would likely register on his face and the last thing he wanted to do was send any signal that might make Adamson feel like he wasn't being understood. He needed this witness to feel as relaxed as possible. Anderson looked at the priest with a steady, interested gaze and often nodded as if he accepted and appreciated what the man had to say. At times, to his own surprise, he actually did empathize with Adamson. Immature and isolated, Fr. Adamson had been so knotted up by rules, prohibitions, obsessions, and shame that he couldn't even consider the damage he was doing. His fear of what might happen if he took responsibility — a fear his bosses seemed to share — drained the truth right out of his life, leaving him a hollow and inadequate man.

Anderson reached the limit of his compassion for Fr. Adamson at the end of the day, when he finally turned to address his behavior with his client Gregory Lyman. As he brought up the young man's name, Anderson could picture Lyman locked up in St. Cloud at age twenty-one. As far as Anderson was concerned, this priest had all but guaranteed that Lyman would have a troubled life when he proved to him that no one, not even a consecrated man, could be trusted. How could he not wind up in serious trouble?

It turned out that Adamson agreed with most of what Gregory Lyman had said in his complaint. Adamson began to groom him on an overnight trip to the St. Paul Seminary where he and other boys from the parish were free to use the gym and other facilities.

"What I remember is his aloneness," said Adamson, as he reflected on the trip.

Adamson recalled that he had focused his attention on the lonesome boy, earned his trust, and was soon training him to be an altar server and giving him rides to church or to the St. Paul YMCA for swimming or basketball. Before the boy turned fourteen Adamson raped him for the first time. Lyman had said he was deeply conflicted by these experiences. He both dreaded and welcomed the attention, and afterward he kept quiet about what happened. The priest didn't dispute any of these facts, and confirmed that as these sexual contacts continued over the course of years, so did Lyman's discomfort.

To hear Adamson tell the story, Greg Lyman never wanted to go public with what had happened and was upset that his parents had pushed the lawsuit forward. When Anderson asked him about the last time he "saw or had sex" with Gregory Lyman, the priest's lawyer made one of his rare objections, noting that it was a "double" question.

"That's a good objection," replied Anderson, positioning himself as both a reasonable man and the voice of authority in the room.

Adamson then revealed that on several occasions Lyman had visited him to ask for cash because he was living on the street and was hungry. All told he gave him about $250. At their very last meeting in prison, "he was terrifically happy to see me," said Adamson. They talked about their shared hope that the uproar would simply die away. Adamson felt "kind of a healing" as they parted and the young man returned to his cell. Within days another prisoner would call Gregory Lyman a "baby raper" and hit him hard enough to break his jaw.

The fact that Lyman was, himself, a sex offender, might trouble jurors if they ever learned of his record, but Anderson knew that most judges would bar this evidence from trial because Lyman was not the one subject to a complaint. And in his own heart and mind, Anderson found it relatively easy to separate his client's acts from Adamson's. Greg had committed his crimes when he was still a juvenile fresh from being victimized by an adult who was his most trusted friend. The criminal justice system had taken these facts into account when dealing with him and, like Anderson, cut him a significant amount of slack. Indeed, the mess that was

Gregory Lyman's life — his crimes, his dismal education and employment record, his sporadic homelessness — was all evidence of the harm done to him by Thomas Adamson.

The real challenge Anderson faced revolved around proving that Adamson was not solely responsible for his acts. This was necessary for two reasons. First, Anderson wanted to expose and change the practices that allowed higher-ups to obscure and enable Adamson's crimes. Second, he wanted to get at the resources held by the two dioceses, which were capable of compensating the Lymans at a much higher rate than any single parish priest. In lawyer's parlance, the dioceses had the "deep pockets."

Reaching into those pockets would require evidence that bishops knew what Adamson was doing and failed to take appropriate action. The priest's own account, offered in the deposition, would be helpful but could also be dismissed as self-serving. What Anderson needed were the names of witnesses who had firsthand knowledge of earlier cases. The groping incident at the Rochester pool was one avenue to explore, but with Fr. Jansen dead, Anderson faced the daunting task of trying to locate and interview dozens, if not hundreds of men who had been boys at the school where Adamson worked at the time of the incident. As he contemplated this task

Anderson heard, in his mind, complaints from his partner Reinhardt, who saw the time and expenses eaten up by the case that, given the status enjoyed by the Catholic Church, was a long shot at best.

Jeffrey Anderson had time to think about his next move against the Church as he flew to London — his first trip across the Atlantic — to meet with two clients. The men had been passengers in a car that had been in a head-on collision with a wrong-way driver named Henry Ebert, whose blood alcohol level was twice the legal limit. Henry Ebert died of his injuries. Anderson's clients were hospitalized. One, Paul Cook, suffered minor injuries and was released in three days. The other, Ray McVeigh, spent three weeks in a hospital bed recovering from a broken arm and multiple internal injuries.

The case might not have gained much attention if Cook was not the former drummer of the Sex Pistols — "the world's most notorious punk rock band" (*Rolling Stone*) — and he wasn't touring with guitarist McVeigh to promote the first album released by their new band The Professionals. The two musicians had just finished playing a concert and were riding in a limousine when the collision occurred. The album, which was titled, ironically enough, *I Didn't See It Coming,* subsequently bombed in record stores. Anderson reasoned that The Professionals had lost sales because the crash interrupted their promotion campaign. To make up for this loss he added a premium to the demands they made from the driver's estate and commenced a negotiation that, due to the distance separating the lawyer and his clients and the novelty of the claim, dragged on for five years.

By the spring of 1986 the case was finally placed on the docket at Hennepin County District Court and Anderson needed to meet with his clients and depose people in the British music business. He took Julie with him. She went sightseeing while Jeff and a defense lawyer named Mark Condon visited with music executives who testified that indeed The Professionals would have sold many more copies of their record if they had been able to promote it.

Condon, who had been at William Mitchell School of Law with Anderson, had also brought his wife to London and they turned out to be fine company at restaurants and nightclubs. On one evening spent with McVeigh at his favorite spot Anderson got, as Julie would say, "ripping drunk." He enjoyed himself so much that he couldn't be roused in the morning. Four years into their relationship Julie took note of Anderson's condition but didn't give it much thought. Although he would always deny he suffered any ill effects from a big night of drinking, Julie considered sleep-late hangovers part of his routine. She dressed, left their hotel room alone, and walked to Buckingham Palace to watch the changing of the guard at 11:30 A.M.

When they returned to St. Paul, whatever bonding Anderson and Condon may have done over drinks didn't make things any easier for Anderson at the negotiating table. On the eve of the trial Condon rejected Anderson's offer to settle for $130,000. Cook and McVeigh told him to withdraw the offer and prepare for battle. They weren't worried about losing. In fact, the closer they got to trial the more determined they became. When, at the last minute, the defense finally offered the full $130,000, they turned it down, saying it was too late.

As court was convened, Anderson saw that Judge Peter Lindberg was in no mood to proceed. He seemed open to the defense lawyers' complaint that they had met the plaintiffs' demands but were rebuffed. Anderson said the offer came too late and his clients turned it down. Lindberg didn't care. He said that if $130,000 had been enough to settle the case at some earlier point, it was enough to settle it now. It was, after all, more money than The Professionals had ever received for a single concert appearance, and in this case they didn't even perform.

Anderson, whose appeal of Lindberg's ruling failed, would always believe his clients had been cheated. He would be grateful, however, for the diversion The Professionals had provided from the frustrating pursuit of Thomas Adamson. Almost two years had passed since Anderson had agreed to represent the Lyman family and he had yet to find a path through the maze of secrecy that was the Church. Anderson needed a break.

7.
FIVE BROTHERS; THREE VICTIMS

"I know what you are trying to do about Fr. Adamson. You will want to talk to Jay Klein. He's a parole officer in Worthington."

"Who is this?"

Jeff Anderson thought he heard the man on the other end of the line take a breath. He asked again, "Who is this?"

"Talk to Jay Klein. In Worthington."

The man hung up.

The lawsuit Anderson had filed naming Thomas Adamson and two Minnesota dioceses had not been publicized. Anderson had purposefully filed it according to the rules of so-called "hip pocket service," which, in a quirk of local custom, put the proceedings under the auspices of the county court while it remained a private matter. This status allowed Anderson to depose witnesses and request documents with the full power of a judge backing him up. It also allowed the Church a chance to avoid scandal by cooperating.

Since no one outside the parties themselves knew about the suit, the man on the phone had to be a Church insider — Anderson guessed he was a priest — or someone so close to Catholic officials that he had been trusted with powerful secrets. Either way, this Deep Throat source was specific enough that Anderson paid a private investigator named Bob Bosse to locate Klein. Bosse, a former police officer, discovered that Klein was indeed a probation officer. He worked for Noble County, in the southwest corner of Minnesota. Both his office and his home were in Worthington.

On a sunny June morning Anderson settled into the driver's seat of his sleek Datsun 280ZX — silver exterior, black leather interior — and drove a hundred miles south on I-35 to Albert Lea, and then turned west on I-90. Bob Bosse occupied the passenger seat beside him. At six feet four inches tall and well over two hundred pounds, Bosse had a way of keeping things calm. Since Anderson was going to Worthington unannounced, he thought a calming influence just might be necessary. As the two men passed through towns named Blue Earth, Welcome, and Alpha, they discussed how to approach a man who was a law enforcement professional and might be wary about their intentions.

Klein wasn't just a probation officer, he was director of corrections for the entire county and he occupied a big office in an old court-house a few blocks from Lake Okabena. An old hand at dealing with inmates and parol-ees, Klein was accustomed to hearing all sorts of strange stories. He also knew how cops and lawyers operated. When Anderson sud-denly appeared at his office, Klein didn't believe that this lawyer from St. Paul had been meeting with someone in the neighbor-hood. But this was the kind of well-mannered lie Klein almost welcomed because it gave him the option to decline Anderson's request for a visit without feeling the least bit guilty. However, with the mention of Fr. Adamson, Klein knew immediately that he wanted to talk.

"My dad and I ran him out of Rochester," he told Anderson.

Immediately agreeing to a formal interview, Klein waited patiently while Bob Bosse fussed with a tape recorder. Anderson took a moment to gauge the man in front of him. Forty years old, Klein was about five foot ten, with a medium build, and blondish-brown hair. Solid Norwegian farmer stock, thought Anderson, the kind of guy who would drop everything to help a neighbor in need. When it became clear that Bosse couldn't make the recorder work, Klein volunteered the one he used to tape his sessions with parolees. With the technical issues resolved, they turned to the subject of the Klein family and Thomas

Adamson.

Klein had been raised in a devoutly Catholic family who lived on a farm outside town. Adrian was one of eight Minnesota communities settled in the nineteenth century by Archbishop John Ireland and his Irish Catholic Colonization Association. Ireland bought 400,000 acres of land, which he sold to people responding to advertisements in church newspapers in the East. Like almost everyone else in the area, the Kleins attended St. Adrian Church and sent their children to Catholic schools. They were friendly with the priests assigned to the region, including Thomas Adamson. And they were not altogether surprised when Jay's younger brother Gene announced he was going to go to seminary.

After he was ordained in the spring of 1974, Gene Klein had trouble getting comfortable with being a priest. Drink helped him until it hurt him and he wound up in a residential rehabilitation program in Rochester. It was there, in late November, that he first spoke of years of sexual exploitation by Fr. Adamson. It had begun in Adrian when he was an eighth grader and Adamson was principal of St. Adrian's school. Once the wall of secrecy was broken, Gene told everything to his parents and his brother Jay, who back then was a teacher and basketball coach at St. Francis of Assisi School in Rochester, where

Adamson was the principal.

Jay Klein was disturbed by what Gene revealed but not shocked. He had worked with Adamson and as he told Anderson, "I noticed that he always checked the seventh and eighth graders for their jock sizes." Klein was most upset by the reaction of his elderly parents, Jim and Rose. Quick to assume responsibility, they were heartsick over the memories of allowing Adamson to take their sons on overnight trips and encouraging them to be involved in activities at the church and school. They felt as if they had pushed Gene into the arms of a sexual predator and were saddened to know that their son had been unable to confide in them.

The truth was even worse than they knew. Within a week another younger brother named Robert would tearfully confess to Jay that he had been molested by Adamson when he was at the same school, but the first incident had been the last. According to Bob, Adamson had said that priests were "given the right by the Church as celibates to have contact with young boys and that's what celibacy means." A third brother named Jack then said that Adamson had attempted to molest him, too, but he had resisted and the priest never tried anything again. A fourth, who requested his name not be published, said he was never molested.

Five brothers; three victims. Jay Klein

telephoned Bishop Watters to report what he had heard and demand that Thomas Adamson be removed from his post in Rochester. He also asked that the bishop move to defrock him, by whatever process was required. According to Klein, Watters had said something about confronting Adamson but insisted that any immediate action would require the priest to confess and cooperate, which was unlikely. Not satisfied, Klein went directly to Adamson and told him, "If you say one more Mass we are going to come up onto the altar and tell everyone what you have done." Adamson left Rochester before the next Sunday. Jay Klein resigned his position at St. Francis School and began the long process of disengaging from the Catholic Church.

Having worked in probation since 1975, Jay Klein knew enough about the law to understand that he was giving Anderson information that would prove that Bishop Watters knew Adamson had had sex with two underage boys and had approached a third. Though the churchmen were never prosecuted due to the statute of limitations, Klein could testify that Watters knew about these crimes and failed in his duty to protect the public from Adamson. Watching Jeffrey Anderson struggle to contain his excitement over what he was hearing, Klein decided to give him a couple more gems.

After his complaint was registered with the bishop, said Klein, "We had a lot of priests call us and tell us to back off." Klein also heard from the elderly priest who had founded St. Francis School. Father Raymond Jansen began their conversation sounding like someone who wanted to defend a fellow priest and scold a layman who had crossed the caste boundary. But as they continued to talk, the old priest said that Adamson had been confronted about his behavior and sent for treatment twice before, but never completed therapy. Jansen had since died, but Klein said the information that Adamson had gotten into trouble *before* 1974 suggested a new line of investigation for the plaintiffs.

Finally, Klein told Anderson about Sr. Tierney Trueman and Sr. Micon Welsch, two nuns who worked at St. Francis School. Welsch had told him that everyone at the school knew not to leave Adamson alone with boys and that she made a point of monitoring the gym when he was in there with children. Sr. Tierney had talked with Klein about Adamson, and was so upset she immediately made the fifty-mile drive to Winona to meet with Bishop Watters. She warned him to remove Adamson before Klein did something drastic. She came back to report to Klein that the bishop didn't react much at all to her visit. He didn't seem surprised or angry, but he did seem "pained."

Watching Anderson make notes on a legal pad, Klein knew which of his revelations struck a chord and took some pleasure in the attorney's struggle to record every important lead. In the years since his run-in with Adamson, Klein's work for the county had brought him into contact with many perpetrators and victims of sexual abuse. The more he learned about the tendencies of offenders — they rarely stopped of their own accord — and the damage they could do, the more he regretted letting go of his complaints about Adamson when he left Rochester. Anderson was giving him a chance to correct this mistake and he was glad for it.

When the attorney and the private investigator departed, Klein stood on the steps of the courthouse and watched them move down the sidewalk. He smiled as he heard Anderson, who was a foot shorter than Bosse and a hundred pounds lighter, chew him out over the tape recorder. He was also amused to see Anderson pump his fist and give Bosse a high five in celebration, no doubt for the breakthrough they had achieved because they had heeded the voice on the phone.

In Stillwater, Julie Aronson ran to the ringing phone and picked it up before the answering machine could seize the call.

"We got 'em!" shouted Jeff in a voice loud enough to overcome the sound of traffic whizzing past the pay phone.

In a hurried voice he told her about the Klein family and the offenses Adamson had committed long ago. Now that he knew the outlines of those incidents he could chase down additional documents and witnesses that would prove Bishops Watters and Roach had knowingly placed a habitual sex offender in parishes where he had access to more victims. The Church would either settle the case for a big sum, or face certain defeat and a higher price at trial.

Listening to all of this, Julie knew Jeff was correct about the case. She was happy for him, but she was also afraid. In victory as well as defeat Jeff had a tendency toward excess and overreaction. On this night he was likely to stop on the way home to celebrate, either at one of the bars downtown or at a friend's house. If not, he might come home and drink even more brandy/sevens than usual. Either way, he would turn this success into an opportunity for oblivion.

Worse would be his response to the ultimate end of this case. Since agreeing to represent the Lymans, Anderson had built his pursuit of the two dioceses into a cause filled with drama and moral imperative. He was right, of course. The Lymans' lawsuit revolved around some profound issues and it was Anderson's ability to frame what was happening as a morality tale that enabled him to

160

cut through all the strange language and arcane Catholic logic that might confuse someone else. But as he generated a sense of mission and urgency, Anderson also made the case so important in his own life that its resolution would be an emotional spectacle, no matter how it turned out.

Julie had seen this dynamic play out before. The decision of a judge or jury would be capped by a party or a night on the town that would transform Jeff into someone very different from the man who made her his partner and confidante over Reuben sandwiches. Raucous and funny, he would become the center of attention and say or do almost anything. Once, on a dare, he had stripped naked and walked down the hill where his house stood to sit on a sidewalk bench. More than once he had flirted with other women so openly that Julie walked out and didn't come back. And even when she stayed at these events she felt ever more uncomfortable as the night wore on and the Jeff she loved faded away, replaced by a character, a stranger who she didn't like very much.

The fear of what came with the end of a big case wasn't something Julie had ever discussed with anyone, and she hadn't yet figured out her feelings in a way that would allow her to explain them. She needed Jeff's approval almost as much as she had craved her father's love and attention when she was a girl, and she was afraid to make him angry.

In time, Julie's feelings would all come out, but for the moment she would hang on through the twists and turns. Within a few days Jeff would propose to her during dinner at the best place in Stillwater, the Matterhorn Room at the Lowell Inn. There, surrounded by cuckoo clocks and beer steins and couples dipping morsels of food into bubbling fondue pots, he offered a ring in a glass of champagne. She said "Yes" without considering the implausibility of her secret hope that he would stop drinking. She was so happy, she didn't care when the restaurant manager wouldn't let her take home the champagne glass as a souvenir.

8.

THE ANGELS HAD TO CRY

Jay Klein was William Hull's nightmare come to life and, as attorney for Fr. Thomas Adamson and the Winona Diocese, he began attacking him in the first minutes of his deposition. Hull objected to everything Klein might say about his dealings with his clients and announced that he would fight to keep most of his testimony from ever seeing the light of a courtroom.

"We are objecting continuously," he declared, "to each question as it is being asked."

With this opening shot, Hull set the mood for a daylong session inside Jeffrey Anderson's conference room at the Conwed Tower. If Fr. Adamson's deposition had been a model of civil confrontation, this one was going to be much uglier. After the first half hour of halting testimony Klein himself stopped the proceedings to complain.

"It really interrupts my train of thought to have you continually objecting," said Klein.

"I guess, Mr. Witness, I am the attorney

and I'll make such objections as I see fit during your testimony," answered Hull.

"It's Mr. Klein."

William Hull never would address the witness as "Mr. Klein." However, as one of the half dozen lawyers sitting on the defendants' side of the table he was forced to absorb the facts that Klein presented. His testimony proved that Bishop Watters had, at best, offered misleading testimony when he said unidentified callers had offered vague complaints about Thomas Adamson. At worst a court might say that the bishop had committed perjury.

In his work, Klein had served for years on a child protection task force. This experience, along with formal training in criminology and psychology, had led him to agree with experts who found wide evidence that sexual offenders rarely stopped seeking new victims and that therapy was rarely successful. "I became more and more aware of the inability to cure pedophiles and I felt very uncomfortable," recalled Klein. Certain "there was a possibility of current or future victims" he had reported Adamson to a national abuse hotline.

Jeffrey Anderson didn't know enough about the international Catholic Church, or care enough about its inner workings, to appreciate the controversies that occupied its leaders

164

in the summer and fall of 1986. In America, where the bishops had just rejected the Mouton-Doyle-Peterson proposal for dealing with sexual abuse cases, their national conference issued a harsh critique of capitalism and its inequalities that provoked howls of complaint from political conservatives. In Rome, engineers turned up the power on radio transmitters beaming church programs to Eastern Bloc communist countries and the Vatican involved itself in politics from the Middle East to Central America and the Philippines. But the most important development of the year, according to a poll of American religion writers, was Cardinal Ratzinger's campaign to discipline theologians and clergy who were tolerant, or even accepting, of birth control and homosexuality.

Homosexuality was such a preoccupation for Rome that in October 1986 Ratzinger's Congregation for the Doctrine of the Faith issued lengthy instructions "on the pastoral care of homosexual persons." This guide for bishops defined a gay orientation as "an objective disorder" and in a not-so-veiled allusion to AIDS, criticized those who advocated for equal rights even though "homosexuality may seriously threaten the lives and well-being of a large number of people."

Ratzinger's document was, in tone and focus, a departure from the more liberal position expressed by the Vatican ten years earlier, which urged Catholics to oppose discrimination against homosexuals. What caused the shift? It was, undoubtedly, inspired in part by the fact that John Paul II and Ratzinger were more traditionalist than their predecessors. However, ample evidence also suggests they were addressing an issue that was not confronted directly in the document but concerned the Church nevertheless: homosexuality in the priesthood.

As the former priest Richard Sipe reported, between 1978 and 1985 widely cited estimates of the proportion of priests who were gay doubled from about 20 to roughly 40 percent. This shift was attributed to many factors, including changing social attitudes that made it easier for people to accept themselves and others as gay. Sipe suspected that this wide variation in estimates reflected the fact that many clergy really didn't understand their own sexual identity. Over and over again he had met men who had engaged in homosexual relationships, some of which were situational and dependent on the fact that these men lived in a sex-segregated community similar to a prison or an isolated military unit. Some denied the sexual aspect of themselves. Others split off their sexual activity, to place it completely outside their stated values. This allowed them to preach the Church's severe moral message to others while hypocritically violating the rules themselves.

In time, the archbishop of Milwaukee, Rembert Weakland, would theorize that for many priests Vatican II had transformed sex "from something negative that leads you into sin, into something positive." Priests loosened their commitment to celibacy. "Summer sessions at Catholic colleges became courtship camps," recalled Weakland. In the same time period thousands of heterosexuals abandoned the priesthood to marry. Among the priests who remained in the Church, a long-standing gay subculture became more significant and slightly more open. Some gay priests sought to be assigned together so they could live as couples in the same rectory. Many vacationed together. However, even as gays came to represent a larger proportion of the priesthood, they were still pressured, under the threat of scandal and dismissal, to keep their orientation and relationships secret.

Ratzinger's letter further isolated gay clergy from the outside world, where homosexuality was fast losing its stigma. Thirteen years had passed since the American Psychiatric Association had declassified homosexuality as a disorder. In a remarkable reversal, the fear and rejection of gay people — called homophobia — had become recognized as a genuine psychological problem. This shift, from the notion that homosexuality was disordered, to the idea that *the fear of it* was the real pathology, was matched by steady progress for the gay rights movement. By the middle of the 1980s homosexuality had been decriminalized in many states and countries. The Democratic Party had added a gay rights plank to its party platform, and both the state of Wisconsin and the City of Miami had made discrimination based on sexual orientation a crime.

In their devotion to attacking homosexuality, Ratzinger and other church officials stood isolated from many of the faithful who knew openly gay priests. In 1986 off-duty priests commonly sought companionship and acceptance in the gay community and they were generally welcome. Richard Sipe, who was conducting a long-term study of celibacy and the priesthood, saw psychological defensiveness and denial at work in the Vatican's effort to criticize and control homosexuality. He also knew from personal experience that celibacy and the sins of sex had created a vast system of mutual blackmail that served, in a perverse way, to strengthen the clerical culture. Under these conditions, priests who had sex of any kind, even alone, routinely confessed and sought absolution from each other. The sanctity of the confessional and the guarantee of forgiveness meant that priests were united in their secrecy. Without the culture of secrecy the entire caste of ordained, special-status men would be revealed to be just like everyone else. With it, they could claim to be holier than everyone else and enjoy the care and comfort of the institutional Church.

Whether it was a matter of theology, homophobia, or even self-hatred, the Church's aggressive approach to homosexuality brought into focus John Paul II's stringent definition of Catholicism. In general, the Vatican under his reign made very specific demands on those who would declare themselves true believers. It was also consistent with what experts would prescribe for religious leaders who might be worried about the fervor of the faithful. Stricter rules may scare away some people who value self-determination, but they also inspire greater loyalty in those who embrace the faith fully. This is why fundamentalist Protestants are generally more vocal about their beliefs and consistent in their church attendance than so-called mainline Protestants. Having given up more to achieve an identity that is both separate from and superior to the population at large, they express their faith with much greater energy. Exceptions, like liberal Catholics who devote themselves to the poor, abound. But as a general rule, conservative faiths that are rigidly rules-based, tend to inspire more loyalty.

For the most ardent traditionalists, fealty to

the Vatican was on par with belief in the holy trinity when it came to defining who was, and who was not, a *real* Catholic. Ordained clergy added this obligation to the many requirements that, if fulfilled, gave them a sense of identity. In Minnesota, the bishops of St. Paul and Winona recognized immediately that with Jay Klein's testimony the potential for scandal increased significantly.

Through the fall and into the winter of 1986, Jeff Anderson and his investigator, Bob Bosse, continued finding and interviewing witnesses, including nuns at schools and parishes where Adamson had worked, and added to their requests for documents. This process uncovered evidence that at least nine boys had been molested by Adamson during his career as a priest. They also discovered that a psychiatrist in Rochester, who had seen Adamson in 1967, had informed the Diocese of Winona that that his condition was "incurable." Matched against Adamson's employment record, which showed him assigned to jobs where he would work with altar boys and come into regular contact with other children for another seventeen years, this evidence was particularly compelling.

Equally compelling were two memos, one dated February 1981 and one dated March 1982, that described in rather exasperated terms the conditions under which Adamson would be permitted to function as a priest.

Both declared "no youth contact" and required him to continue getting psychological care. The second of these documents was signed by Adamson and Archbishop Roach, and was titled "Special Agreement Between Archbishop Roach and Reverend Thomas Adamson." Although this document was intended to stop the criminal behavior of a priest who was sexually violating children, it resembled nothing more than the kind of contract a parent might draw up to bind a misbehaving boy to his promise of improved behavior.

As Anderson's investigation and discovery request revealed embarrassing secrets and threatened them with scandal, the bishops carried on in public as if nothing unusual was happening. In December Archbishop Roach publicly criticized Minneapolis city councilwoman Barbara Carlson for announcing that she would give her unmarried children and their friends condoms for Christmas. The archbishop said that because of Carlson "in Minneapolis the angels had to cry." Carlson, a Catholic, said she was far more concerned about unwanted pregnancies and AIDS than angels. "The archbishop may want to think everyone is virtuous and they're saving themselves for the holy sacrament of matrimony," she added. "But that's a delusion."

On Christmas morning the Minneapolis

Star Tribune published an interview with the archbishop that allowed him to discuss his spiritual life at length. He explained that he began every day with a 6:30 A.M. walk during which he prayed, and he credited the serenity prayer of Alcoholics Anonymous for helping him maintain sobriety, a requirement that arose after his conviction on charges of driving while intoxicated in 1985. The serenity prayer advises people to fix problems they can fix and recognize those they are powerless to address. "The very important part of that is the wisdom to know the difference," noted Roach. "I apply that many times in the day, to many things in the day, to the things that I do. Many things I just can't fix, and I tend to be a fixer. If I get battered often enough with enough things I can't fix, but I think I should, I'm going to be burst apart."

As the Christmas season passed and 1987 arrived, Bishops Roach and Watters moved to fix the Lyman problem, authorizing their attorneys to make a settlement offer. When Jeff Anderson took the call he was stunned by the amount — $1 million — and by the single requirement attached to the cash. As he later recalled it, Bill Hull, who represented the Diocese of Winona said, "I'm authorized to make your client an offer to $500,000 but they'll go to a million. Will you take it please? Your client will, of course, sign the usual confidentiality agreement."

Anderson was surprised by the number. He had never reached a million-dollar settlement in any of his previous cases. He quickly calculated that, depending on expenses and other variables, about $350,000 of it would go to his firm, which his partner would surely appreciate. He then took a deep breath and considered the "usual confidentiality agreement." He had never entertained a request for such an agreement. And if there was such a thing as a "usual" agreement that settled this kind of claim, then the Church must have settled and kept secret many previous cases. A secret settlement would mean no one would be alerted to the possibility that priests could sexually abuse children. Anderson spoke before thinking. "Signing will make us as bad as your client," he said.

Hull ignored the insult and reminded Anderson that he had a duty to take the offer to his client. Considering the fact that Lyman was jobless, drifting between his parents' home and the street, and selling plasma for the cash, a million dollars might be more than enough to overcome his moral outrage. Anderson called his client and set up a meeting at his parents' house the next day. He couldn't sleep at all during the night, considering how much Lyman needed the money and how wrong it would be to keep a settlement secret.

When the two men met, Anderson told Lyman to sit down. Before he spoke Anderson shed a few tears, partly out of exhaustion and partly out of fear for other child victims. He then told his client about the million dollars and the secrecy agreement, and finished by saying that he wanted to reject the offer on moral grounds and make a public filing of the lawsuit. With this strategy they could alert the community to the problem of clergy sexual abuse and cover-up inside the Church. Of course a trial would also bring the possibility of total defeat, Anderson had to add.

"But as your attorney I'd advise you to turn them down, file the lawsuit, and make this thing public."

Lyman didn't respond right away and his silence made Anderson tremble with anxiety. Finally Lyman said, "Do it, but do it fast before I change my mind."

Anderson left the meeting thinking about who he would call, and in what order. First would come the Winona Diocese's attorney, so that the offer would be rejected in a clear and formal way. Then he would contact every reporter he knew to tell them he was about to file a newsworthy suit at the Ramsey County Courthouse. He then left his office, complaint in hand, determined to file it with the clerk before Greg Lyman could call back and claim the $1 million.

As Anderson expected, the press was very interested in the suit and it was reported on local TV news broadcasts and in both the St. Paul and Minneapolis dailies. When asked to answer reporters' questions, the bishops declined, although they issued a statement that lamented "the damage done to the young man" and noted how the Church was "growing in its awareness of the problems of sexual abuse."

Although they intended to sound like humble and caring pastors, the churchmen immediately ran into the paradox in the competing roles they had to play. Catholics expected them to act like true Christians, which required them to honestly confront all sin, including their own, and to protect their flocks. However, they were also defendants in a high-stakes lawsuit that threatened the finances and reputation of an institution they had vowed to protect. A creatively wary defense attorney might even imagine ways that the Lyman suit could lead to criminal charges against both the perpetrator Adamson and the bishops who could be viewed as his co-conspirators in covering up his assaults.

On the day after they stood as kindly pastors, the bishops seized the role of defendants. Bishop Watters went back to reporters to deny "all allegations of negligence, fault, or wrongdoing" on the part of the Diocese of Winona. Joan Bernet, spokeswoman for the St. Paul Diocese, said officials there had no knowledge of Adamson's criminal past when he came to work there in 1976. As for crimes committed after his arrival, which were reported to the Church, Bernet said the law did not require bishops to notify police, and parents had requested that no report be made to the authorities.

Bernet was technically correct in describing the bishops' status as clergymen, but as the ultimate authorities over Catholic schools they may have been required to report abuse as educators, who had been so-called mandated reporters since the early 1970s. Across the nation lobbyists for the Catholic Church and other denominations had fought being covered by such "mandated reporter" laws, arguing they would intrude on religious practices like confession. In Minnesota and most states they had succeeded, and these exemptions meant that bishops might hide a priest's assault on a child and escape being prosecuted themselves. Of course nothing prohibited a bishop from urging others to go to the police in order to protect other children from a predator, but in Adamson's case, and many hundreds that would follow, this option was never taken.

Rather than pursue the facts in hopes of stopping a possible predator, the bishops in Minnesota had sometimes actively avoided knowing the truth. Fr. James Fitzpatrick, who served in Winona, would testify that his superiors had ordered him to ignore early complaints against Adamson. Without real investigation, reports remained unfounded and could thereby be dismissed. In their letters, they communicated so obliquely that even under the pressure of discovery orders from a state court, they could continue to claim they hadn't known key facts. As the bishops shifted from expressing concern for the victim to denying responsibility, Jeff Anderson stood coolly on the sidelines, offering no quotes for the reporters who rang his phone. The filing spoke for itself, and in their wildly swinging struggle to respond the bishops accomplished more for his client in the court of public opinion than Anderson ever could. The publicity also inspired other families who had been traumatized by predatory priests to contact Anderson.

Three days after he filed the Lymans' papers, Anderson heard from several young adults who said they had also been abused by priests. One single mother called to say that her teenage son had been molested by Thomas Adamson. John Doe, as he would be called due to his age, had followed a path that was similar to Greg Lyman's. Lonesome and struggling in school, he was befriended by Adamson, who then sexually assaulted him. Disturbed by what had happened, he became withdrawn and even more isolated. He too was caught committing a burglary and it was this arrest that prompted him to reveal what Adamson had done.

In his first meetings with John Doe and his mother, Anderson was struck by how similar the boy was to Greg Lyman. Lawyers learn that they never get "perfect" clients free of their own troubles, but the pattern of victim-turned-perpetrator was truly remarkable. As Anderson was coming to know, sexual abuse often echoed in his clients' lives in ways that would shock people who had never investigated this kind of crime. Much of what Anderson discovered came from a fast-growing body of literature on the subject. He also received an informal education from various experts he retained. In Gregory Lyman's case he had hired a psychologist named Susan Phipps-Yonas, Ph.D., to evaluate his client so that he could gain some understanding of the damage done by Thomas Adamson.

When Phipps-Yonas earned her doctorate in 1978, her profession considered incest almost nonexistent and the long-term effects of child sexual abuse were poorly understood. By the mid-1980s new research and her own work with hundreds of cases referred by local courts had persuaded her that all forms of sexual abuse were far more common than she once believed. She also noted that individual victims reacted to sexual violation in very different ways. Some appeared to show little negative effects. Others were devastated by shame and feelings of betrayal and wound up enduring lifelong struggles with depression, paranoia, substance abuse, and other symptoms. Determining exact cause and effect was impossible, of course. But she saw so much suffering in victims that she became certain that sexual abuse could lead to depression, paranoia, drug and alcohol addiction, and even suicide.

Phipps-Yonas saw Gregory Lyman nine times and reviewed his medical files and court record. She discovered that Gregory was adopted by the Lyman family when he was five months old, and he had begun life in a family troubled by violence. It would defy credulity to say that a child born in rough circumstances was somehow doomed to be a victim of sexual abuse *and* become a perpetrator himself. However, in the course of their careers, both the psychologist and the attorney learned to expect disturbing and distressing surprises, including victims who had been abused by acquaintances or relatives before being assaulted by priests. In almost every case of clergy abuse Anderson had to deal with what he called "the ordinary chaos" of trauma victims and their families. As Dr. Phipps-Yonas would explain to him, sexual predators often pursue troubled children as victims in the same way that armed robbers target banks. Lonely, isolated, and depressed boys and girls who come from chaotic families yearn for attention and are more vulnerable to being targets of sexual violence. Since these same children often have trouble in school, or with the police, they have a record of problems that make them less credible should they ever complain. The same is true for parents who may not supervise their children closely because they are overwhelmed by life or suffering from a psychological disorder or addiction. These mothers and fathers have trouble recognizing a son or daughter's suffering.

In the case of John Doe, Anderson noted that the victim and his mother were both active alcoholics. Relying on what he had learned in his own aborted rehab stint and from his friend Grant Hall, he had pressed them to join Alcoholics Anonymous. Eventually this kind of intervention became routine for Anderson, who estimated that about 80 percent of his male clients had problems with drugs or alcohol or both. Arguing "I can't help you unless you are willing to help yourself," he would require them to seek help as a condition of their working relationship. Invariably his clients chose to enter treatment or join AA in order to continue working with Anderson and pursuing their cases.

At the time when he counseled John Doe and his mother to get help, Jeffrey Anderson's own alcoholism was practically roaring with strength. On many nights he went to a bar or club after work where he lost track of time in all the laughter, flirting, and storytelling. Having consumed enough alcohol to overcome his well-developed tolerance, he was nevertheless able to drive the twenty miles to Stillwater on instinct. His skills were so sharp that he was able to keep his car going in a straight line, but speed was another matter entirely. Once, after a party, he was stopped by a police officer who clocked his car going over eighty miles per hour. Like many, the cop who stopped Anderson knew him and liked him. He let him go.

In Stillwater he often drank until he fell asleep. When this happened his dreams became a torture chamber. On one night he found himself lying naked on a cold stainless steel table in a white tiled operating room. Bright lights overhead practically blinded him and he could hear the sound of running water. Suddenly a surgeon wearing a medical mask appeared beside the table, scalpel in hand, announcing the start of an autopsy. Although his heart beat wildly and his mind screamed with fear, Anderson was unable to move or make a sound as the knife began to cut.

This night's terror episode ended as Anderson shouted, leaped out of bed, and smashed through the glass of the French doors of the bedroom he shared with Julie. He awakened, terrified and trembling, with blood streaming from his hands and arms. Anderson's parents, who happened to be staying overnight in Stillwater, raced to see what was happening and found Julie comforting their son as he emerged fully from the dream and realized where he was, and what was happening. He explained to his parents that he had experienced this kind of vivid and disturbing dream before and that they were probably the product of stress and excess fatigue, and since they invariably passed, there was nothing to worry about. He was not convincing. Common sense suggested something deeper and more serious than simple stress and fatigue had caused Anderson's terrifying dreams. And who was to say that the next night's terror wouldn't leave him with more serious injuries?

Julie tried to tell her husband to beware of the stress he faced in his work. No one who immerses himself in the trauma suffered by victims of sexual abuse emerges unscathed. As several victims and their families came to his office Anderson listened to them tell stories of assault, shame, and betrayal that filled him with anger and concern. His clients were exceedingly wary people who could drift to the edge of paranoia. They would telephone him to demand reassurances, accuse him of ulterior motives, or dismiss him as their lawyer only to hire him back in an hour, a day, or a week. Understanding that he couldn't expect their automatic trust, Anderson took every one of their calls, listened carefully, and tried to keep his clients on an even keel. Invariably the fears and anxiety would subside and the clients were reassured, but the process would consume valuable hours and even more valuable energy.

The work of managing so many traumatized clients would drain anyone, but Anderson insisted to Julie he wasn't much affected. Although he might not say it out loud, deep down he believed that he wasn't like other people. A workout fanatic, he thought that his sessions in the gym and a naturally resilient constitution protected him from stress. Julie could see in his drinking and his nightmares that this wasn't true. But given their age difference and his argument skills, she couldn't get him to agree. His drinking was not out of control, he would say, because it hadn't affected his work. Indeed, he was functioning at such a high level — taking on new cases, pushing them forward effectively — that this "proved" that nothing was wrong. After arguing to the point of exhaustion Julie would back down, but when she was alone her fears would bring her to tears.

Ten days after filing the Lyman complaint Anderson went back to the courthouse with the John Doe lawsuit. The papers noted that the victim was thirteen when Fr. Adamson first molested him in 1982. At that time Adamson was working at a church called Risen Savior in the suburb of Apple Valley and, according to Anderson's filing, he developed a "big brother" relationship with the boy. The crimes against John Doe were relatively recent but still outside the three-year statute of limitations, which meant that Adamson would once again escape arrest on criminal charges. However, it helped Anderson advance his claim that the Church had knowingly harbored a serial offender.

The St. Paul *Pioneer Press* gave the news of the lawsuit front page display and ran a separate article that explained, in detail, Anderson's claim that higher officials knew Adamson was a sexual predator long before his clients were abused and nevertheless allowed him to hold jobs that brought him into contact with children. All but forced to respond, the Church broke a two-week silence as the chancellor of the Diocese of St. Paul called the press to the chancery. Bishop Robert Carlson said his boss, Archbishop John Roach, didn't know the truth about Adamson until he confessed in 1980.

Struggling to explain how they could have allowed a man charged with molesting children to work with them so closely, church leaders offered the kind of convoluted explanation that would be the hallmarks of the hierarchy's arguments in hundreds of cases to come. They would say they had relied on psychological experts who had assured them that sexual offenders could be controlled. They also claimed they were denied key information because of doctor-patient confidentiality. Of course, the psychological community was not in agreement when it came to sex offenders and the majority of experts warned that most could not be thoroughly "cured."

The irony of the Church hiding behind mental health experts was evident to anyone who knew about Catholicism's historical rejection of psychology and psychiatry. Many American church leaders, most notably the famous archbishop/broadcaster Fulton Sheen, had long made a point of insisting that faith and religion were superior to anything that might be offered by therapists, doctors, or analysts. In the 1950s and 1960s Sheen frequently criticized what he called "Freudianism," arguing that it was a way to "deny any personal responsibility," and he repeatedly taught people to apply willpower and prayer to ease mental suffering.

As a whole, the American bishops rejected whatever wisdom psychology might offer to clergy when they chose to ignore the 1972 Kennedy and Heckler report. Ironically enough, this document's existence meant that anyone filing a lawsuit alleging improper

185

conduct by a priest could claim that Church officials had been forewarned of a problem. However, claims against individual priests and their dioceses would require more specific evidence. In the John Doe case this proof resided in "secret archives" that contained sensitive information and could only be accessed by the highest officials in a diocese. In St. Paul the archive was in the basement of the chancery. Two keys existed. One was kept by Roach. The other was held by his second-in-command.

The secret archives intrigued Jeffrey Anderson almost as much as the conflict between Bishop Watters of Winona and Archbishop Roach in St. Paul, which was revealed in letters between them. At issue was the question of how much Roach knew about Adamson at the time he was sent to St. Paul. In the letters Watters suggested that he had informed Roach fully — giving him information on charges that Adamson abused minors — at the time of the priest's transfer. Roach insisted that he was told Adamson "had a problem with homosexuality" but not that he had sexually assaulted minors.

This conflict came to a head when Roach drove to meet with Watters in private at a convent halfway between their home cities in the Mississippi River town of Frontenac. Designed and built to resemble an Austrian castle, Villa Maria was a looming stone building topped by red tile roofs. The entrance to the convent was flanked by stone towers five stories high. Inside the bishops found a small conference room where they spent ninety minutes hashing out their differences. In the end Watters's recollections changed. He agreed that in fact he had failed to inform Roach of the true extent of Thomas Adamson's problem. It was around this time that he also decided that he would leave his office, even though he was four years shy of the usual retirement age of seventy-five.

Roach's description of the meeting at Villa Maria made it sound like they had conspired to get their stories straight. It also highlighted the trouble they might encounter if the case went before a court. After Roach's deposition, the two dioceses and their lawyers made another push for a settlement. With the Lymans' complaints against Adamson now out in the open, Anderson and his clients were satisfied that the community had been alerted to the problem of predator priests and a measure of justice had been achieved in the shaming of the Church. They accepted the $1 million payment offered, which would be paid to Greg in small sums as an annuity. But Greg refused to sign any agreement to keep the settlement confidential and the facts of the case were made public.

The Lyman settlement made headlines and

cemented Anderson's status as a lawyer who would fight the Church. It also announced, to certain of his friends, that he had shifted his thinking when it came to sex. A former client, Tim Campbell, who worked for the local gay newspaper and once regarded Anderson as a hero, was disappointed. On a cold winter day he encountered his old friend Anderson walking down one of the narrow skyways that connect the upper stories of buildings in downtown St. Paul. Campbell was delivering papers. Anderson was on his way to a meeting.

"I see you've changed sides," said Campbell with a sharpness in his voice. When Anderson asked him to explain, Campbell said that Anderson was no longer "pro sexual" and that he had "gone for the money" by filing suits based against the Church.

Campbell didn't think that priests like Adamson were doing something that was, by definition, always wrong. He believed that some teenagers were capable of consenting to having sex with an older man and that a certain hysteria was being created by parents who overreacted to harmless sexual episodes and lawyers who sought to profit from suits.

The comments and Campbell's attitude caught Anderson by surprise. After an icy parting he thought about the exchange. Society as a whole had become less tolerant and more punishing, at least when it came to public policy and sexual behavior. In years gone by, Anderson would have likely agreed to represent a gay priest who had been arrested looking for sex in a public washroom. But that kind of case, which would have involved a voluntary arrangement between strangers, was different from one in which a trusted pastor uses his position to manipulate a twelve- or thirteen-year-old into repeated sexual encounters. People like Campbell could say what they would about harmless sex, Anderson thought, but when a priest violates a minor sexually, *"it is bound to fuck the kid up."*

Given the formidable power of the Catholic Church, Anderson didn't feel any less radical in his role as an attorney for young people who had been raped than he did when he defended gay men rousted out of a bathhouse. As far as he could tell, predator priests used their status and authority to commit crimes and the institutional Church brought its power to bear against individuals who complained. And so what if these cases brought big paydays? The money freed Anderson from financial worries and financed the aggressive pursuit of new cases.

The potential for more big settlements grew as every week brought Anderson calls from adults who had been victimized as children and from parents who said their sons and daughters had been abused by both Catholic clergy and Protestant ministers. Some of these cases fell outside the three-year limit set by Minnesota's statute of limitations and the Church could use this factor to deflect a claim of simple negligence. However, if Anderson could show the Church had acted recklessly, or committed an intentional fraud, he wouldn't be bound by the strict terms of the statute of limitations. He could also push for payments far in excess of a $400,000 limit the state legislature had placed on claims of emotional distress caused by simple negligence.

In tort law, where the courts settle disputes over everything from car accidents to defective medical devices, plaintiffs' lawyers routinely search for the kind of evidence that would elevate a case above simple negligence. When a court recognizes recklessness and fraud it says, in effect, that the defendants may have committed a more serious offense, both morally and materially. If found guilty, defendants who commit fraud or act recklessly may be required to pay punitive damages far in excess of the penalties assessed in cases of negligence. A Catholic equivalent might be seen in the distinction between venial and mortal sins. The former is slight and readily forgiven. The latter is serious and requires deliberate and profound repentance.

A bishop who knew, or should have known, that a priest posed a threat to children but left him in ministry could be considered reckless. If he worked with others to deflect complaints and cover up accusations, then he may have also conspired to commit fraud upon every family in a parish. No legal scholarship would be required to determine that a bishop or church that allowed a boy or girl to be victimized under these circumstances broke an important trust. It would be obvious to anyone.

If Anderson could bring a case involving recklessness or fraud before the members of a jury, he might well persuade them to send a message to priests and bishops everywhere in the form of a big punitive damages award. Among the many victims who came to Anderson in the wake of the Lyman case, one stood out. The John Doe who was abused by Fr. Thomas Adamson after higher church officials had heard previous complaints seemed to be a victim of both recklessness and fraud.

For the Church, words like "fraud" and "recklessness" brought not only financial risk but also greater public scandal. If Anderson was involved, there would be no way for the Church to escape this shame because he would make every filing public. This step was part of a process he was crafting into a standard operating procedure. The Anderson method would begin with long interviews of victims and their loved ones. He would then confirm the basic facts with his own investigation and file suit to begin the discovery process. With or without Anderson's encouragement, news reporters would invariably learn about the complaint against the Church. Because previous cases had established the fact of clergy abuse, the press no longer shied away from covering the issue. Instead, abuse claims against supposedly celibate men of God became a staple of the news business and the resultant scandal — something the hierarchy dreaded — was inevitable.

Anderson's use of the press was by no means unique. Lawyers have long sought to influence justice by molding public opinion. In this case, Anderson wasn't trying to affect a specific jury. He was, instead, trying to get the public accustomed to the idea that a priest just might molest, assault, and even rape a child and his higher-ups might conceal the crime and allow the assaults to continue. These concepts were so alien to most people that only repeated and regular coverage of the issue could open enough minds that Anderson might win a jury trial, should one come along. Toward this end, he cultivated local reporters and when calls came in from out-of-town papers and broadcast outlets he agreed to be interviewed whenever asked.

One of the most comprehensive reports written at this time was published by the Knight Ridder News Service and appeared in papers across America. Reporter Carl Cannon noted the pattern Anderson had found repeated in twenty-five dioceses where church officials decided against reporting assaults on children by priests and transferred molesters to parishes where they continued to have access to children. To support his articles Cannon had researched cases from coast to coast. He had also found Thomas Doyle, who gave him the report he had written with Ray Mouton and Michael Peterson. Doyle said he had concrete evidence on about two hundred priest abusers and predicted more scandal to come.

"I got a call from a nun today in Missouri who's got a priest doing this stuff to kids," he told Cannon. "She can't get anywhere with the bishop. She doesn't know where in the Church to turn."

The St. Paul *Pioneer Press* published Cannon's investigation and added a sidebar stressing the local angles on the story. Jeff Anderson was featured prominently and the report prompted more calls from people who had been abused by priests. Most had never shared their stories with anyone because they remained attached to the Church, blamed themselves for the crimes, and feared no one would believe them. Those who did act typically contacted Church officials who discouraged them from reporting priests' crimes to police. Bishops assured victims they would

193

keep accused priests away from children but they rarely did. Those victims who later turned to attorneys when they realized they have been ignored by the Church hoped that the legal system would give them both justice and some sort of relief from the aftereffects of incidents of rape and molestation. Anderson could only promise that he would try to hold abusers and their enablers accountable in court. Other sorts of recovery — psychological, spiritual, or social — would depend mainly on their own inner resources.

9.
"WHAT DID THE PRIEST DO TO YOU, GREG?"

When he got his first settlement payment, Greg Lyman bought a Chevy Camaro IROC-Z, spent thousands of dollars entertaining himself and friends, and gave away thousands more. By November 1988 the car was the only thing left, and the next annuity check wasn't due for months.

Broke and disconnected as ever, Lyman drove to a for-profit plasma bank to make a donation and get some cash. Inside the clinic, he checked in with the receptionist, who handed him some paperwork. He took a seat in the waiting area, clipboard in hand, and began to write his answers to the questions on the form. A television suspended from the ceiling blared the theme music for a program. Lyman ignored the music and the barking of the host and concentrated on the form. Then something made him look up at the screen. There he saw himself, seated on the set of a TV talk show. The host, Geraldo Rivera, was asking, "What did the priest do to you, Greg?"

Around the age of 12 or so, he and I went to a YMCA. And I was an altar boy at the time. And the first time I was ever touched, he began stroking my penis in a sauna, I believe it was, at the YMCA.

Rivera was among the first national television talk show hosts to devote an entire program to the scandal of sex crimes in the Catholic Church. In fact, he aired two hour-long programs that brought together victims such as Lyman with Jeff Anderson, the journalist Jason Berry, and Thomas Doyle, who was not in the studio but appeared in a video report introducing the subject. These programs, plus one presented by the talk show host Phil Donahue, would prompt viewers across the country to report to the Church, police, and private attorneys that they too had been raped or molested by priests. They also marked the true beginning of the national broadcast media's role in a scandal that would become much bigger than even an insider like Doyle could predict.

Historic as it may have been, Greg Lyman's glimpse of himself on the TV screen only made him feel self-conscious and a little afraid. He glanced around the room to see if anyone else waiting to give plasma had noticed he was the "victim" on the TV set. To his relief, the others in the room didn't seem to make the connection. He got up quickly, put the clipboard on the seat, grabbed his jacket, and left.

The plasma donors who remained in the waiting room saw Geraldo Rivera's blunt-edge interview method focused on a young man who was presented as a representative of all the boys ever abused by priests. It was not the role anyone would knowingly choose for himself and Greg Lyman struggled to maintain his dignity. At one point he said, defensively, "There was no anal penetration." At another moment, his face flushed red as a man in the audience said, "You should have known that something was wrong."

Rivera, who was standing in the audience, turned toward the stage and the panel of interview subjects. "Greg, you take a shot at it," he said. "I know it's a tough question but obviously the audience is asking it."

"I was naive," answered Lyman. "My mom and dad, you know, sex was a bad word. I was never taught. And I trusted the priest . . . I wish I would have had some education, some, 'this is right and this is wrong.' "

"Help him out, Jeff," said Rivera, looking directly at Anderson.

"The power of the priest to a Catholic family, to a twelve-year-old boy, is an amount that's incredible, and what he says goes," said

Anderson. "He didn't know how to get out of it. He didn't have the strength, the ability, or the experience to get out of it and that's why it's called rape, and that's why it's criminal."

Viewers who watched the entire episode of the program, which was called simply *Geraldo,* would hear Anderson, Berry, and Doyle struggle to describe the breadth of the crisis. Berry, who suggested the title Rivera attached to the show — "The Church's Sexual Watergate" — noted dozens of cases he had uncovered and many millions of dollars paid in settlements. Doyle, whose career ambitions had been dashed by his efforts to push the Church toward reforms, stressed the hypocrisy of the hierarchy. "It's difficult to preach the sanctity of marriage and family," he noted, "when, at the same time, the appearance might be given of condoning highly illicit activity within our own ranks." Anderson's role allowed him to pose as a crusader and describe the pattern of behavior — secret settlements and quiet transfers of problem priests — that left the Church vulnerable to legal claims.

At the New York studio where the program had been taped, Lyman, Anderson, and Berry attended a brief post-performance gathering where the host thanked all the guests. Berry took the opportunity to chat with Anderson, who had already impressed him as a bulldog

198

litigator. The two men were becoming friends, of a sort, and they admired each other as truth-seekers. Of course pure idealism does not reside in any human being, Berry thought. In Anderson's case, principle was surely blended with a desire for wealth, fame, and the sheer pleasure that comes with victory.

In the end, the exact measure of all the drives that motivated Anderson as he tried to hold Church leaders accountable wouldn't matter as much as the result. Berry could reach a similar conclusion about himself. After all, he had accepted Rivera's offer to appear because he wanted to alert the public to an important issue, *and* because the publicity might help him persuade a publisher to give him a contract for a book he had begun to write. The show's host was also propelled by varying motivations. Geraldo Rivera would claim that his program served a greater good by keeping the public informed, but as any regular viewer would attest, the program was also a showcase for sensational topics and the host's pugnacious techniques.

Rivera sometimes paid a price for his aggressive style. Jason Berry got a closer view of this dynamic when he ran into a fellow Louisianan, Michael Palasch, on his journey home. The two men had actually met a day earlier when they shared a limousine ride from the airport to the hotel where the *Ger-*

aldo show put up their out-of-town guests. Director of a racist group called Skinheads of National Resistance, Palasch complained to Berry that the program taping he was supposed to attend was postponed when members of the radical Jewish Defense League threatened violence if Rivera proceeded with planned interviews of neo-Nazi leaders. According to Berry, Palasch doubted whether the taping would be rescheduled. In response Berry reassured him with both sympathy and irony, "Geraldo's a man of his word."

Geraldo was a man of his word. He brought Palasch back for a panel discussion of the neo-Nazi movement that ended in a chair-throwing melee. Ten days later Rivera wound up on the cover of *Newsweek,* his scabbed and broken nose serving to illustrate the magazine's article titled "Trash TV." It may have been trash in *Newsweek*'s view, but the *Geraldo* program did reveal truths about important issues that more staid media outlets would soon address more aggressively. Among these were the threats posed both by violent racist extremists and by priests committing sexual assaults all around the world.

Geraldo and other TV programs that focused on the sex abuse scandal in the Catholic Church — *Donahue, Oprah,* etc. — had a profound effect on men and women who had been molested or raped by priests when they were young. With each broadcast more victims began to connect their early trauma and later trouble in their lives. Hundreds and eventually thousands would turn to the Church, psychotherapists, and lawyers in an attempt to find some peace and justice.

A relatively new phenomenon, the shows relied on a formula that began with individuals who spoke about compelling issues — medical disorders and tragedies were staples — that were confirmed by writers and experts whose attention made the subjects more worthy of consideration. These authorities typically appeared alongside the people who shared their personal experiences. If possible, opposing views were added to create tension and drama. Books that served as the basis for programs were highlighted throughout the hour and at the end of a program viewers were offered phone numbers for agencies and groups related to the subject at hand.

The programs varied in style depending on the personality of the host. Geraldo Rivera was a tough-guy reporter and he tended to emphasize exposé and scandal. Highly empathetic and emotive, Oprah Winfrey took a more psychological approach, which led to hours filled with tears and what she called "healing" as guests described their ordeals and found affirmation and acceptance. Hugely popular, Oprah spoke a language of self-help and informal spirituality to become one of the most influential women in the world.

Eventually, Oprah and the others would provoke a backlash from social critics like Wendy Kaminer, who would write that "talk shows have helped transform victimhood into a kind of status symbol." But in the short term, these programs contributed to a groundswell of support for people who wanted to declare themselves on a variety of issues. Very quickly the term "survivor" replaced the word "victim" as guests announced that they were "in recovery" from some form of abuse or dysfunction. For people who had been abused by priests, the shows suggested that they were not alone, and that the world would not be entirely hostile to their claims.

Critics who saw in these programs a threat to traditional mores were correct. In general, the talk shows offered encouragement and acceptance in ways that eroded the power of the usual authorities and boosted individuals. Minorities of all sorts found support as did just about anyone who stood up for his or her rights. Catholic Church officials rarely appeared on shows that dealt with abusive clergy and supporters of the faith often came across as defensive. In contrast, advocates like Jeffrey Anderson seemed dynamic, compassionate, and trustworthy. Each time he appeared, Anderson received a flurry of phone calls from people who had been sexually abused as children and wanted a lawyer.

As he took on cases and filed suits in more than a dozen states, Anderson ran up against different statutes of limitation and challenges to the claims of his clients. In Minnesota the law permitted adults who said they had been abused as children to make a claim within three years of turning eighteen. Lawyers tried to overcome statutory limits with two arguments. In some cases they said their clients suffered from trauma-induced amnesia that was overcome only through psychotherapy. In others they argued that their clients didn't realize the extent of the harm caused by their abuse until they had psychological difficulties later in life. Both phenomena proved "delayed discovery" — an established exception to statutes of limitations — because the damage done by abuse was like a virus that lay dormant and didn't show itself until years after time limits ran out.

Claims of delayed discovery by victims of sexual abuse faced tough criticism from defendants. Expert witnesses disagreed about the way memory functions and cast doubt on the idea that someone could forget abuse and then recall it reliably in adulthood. Plaintiffs suffered a major setback when the Supreme Court of Washington state considered *Tyson v. Tyson,* in which a twenty-six-year-old woman tried to sue her father for sexual abuse. State law allowed for a claim to be made after a child victim turned twenty-one and before he or she turned twenty-five. The court noted a lack of corroborating evidence and ruled that it wouldn't rely on psychiatric testimony to waive the statute and allow the case to go before a judge.

The decision in *Tyson v. Tyson* gave pause to any lawyer considering a case outside a statute of limitations. A solution came in 1988 when a woman named Patti Barton, who alleged abuse by her father, lobbied the state legislature in Olympia to change the law. Barton succeeded as the Washington House and Senate approved a new statute that allowed adults to sue once they recognized they had been harmed, no matter their age. Once it was signed into law, Barton began traveling to other state capitols, with the statute in hand, urging lawmakers to give their constituents the same rights.

In Minnesota, the statute of limitations was attacked first by a lawyer named Mark Douglas, who had been molested by a family friend when he was a boy. Jeffrey Anderson joined Douglas in pressing the case with William Luther, chairman of the judiciary committee of the Minnesota Senate. Luther sponsored a bill that recognized delayed discovery and gave people the chance to sue, no matter their age, within two years of realizing their psychological suffering was linked to assaults they endured as minors. The legislation passed both chambers of the state legislature without attracting any press attention. Anderson was invited to attend the signing and have his picture taken with Governor Arne Carlson. Anderson passed on the picture, but he got a copy of the bill with the governor's signature.

On the day after the new law was signed and took effect, Anderson carried his copy into a county courthouse thirty miles west of Minneapolis where he had brought a suit against a minister in the Evangelical Lutheran Church of America. The Church was represented by Patrick Schiltz, who had recently returned to Minnesota from serving as clerk to Supreme Court Justice Antonin Scalia. Schiltz had asked the judge to dismiss the claim based on the old statute. When Anderson handed the judge the document, and Schiltz got a look at it, he agreed that his motion had become irrelevant. The new law kept the suit alive and Anderson eventually obtained payment for his client in a settlement.

Variations of the law were passed in eight more states, and they deprived defendants of the main tool they had used to block lawsuits. With firmer ground to stand on, Anderson took on dozens of additional clients. In each case bishops were forced to consider the damage a trial might do to the reputation of the Church, and the possibility they might lose. The prospect of a jury hearing how a priest abused his trust in order to sexually violate a child, and the damages they might award, motivated many dioceses and religious orders to settle claims.

The settlements Anderson negotiated in this early period ranged from tens of thousands of dollars to in excess of a hundred thousand. Since he was working in a new area of law, he depended on his clients to judge whether the amounts offered were sufficient. Most were adamant about hearing Church officials acknowledge their injuries, removing priests from ministry, and protecting others from harm with a public disclosure of records. The first condition was met when Church officials agreed to pay a claim without receiving a confidentiality agreement. The second condition was a more difficult matter. As Anderson learned, priests enjoyed certain protections under canon law and could appeal a bishop's sanction to Rome, where the bureaucracy worked very slowly. In the meantime they could move from diocese to diocese and even from country to country without much fear that their past would be known. Release of documents, the third condition, was the most difficult for Anderson to achieve. Every local bishop would respond differently to demands for records, and often their responses would be based on the concern that they might release information that would lead to more lawsuits or even criminal charges.

The workings of the Catholic system, which was governed by its own canon laws and steeped in ancient traditions, were a constant puzzle to an outsider like Anderson. He was often stumped by Latin terms and confused by the varied powers of the hierarchs. Understanding it all would require an advanced degree or expert help. As Anderson would recall, in his search for assistance he tracked Tom Doyle to Indiana, where he was a chaplain at Grissom Air Force Base. His home phone number was listed and Anderson called him one evening.

Tom Doyle had already helped a San Francisco lawyer who called him for advice on a case that was settled before he could appear as an expert witness. Like the few media interviews he had done, the process had given Doyle an emotional boost because it was a chance for him to use what he knew to help a family and push the Church to face its problems. But these occasional opportunities weren't enough to ease the feeling that he was drifting sideways through life.

It wasn't that he was unhappy with chaplain's work or the Air Force officers. As a pastor, Doyle had never felt more comfortable than he did counseling military men, and he had plenty of friends at Grissom, including a few who liked to go shooting with him. Sometimes Doyle and his buddies shot targets they set up in some friendly farmer's field. He would bring a few special guns from his collections — a .347 Magnum, an M16, an AK-47 — and they would compete with each one. They also helped with the eradication program that dealt with animals that posed a problem to aircraft. (With the right scope Doyle could hit a groundhog at 300 feet.) But the camaraderie Doyle felt with his friends, and the satisfaction he received in his work, didn't settle his soul. Too often he was almost overwhelmed by fear, anxiety, and even depression. When this happened during the day he went home for lunch, drank a half bottle of wine, and a chased it with a swig of Listerine. In the evenings he would escape with a drink, and then another, and then another.

On the night when Jeff Anderson called, Doyle was only partway into his off-duty drinking routine and he was still sober and alert. He knew who Anderson was, and had assumed that one day they would meet. Doyle shared with Anderson his thoughts about what he called "clericalism," which he described as a Catholic mind-set that elevated ordained men above all others and led, inevitably, to corruption. On the other end of the line Anderson could feel Doyle's disillusionment and sensed, also, a bit of anger. Without much prompting Doyle said he believed that children were still vulnerable to sexually dangerous priests and that the Church hierarchy was still not facing its problems squarely. He agreed to help Anderson any way he could.

10.
THE MEASURE OF THE ELEPHANT

The rent tested Barbara Blaine's faith.

Her hero Dorothy Day, the founder of the Catholic Worker movement, taught that God will provide. But in Blaine's experience it wasn't God who paid to house and feed the homeless of Chicago's North Side. Rent, groceries, utilities, and other expenses depended on the money she and her partner Gary Olivero begged from donors and earned at jobs outside the eight-bedroom Catholic Worker House they ran near Loyola University. (Begun during the Great Depression, the American Catholic Worker movement includes about two hundred independent local groups of laypeople who voluntarily live in poverty and offer services to the poor.)

A bit older than Blaine, Olivero was a slightly built man who wore big, black-framed glasses and threw himself into causes with total abandon. Blaine was a bit more nuanced in her commitment. She often wondered if God was sending some sort of ironic message by requiring her to work nights at a city-run homeless shelter just to keep the shelter she had established going.

If God was saying anything, it was that everyone — even a selfless Christian on a mission — needs help from time to time. Catholic to the core, Blaine naturally looked to the Church, which had officially declared itself aligned with her cause. In the mid-1980s the otherwise conservative hierarchy maintained a ferociously liberal commitment to social programs that benefitted poor people. Chicago's Cardinal Joseph Bernardin, who met people with a "call me Joe" warmth, frequently called on Catholics to muster as much passion for the poor as they expressed in opposition to abortion. "To stand for life," he told one audience in 1985, "is to stand for the needs of women and children who epitomize the sacredness of life."

Determined that Bernardin follow his own values, Blaine went to see the officials who controlled the property of the archdiocese to ask them to give her one of their empty buildings to use as a shelter. A social worker by training, Blaine was a familiar kind of Catholic woman. Polite and respectful, she was nevertheless demanding, relentless, and willing to bully them with the Gospel. Her stubbornness stood in contrast with her appearance. A short, auburn-haired woman with fair skin and a ready smile, she was almost thirty but could have passed for twenty. Her voice was soft and agreeable and she always apologized for taking up anyone's time. But what she said about the sin of letting perfectly good buildings stand empty while women and children lived in cars would have shamed a saint.

After realizing Blaine wouldn't go away until they accommodated her, Church officials gave her an abandoned convent on the South Side of the city. Three stories high and flanked by a small gray yard, the place required some updating but it was solidly built and closer to the population served by the Worker House. By 1985 its thirty rooms sheltered dozens of women and their children along with a couple of elderly men, one of whom needed around-the-clock, hospice-like care. A big ground-floor kitchen fed all these people and more who came in off the street. A food pantry served neighbors who came by the hundreds for free groceries. Like all Catholic Workers, Blaine was paid $10 per week.

At the time, Barbara Blaine considered her impoverished Catholic utopianism a natural extension of the faith she was born into in Toledo, Ohio. Life in her childhood home was measured by first communions and confirmations, which were conducted at a church the family helped to found. The eight Blaine children went to Catholic schools.

Priests and nuns were family friends. On most days one or more members of the family performed some sort of volunteer service at the church or school.

In Chicago, Blaine's typical day would begin with bathing and dressing an elderly man named Ray Matthews, who had chosen the Worker House as the place where he would die. She would then oversee breakfast and dispatch a dozen or more children who lived at the house and attended nearby schools. Their mothers then needed help with job applications or welfare forms and at 11 A.M. Blaine took to the sidewalk to greet the crowd assembled for the food pantry, which opened at 11:30. By nightfall she might welcome a new family, dash to the emergency room with a sick child, or organize the kids to make decorations for an upcoming holiday.

Eventually Blaine would recognize she had lost herself in a kind of obsessive-compulsive form of sacrifice. ("A culture of the martyr" was what she would call it.) The demands of this life were so great that she rarely had a moment to think about herself. Of course this oblivion was perfect for someone who was afraid of the past and her own feelings. In the name of doing good she lost herself in others and let things like friendships, social calls, and even the mail slide for weeks or even months. In the summer of 1985, in a rare moment when no one else demanded

213

her attention, Blaine sat down with a stack of magazines, newsletters, and papers that had gone unread for many months. Included were back issues of the *National Catholic Reporter.*

Leafing through the *Reporter,* Blaine found Jason Berry's first article on Gilbert Gauthe. As she read, her heart began to race and she broke into a cold sweat. Suddenly she felt unable to take a breath. She became light-headed and gasped for air. As she put down the paper she realized she had seen adults and children with the same symptoms. Though each one of them had insisted they were having some sort of cardiac episode they were, in fact, having panic attacks. Coming on as she read an article about priests raping children, her panic attack was a signal from the girl she once had been, who wanted someone to acknowledge her experience, her pain, and her existence. As an adult Blaine knew only that she needed help. She sought it through psychotherapy.

In therapy Barbara Blaine would finally tell someone how she had been stunned into silence as a priest explained that she was "closer to Jesus" than anyone he knew and proceeded to kiss and then undress her. At last she told how Fr. Chet Warren had blamed her, a thirteen-year-old, for his sexual assaults. She was "too beautiful" to resist, he had explained. Then he told her that through sex they had become spiritually "engaged" and that after their lifetime of service to the Church — he as a priest, she as a nun — they would be married in heaven. Overwhelmed by divergent feelings she was too young to sort out — guilt, attachment, fear, pleasure — Blaine had said nothing and tried to erase what had happened from her memory.

All of it, from the seduction to the silence, would be textbook stuff in the eyes of experts in sexual abuse. For Blaine it was a devastating interruption of her adolescence that left her with symptoms of posttraumatic stress disorder. Eventually she would connect her anxiety, fearfulness, and low self-esteem to Chet Warren and learn to live with PTSD. In the meantime the ever-practical Blaine would try to hold him accountable and make sure he wouldn't victimize anyone else. She called Warren's superiors at the provincial headquarters of the Oblates of St. Francis de Sales in Toledo. They agreed to see her on Halloween day, 1985.

Days before Blaine's appointment in Toledo, the kids at the Worker House used blunt scissors and big waxy crayons to turn construction paper into grinning pumpkins and arched black cats, which they taped to the windows and walls. When the holiday arrived Blaine helped get the kids off to school and then set out for Ohio in a car she had borrowed from a friend. The five-hour drive gave her time to consider what she would say. No longer ashamed, she was determined that the truth be told and she hoped that the provincial of the Oblates would do all the right things.

At their meeting Blaine recalled for the provincial her family's life in the Church and then described what had happened with Chet Warren. She then asked him to immediately bar Warren from working with children.

"At first they acted like they believed me," recalled Blaine, years later. "It was almost like they were expecting it."

While the Oblates didn't challenge Blaine's claim of abuse, they quietly pressed her on the details. Perhaps it didn't begin when she was thirteen, he said. Maybe she was fifteen, or even sixteen. She resisted this suggestion. They then asked her to attend a series of six psychotherapy meetings with Warren and a psychotherapist named Mary Morgillo. These sessions would somehow contribute to her "healing," he said.

Still a good Catholic, Blaine dutifully went to two of these sessions. At the first of these meetings, Warren admitted he had sexually violated her beginning when she in grade school. However he insisted on challenging the details of what had happened and when, in order to make it seem like she had been older. He also sifted and reinterpreted events in ways that made her partly responsible and identified him as not just a perpetrator but also a victim. She stopped attending when, before the third session, she was informed that Warren had been excused because he told his superiors the sessions made him uncomfortable.

Chet Warren continued working as a priest. Blaine involved herself in group therapy with other victims of sexual abuse and continued individual sessions with a counselor. She also telephoned Jason Berry to ask about the broader issue of sexual abuse in the Church and to ask if he knew of any self-help groups that might offer support to victims. He said no such groups existed. The call prompted her to eventually start her own.

Self-help and organizing came naturally to Blaine, but progress in this instance was exceedingly slow. Victims of sexual abuse by priests tended to keep quiet about it and the few who filed lawsuits usually did so as "John" or "Jane Doe." With the Internet still years away, Blaine painstakingly scoured the press for reports on clergy abuse and telephoned every reporter who published a story and every lawyer who filed a claim. Most refused to even pass her name along to other victims. A few, including Berry, were happy to tell victims about a woman in Chicago who wanted to talk with them. In this way Blaine heard from a few dozen people — she imag-

217

ined they represented a large proportion of all the victims in America — and added their names to the rolls of a group she called, for lack of a better name, The Victims Network, then later SNAP — Survivors Network of those Abused by Priests.

On St. Patrick's Day 1988 Jason Berry appeared on the *Donahue* show with reporter Carl Cannon of Knight Ridder newspapers. When the program's producers told Berry they expected viewers to contact the show for more information, he suggested they refer them to Blaine. They went a step further, flashing a notice at the end of the show that directed viewers to call The Victims Network at a Chicago number. The number rang one of two lines at the Catholic Worker House in Chicago.

Blaine answered the first call just minutes after *Donahue* aired in the Eastern time zone. The man on the other end of the line told her a bit about how he had been molested by a priest and asked about what help she could offer. She explained that she was just beginning to gather names and telephone numbers so that victims could find each other. The man agreed to have his name on the list and as he said good-bye gave Blaine permission to share his contact information with other victims from his state. As soon as Blaine put down the receiver the phone rang again. Before the night was over she would fill several sheets of paper with names and phone numbers. The phone would continue ringing for the next couple of days. Blaine began to imagine a true network of local chapters, something like the organization of Alcoholics Anonymous, serving perhaps a few hundred people with similar experiences and needs to support each other.

As she connected survivors around the country who provided each other with support, some told Blaine about another Chicago-area woman who was working on the issue of clergy abuse. Jeanne Miller was crisscrossing the country promoting a book, written under the pen name Hilary Stiles. Her son and other boys had been propositioned by a priest. When she complained, she was stonewalled by the Archdiocese of Chicago. The book was nothing less than an indictment of the Church on charges of criminal conspiracy for covering up the sexual crimes committed by clergy. When Stiles first began to speak out in her parish she was met by hostility and criticism, but every time she appeared on TV she heard from dozens of people with similar experiences. Several people, including Berry, urged Blaine to call her.

Jeanne Miller's alter ego Hilary Stiles wore a dark wig, blue contact lenses, and heavy makeup that made her look like the glamorous novelist Jackie Collins. Though based on Miller's experiences with the Chicago Archdiocese, *Assault on Innocence* was offered as fiction. In TV appearances Stiles claimed that a real-life Chicago priest named Robert Mayer had tried to molest her son during a weekend outing at a lake house. Miller telephoned the mothers of three other boys who had been at the house. Two refused to consider what she had to say. The third believed that her son was actually molested by Mayer. Together the two mothers investigated and heard that the priest was giving drugs and alcohol to boys in the parish and inviting them to his quarters in the rectory. When the women complained to church authorities they were met with denial and resistance. Miller filed a lawsuit. The chancellor of the archdiocese called the women to an evening meeting in the basement of a church. There, seated at a folding table setup beneath a harsh overhead light, he threatened them with excommunication.

Miller was not deterred. She started attending church in another town and mortgaged her home to pay her lawyer. Her husband begged her to stop. He wanted to return to their parish and the life they had known before. She refused. Cardinal Bernardin moved Mayer to another Chicago suburb, Des Plaines. Soon the Des Plaines police were at her door with questions about Fr.

Mayer. Bernardin's prescription for a geographical cure had failed. As her husband protested, Miller renewed her campaign to have Mayer disciplined. The Church resisted and at their parish the Miller family was shunned as troublemakers.

Compared with Barbara Blaine, Jeanne Miller was an unlikely crusader. She was not an activist. She had never worked as an advocate of any sort, nor had she tried to follow the social gospel of the Catholic Workers. For the most part she had lived as a traditional believer who loved the Church and was devout in her attendance at Mass, confession, and holiday services. In fact, the firm structure of the institution had always appealed to her as an antidote to the chaos she had known during her peculiar childhood.

Jeanne Miller was the grandchild of a brilliant but domineering woman who founded Moreland Realty, a development company that built thousands of homes in Chicago's western suburbs in the years after World War II. Her parents, so good-looking that they could have worked the fashion runways in New York, were employed as sales agents at Moreland subdivisions. However, they were more than salespeople. Required to live in Moreland model homes, they were on-duty all the time, welcoming serious shoppers and the merely curious, at all hours of the day or night. With their children they posed as the model family in Moreland's newspaper ads. When all the houses in a particular development were sold, they moved on to the next one.

Behind the veneer of perfection that the Millers presented to people shopping for homes, Jeanne's family struggled with the stress that came with their dependency on her grandmother and moving a dozen times in as many years. Both of her parents were alcoholics, and her mother became addicted to prescription drugs. As a teenager Jeanne pleaded for her grandmother to help, but she was ignored until the day her mother put on her best clothes, leaned over the muzzle of a shotgun, and stretched out her hand to push the trigger. The suicide attempt failed. Jeanne discovered her mother was in the hospital, and why, when she got home from school. As she started to cry, the local parish priest told her, "Don't be so selfish." Two weeks after she returned home, Miller's mother succeeded in killing herself by drinking drain cleaner.

Jeanne Miller never forgot how her pleas for help with her mother were ignored. As a mother herself she couldn't tolerate having her concerns about Robert Mayer ignored by the archdiocese. As the proceeds from her second mortgage ran out she sold her jewelry in order to continue to press her claim against the Church. When she finally reached the limit of her resources, Miller agreed to negotiate a settlement. The archdiocese paid her $15,000, which was about half the debt she owed her attorney, and Bernardin agreed to meet with her. In the spring of 1985 she went to his office in the Loop district of Chicago. As she would recall it a few years later, "Bernardin pointed to a stack of papers on his desk, and told us they were sexual complaints against priests and that they took time to investigate. We said the whole issue of pedophilia needed to be addressed. He said our case had forced them to do that. He told us, 'It's still a mystery how your case got so out of hand.'"

In her book *Assault on Innocence,* Miller/ Stiles confronted the problem of priest predators and cover-up more directly and personally than any previous author. When the small press that issued the book failed to give it a publicity campaign Miller assumed the job herself, mailing out hundreds of copies accompanied by a letter packaged in a mailing tube that looked like a stick of dynamite. More than a dozen producers invited her to appear on television. Whenever "Hilary Stiles" was interviewed on local TV, viewers responded by the hundreds. She referred victims looking for legal help to Jeff Anderson. To others she offered a sympathetic ear. After a few months of this, Miller began to feel like one of the blind men in an ancient

Indian proverb. Each one feels part of an elephant — trunk, tail, ear, mouth — and fails to identify the animal's true size and mass.

When Barbara Blaine called, Miller listened attentively to her description of how Chet Warren had abused her and to Blaine's report on how the Oblates of St. Francis had done nothing concrete in response to her complaint. Miller had already learned that people who "come out" as abuse victims and meet resistance in the Church feel traumatized all over again. Disillusioned and isolated, many needed to talk and talk about their experience. She heard this need in Blaine, and allowed her to vent as long as she wanted. She also detected in her a certain energy — outrage mixed with the need to "do something" — that might make her an ally.

At the Catholic Worker House, Barbara Blaine kept the phone lines tied up for more than an hour as she soaked in the kind of affirmation she had never felt from anyone else who had heard her story. Here at last was someone who was just as committed to Catholicism as she was; who also knew the disillusioning truth about priests and bishops and sexual abuse. But as Blaine found understanding and empathy with Jeanne Miller she was interrupted, several times, by staff and house residents insisting she get off the phone. "When they said 'It's really

224

important,' " recalled Blaine, "I said, 'So is this.' "

As Blaine finally finished her conversation with Miller she made an effort to control the irritation she felt about all the interruptions. To her surprise, the people who had been pestering her were, at first, hesitant to explain themselves. Then, in a rush, they told her there had been an accident. A tractor trailer had smashed into the car Gary Olivero had driven to Catholic Charities to pick up food. Before the day was done, the city's Catholic activists would be mourning his death.

Like Jeanne Miller, Richard Sipe had touched part of the elephant — perhaps more of it than anyone — but he still wanted help to understand all of its dimensions. He felt this way despite his decades-long study of the clergy and sexuality and a lifetime spent inside the Church. The fourth of ten children from an intensely Catholic family in small-town Minnesota, Sipe was thirteen years old in 1946 when he enrolled at a Catholic seminary in Collegeville, Minnesota, where the Benedictine order also maintained an abbey and a college. When he was a novice monk the book *Client-Centered Therapy* by the renowned psychologist Carl Rogers began what would become Sipe's lifelong interest in the nexus of spirituality and psychology.

In the 1950s, St. John's Abbey became the

site of early collaborations between clergy and mental health professionals, two groups that rarely came together. The sessions were directed by a priest named Alexius Portz, who believed the two disciplines had common concerns. To encourage openness, he restricted the meetings to the participants and barred the press and college community. Sipe got the job of running the equipment that recorded the lectures. To minimize the distraction, he was posted behind a closed door, with cords running under it to microphones. What he heard confirmed much of what he had begun to think about human nature.

When he was later ordained as a priest, Sipe first served as a teacher at a Catholic high school in Cold Spring, Minnesota. He continued his own academic work in counseling at the University of Minnesota, St. Cloud and St. Thomas University in St. Paul. As he worked as a counselor and as a priest hearing the confessions of both clergy and laypeople he noticed that individuals were practically tormented in their efforts to live according to Catholic teachings on sex. This was especially true for clergymen like himself, who were supposed to maintain absolute celibacy.

In 1964 Sipe spent a year in training at the Menninger Clinic in Topeka, Kansas, and he then went to the Seton Psychiatric Institute in Baltimore, where he eventually settled into work as a therapist and professor at St.

Mary's Pontifical Seminary, which served more than five hundred students from all over America. It was in Baltimore that the anthropologist Margaret Mead, visiting to give a lecture, pushed him to consider the Catholic clergy to be members of a discrete culture and to write about what he was observing in ethnographic, rather than psychoanalytic, terms. The proposal implied that just as Mead had famously revealed universal ideas about sexual liberation in her popular books on isolated societies in the South Pacific, Sipe might teach the wider world something through an exploration of the clergy subculture.

At the moment when he met Mead, Sipe was beginning to come to terms with his own status as a priest. Though firmly Christian, and Catholic, he had never been comfortable with the kind of obedience required by the hierarchy. Throughout his life as a monk Sipe had talked often with superiors and peers about how the all-but-blind obedience required by the Church grated against his internal (perhaps very American) resistance to authority. Try as he might, Sipe could not submit with a happy heart. Indeed, the more he succeeded at being obedient, the more depressed he became. Psychotherapy led him to conclude that he would have to leave the priesthood to resolve this conflict. By 1970 he was a layman married to a psychiatrist and former nun named Marianne Benkert, M.D., but he continued to serve Catholic institutions as a therapist who treated clergy.

By 1988, Sipe's long experience with ordained men who suffered from alcoholism, drug addiction, and psychological and sexual problems was probably unmatched in the world. But as often as he heard about priests who had secret children, or bishops who paid for abortions, Sipe continued to be surprised by what he learned in both therapy sessions and contacts with colleagues and church officials. As a social scientist he approached every case fully open to the idea that a priest or a bishop was the man he claimed to be. He also looked for confirmation, or contradictions to his findings from every available source. When he learned that Jeanne Miller had files full of letters from people who had been victimized by clergy he contacted her and flew to Chicago read them. His wife Marianne, who had seen the same kinds of patients and was his partner in the exploration of sexuality in the Catholic world, accompanied him on the trip.

In Miller's papers were letters from men and women of all walks of life, detailing everything from violent rapes committed by priests to longtime "marriages" to Catholic clergymen complete with children and grandchildren. "Those files provided validation of all that we had been learning in our practice,"

228

recalled Sipe, many years later. "Hundreds of people had written to tell her about their experiences with priests, and what they said was remarkably consistent with what priests and bishops had been describing from their point of view."

In fact, Catholic clergy tended to share complex and sometimes contradictory views of sex and celibacy that would have surprised laypeople, especially non-Catholics. While priests were supposed to abstain from all types of sex, a so-called "housekeeper syndrome" was widely discussed among bishops and priests who winked at ordained men who were obviously involved with women who worked in their parishes. Church leaders also made distinctions about age that varied from the civil law. While most states regarded anyone under sixteen or eighteen as a legal minor, the Church considered seven to be the "age of reason" and determined that a girl or boy could grant sexual consent somewhere between age twelve and fifteen. This kind of thinking provided the context for Milwaukee Archbishop Weakland's mixed statement on the sex abuse crisis, which he offered in an article published in 1988.

After explaining that abusive behavior is "rarely containable" and noting that offending priests should be removed from pastoral duties, Weakland spread the blame a little further. He warned that "we could easily give a false impression that any adolescent who becomes sexually involved with an older person does so without any degree of personal responsibility. Sometimes not all adolescent victims are so innocent; some can be sexually very active and aggressive and often quite streetwise."

For an archbishop speaking for a Church with strict public positions on all sorts of moral issues — abortion, the ordination of women, homosexuality — Weakland's position on priests who engaged in sex with minors was notably ambivalent. However, Sipe saw that it was consistent with the forgiving attitude clergy assumed when dealing with their own behavior. After thousands of confidential interviews with clergy at all levels Sipe developed some estimates of sexual issues among clergy. These figures were based not on a tabulated survey or scientific sample, but on his own deep experience with a significant number of priests. Extrapolating from this base, Sipe concluded that fewer than 2 percent of American priests ever managed to sublimate their sexual urges to the point where they were truly celibate. More remarkably, he estimated that at any given moment about 20 percent were involved in relationships with women, 10–13 percent were sexually active with men, and 6 percent were either occasionally or regularly violating adolescents or children.

As Sipe finished his book in 1989, he had met with more than a hundred priests who had exploited underaged victims and knew of one psychiatric center — St. Luke Institute in Suitland, Maryland — that had evaluated one hundred and thirty priests in a less-than-one-year period and diagnosed seventy-two as pedophiles. He believed that the culture of the clergy, which was organized around secrecy and privilege, made the priesthood attractive to men with serious sexual problems. Canon law allowed for the Church to remove an accused priest from ministry but Sipe knew that fear of scandal and a shame-based theology of sex made it impossible for the hierarchy to respond quickly and decisively. As a psychotherapist Sipe saw the devastating effects of abuse on victims and considered the Church responsible for helping them. As a Catholic who valued the institution, he wrote that "to survive" the Church needed to reassess basic beliefs that had stood for centuries.

The crisis, which Sipe thought he understood, got much bigger between the time when he finished his manuscript and chose a title — *A Secret World: Sexuality and the Search for Celibacy* — and its publication in the fall of 1990. In the Canadian province of Newfoundland a Church-sponsored inquiry criticized Archbishop Alphonsus Penney for ignoring accusations of sexual abuse against

231

twenty priests and layworkers at a Catholic orphanage called Mount Cashel run by the Irish Christian brothers of Canada. Penney resigned saying, "We are a sinful church. We are naked. Our anger, our pain, our anguish, our shame are clear to the whole world."

In time more than a hundred men would say they were abused at the orphanage and eight brothers would be convicted of sexual offenses against minors. Almost $30 million (Canadian) would be paid to victims by the order and government agencies that sent boys to the orphanage. The judge who sentenced one of the brothers to twelve years in prison for his crimes told him, "You are a disgrace to the order and to humanity." In time the orphanage itself would be torn down and the site would be covered by a supermarket parking lot.

Although it was the largest scandal to date in North America, events in Newfoundland were not noted in press reports on Richard Sipe's book, which he reviewed in a talk at the annual meeting of the American Psychological Association in August 1990. Instead, the press seized on the opportunity to address the broader issues of sex in the Church and the lives of priests. In dozens of interviews Sipe was astonished by the curiosity of journalists who seemed full of questions that they had never felt free to ask anyone else.

The interviews, which were full of pointed

questions about controversial topics, made full use of Sipe's skills as an academic, therapist, and former priest. However, he found he liked talking with reporters who reached far more people with their words than Sipe's book might ever touch. He came to see the journalists as a bridge that might bring his ideas further into the world. They came to rely on him as a guide through obscure corners of the Church and an interpreter of the ordained psyche.

A Secret World was welcomed by the mass media, but it met sharp criticism in other circles. A spokesman for the Catholic Church insisted that Sipe's methods were flawed because he did not conduct a random survey and his conclusions couldn't be applied to the overall ranks of the clergy because his information came from sexually active priests. (The assumption here was that most priests were successfully celibate.) This criticism was seconded by the famous sociologist/author/priest Andrew Greeley, who said that Sipe's book offered "wild" guesses instead of scholarship.

Greeley was famous for his own evaluations of Catholic America, which depended on annual surveys, which he often used to counter negative stereotypes about Catholics. Given the difference in their approaches — Greeley deployed surveys while Sipe dove deep into the lives of priests — his critique was an

apples-to-oranges exercise, but he pressed it
nevertheless. In an opinion piece published
by the *Los Angeles Times* he declared that
Sipe's book marked the arrival of a "silly
season" for commenting on sex and the
Church. Setting aside the elevated power and
status priests claim for themselves as ordained
men, he compared clergy who struggle with
celibacy to married men who have trouble
being faithful. He wrote:

Someone ought to say that when a man
like Sipe, who abandoned his own priestly
commitment, accuses those of us who
honor it of not doing a perfect job, one
hears a bit of axe-grinding in the background, a touch of self-justification, a
smidgen of guilt and defensiveness.

After the column was published, Sipe heard
from academics, media figures, and prominent Catholics around the world who told
him they had been contacted by Greeley, who
continued his attack in private. Greeley apparently resented how Sipe, an ex-priest, had
dissected his former brothers and invited the
public to view what he found. Greeley rejected the notion that a psychological/
anthropological approach would yield meaningful insights, and suspected Sipe harbored
some deep antipathy toward celibate priests.
However, a careful reading revealed that Sipe

actually respected the few true celibates he had encountered, describing them as flexible and good-humored men who were "brave, courageous, and devoted." Still, he saw so much suffering related to the way the Church handled sexual issues — the problem of pedophile priests being just one example — that he couldn't understand why the hierarchy wouldn't consider examining certain beliefs.

The gap between the nuanced conclusions of *A Secret World* and the response it provoked from the Church and critics like Greeley might be explained by the fractured quality of the sexual abuse crisis. Depending on one's perspective, the Church was embroiled in a spiritual struggle over sex, a conflict between democracy and monarchy (which was how Jason Berry saw it), or a legal war over the crimes of priests. The crisis involved all three of these battles and more, but this fact made talking about what was happening a difficult task even for sophisticated observers who were willing to discuss sex, religion, politics, and money, all at once.

Any attempt to consider the wave of sexual abuse claims and its true meaning was further complicated by the structure of the Church and its many institutions. With hundreds of dioceses and thousands of other entities — orders, schools, parishes, hospitals, colleges, seminaries, etc. — the Catholic Church exists in so many pieces that it was practically impossible to confront any major issue in a comprehensive way. Most of these divisions and subdivisions in the Catholic community could claim financial independence when it suited them, and seek the shelter of the law's special provisions for religious activities.

Because they were the main employers of priests, diocesan officials and the leaders of religious orders were more likely to find themselves dragged into abuse cases. As news about Gauthe, Porter, Adamson, Mount Cashel, and other cases shocked the public, the Catholic bureaucracy had struggled to respond. Along the way American bishops seemed to reach an informal consensus on the psychological problems of abusive priests. In their view, most of these men were actually expressing homosexual desires with young people who had passed puberty. While illegal, this practice, which was called ephebophilia, was regarded by them as something less disturbing than classic pedophilia. The bishops also embraced the notion that these priests could be treated effectively at places like St. Luke's or various Paraclete centers. As they sent accused priests to these facilities, bishops could appear to be addressing a problem while they also bought time for themselves and the accused. Not coincidentally, a priest could be spared prison time if, while he was in treatment, the statute of limitations on an offense expired.

The consensus of the bishops, when it came to priests and sexual abuse, was voiced by auxiliary bishop Alexander James Quinn of Cleveland to an April 1990 gathering of canon lawyers. Quinn, who had worked with Doyle, Mouton, and Peterson, told his fellow priests that the problem of sexual abuse was no more common in the Church than it was in the society as a whole. "We knew it was there, before," he said of the problem, but in the past decade it had become "discussed publicly."

Noting that in every case a bishop is caught between his role as "chief pastor" to lay-people and "father of his priests" he stressed that no harm be done to a ". . . brother priest who may be suffering from an illness and may also be innocent . . ." When valid claims arise, Quinn added, Church officials should act as caring pastors. "If we're going to save ourselves, we're going to save ourselves big," he said. "Let's be pastoral."

A civil attorney as well as a churchman, Quinn advised the men at the conference that the Church was vulnerable to lawsuits on many different fronts. Where once it enjoyed "almost complete immunity" from lawsuits it now faced "a tort litigation boom," said Quinn.

Although he didn't mention the case by name, a United States Supreme Court ruling handed down one week prior to the canon lawyers' conference had set the conditions for the "boom." At first glance *Employment Division v. Smith* seemed to have nothing to do with the Catholic Church or clergy abuse. The case involved an American Indian claim that the use of the illegal peyote mushrooms should be permitted because the drug was used as part of a spiritual practice. By siding with the State of Oregon, which outlawed the drug, the court signaled that the First Amendment did not allow religious groups to define generally illegal practices as religious activities and therefore be exempt from regulation. The conservative Catholic justice Antonin Scalia wrote that such exemptions would "make the professed doctrines of religious belief superior to the law of the land, and in effect to permit every citizen to become a law unto himself."

In *Smith,* Scalia signaled that Churches and other religious groups enjoyed no special exceptions from the laws that applied to all. Where clergy abuse cases were concerned, the ruling seemed to suggest that like any employer or supervisor, dioceses and bishops bore some responsibility for the conduct of rank-and-file priests. Like other employers, Church officials bore some responsibility to the public for the men they sent to serve them, and they could be charged with negligent supervision and blamed for the emotional distress caused by an abuser's crimes.

The *Smith* decision was just the latest in a series of legal developments that had shaken church officials who had been accustomed to special treatment from the legal system. The clergy abuse cases brought in Louisiana and Minnesota had shown that even confidential personnel files could be subpoenaed by lawyers suing on behalf of victims. Under these new conditions, said Quinn, bishops and other administrators needed to be much more careful about the documents they collected and preserved. He recommended that they review their files routinely and either dispose of controversial items or use the Vatican status as a sovereign state to hide them from subpoenas issued by plaintiffs' lawyers.

"Comb through your files," said Quinn. "If there's something there that you really don't want people to see you might send it off to the Apostolic Delegate because they have immunity to protect something that is potentially dangerous or that you consider to be dangerous."

As he spoke of the Church and the abuse crisis, Quinn presented a picture of a besieged, even persecuted institution hard-pressed to defend itself. But he also offered a bit of macabre history that was intended to startle but reassure the men he had counseled. He recalled a New York case in which a Catholic priest arranged an illegal abortion for a woman he had made pregnant. When the woman died, Fr. Hans Schmidt and the dentist who did the operation dismembered her body and "part-by-part" dropped her off the side of a ferry boat. A jury rejected Schmidt's insanity plea and he was executed.

Reassured when Quinn told them the case was from 1913, some of the men in the room chuckled as he explained that the State of New York judicial system "did all the penal work" and saved the Church the bother of disciplining Schmidt. Quinn's point was that the "diocese didn't have to do anything more than survive that, and I suppose it will survive some of these other things."

Borrowed in large part from 1913, the strategy Quinn proposed for the modern sexual abuse crisis was reported by Jason Berry in the Cleveland *Plain Dealer* and the *Baltimore Sun.* (Editors at *The New York Times* and *The Washington Post* both turned down the piece, which meant it received less notice nationally.) Berry called Quinn before writing about the bishop's remarks. In their conversation, Berry recalled that Tom Doyle had warned against using the Vatican's diplomatic privilege to dodge civil responsibilities because such a scheme, if discovered, might cause an international incident.

"Whatever I said is my own opinion,"

Quinn snapped at Berry. "It was never discussed with the nunciature."

11.

WILLFUL INDIFFERENCE

Having aided Richard Sipe's research, Jeanne Miller welcomed his book and the increased attention it brought to the issue of clergy abuse. Sipe referred to her the people who contacted him about problem priests and as this number grew, Miller thought about creating a formal organization that might do more, in terms of education and advocacy, than she could do as an isolated individual. Moving slowly, she picked a name for her group — Victims of Clergy Abuse Link-up — and began having meetings at her suburban home. At these sessions abuse victims and their supporters talked mainly about ways to reform the way the Church dealt with problem priests and to find justice for victims.

Perhaps because she was a victim herself, Barbara Blaine was more interested in forming a mutual support network for people struggling with the aftereffects of clergy abuse. And since she was already experienced as a social activist, she didn't need to think much about organizing. From the day that the *Donahue* show brought that first flood of phone calls she began refining the self-help model to create something for abuse victims. She changed the name of The Victims Network to: SNAP, which stood for Survivors Network of those Abused by Priests. Even though she wasn't especially picky about terminology, in choosing to use the word "survivor" Blaine signaled that she was sensitive to those who didn't consider themselves "victims" and preferred to emphasize their recovery from the effects of abuse.

When she had collected enough names to draw a decent crowd, Blaine found a Holiday Inn in the suburbs of Chicago that would give her free use of a conference center if she could guarantee that a certain number of hotel rooms would be taken by SNAP members. Fewer than twenty people arrived for the Friday night registration but Blaine conducted a press conference that prompted another fifteen or twenty to show up for the Saturday session. The agenda included talks by a therapist, a local lawyer, and a nun who addressed the spiritual impact of abuse. Before group discussions began Blaine established ground rules to encourage openness.

"We're a self-help group," she noted. "You don't get to tell others what to do. You are not allowed to give advice. We don't make judgments. There are no right and wrong statements. We are making a sacred commitment to each other. Everything said in this room is confidential."

Safe among people who shared their experiences, participants told their stories and discovered they had much in common. To a person, victims had been vulnerable to a persuasive and manipulative authority figure and so ashamed or traumatized by what occurred that they kept it secret. Most were only able to connect the abuse to later problems such as depression or addiction after entering treatment or reading about the long-term effects of sexual trauma. The survivors who spoke also told consistent tales of Church leaders who denied or downplayed what they reported and moved slowly, if at all, to help them.

More meetings would follow the first gathering and Blaine would slowly acquire the skills to respond when someone needed more than the self-help model could provide.

At a meeting in Rhode Island, the decorative candles Blaine brought to distribute as gifts brought one woman to tears. Candles had been used by the priest who molested her.

Unexpected reactions gave the members of SNAP opportunities to learn about the nature of sexual trauma. The candles in Rhode Island had triggered a psychological flashback in the woman who associated them with her abuse, making her feel as she did when she was molested. In another telling case, a woman named Anne, who belonged to the Chicago chapter, asked others to help her tell her parents about what she had suffered as a child. On the day Anne chose, SNAP members went to a park and watched from a nearby picnic table as their friend explained what she remembered to her parents. According to their plan, they would be available if the woman's parents reacted negatively. As it turned out the woman's mother and father already knew what had happened. Their daughter had reported it when it occurred. At the time they had found other parents whose children had also been abused and forced the priest to leave the parish.

The memory gap that allowed a woman who had been molested as a girl to forget she had once told the truth about it illustrated one of the major controversies that arose around all types of child abuse claims in the late 1980s and early 1990s. On one side of this issue stood therapists, victims, and others who would consider Anne's experience and say it proved that someone could forget an assault, or even a series of assaults, but still suffer from the effects. Indeed, they would consider memory loss a hallmark of trauma and be unsurprised when incidents were recalled in the safety of adulthood. On the other side of the controversy gathered a number of people accused of abuse, a handful of psychologists and social scientists, and defense lawyers who raised a host of questions about the reliability of memory. These skeptics could point to cases where suggestive questioning had apparently led children to allege abuse by preschool teachers and argue that this event threw all such allegations — against teachers, parents, clergy, and others — into the category of mass hysteria.

For the media, the broad argument over memory offered an opportunity to speculate about the frightening prospects of innocent caretakers railroaded into prison by false testimony produced by unreliable, if sincere, witnesses. For people who claimed to have been abused by priests, the controversy made the pursuit of corroborating evidence even more essential. Here, the nature of sexual abuse actually favored victims. As many studies had shown, most offenders abuse a number of victims — Gilbert Gauthe admitted to more than a hundred — as they compulsively seek to replace those who grow older and cease to be attractive to them. This practice produces large numbers of potential witnesses who might come forward once an initial complaint is made and reported in the press. Jeff Anderson saw this dynamic play out in his first case of clergy abuse and in almost every one that followed. The American public got a sense of this process when Frank Fitzpatrick served the role of first reporter against James R. Porter, a priest who had molested him when he was a ten- or eleven-year-old boy in Massachusetts.

A private investigator, Fitzpatrick had put what happened to him out of his mind until 1989 when, at age thirty-nine, he was flooded with memories. Using his professional skills, he tracked down Porter, who had left the priesthood, married, and settled in Minnesota. In telephone conversations that Fitzpatrick recorded, Porter confessed that he had molested many children. When Fitzpatrick asked if Porter recalled "me in particular" the former priest answered, "No, I don't remember names." Fitzpatrick noted that Porter had traumatized the children he molested. Porter replied:

I don't take it lightly. God Almighty, it can make you sick. If I keep dwelling on it, I'd go crazy. So what I have done, is I have just invented my life as best I can, and tried to live in a Christian, Catholic way. It's been marvelous, how I've had no difficulty whatsoever.

After he obtained Porter's confession, Fitzpatrick placed an advertisement in Massachusetts newspapers — the headline read "Remember Father Porter?" — asking for other victims to contact him. He heard from eight others who said that Porter had raped or molested them when they were children. With some more digging Fitzpatrick discovered that Church officials had known that Porter was molesting children in the 1960s. After parents complained he was sent to a Servants of the Paraclete psychiatric center in New Mexico, where he was treated for this problem. Even during his treatment, Porter acted as a priest in New Mexico. Upon his release Porter returned to ministry in Bemidji, Minnesota. No parish where he worked was ever informed of his past.

In late 1990 Fitzpatrick went public with what he discovered, speaking first at a forum in Rhode Island and then to the press. Soon he was represented by Boston-based attorney Roderick MacLeish Jr. Within a year, nearly fifty people would join a lawsuit MacLeish filed against the Diocese of Fall River, Massachusetts, where Porter had been posted. MacLeish's filing was followed by a similar one Jeffrey Anderson filed with a co-counsel in New Mexico, where Porter had molested children while being treated by the Servants of the Paraclete. Anderson also sued in Minnesota where seven men, most former altar boys, claimed Porter had molested them when he worked in Bemidji.

In Porter, Anderson and the other lawyers were dealing with the first priest in the brief history of the scandal who actually admitted from the start that he was a serial pedophile. For victims who tracked the issue, Porter affirmed what they had been saying about the way the Church mishandled complaints. In Chicago, SNAP founder Barbara Blaine heard about a press conference Anderson planned and got it in her mind that she wanted to attend to support the victims who had decided to speak out. After dinner was served and residents of the Worker House began to settle in for the night, she asked a woman on the staff if she would drive with her to St. Paul. Helen O'Neil, who had come from Great Britain to work at the Chicago house, agreed and the two women set off on the seven-hour drive.

As they drove and looked out over the darkened rural landscape, O'Neil and Blaine talked about the problem of sexual abuse and how it could erode a victim's self-confidence, and ability to trust others. O'Neil had had some troubling experience with abuse that she intended to leave behind when she moved to the States. However, when Blaine told her about SNAP she felt called to help. So much for escaping the issue. As the sky began to lighten, Blaine and O'Neil pulled into a highway rest area to park the car and nap. When they awoke they found a hotel where they used a lobby restroom to wash up and change clothes. Then they got back on the road.

In St. Paul the two women found the site for the press conference, followed the crowd of reporters inside, and stood in the back to listen. Watching Anderson, Blaine thought his expensive suits and well-styled hair made him look a little too slick. But he seemed to understand the way the Church handled abuse cases, emphasizing damage control over care for victims, and she could tell by the way Anderson's voice wavered as he discussed his clients that his concern for victims was heartfelt. The men who spoke at the event recalled how Porter had won their confidence and then exploited it.

After the press conference Blaine spoke to the victims, some of whom had cried before the television cameras. She told them she thought they were brave and she was grateful that they were speaking publicly, because few did. She told them about SNAP and offered her support. She then fell into a conversation with a television producer. As they talked about James Porter and the fact that he lived nearby, the producer and Blaine decided to drive to his home to see if he would talk on camera.

Oakdale, Minnesota, was a fifteen-minute drive from downtown St. Paul. Porter lived in an ordinary subdivision of neat houses with carefully trimmed lawns. Blaine and the television crew found his home, circled the block, and then stopped in front of it. With a cameraman recording them, they knocked on the door. When it opened a boy, Porter's son, stood shyly and explained that his father wasn't home. Looking over his shoulder, Blaine could see James Porter's reflection in a mirror. He was standing behind the door. She chose not to say anything about what she saw. Instead, she said, "If your dad touches you it's wrong, and it's okay to tell."

When the door closed, Blaine and the TV crew walked back to their vehicles and she told them what she saw. She and Helen decided to walk up and down the street to knock on doors and explain to Porter's neighbors, "You have a child molester living here." Before they departed they drove past Porter's home again and caught sight of him in the backyard. He may have been hanging laundry. He may have been pretending to hang laundry while looking out for trespassers. Either way, Blaine thought she might have caught his eye.

In a matter of months James Porter would become the public face of the national clergy abuse crisis. As roughly two hundred victims came forward he would be featured on an ABC television network news program and vilified in the print media. *The Boston Globe* would reveal how Church officials, including Pope Paul VI, knew of Porter's criminal tendencies, if not his specific crimes, in the 1960s and 1970s. Porter even confessed to his offenses in documents he sent to the Pope as part of his request to leave the priesthood. "I used my collar as a sword and a shield," he wrote.

When Boston's Cardinal Law first spoke of the scandal he acknowledged the betrayal Porter had practiced, but added that the Church should "respond both to victim and betrayer in truth, in love and reconciliation." Ten days later Law would announce, "I'm absolutely fed up with the media coverage of this case of twenty-five years ago." Insisting that the press overplayed the story while ignoring the positive work of the Church he added, "By all means we call down God's power on the media, particularly the *Globe*." If God responded to Law's call, it wasn't apparent to anyone in New England, where the Porter case filled the airwaves and dominated the front pages of local newspapers.

With Frank Fitzpatrick's investigation of James Porter, a victim had managed to turn the tables on a perpetrator by capturing his confession. But while Fitzpatrick's dramatic actions brought a surge of publicity to the cause of abuse victims, a less noted development would have a much greater effect on the larger confrontation between the Catholic Church and the law. In this case, Jeffrey

Anderson had gone back to court with a new complaint against Fr. Thomas Adamson and included claims for punitive damages on the grounds that the dioceses of St. Paul and Winona had committed both fraud and reckless negligence. Coming in the wake of the Supreme Court's *Smith* decision, the trial would be the first in which the First Amendment offered scant protection to bishops who might claim that all of their activities were religious in nature.

The plaintiff in this landmark trial was the John Doe who had come to Anderson about Fr. Adamson after Greg Lyman settled his case. Doe had recounted years of abuse, beginning at age thirteen. On some days, he said, Fr. Adamson had violated him as many as six different times. In the suit Anderson would argue that this victimization had contributed substantially to addictions and other mental health problems that had plagued Doe into adulthood and made his outlook for the future terribly bleak. To date he had been unable to secure a job or a home for more than a few months at a time.

Doe's personal problems made him a difficult client, but he was also one of the most determined young men Anderson had ever met. From the start he wanted to make Church officials disclose everything they did, and failed to do, about Adamson in the years leading up to his abuse. Toward that end, he authorized Anderson to reject every settlement offer that came along and force the bishops of St. Paul and Winona into an actual trial. In the months leading up to trial, Church lawyers offered various amounts of cash, hoping to settle the case. By the fall of 1990 the offer reached the $1 million mark. Anderson agreed with Doe's decision to reject it.

The hard negotiating stance, which began as a matter of principle, gradually became something more. As Anderson mined documents for leads and deposed witnesses he found facts that were never discovered in the Lyman case. The most important new evidence showed that a lower-ranking bishop in St. Paul named Robert Carlson had repeatedly warned Archbishop John Roach about Adamson's relationships with boys. Bishop Carlson had clearly wanted Adamson barred from any work that might bring him into contact with young people, and had been frustrated by Roach's reluctance to act more decisively.

Other documents noted the names of nuns who worked with Adamson and suspected he was sexually abusing children, and made their concerns known to higher-ups who did little in response. In her deposition Sr. Patrice Neuberger testified that she was not the first to warn bishops about Adamson and she had been assured that "something will be done."

Nothing was done, and John Doe was subsequently violated by Fr. Adamson.

Finally Anderson discovered that a psychiatrist chosen to treat Adamson had concluded that he didn't have to report Adamson's sexual contact with adolescents to criminal authorities because higher Church authorities were already "aware of it." A devout Catholic, Joseph Gendron, M.D., was one of two experts Archbishop Roach relied upon to manage Adamson, even though he had no special training in sexual abuse or pedophilia. The other was a priest who was also a psychologist. Both men seemed to place their loyalty to the Church above their responsibility to safeguard the community.

Altogether, the evidence showed that officials in two dioceses had received repeated warnings about Adamson over more than two decades and yet failed to keep him away from children. For Anderson the pattern met the standard to claim that Church officials were guilty of "reckless disregard" and "willful indifference" negligence in the supervision of Adamson and fraud in their relationship with parishioners who trusted that the Church was a safe place for children. These claims raised the stakes in the case to the point where the jury could award punitive damages, well in excess of the amount that would compensate Doe for his losses.

No Church officials had ever paid punitive

damages for negligence. If Anderson succeeded in winning them in this case, it would establish that bishops were direct supervisors, responsible for their priests, and liable for how they managed them. This precedent would open the door to multimillion-dollar verdicts across the country. As the trial date approached and their offers of a settlement were rejected time and again, the legal team for the Church added a new member to manage the trial itself.

Theodore "Ted" Collins was a committed Catholic who had attended seminary as a teenager but gave up his dream of becoming a priest because he couldn't accept celibacy — he referred to it as "putting on the tin underpants" — and the regimentation of clerical life. In adulthood he attended Mass more than once a week, and was certain, in his soul, that despite its problems the Roman Catholic Church was perhaps the greatest source of goodness in the world. It deserved a vigorous defense.

As a lawyer, Collins owned the respect of his peers. Gifted at argument and examining witnesses, he loved appearing before judges and juries and he had extensive experience as both a defense lawyer and a prosecutor. In the 1970s he was frequently tapped to help the government with key cases, including the prosecution of cop killers and the teenager who bombed a Dayton's department store in

1970 as an act of political protest.

Coming late to the case, Collins was struck by the naive way the bishops had responded to Thomas Adamson's crimes. Threatened by scandal, they had thought they could quietly manage the case and preserve the image of the Church. Then, in depositions, they were trapped by their own words as they struggled to reconcile their duties as moral leaders and shepherds with their actions. Looking ahead to the trial, he knew how Jeffrey Anderson could cite the Church's own documents to suggest negligence and turn Carlson, Roach, and Watters into his star witnesses to prove the claim. That was the way he would try the case, if he were on the other side.

John Doe's case, *John Doe 76C v. Archdiocese of St. Paul and Minneapolis and Diocese of Winona* was heard in a small, redbrick county courthouse in the small town of Anoka. In the pretrial jury selection process both sides tried to exclude men and women who may have leaned against their positions. In the process they wound up asking potential jurors about their religious backgrounds, educations, and whether they watched *Oprah* or *Donahue* and how those programs may have influenced their thinking about sexual abuse. The cultural significance of talk shows was revealed when a lawyer, unable to recall a host's name, asked, "What's the lady's name

257

that lost the weight?" and prospective juror number one hundred and fifteen immediately replied, "Oprah Winfrey." The same juror noted she had seen Jeffrey Anderson on a television news program. "I remember his smile," she explained.

The trial, which ran from November 3 to December 8, 1990, marked only the third time a civil complaint against a Catholic priest had gone before a judge and jury. As the local media descended upon the courthouse, TV vans lined the street outside and telescoping masts were raised to transmit reports. Inside, the first row of the public gallery filled up with reporters who sat with notebooks and pens.

The facts of the crimes were not much in dispute. From the start Adamson admitted he had molested Doe and the two dioceses accepted some responsibility. The battle would be fought over how to measure the harm done, apportion the blame, and determine whether punitive damages would be paid. Anderson would press the point that the bishops were guilty of willful indifference because their cover-up had endangered the children whom Adamson attacked. Why hadn't they acted to stop Adamson when they first heard a complaint? Why hadn't they ministered to the victim and his family as if they were pastors?

In pretrial hearings, Judge Phyllis Jones

ruled in favor of the defense on the majority of the motions, including its request to tell the jury about abortions obtained by more than one of John Doe's adult sexual partners. As one defense lawyer explained, the point he wanted to make was that the priest's victim had problems with "sexual compulsivity" and problems with "responsibility" that might mitigate his client's responsibility. Anderson, while noting that the issue of abortion "is explosive," failed to have the record kept out of evidence. In the same pretrial process the judge barred many of Anderson's more powerful exhibits, including testimony from a witness who said a bishop had refused to confront Adamson after complaints by saying "little boys heal."

Twenty years later, Anderson's frustration with Judge Jones remained fresh. He recalled that at one point when the judge ruled against him and then announced a recess for lunch, Anderson rose to challenge the lunch break. "I said, 'Judge, the decision you just made is so erroneous, we have to have everything on the record.' " When she brushed him off, Anderson then spoke directly to the court reporter telling her "You're staying." Jones reminded Anderson that the reporter worked for her and the argument ended as both women departed.

When the evidence issues were finally settled, Anderson used his opening statement to explain to the jury that "this is not a case against Fr. Thomas Adamson. This is a case against those in the Church who had the power, who had the ability to prevent this from ever happening. For it was they who placed Fr. Adamson at that location, in that position of power and of trust, with knowledge that he had abused boys in the past."

In style, as well as substance, Anderson mixed formalities with the kind of language jurors might find familiar from television dramas. For example, he noted that, "Bishop Loras Watters continued to place him [Adamson] in other parishes within the Diocese of Winona until it became too hot because of the threats of the Klein family." The "heat" Anderson described was created by the possibility of disclosure. The choice of words allowed Anderson to speak of the bishop as if he were a crime boss.

From this beginning, Anderson put on a case that set a template for almost every clergy sex abuse trial to follow. He brought Jay Klein up from Worthington to testify about the complaints his family had lodged in the 1970s. Then he called on psychologist Susan Phipps-Yonas to describe how Adamson's betrayal had devastated his client and contributed to his many adult problems. Another expert, psychiatrist Martin Blinder, said that when he examined Doe he found "a twenty-four-year-old man whose growing up was arrested in adolescence. He can never recapture those lost years." He added, "I think for the most part he will always be crippled in some way."

Defense attorneys presented their own expert witness, a psychiatrist named Barbara Long. Dr. Long had visited with the victim once and consulted medical records provided to her by defense attorneys. In her report of roughly nine pages she devoted just eight lines to sexual abuse. The rest was focused on the notion that John Doe was profoundly disturbed before he ever met Fr. Adamson. Describing him as only "moderately" affected by Adamson's assaults, Long suggested that Doe suffered from a personality disorder that was the product of genetics as well as his early relationships with his mother. Long also speculated that Doe may have enjoyed the sexual encounters with Adamson and suggested that he would have become an addict even without the experience of abuse.

Under cross-examination, Anderson led Long to disclose that she had no particular training in the area of sexual abuse, nor had she written any papers or conducted any research on the subject. He also attacked her suggestion that his client carried, from his family, a pre-existing genetic inclination toward mental illness. In fact, as Long had to agree, she had seen no records to indicate mental illness on either side of his family. As

Anderson reminded her that Fr. Adamson had abused his client countless times, including six episodes in a single day, the psychiatrist softened her testimony. Eventually she agreed that much of the young man's trouble could be attributed to years of sexual involvement with a middle-aged priest.

"What we don't know," she hastened to add, "is what this means and whether it's a significant or a relatively minor causal factor."

For Jeff Anderson, who faced Ted Collins and a small flock of additional defense attorneys, the trial became a marathon. Every morning, for six weeks straight, he rose in the darkness before dawn and picked out clothes that he hoped would communicate authority but not excess. He paired dark suits with plain shirts and ties that were bright enough to help the jurors stay alert and focused on him through the long days of work.

Leaving Stillwater before 7 A.M., Anderson drove for an hour to reach the courthouse. On the few days when his wife Julie could sit in the gallery and watch, he found support in her smile. Otherwise his only ally was his young associate Mark Wendorf, who helped manage the flow of documents and labored to keep track of witnesses and their testimony. In the evenings Anderson would leave the courthouse to discover the sun had already set. He drove home to dinner and long conversations in which Julie served as his sounding board for new lines of questioning. Late at night he would drink as a reward, and in order to come down from the excitement of the day and find his way to sleep.

The local press made much of the fact that Fr. Adamson appeared as a witness and confirmed that his superiors knew he was a danger to youngsters. However, more important testimony came from Adamson's higher-ups. First, Bishop Robert Carlson recalled how he had twice warned his boss, Archbishop John Roach, that "the archdiocese would regret it" if Fr. Adamson were not fired for having sex with boys. Then Anderson called the archbishop of St. Paul, who had assumed responsibility for Adamson when he departed the Diocese of Winona in a cloud of suspicion. For more than a decade he had allowed him to remain a priest in contact with young people, despite multiple warnings that he was a danger.

A small man with thinning hair and a big smile, John Roach was beloved by Catholics in Minnesota and widely respected in the national Church. At seventy years of age he had spent forty-five years in the priesthood. Except for his own arrest for drunk driving, he had never been involved in a public scandal.

On the stand, Roach repeated points made many times before in the sex abuse crisis.

Mistakes had been made, he said, but like the rest of society the Church hadn't been well-informed on the nature of sexual abuse. He also said that he had relied on experts whose advice turned out to be wrong. When questioned about the meeting that he and Bishop Watters had to discuss their recollections of the Adamson case he insisted they got together "not in a conspiratorial sense, but to make sure we were remembering the same thing."

Nervous under Anderson's questioning, Roach insisted that the diocese was not guilty of willful indifference to children. "That is not tolerable," he said. "That is not true." He also tried to present himself as a compassionate shepherd who was genuinely concerned about the people in the Church. However, he came across as more of a protector of the clergy than a pastor of the people.

"I want to help people," he said at one point, "but I *really* want to help priests."

With this statement, Roach made one of Anderson's key points — that in his heart, the bishop placed a higher value on the welfare of ordained men than he placed on the well-being of children.

The final witness in the trial spoke about the assets of the two dioceses, which might be available to pay damages and penalties. Anderson left the questioning to his associate Mark Wendorf, who led a consulting accountant named Kevin Bergman through an analysis of audited financial statements submitted to the court. Bergman noted that between St. Paul and Winona, the Church held almost $16 million in unrestricted funds and $27 million worth of real estate. The latter figure was based on dated valuations, but when Wendorf prodded Bergman to estimate current values, Judge Jones stopped him. However, she did allow the defendants to point out that $2.5 million in excess pension funds might be unavailable to the Church due to regulations governing the plan.

Although they had signaled their confidence throughout the trial, and even withdrew their settlement offer, the defense team concluded with a remarkable admission. The Church *was* guilty of negligence, the lawyers said, but not of "willful indifference," which would permit the jury to levy punitive damages. If the jury disagreed, they added, they should confine the penalty to a modest six-figure sum. To back up their call for restraint they blamed Doe's alcoholism and his parents, who entrusted Adamson with their son at a time when the boy showed signs of psychological problems. They may not have been primarily responsible for the abuse but, they said, they deserved a portion of the blame. (This kind of blame-shifting would become a staple of Church defense in future cases, traumatizing many parents. Some Church lawyers would even maneuver to make parents co-defendants in cases brought by their own children.)

In his closing argument, Jeff Anderson countered the defense claim about John Doe's alcohol problem by pointing out that Fr. Adamson had given him his first drink, when he was thirteen. He then compared the bishops' supervision of Adamson to the Ford Motor Company's decision to continue selling the Pinto automobile after engineers determined that the car's gas tank would explode in some minor collisions. Just as the Pinto was a defective car, he said, Adamson was a defective priest "entered into the stream of religious commerce." At the same time, the Church made efforts to avoid a scandal. "They were successful in protecting their image for many years," he said. "They were successful in protecting this priest for many years."

Knowing that the jury would be challenged to put a dollar value on his client's loss and on the appropriate penalty that should be paid by the Church, Anderson did the math for them. He estimated Doe's emotional distress, embarrassment, and financial losses had to be worth more than $2 million. If the jury agreed, and wanted to send a message to society about abuse inside religious institutions, they should consider the danger Adamson had posed to the public and add the punitive damages equal to the amount recently paid to a young man who had been severely injured in a Pinto accident — $3.5 million.

The total figure — $5.5 million — was an easy-to-remember number and represented a third of the available cash held by the two dioceses. If the jurors considered it excessive, Anderson urged them to reflect on the damage done to Doe's sense of self-worth, his ability to relate to others, and his prospects for a happy life. Recalling how Fr. Adamson had drawn a thirteen-year-old into years of sexual victimization, Anderson concluded, "Short of murder, perhaps nothing is worse than what he did."

A unanimous vote was required for the jury to reach a conclusion and during the first day of deliberation none of the lawyers involved in the case expected they would reach one. The case they had heard was complex and the verdict they would render might send a signal across the entire country. For three days they considered the case quietly. On the fourth, the jurors demonstrated a bit of weary anxiety when they complained about a microwave antenna raised by a TV truck crew. Worried that the equipment on the mast might pick up their conversation, they asked the judge to order the truck moved. She did.

Finally, five days after they were asked to compare a priest to a Pinto, the jury sent word that they had finished their work. When the parties gathered in the courtroom the only one who didn't appear was Fr. Adamson, who had been present through the entire trial. A cadre of five lawyers and several clerics sat on the defense's side of the courtroom. John Doe sat beside Anderson and Wendorf while his parents took seats behind them. Doe burst into tears as the verdict was read.

On the matter of compensation, the jury found that Doe deserved $855,000. On the question of willful indifference they agreed that the bishops were liable and the Church should be punished by an additional penalty of $2.7 million.

In the courtroom John Doe embraced both of his lawyers and then turned to his mother and father, who had listened while defense attorneys blamed them for what happened to their son. His mother had believed the jurors were "people like me, down to earth" and suddenly she felt as if "something was lifted off of me." His father immediately imagined the news of the verdict rippling across the country as a warning to other bishops trying to deal with criminal priests.

Church officials and their lawyers were stunned by the size of the awards. Insurance would pay the compensatory damages, but the additional $2.7 million was not covered by any liability policy. The defense attorneys told the press they would ask the judge to overturn the verdict or strike the punitive damages from the award.

The Anoka jury's verdict was delivered on a Friday night, which was convenient for a lawyer who would celebrate to excess. By 1990 Jeff Anderson had switched from brandy/sevens to blue martinis — a combination of vodka and blue curacao — which he could consume in great quantities at a party he held in his office. Under the influence of this bright blue concoction he was able to laugh, almost uncontrollably, about the foibles of the judge who had tortured him through the trial. He was also able to imagine, with some excitement, the improved prospects for other cases he had undertaken on behalf of abuse victims across the country.

Julie Anderson stood a bit to the side during the celebration. In the years since she had been married, she had outgrown her interest in big parties and become even more convinced that her husband had a serious drinking problem. With the self-help movement in full swing the media was full of information on the subject and she had built a collection of books on alcoholism, codependency, and relationships. In her mind the evidence of her husband's addiction was overwhelming. But no amount of information made it any easier for her to talk about what she believed. On one level she dreaded even attempting to argue with a man who was so gifted at persuasion and denial. On another, she sensed that if she ever succeeded in getting through to him, and he somehow quit drinking, *everything* would change.

Uncertain she was ready for the seismic shift that would come with sobriety, Julie would begin conversations but then feel overwhelmed and retreat. She was able to write down her concerns, and she gave him letters that described her loneliness and fears. Her husband seemed sympathetic when he read them, but as far as she could tell, they had no lasting effect.

The need for some change seemed all the more urgent to Julie because a new member of the family had arrived at the house in Stillwater. Two months before the Doe trial she had given birth to her first child, a son who was named Darrow (after the famous lawyer) and the new responsibility had made her even more wary of her husband's wild ways. She was having more trouble accepting her husband's absences and erratic behavior, and she knew that on some level he understood that something was wrong. Julie had noticed that when his sober friend Grant Hall came to visit after Darrow's birth, Jeff had hidden a bottle of vodka he had just brought home. Nothing had been said about this little sleight of hand, but it spoke volumes nevertheless.

On the day after the verdict, friends and

colleagues who had missed the news on Friday night called to congratulate Anderson after they read about it on the front pages of the local papers. Most, if not all of them, had made a rough calculation of the fee that Anderson might collect on the award, but he wouldn't let them talk about this aspect of the victory. Besides, the appeal promised by the defendants would be heard by the same Judge Jones who had run the trial. Given her previous rulings, Anderson expected her to ratchet down the jury's numbers. One friend, an attorney named Lee Daly, came to the Andersons' house on the hill in Stillwater and told him to prepare "to move this whole thing forward." Daly saw the issue of abuse unfolding as a national cause. Anderson told him he was too exhausted to even consider a strategy for the future.

Soon, however, Anderson began to see the clergy abuse cases as part of a larger, liberal trend in human affairs. Just as bishops, cardinals, and the Pope saw themselves as defenders of constant truths, Anderson saw himself as an agent of equality. In his view, overly broad readings of the First Amendment had allowed the Church to operate outside the rules of decency and become a power unto itself. Given what he knew about human nature — including *his own* nature — he was sure that under these conditions any group of men would come to abuse their privileges. This is what had happened in the case of sex, crime, and the Church.

Previous efforts to limit the scope of First Amendment protections for religion had failed, but there was something about the rape and sexual abuse of children that moved the legal system to reconsider the balance. The cases in Louisiana, the *Smith* ruling, and now the Doe decision had not only changed the balance, but had broken the cover of secrecy that allowed bishops to hide complaints and shuffle abusive priests from parish to parish, exposing vulnerable children with every move. Without this cover, ordinary Catholics would be able to see the values of the hierarchy at work as they dealt with sexual sins inside the priesthood, and they could judge for themselves both the men and their principles. For his part, Anderson would be happy to pursue one case after another until the institution itself changed in ways that would put an end to the crisis.

In the months that followed the John Doe verdict, Judge Jones held hearings on the jury's award and then slashed the total to a little over $1 million. This result was just about equal to the highest settlement offered by the defendants before trial. Considered one way, Jones's actions deprived Doe and his attorneys of any reward for the extra effort they made during the six-week trial. They had risked losing it all, and endured all those days and nights of stress, to wind up right where they had started.

But while the plaintiff and his attorneys could fault Jones on the dollars, they could find some affirmation in what she had to say about the jury's answers to the key questions posed at trial. Jones had noted that the bishops *were* responsible for protecting Church members from criminal clergy and she had rejected the defendants' claim that they enjoyed First Amendment protection from liability. "The interest of the state in the health and welfare of its citizens, particularly its youth, overrides the religious interests enumerated by defendants," she wrote.

Anderson appealed the reduction in the award, but the Minnesota Supreme Court upheld Judge Jones's reasoning and her decision to reduce the penalties levied against the two dioceses. Though not close to the seven-figure amount he could have earned based on the jury's original award, Anderson's fee would fund his work on new cases and reassure his partner Mark Reinhardt. Although Reinhardt had supported the investment of time and money in the clergy cases, he had also fretted about the revenues lost as more ordinary cases — like personal injury claims — were set aside.

For Anderson's client, the money was an acknowledgment of his injuries and it promised to make some aspects of life easier, if only in the short term. Anderson would advise Doe to invest the small fortune wisely and husband it for the future, but based on his experience with some other clients, Anderson couldn't feel confident that he would. Indeed, as Anderson considered the path followed by his other abuse clients who had received a substantial award, he found himself worrying about whether the cash might do more harm than good. Anderson continually admonished him to stick with his commitment to sobriety and Alcoholics Anonymous. It didn't occur to him to consider taking his own advice.

Greg Lyman had given Anderson reason to fear how Doe might act under the influence of more than half a million dollars. In periodic conversations, Anderson had continued to counsel Lyman to get help for his psychological problems and support for his effort to stop drinking. None of what he said worked. In the months leading up the Doe trial, Lyman had begun drinking heavily and acting impulsively. Although he had established a relationship with a young woman named Annette and together they had brought a child into the world, Lyman showed few signs that he was settling down or even recovering from the effects of abuse. Instead he talked angrily about how he had been betrayed and exploited. Obsessed with the idea that Thomas Adamson was living freely and potentially abusing new victims, he often ranted about how "someone should do something."

Barred from working as a priest, Adamson had fled Minnesota for a small town in Wisconsin where he worked as a hotel clerk. When Lyman learned where he was, he told Annette that one day he would travel to Wisconsin and kill him. She didn't take him seriously until he went out one morning and didn't come back.

Adamson's new home was close to the city of Eau Claire. Lyman went there, got a room in a motel, and started drinking. After writing a note that that included the lines "he has to die" and "unfortunately, with his death will come mine," Greg went to a K-mart store where a clerk refused to sell him a shotgun and a box of shells. His next stop was a downtown tavern called The Wig Wam, which occupied a two-story, redbrick building three blocks east of the river that cuts the city in two. He was thoroughly drunk when local police arrived to question him. Customers in the tavern said he had been talking about Adamson and what he planned to do. When they searched Lyman's Camaro the police found an eight-inch hunting knife and a baseball bat. In his motel room they discovered the note. It was at that moment that they arrested him.

The Eau Claire officers had been alerted

by a call from the police in St. Paul, who relayed a warning they had received from Lyman's girlfriend Annette. When Greg went missing she told them about his threats. She didn't think he was capable of hurting anyone but she was worried that he might find some other sort of trouble. "He never really recovered," she said about the abuse he had experienced. "There's been a lot of pain."

Local lawyers helped Greg Lyman persuade a judge that he never would have followed through on his threats. The original charge, attempted homicide, was reduced to attempted battery. Lyman was permitted to plead guilty, sentenced to three years' probation, and barred from returning to the state during this period. At the time Lyman thought he had manipulated his attorneys, the prosecutor, and the judge into giving him what he wanted. Many years would pass before he would realize that in this moment of crisis he had talked himself out of what he really needed: placement in a psychiatric facility.

12.
AN ATTITUDE OF RESISTANCE

After the complaints brought by John Doe and Frank Fitzpatrick, the threat that the Catholic Church faced in the problem of clergy who abused children was clear. In the Doe case Judge Phyllis Jones, with the backing of the Minnesota Supreme Court, had established that abusive priests were like exploding hatchback cars and their bishops bore some responsibility for the damage they did if they let them loose on an unsuspecting public. Fitzpatrick, with his knack for investigation, organization, and public relations, had shown how the exposure of a single sexual predator could create a truly national scandal.

First told in New England and Minnesota, the James Porter story become the subject of a July 1992 exposé on the ABC network television program *Prime Time Live* and the focus of intense national press coverage. Landmarks in the case, including Porter's September 1992 arrest and incarceration in Minnesota and later prosecution in Massachusetts, brought opportunities for news-papers, magazines, and broadcasters to review the entire tortured history of the case. Days after the report aired, the victims support group SNAP held one of its weekend sessions in Boston. Organizers Barbara Blaine and Helen O'Neil found themselves surrounded by reporters as they arrived at the local Catholic Worker House in the South End neighborhood. In the summer of 1992 the local media's appetite for the story was so intense that Blaine and O'Neil awoke at the house the next morning to find TV crews camped in the front hallway. After crawling out of her sleeping bag, Blaine trundled to the bathroom in her pajamas where she showered and dressed before being interviewed under bright TV lights.

At the conference, which was held at Boston University, Blaine, O'Neil, and a SNAP leader named David Clohessy met victims from across New England. Many had decided to speak about being abused by priests after they read or watched news accounts featuring Frank Fitzpatrick and James Porter. As the number of his named victims had passed fifty, Porter made things even worse for the Church by answering questions from journalists and even admitting, before TV cameras, that he had lost track of the number of children he had raped or molested.

In Massachusetts, lawyers representing

Porter's victims were boxed in by an unusual law that protected charitable institutions like Churches from suits that might ruin them financially. This so-called "charitable immunity" capped the amount an individual could receive in a lawsuit at $20,000. Noting this limit, editorial writers at *The Boston Globe* called on the Church to do more to police its priests and care for victims. A good start, added the *Globe,* could be found in the Peterson-Doyle-Mouton report of 1985. Specifically, the paper called for creation of a national crisis team, as that report recommended, which would intervene whenever abuse cases arose.

At the height of the outcry over the Porter case, several polling organizations tested Catholic opinion and confirmed a growing separation between the views of laypeople and church leaders. *Time* magazine found that more than 60 percent of everyday Catholics believed priests should be allowed to marry and that women should be eligible for ordination. The Gallup poll found even greater support for women priests and that more than 70 percent wanted priests and laypeople to get involved in the selection of bishops. Gallup also found that Catholics were not much different from their fellow Americans on the matter of abortion, with 45 percent supporting general access to the procedure during the first trimester of pregnancy, compared with 47 percent for all respondents. Only 17 percent said adults should follow all the dictates of the Church when it came to sex and reproduction.

Of course, Churches are not ruled by public opinion polls. Indeed, they often stand as defenders of eternal truths and bulwarks against moral fads. And in every era the hierarchs of the Catholic Church had faced the challenge of separating ideas that offered valid new understanding and passing trends. Historically this sorting-out required years, decades, and even centuries. Almost three hundred years would pass before Galileo, declared a heretic after he said the Earth was not the center of the universe, would be fully exonerated by the Church. During that period, all of civilization moved toward Galileo's science and Rome's credibility suffered.

In the modern age of instant worldwide communication and a global hunger for democracy and individual rights, the Church faced continuing pressure from science and an overall resistance to centralized authority, whether it was wielded in Moscow, Washington, or Rome. An ordinary American of the late twentieth century could know more about what was happening in the wider world than the most informed experts in previous generations. And as the polls indicated, they considered themselves rather autonomous when it came to moral issues, great and small.

This attitude of independence was not confined to the United States. In the early 1990s it arose in Ireland, which was the most important bastion of Catholicism outside of the Vatican itself. (This was Pope Paul VI's description of the country in 1978.) The flashpoint of Irish skepticism came in 1992 when a court, following laws supported by the Church, prevented a fourteen-year-old rape victim from having an abortion in Great Britain. The Irish Supreme Court overturned the decision in early 1992.

Months later the press revealed that a prominent bishop named Eamon Casey had fathered a child with an American woman and used Church funds to support them in the United States. The episode energized a national movement to separate Church and state in Ireland, where the two were more intertwined than in any place in Europe. It also focused attention on the sexual ethics of Church leaders. As one Irish sociologist noted at the time, the Irish public wasn't concerned as much about Casey's sexual behavior as it was about "hypocrisy about parenthood, about the way a man treats a woman and a child."

After Casey resigned, America's bishops put the status of women and sexual abuse committed by priests at the top of their agenda when they met at Notre Dame University in

South Bend. The bishops had spent nine years working on a statement — called a pastoral letter — outlining their views on women in the Church. According to one Jesuit scholar, who was expelled from the Church for publishing his data, 40 percent of the bishops had come to support the ordination of women as deacons and 14 percent thought they should be allowed to become priests. These figures represented an increase of more than 40 percent since 1985, and a significant divergence from the Pope's position. At Notre Dame this divergence helped to stall progress on the document.

The bishops used a closed-door session to consider the sex abuse crisis and afterward the president of the conference called for a prompt response to complaints, compliance with civil law, removal of an accused priest — "if evidence is sufficient" — and help for victims and their families. As individuals, bishops had been asking the Vatican to streamline the canon law process for dealing with abuse cases and give them more tools with which to act. However, as a group they had not been assertive. In 1989 an executive committee had recommended immediate treatment for those involved in abuse cases but did not address the criminal aspects of abuse. The committee also attempted to deflect attention by noting that parents and stepparents were more likely to abuse children than priests. The truth of this claim was subject to debate, and the impulse to state it made the bishops seem insensitive.

After the bishops' private discussion, Archbishop Daniel Pilarczyk of Cincinnati struck a more pastoral tone as he spoke of the "pain and the hurt" caused by priests who broke their vows with minors, and promised to "break this cycle of abuse." But he also modified his apology by noting, "Until recently, few in society and the Church understood the problem [of sexual abuse] well."

If by "until recently" the bishop meant until the late 1970s, he was mostly correct. Until then, few experts understood the scope of the incidence of sexual abuse or the persistence and power of the compulsions that drove most sex offenders. However, it was also fair to say that since Doyle, Mouton, and Peterson distributed their report in 1985, no bishop or diocese could claim to be unaware of the breadth and depth of the problem among Catholic priests.

The bishops approached the acts committed by priests and the scandal control practiced by higher officials within a framework of sin rather than crime. Instead of punishment for pedophile priests, Pilarczyk spoke of "healing and reconciliation" as if the Church could serve both the victims and perpetrators equally. This thought was consistent with Catholic theology, which emphasized the commonality of sin and forgiveness for all, and considered the salvation of the soul the Church's main purpose. It also reflected past practices in many jurisdictions where police and prosecutors had allowed the Church to handle complaints against priests internally. If victims didn't insist on charges being brought, cases would be dropped as offenders were transferred and bishops counseled forgiveness.

But just as the bishops considered the sex abuse crisis through the lens of their theology, victims of abuse weighed the Church's response against their own experience. Barbara Blaine heard in Pilarczyk's statement an echo of the bishop in Toledo who asked her to attend counseling sessions with the man who stole her adolescence. In her eyes, statements like these meant the hierarchy was equivocating, manipulating, and evading. For Jeanne Miller, however, Pilarczyk's apologetic commitment to act was cause for real optimism. Miller still believed in the Church and expected some top officials to become her allies. She was already building bridges to them, and with the first national gathering of VOCALink-up set for the fall of 1992 she hoped true reform was in reach.

The list of speakers Miller recruited for the conference amounted to a Who's Who in the world of clergy sex abuse. Besides Jeff Anderson, who would address the legal issues, Miller lined up Thomas Doyle, Richard Sipe, Andrew Greeley, and Jason Berry. Berry had continued to write about the Church and sexual abuse for newspapers across America, investigating cases from coast to coast. Along the way he wrote a book that was rejected by thirty publishers until Greeley sent it to a friend at Doubleday. In late summer of 1992, Doubleday's publication of *Lead Us Not Into Temptation* provided readers the first comprehensive account of the crisis to date. The book established Berry as an independent authority and a truly authoritative source for journalists and TV talk show hosts.

Berry was an appealing expert because he operated outside the institutional Church and had no personal links to the problem of sexual abuse. However, he was hardly a disinterested observer. Catholicism was a foundational part of his identity. His first daughter Simonette had been baptized in the Church shortly after her birth in 1984 and when his second child Ariel arrived in 1991 she was baptized too. Born with Down's syndrome, Ariel brought some special challenges for her parents, including a sobering diagnosis of a pulmonary defect that was certain to shorten her life. As Berry absorbed the realities of Ariel's condition he found himself drawn closer to God, praying for her survival when he attended Mass at his neighborhood parish.

Both a Catholic and an investigative reporter, Berry dealt with many of the most painful aspects of the abuse crisis every day. Lawyers sent depositions that were filled with the awful sexual secrets of the priesthood and victims telephoned with even more disturbing accounts of their victimization as children and the aftereffects of the trauma. "I felt a lot of anger over the hypocrisy," he would later recall. But at the same time he knew many priests and nuns who lived out the higher aspiration of the Church and offered their prayers and support to him and Ariel. Their example of Christianity, as well as supportive friends and psychotherapy, helped him carry on. Believing the Church belonged to him as much as it belonged to anyone, he refused to give up on it.

Because they held out hope for change in the Church, Berry and the others didn't blanch when Jeanne Miller told them she hoped that Chicago's Cardinal Bernardin would also speak at the conference. Miller had been meeting Bernardin in private, at his mansion, over the course of a couple of years. In that time she had explained how she had felt more betrayed by the diocese's defensive response to her complaint than she was by Fr. Mayer's behavior with her son. While diocesan officials had deflected Miller's complaints, Mayer had gone on to molest other children. He was removed from his post as a pastor in 1991 only after a thirteen-year-old girl complained about him touching her.

On the day after the girl's complaint became public, Cardinal Bernardin appointed a three-person panel, which included a retired judge and a social services expert, to review personnel files and the way complaints about priests in Chicago were handled. This panel found fifty-nine priests had been accused of sexual crimes. In the summer of 1992 Bernardin announced that six of these priests had been removed from parish duties and eight more were in the process of being removed. He set up a telephone hotline for abuse complaints and finally, in the summer of 1992, agreed to address the first VOCALink-up conference at a hotel in the suburb of Arlington.

Despite the archdiocese's stumbles on Mayer and other cases, no top-ranking member of the hierarchy had done more to address the abuse issue than Bernardin. Unlike Boston's Cardinal Law, who had flushed with anger at *The Boston Globe,* Bernardin spoke in humble terms, noting "mistakes for which I am truly sorry." Then, two months before the VOCALink-Up conference, Bernardin established a permanent panel of five laypeople and three priests who would review complaints and report to him alone. He also volunteered to name a board of overseers who would be required to report complaints

287

to child welfare authorities, and agreed that any priest found to have abused a child would be barred for the rest of his life from any work that might bring him into contact with children.

Bernardin's plan was in part a response to criticism from Cook County state's attorney Jack O'Malley. In the midst of a reelection campaign, O'Malley had attacked the Church for using constitutional arguments (freedom of religion) to resist cooperating with authorities on criminal matters. When it was announced, O'Malley welcomed Bernardin's review board as a step in the right direction. However, Jeanne Miller believed Bernardin was trying to construct a system that he could control in the way that bishops had historically controlled the resolutions of complaints. "There's still a real duplicity there," she told the Chicago press. "I think it's a prettier version of the same thing."

In politics they would say Jeanne Miller's tough talk "played well" with her "base" of support in VOCALink-Up. It did not play well with Bernardin, who immediately broke his commitment to attend the conference. When Miller called his home to ask if he would discuss the matter, the nuns who answered were as friendly as ever, but after they checked to see if he would take Miller's call they came back with an apology. The cardinal wasn't available and they didn't know when he would be.

Among the three hundred people who filled the ballroom at the Arlington Hilton for the VOCALink-Up convention were some who worried about good priests who would suffer by association with the abuse crisis. Others believed that Bernardin's change of heart was a sign that the hierarchy would never give up its elevated status. Thomas Doyle had concluded as much because of the tough tactics lawyers for the archdiocese had employed when he was deposed as an expert witness for a thirteen-year-old boy who said he was abused by a priest at age seven. The deposition was adversarial from the start. Years later Doyle recalled:

> The lawyer for the archdiocese asked me the same question for about the eighth time and I said to her, "No matter how many times you ask me that I'm going to give you the same answer. Don't you understand English?"

The deposition experience convinced Doyle that no matter how gently Bernardin ministered to the victims of abusive priests, officials of the archdiocese would fight every attempt to hold the Church accountable and to protect its assets.

At the hotel in Arlington, the men who

knew best how the clergy thought and acted were among the least optimistic. After describing his own failed effort to help the bishops, Doyle said he was skeptical about the hierarchy's ability to even recognize the scope of the problem they faced, let alone deal with it effectively. Andrew Greeley, the only man who appeared in clerical black, sounded more like Richard Sipe's ally than his critic. (The two men greeted each other cordially and no mention was made of Greeley's earlier attacks on Sipe's work.) Greeley spoke of "the sexually maladjusted priest who has been able to abuse the children of the laity and thus far be reasonably secure from punishment. There is no power of church or state that is willing to force priests to be accountable for their behavior." Priests inhabit an "immune class," he said, which is protected from "sanctions of both church and state" by the "rules of the club." (A few months later Greeley would back up his words with a study estimating that the Church was spending $50 million per year on the sex abuse scandal and that as many as 100,000 American Catholics had been abused by priests when they were young.)

Greeley and Doyle represented the outraged but loyal priests who remained inside the clerical culture hoping to change it. It would be left to Richard Sipe, *former* priest, to suggest something more radical might be required. Not quite ready to abandon the Church, he nevertheless raised the notion that Catholics who spoke out against abuse stood at the beginning of a process that might lead to profound changes in the Church. He did this with the first words he spoke, which referenced the place where Martin Luther spoke out against corruption. At this gathering where scattered advocates and agitators first came together as a true movement, Sipe smiled and opened his arms and said, "Welcome to Wittenberg."

Perhaps the best-informed expert in the field, Sipe said that the Church was run by clerics who inhabited a world "in which men are revered and powerful and boys are treasured as the future of the Church." However, as celibates deprived of intimate relationships, many of these men never leave "a preadolescent stage of psychosexual development," said Sipe. Those who would abuse minors could not be screened out because they evolve into this behavior as "products of the system." The same system was unable to acknowledge the problem raised by victims of abuse because any effective response would include a reconsideration of basic assumptions about gender, sex, and the credibility of the Catholic Church.

The paralyzing power of the Church's dilemma was made clear to Sipe when he attended a conference at the Vatican where he heard dozens of expert opinions of celibacy. The official Church position was argued by a cardinal named James Francis Stafford who said that married men could not function as priests because in conducting Mass they would commit adultery against their wives. In this paradigm, the celebration of Mass became a spiritual/sexual event shared by the priests and the Church, which becomes his symbolic sexual partner. Sipe saw danger in this type of talk, which made him wonder if certain clergy weren't doing more harm to themselves than was being done by outsiders. The wider society was already reconsidering the status of the Church in law, the moral authority of its bishops, and the trust enjoyed by priests. This process, enabled by the mass media, would continue as lawyers used the courts to pry evidence out of Church archives and victims organized to share what they knew and discover additional routes into the clerical culture. In time, said Sipe, "When the whole story of sexual abuse by presumed celibate clergy is told, it will lead to the highest corridors of Vatican City."

Slow moving and defensive, the Church was not organized to respond to the hundreds of scandals that threatened to explode like so many wildfires across the Catholic landscape. As someone who still valued the institution, Sipe hoped for a brave change in thinking — perhaps one dictated from the top — that would begin a new, modern era of equality and respect among believers. If this happened, outspoken victims of abuse could actually "save the Church and its priesthood from destruction." Otherwise, said Sipe, the Church faced a fate similar to that of the steamship *Titanic,* which was grand and indestructible until the moment it wasn't.

13.
THE MEANING OF MEMORY

With hands and feet numbed by wind-driven sleet, Barbara Blaine walked the sidewalk in her mother's green wool coat, which she had borrowed as she passed through Toledo on her way from Chicago to Washington, D.C. Although the inked letters were dissolving, the people in passing cars could still make out the message — "Child Rape is a Cardinal Sin" — on the placard she held in her hands. Nearby, another victim of clergy abuse held a sign that announced, "Priests Are Not Above the Law." In time these slogans would be staples at demonstrations mounted by the Survivors Network of those Abused by Priests, but in November 1992 they were new and disturbing to read.

The picketers at the Omni Shoreham Hotel in Washington, D.C., wanted to be heard by the bishops of the Catholic Church in America, who had gathered there for one of their semiannual meetings. In general, the demonstrators still hoped that the Church was a holy institution that would hear them and change its ways. Based on her experience with the Oblates, Blaine was wary of the hierarchy, but she believed that the high-ranking men of the Church were misinformed and perhaps ill-served by lawyers and underlings. She hoped that victims of abuse could educate them and that this education would change the way they responded to cases.

Others had come to the meeting of the National Conference of Catholic Bishops with similar intentions. Members of the Women's Ordination Conference wanted to be heard before the bishops approved a pastoral letter outlining their stand on the status of women. Gays and lesbians, who sought the same sort of rights and respect accorded by the Church to heterosexuals, also hoped to get a hearing. They arrived with a petition signed by Catholics opposed to the Vatican's position on gay rights. It bore 12,000 names.

A few bishops and cardinals seemed receptive to these causes. Cardinal Bernardin of Chicago had issued a statement affirming "the fundamental human and civil rights of persons who are gay or lesbian." In the same paper he had said that while he could not "endorse" homosexual activity he recognized "the inviolable dignity of a gay or lesbian person and the goodness to their stable, loving, and caring relationships."

Slightly built and ever-smiling Bernardin represented for many a more flexible Catholicism suited to the times. Along with bishops Rembert Weakland of Milwaukee, Thomas Gumbleton of Detroit, and Philip Francis Murphy of Baltimore he was one of a handful of hierarchs who seemed open to a conversation about the way the Church approached sex and gender. Murphy had recently published an article favoring ordination of women. In it he recalled visiting a Catholic school classroom where he asked children how many sacraments were offered by the Church. A little girl answered "seven for men and six for women" because females were denied ordination. Murphy wrote that the child's answer was correct, but the practice was wrong because "justice demands" equal treatment.

Although men like Murphy and Bernardin gave her hope, Blaine understood that compared with the national community of Catholic women, and the gays and lesbians who numbered in the millions, a small, less-than-organized band of sexual abuse victims seemed unlikely to move the bishops to act. As the conference began, the bishops signaled they would not meet with the sidewalk picketers. Then, on the first afternoon of their meeting, they changed their minds and sent an invitation. They wanted to hear what the demonstrators had to say. Immediately.

On the sidewalk about a dozen of the men and women near Blaine suddenly dropped their signs and began to scurry across the lawn toward the hotel entrance. A few even ran to reach the brass-trimmed doors, which opened to let them into the lobby. Struck by how eager, and even giddy her fellow picketers had become, Blaine realized they were still deeply affected by the status of the powerful men inside the hotel. A moment before, they were determined to shame the bishops. Now they wanted nothing more than to be welcomed into their presence.

Inside the hotel men in black stood in small groups or moved from one meeting room to another. Some held folders filled with papers under their arms. A few sipped coffee from cardboard cups. The picketers were directed to a small meeting room where eight were permitted to meet with Cardinal Roger Mahony of Los Angeles and two bishops, Alexander Quinn of Cleveland and Harry Flynn of Lafayette, Louisiana. (Jason Berry, who dealt with Flynn when he was transferred to Lafayette after the Gauthe scandal, would recall him as comparatively open-minded.)

Barbara Blaine found it strange that the bishops welcomed TV news crews to film the meeting, which took place in a small conference room. Mahony held his hands together, as if in prayer, and tilted his head as he listened to several of the men and women describe their experiences. Hovering behind the speakers, sound technicians hoisted up microphones attached to long poles and struggled to position them to pick up the conversation.

Many of the survivors who spoke shed tears. Others asked for the bishops to worry less about defending the institutional Church and more about Catholics who had been abused. In one of the few sharp exchanges, Blaine asked Mahony about a woman named Rita Milla, who had been sexually violated by seven Los Angeles priests. As she spoke, Blaine felt her hands and feet, which had been chilled by freezing rain, tingle and ache as they thawed in the warmth of the meeting room. She also felt a familiar sense of outrage over what had happened to Milla, who was a teenager when one of these priests made her pregnant. Fr. Santiago Tamayo sent her to his family in the Philippines. The diocese then urged Tamayo to flee the country, and paid him while he stayed abroad for four years.

In Los Angeles, Mahony had acknowledged the facts of the Milla case but had said any apologies should come from "the people who did the actions." In Washington the cardinal wouldn't answer Blaine directly, but he did shift on the matter of apologies. At four different points he offered some form of regret and sorrow. Around him many heads nodded in response but one of the victims did express some skepticism. Ed Morris, who said he had been raped at age fourteen said, "As my abuser used to tell me: 'The road to hell is paved with good intentions.'"

After the forty-minute session, Mahony reported to his fellow bishops that the meeting "was one of the most moving experiences I have ever had in my seventeen years as a bishop." He urged them to "show loving concern and healing" for the victims of abuse, and to refrain from "legalistic protecting of erring priests." He noted that he had apologized several times on behalf of the Church, and he recommended that every bishop pay closer attention to the concerns of those he described as "victims of priestly misconduct." He added, "You and I know many victims of sexual misconduct across the land. People are looking for accountability. We have much to learn from those who are hurting and aggrieved."

The victims who met with Mahony responded gratefully. Frank Fitzpatrick, the private investigator who had tracked down James Porter, told reporters, "We achieved all that we could with this meeting. In a perfect world we would have sat down with all the bishops but we sat down with three and that's a start."

Barbara Blaine was not so generous in her private assessment. To her ear, Mahony's sentiment was a lukewarm response expressed in the kind of obtuse language that minimized the damage done by abusive priests. The people he had met were raped as children by trusted men of God. Some had wept as they spoke. To observe that they were victims of "erring priests" or "priestly misconduct" seemed strangely cold. Mahony had listened, but not with his heart, thought Blaine. Nothing else could explain why he showed no anger toward the perpetrators and expressed no urgency about how bishops should respond. He had not promised any action or committed to further meetings with victims. However, he had succeeded in seizing the high ground before the national press.

On the same day as Mahony's meeting with the picketers, other church officials had held a similar impromptu conference at the hotel with gay and lesbian activists. The next morning the two events were reported together in major newspapers across the country. It was a public relations coup for the bishops, who managed to squeeze two difficult issues together and made their openness the most remarkable aspect of the story. Two days later, as they closed their conference, the assembled men of God pledged to reevaluate their polices on sexual abuse and agreed that the Church should offer:

- **Prompt response to accusations**

- **Swift suspension of an offender if the evidence warrants and referral for medical treatment**

- **Full reporting to the civil authorities and cooperation with investigators**

- **Emotional and spiritual support for victims and families**

- **Forthright public explanations within the limits of individuals' privacy**

Policy reviews had been promised in the past and the five guidelines were no different from the principles voiced by top leaders in the years since the crisis began. Moreover, as outgoing conference president Daniel E. Pilarczyk of Cincinnati noted, such resolutions and recommendations were not binding on any individual bishop. As a national group, the bishops' conference was not responsible for anything done by a diocese or order. Similarly, the Pope and other Vatican officials could distance themselves from responsibility for the actions of individual clergy and local Catholic organizations. Vatican officials might hold the power to defrock a priest, but they could deny all civil legal responsibility for them, even when they acted as representatives of the faith and its institutions.

Anyone who tried to figure out where the ultimate decisions were made in the Catholic Church would not find easy answers. On matters of faith and morals, individual believers were encouraged to think for themselves and the Pope often sought advice from gatherings of bishops. However, the final word on religious matters resided always in Rome and this was especially true whenever John Paul II issued teaching documents, called encyclicals, which were then wielded to discipline theologians and others. Thinkers who were too independent could be stripped of their status as clerics or teachers and even excommunicated.

As he observed the way the Church worked, Jeffrey Anderson began to conclude that in fact all important decisions were made at the Vatican and anyone who said this wasn't true had to ignore that the Church was a monarchy with the Pope its ruler, requiring absolute obedience and secrecy. This belief was based on his review of thousands of documents and dozens of depositions by Church officials, including bishops and cardinals.

When it came to operating in the larger society, especially in civil legal systems, the Vatican claimed diplomatic immunity as a sovereign nation while local Church authorities sought to protect themselves from liability by a variety of means. Within their dioceses bishops often oversaw dozens of different corporations, which allowed them to protect various assets so they couldn't be sought in payment of a court judgment. When it was useful, they described priests as independent agents, only nominally under their control. And wherever the law provided special status for religious activities — as the United States Constitution does — they would claim they were acting as a matter of faith.

Under these conditions, the Pope and the American bishops could seek to avoid liability when individuals filed lawsuits but command respect and attention as religious authorities. In the 1980s and 1990s John Paul II used this status, and his enormous talents as a public person, to attract the kind of welcome associated with conquering heroes. The American bishops accomplished the same thing, on a smaller scale, when they sent a delegation to meet with abuse victims and invited the press to attend. Calm, kindly, and authoritative in their immaculate black suits, Mahony, Quinn, and Flynn seemed like very important men who had been generous with their time and attention.

As Barbara Blaine considered what happened at the Omni Shoreham she concluded that people who literally ran to meet with a few higher Church officials weren't likely to carry the fight for change in the Church. What seemed to them like a victory had actually been a setback. Blaine found agreement with her friend David Clohessy, who had come to Washington from Missouri to get soaked on the sidewalk.

Clohessy had experienced memories of being abused by a priest named John Whiteley after watching the film *Nuts,* in which Barbra Streisand plays a character who was sexually abused. For years Clohessy had managed to wall off memories of Whiteley in his mind. Common to people who experience trauma, this coping mechanism is typically an unintentional process and it doesn't save a victim from the aftereffects of abuse, including depression and problems relating to others. Prompted by the film, Clohessy reconsidered what had happened to him and the harm it had caused and took legal action.

A public relations expert and political activist, Clohessy had been represented by Jeff Anderson in a suit he filed against the Diocese of Jefferson City, Missouri. The claim depended on a new state law, enacted in 1990, that allowed adults to sue for childhood abuse within three years of the time when they realized they had been harmed. A few weeks before Clohessy went to picket in Washington, the judge hearing his complaint threw it out, declaring the law was unconstitutional because it was retroactive. Clohessy's appeal to the state supreme court would fail; however, over time he would become one of a handful of national leaders in the victims movement.

In the early days of SNAP, before the World Wide Web made keeping current easier, Clohessy sent out regular packets of articles about clergy abuse, which he gleaned from newspapers and magazines and then copied at his own expense. Like a pre-Google news alert system, the packets informed Blaine, Jeff Anderson, Jason Berry, and others of developments in cases all over the country. With this information, supplemented with telephone calls, faxes, and occasional gatherings, they could look for patterns in the way bishops and their attorneys responded to claims.

While activists and attorneys struggled to keep up with developments by tracking cases nationwide, the general public received only occasional notice of a lawsuit filed here or a settlement reached there. And in the years since Gilbert Gauthe and the suits in Lafayette, only a handful of national print and TV reports had suggested that a broader, systemic problem might be emerging. The lack of information, and more important, context, explained the silence that greeted one of the most shocking moments of performance that was ever presented on television.

The shock came as Irish singer Sinéad O'Connor appeared on the program *Saturday Night Live.* On October 3, 1992, she came onto the stage with her head shaved and dressed in white lace. After waiting for the audience to settle she sang Bob Marley's "War," which was based on a 1968 speech given by Ethiopian emperor Haile Selassie. O'Connor changed the lyrics to make it about child abuse and at the end, where Marley's verse cries "Good over evil! Good over evil!" she held a photo of Pope John Paul II in front of her face. She then said, "Fight the real enemy" and tore it to pieces.

In the audience, no one reacted. In the production control room technicians broke with their routine and did not switch on the applause sign.

In the weeks following O'Connor's appearance, she was alternately castigated and defended by politicians, writers, and other performers. Executives at the TV network that aired the program said the act was a surprise and disavowed O'Connor's sentiment. Many Catholic laypeople and clergy called her bigoted and demanded an apology. In some corners of the media, columnists and commentators tried to understand what O'Connor was saying and eventually connected her demonstration to Church policies on sex and gender and its responses to abuse claims. Although her act was called a "stunt" and a "prank," as she ripped up the Pope's picture O'Connor had prompted millions to consider an issue that previously occupied the edges of public awareness.

Among survivors of clergy abuse, O'Connor provoked both admiration and confusion. Those who still hoped to stay in the Church and see it reform didn't know whether to welcome the attention she brought to the way the hierarchy regarded children or to distance themselves from her. Of course none of them knew that in Ireland Church leaders had already formed a committee, chaired by Bishop Laurence Forristal, to plan a response to *future* public accusations of clergy abuse. And only those who had taken a critical eye to Irish Catholic attitudes about children — those vessels of original sin — would have grasped O'Connor's later explanations for her act. In a public letter she wrote about her own experience of being abused as a child and that in Ireland "the Catholic church has controlled us by controlling education, through their teachings on sexuality, marriage, birth control and abortion, and most spectacularly through the lies they taught us with their history books . . . My story is the story of countless millions of children whose families and nations were torn apart for money in the name of Jesus Christ."

With more than a hundred cases in sixteen

states, Jeff Anderson had little time to reflect on the Irish Catholic experience or the larger public attitude toward the Church. He was too busy dashing from state to state, trying to advance claims that the Church sought to block at every turn. In many jurisdictions he ran into the same issues involving statutes of limitations, the injury suffered by victims of abuse, and questions of liability. By 1992 laws had been changed in about a third of the states to accommodate the concept of "delayed discovery of injury" and give claimants more leeway to file suits. However, these statutes did not resolve disputes over the supervision of Catholic priests or settle widespread doubts about the nature of memory. Outspoken critics challenged the notion that traumatic incidences were sometimes forgotten or repressed as the human psyche sought to overcome the effects or that these memories could be recovered through hypnosis and other methods.

The debate over memory boiled most furiously around cases in which children may have been coaxed to accuse adults of terrible crimes. Research psychologist Elizabeth Loftus, who said she could prompt a five-year-old to recall "a bear that wasn't there," began warning the public and trial courts in the 1980s of the suggestibility of children. Loftus said that she had been sexually molested as a young girl but played down any effects it may have had on her life.

In her work, the professor studied the variability of memory and came to believe that outside influences can change how individuals recall events. Loftus questioned whether people who were traumatized ever forgot what happened to them only to remember the events later in life. She received support from social psychologist Richard Ofshe, who openly criticized psychotherapy that produced "recovered memories" of abuse not previously acknowledged by patients. Both served as expert witnesses in trials. By the mid-1990s Loftus would be charging $400 per hour for such services. She would also provoke ethics complaints to the American Psychological Association from victims whom she challenged in court and in the press. In one complaint to the APA, an incest victim objected to Loftus characterizing her memory as "fantastical" even though her sister also recalled being abused by their father. The APA took no action on the complaint. Loftus subsequently resigned from the organization, though she said her decision was not connected to the complaint.

As skeptics and expert witnesses, Ofshe and Loftus followed a trail pioneered by a less well-known psychologist from Minnesota named Ralph Underwager. A minister as well as a therapist, Underwager began testifying on behalf of defendants in abuse cases in

1984. In a 1989 book called *Accusations of Child Sexual Abuse* he and his wife Hollida Wakefield argued that most accusations of abuse in childhood were based on false memories suggested by incompetent or malevolent psychotherapists. Underwager and Wakefield were widely rejected by the scientific community, and a scathing review of their book in the *Journal of the American Medical Association* found it of full of "unsupported statements." Nevertheless, by 1992 Underwager and Wakefield had been permitted to testify as experts in more than two hundred court cases. They also joined Ofshe and Loftus on the advisory board of the newly formed False Memory Syndrome Foundation (FMSF), which was devoted to challenging claims of childhood abuse.

The false memory foundation presented itself as a kind of counter-movement to those who advocated most actively for the rights of people who claimed to have been abused as children. In 1994, Paul McHugh, a psychiatrist based at Johns Hopkins University, offered a comprehensive outline of the group's views, which included references to mass hysteria and warnings of "pseudo-memories" that may be confirmed by professionals and others predisposed to blame sexual abuse for a subject's psychological problems. McHugh called for interventions to halt the "jug-

310

gernaut" of abuse claims, including media campaigns to alert the public of the risk of pseudo-memories.

While credentialed experts like Dr. McHugh provided the FMSF with informed skepticism about abuse claims, the energy behind the organization came from the group's founders, Pamela and Peter Freyd. Their daughter Jennifer had accused Peter Freyd of incest in 1990.

The Freyds were no ordinary family. Peter was a tenured professor of mathematics at the University of Pennsylvania. His daughter Jennifer earned a Ph.D. in psychology at Stanford and became an expert on trauma and memory. She would coin the term "betrayal blindness" to describe how a child who must depend on an adult for survival would seemingly forget traumatic abuse in order to continue living under that person's care. Memories of such abuse might emerge in adulthood, when a victim no longer depended on an abuser's attention. Freyd claimed to have experienced this psychological mechanism herself, and allegedly recalled her father abusing her when she was a child, an accusation that her parents denied. Once a personal matter, the Freyds' conflict became a public battle and the members of the family were regarded as heroes or villains by the factions in the larger debate.

Aided by a surge of publicity, the FMSF

grew quickly and its supporters promoted the idea that a practice they called "recovered memory therapy" was producing a rash of abuse claims against people who had done nothing wrong. Members of the FMSF were also critical of recent books on incest and sexual abuse, especially *The Courage to Heal,* which became popular among people who reported being abused. The authors of *The Courage to Heal* were creative writing teacher Ellen Bass and her student Laura Davis, who was a victim of incest. Neither one had professional credentials in mental health. The book began what Loftus would call an "incest book industry [that] has published not only stories of abuse but also suggestions to readers that they were likely abused even if there are no memories."

In the FMSF's analysis, many of those accused were actually victims of books like *The Courage to Heal* and of misguided therapists and investigators who manipulated both adults and children and ultimately destroyed relationships, reputations, and even the finances of innocent people. The grueling McMartin preschool case, which yielded no convictions after seven years of investigation and proceedings, was cited as a case in point. Others included accusations of satanic ritual abuse (SRA). This subcategory of claims included charges that Satan worshippers killed children in sacrificial rites that were kept secret thanks to a vast conspiracy.

Although rumors of these rituals circulated widely, studies by both law enforcement experts and social scientists found no evidence of either the rituals or the conspiracy. However, the absence of proof didn't inhibit lecturers and authors who fanned the flame of fear at conservative churches or authors seeking publicity for books. In 1989, *Oprah* introduced millions of Americans to Lauren Stratford and Michelle Smith, who had both published memoirs of satanic abuse. Eventually both stories would be thoroughly discredited by independent journalists. Of course, compared with *Oprah*'s audience, the readership for these accounts was minuscule and the SRA scare would linger for most of the 1990s.

Unsubstantiated claims of satanic ritual abuse and notorious prosecutions, like the McMartin case, made perfect targets for FMSF publicity campaigns and skeptics who warned that therapists were somehow encouraging people to fabricate tales of abuse. However, truly false allegations remained almost as rare as SRA and aside from isolated practitioners "recovered memory therapy" never emerged as an actual method of psychotherapy. Similarly no real authority ever recognized a "syndrome" that produced fabrications of abuse. Instead, this phenomenon remained an artifact of the false memory foundation and its supporters who became steadfast skeptics when it came to sexual abuse claims and reliable allies to those who said they were unjustly accused.

With experts and family members engaged in open, heated disputes about such difficult issues — child abuse, psychotherapy, the reliability of memory — public attention was diverted from the aspects of sexual abuse, trauma, and memory that were well established. By the mid-1990s, more than thirty different studies would confirm that people abused in childhood could experience periods of "forgetting" or "traumatic amnesia." (By 2012 the number of academic articles supporting the phenomena would exceed three hundred and fifty.) Clinicians wouldn't necessarily describe these mechanisms as "repression," which suggested some kind of active choice. Instead they noted that shame and embarrassment often led victims to deny those episodes of abuse in their own minds until they recalled them in detail during treatment or after some triggering event, like viewing a movie. In nearly all cases, victims reported that they hadn't actually forgotten what had happened to them but had *tried to forget* in order to move on with their lives. This last point was often blurred or ignored in press coverage of lawsuits and the broader issue of sexual abuse.

As the most visible victims of sexual abuse, men and women who had been raped or molested by Catholic priests embodied the struggle to understand the cause and effect of sexual abuse. Clergy abuse cases moved judges and juries to gradually recognize the trauma suffered by victims and the many ways that unaddressed experiences can harm individuals. Plaintiffs' attorneys emphasize the "delayed discovery of harm" by their adult clients and this concept was accepted by some, but not all, courts and state legislatures. But while this concept permitted people to bring complaints, they still had to present evidence that they had been harmed in specific ways by specific people. Here the bureaucracy of the Catholic Church aided plaintiffs by preserving the documents that proved crimes had been committed.

Despite the urgings of Bishop Quinn, who had recommended proactive review of sensitive documents, employment files held in church offices around the country were filled with notes and formal reports on sexual crimes committed by hundreds and perhaps thousands of priests. By early 1993, more than four hundred American priests stood accused in either criminal or civil proceedings and lawyers across the country were using discovery and court-issued subpoenas to access incriminating records.

In Minnesota alone, Jeff Anderson used confessions and Church documents to negotiate payments for the victims of half a dozen different priests, including a visiting preacher from Tanzania and a charismatic pastor known as the "Polka padre" because he played polka music at his services. Anderson's clergy abuse practice grew to twenty-seven states and counted more than two hundred clients. In many cases he partnered with local attorneys who called on him for expertise.

When Anderson heard from potential clients in California, he worked through a network of trial lawyers to reach a prominent litigator named Joseph Dunn, who allied with him to sue on behalf of men who said they were abused by a friar at Catholic schools in Fullerton and Anaheim. In Colorado he helped a Boulder-based attorney named Scott Lasch sue the Diocese of Pueblo on behalf of a man who said he was infected with HIV by a priest who first drew him into a sexual relationship when he was sixteen years old. In New York City, Anderson helped bring a case against the famous priest Bruce Ritter. The founder of Covenant House, which served homeless and runaway youth, Ritter left New York for India. The case was dismissed on the statute of limitations.

Anderson wasn't alone in this legal arena. In New Jersey and California other lawyers developed regional practices in this area of law. Most of these came into being after a particular scandal became public and victims were moved to report what had happened to them. In New England, for example, attorneys Roderick MacLeish and Mitchell Garabedian came to represent dozens of people who had claims against James Porter, and then heard from people who claimed to be abused by other priests in Massachusetts, New Hampshire, and Rhode Island. Other religious groups were also affected as individuals came forward to describe abuse by rabbis, ministers, and elders. One insurer reported two hundred claims of sexual abuse against individual Protestant pastors and churches.

But while others confronted the problem of abuse in the context of supposedly sacred relationships, the Catholic Church remained the focus of mass media reports, and Jeff Anderson stood as the institution's main antagonist. The Church held this special status because its problems were so much more widespread and because it stood as a highly organized institution with a theology that stressed, more than most, the importance of sexual control. Anderson maintained his standing by traveling the country to take on ever more cases and adding staff to his firm to keep up with the workload. He also responded whenever the press called, answering questions with blunt and imminently quotable lines.

When the general counsel to the bishops' conference said "lawyers should stay out" of abuse cases so the Church could provide "healing and reconciliation," *The New York Times* offered Anderson an opportunity to respond. He noted the Church's failure to control abusive priests like Porter, who had victims in five states, and suggested he still had a role to play. "When they get the rats out and clean the basement I'll be out of business," he said. "That's my goal: not to have to do any more of this."

Critics, including the loyal Catholics who sent Anderson letters calling him "scum maggot" and the "Antichrist" wouldn't have believed that Anderson wanted out. Considering his fees from judgments and settlements, which ranged from 33 to 40 percent, it was easy to estimate Anderson had made more than a million dollars by suing the Church. Didn't the money motivate him? "I like getting paid," he admitted. "But that isn't what motivates me."

In fact, given the disturbing nature of the crimes and the quality of his clients — many were demanding, psychologically fragile, and erratic — a lawyer with Anderson's talent and drive could have found easier ways to get rich. He persisted because he believed in the cause.

Had he been raised Catholic, Anderson

might have found it all too disillusioning. But as an outsider he never expected priests and bishops and cardinals to be different from other men. And as far as he was concerned, the Church was acting like any other large, powerful institution intent on self-preservation. Moving it to change would require a long fight, but he was willing to conduct it. In the meantime, he wasn't especially disturbed by what he saw and heard. Others who joined the cause couldn't say the same.

14.
THE PENDULUM SWINGS

With winter just weeks away, the Indiana sky turned dark by the time Tom Doyle got home from work. After putting down his keys and stripping off his military fatigue jacket he grabbed a glass and opened the refrigerator to tap the three-liter box of wine he kept on the shelf. With glass in hand he sat down in his living room where he could look out a back window that faced some woods. On good days he thought the quiet land was beautiful. On bad days he saw only blackness streaked with gray, and he could hear in his mind the nuns who taught him in grade school declaring, "Hell is the absence of hope."

The hell that is hopelessness had crept up on Doyle over the years. Its source was a mixture of profound doubt about his life choices — ordination, obedience, then defiance — and anxiety about the future. Military duty was satisfying. He had never met a group of men more honest and forthright than his fellow officers. But at the end of the day, when others went home to wives and families, Doyle was met by silence and his own thoughts. Sometimes he would turn to the writer John Dominic Crossan, an ex-priest who wrote about a Jesus who was a radical and independent thinker. But when Crossen couldn't help, Doyle found himself thinking about suicide.

Instead of taking action, he would drink himself to sleep. When he woke up, he would be grateful to see another day.

Doyle was finally forced to deal with his drinking problem one night when he went out to a nearby bar. As he headed home the state police saw his black Jeep Cherokee weaving down Indiana Highway 31 and gave chase. When the red lights of the cruiser flashed in Doyle's rearview mirror he automatically took his foot off the gas, pressed the brake, and steered off the pavement.

Doyle had been pulled over before, but this time was different. Instead of warning him and letting him go, the officers asked him to get out of the car. The alcohol on Doyle's breath was enough to land him in the back of the patrol car. A tow truck was summoned to haul the Cherokee to an impound lot. Doyle was deposited at the Howard County Jail, where he spent the night locked up. In the morning he posted bail, called his office to report what had happened, and took a cab to get his Jeep. Unsure what to do, he went home. Moments after he arrived a car pulled up outside. It was Phil Fain, the senior chaplain at Grissom Air Force Base. Doyle was in the yard before Fain got out of his car.

"Phil, I need help," said Doyle.

"We're going to help," answered Fain.

The help came at a price. Doyle would be required to undergo a psychological evaluation and accept a formal letter of reprimand. That night he went to his first meeting of Alcoholics Anonymous in Kokomo. About fifty men and women attended the meeting, where a handful rose to talk about their struggles with sobriety and the conversation was filled with slogans — "Let go and let God" — and references to the Twelve Steps. At the end, the assembly stood, joined hands, and recited the Serenity Prayer. Doyle felt both inspired and completely alone. As he turned to leave, an elderly man offered his hand and said, "You're in the right place."

The state of Indiana allowed Doyle to drive while his case was pending trial, but the Air Force required him to park outside the front gate at Grissom and walk onto the base. The shame he felt as his colleagues watched him walk to work was worse than the headaches, muscle aches, sweats, and sleeplessness that came as he suddenly stopped drinking. He went to AA meetings at lunchtime and after work and announced to Fain "for the first time in my life I think I've found God."

Doyle's superior officers offered him a stint in residential rehabilitation. Doyle accepted and his base commander, Daniel Goddard, drove him the nine hours to a place called Guest House, in rural Minnesota, where Catholic clergy got sober with a combination of individual counseling, group therapy, diet, and exercise. Pushed to confront his own feelings, Doyle had to admit that he was furious with his superiors in the Church and deeply depressed by their response to the sexual abuse crisis. The rejected report to the bishops, Michael Peterson's death, and the grief he encountered in victims of pedophile priests all flooded his mind.

"I have to admit," he finally told a counselor, "that I'm developing a real antipathy toward guys in miters."

Doyle felt divided, right down to his soul, by his work with lawyers for people suing the Church and his commitment to the priesthood and his Dominican order. Under canon law he was permitted to help Jeff Anderson and others. And Doyle was good at making himself look strong and certain as he defied bishops who insisted that he stop. But until he encountered this issue, he had been a man of the system, comfortable within a rigid, rule-based organization of rank and order. Now as the only active priest in the world willing to testify about the Church for sexual abuse victims, he felt isolated and insecure.

Ironically enough, Doyle would find salvation in two places where rules and rank were of enormous importance. In the fellowship of AA, the rules required complete abstinence and a wholehearted commitment to the Twelve Steps. In the military, pay, privilege, and responsibility corresponded directly with rank. However, in both of these institutions the rules also guaranteed a certain equality and respect for conscience that allowed for a wide variation of opinion. This was especially true in the Air Force, where Doyle found that the rule of law and, ultimately, civilian oversight, prevented any general from acting like a pope.

As an Air Force chaplain Doyle was paid by the government, not the Church, and with good performance he could climb in rank and pay grade. He also discovered among military officers a kind of open-mindedness that he never knew among fellow priests. A three-star general about to retire pulled Doyle aside and told him, "You need to know the Air Force is behind you." He got similar encouragement, even after everyone found out about his time in rehab. Doyle's only slip after his rehab visit occurred when he inadvertently drank wine from a chalice at communion. "I was distracted about something and wasn't thinking," he would recall. "Both times I called my sponsor, drank about a gallon of water, and headed right to the gym for a vigorous workout."

Jeff Anderson had talked on the phone with Tom Doyle more than a dozen times, and Doyle always seemed alert and fully present. Meeting him in person for the first time at the VOCALink-up conference, Anderson had seen a relaxed and confident man. He seemed more like a friend from the old neighborhood in Edina than a priest or an Air Force officer. As they sat together in the hotel bar, Doyle cussed and swore and cracked jokes about bishops, and he seemed to hold his alcohol extremely well. Anderson had no idea that Doyle felt the hopelessness that would lead to dark nights of suicidal planning and roadside arrest.

But then Anderson hadn't faced his own drinking problem. Life had been too good for that. Thanks to Julie, Darrow was growing up nicely and renovations were progressing at the big house on the hill. The job was done floor by floor and took more than a year and half. With her husband traveling much of the time, the task of managing the work fell mostly on Julie, who welcomed the distraction from her growing worries about her husband. He couldn't sleep at night unless he drank, and sometimes he didn't so much fall asleep as pass out. Asleep, he would suffer from violent nightmares. In one recurring dream he drove his car at speeds in excess of a hundred miles per hour. Unable to see clearly as the car careened from side to side, he felt terrified that he might cause a fatal wreck, but was unable to stop.

The dream was just a sleeping version of a waking fear that Anderson had set aside a hundred times or more as he left a bar or club and got in his car to drive home. When sober, he did worry about the possibility he might hurt someone or himself, and in truth an accident might have forced him to consider his drinking, but it never happened. Instead, he pressed his luck and somehow avoided disaster. The same dynamic governed his marriage. Anderson was so emotionally attached to his wife that the thought of losing her was almost impossible to consider. He couldn't or wouldn't stop partying, but he did make sure he came home when he said he would. When Julie was unable to contact him as he traveled, he would claim to have been with clients or say he was working overtime at hearings or depositions. On one morning Julie and Darrow sped to the airport before dawn to meet his overnight flight from Hawaii, only to discover he had never gotten on the plane.

More than ten years younger than him, and plagued by her own insecurities, Julie Anderson tended to back down during conflicts and accepted her husband's excuses rather than engage in a protracted debate with a man who could practically bend a jury to his will. Also, with the demands of motherhood she found a new focus for her attention. These responsibilities grew when Darrow was joined by twin brothers who arrived prematurely in February 1993. After weeks in the hospital Casey and Drew came home and absorbed much of their mother's emotional energy. Doubts about her husband receded except when a new incident arose or she enjoyed a rare moment to herself. Then, while driving alone or wheeling a cart through the aisles of the local Cub Supermarket in the middle of the night, Julie found herself overwhelmed by doubts and fears.

Few people outside the Andersons' marriage had any reason to believe anything was wrong. In the early 1990s Jeff Anderson was one of the most famous attorneys in the Twin Cities. He appeared often in the national press, talking about clergy abuse, the reliability of memory, First Amendment issues, and the nuances of sexual abuse. He also published articles in legal journals and appeared as a panelist at national conferences on religion and the law. In 1992 Anderson faced off against the bishops' lawyer Mark Chopko at a forum sponsored by the American Bar Association. With a hundred attorneys in the room Anderson all but issued a battle cry as he warned church officials who tried to hide abusive priests that, "We're go-ing to get you."

To keep up with the pace of travel, work, and play Anderson followed a demanding daily exercise regimen that included both running and muscle-building exercises. The workouts, combined with God-given hyperac-tivity, gave him an extraordinary capacity for work, but even an iron man has his limits. Anderson met his on a sunny summer day when he and Julie went to Bloomington to join a charity road race.

The course covered ten kilometers, which was a distance the Andersons had run before quite comfortably. As he pinned on his number and moved toward the starting line with his wife, Jeff began to feel light-headed. Then, when the race officials called for the runners to get set, he suddenly dropped to the ground, convulsing in what seemed to be a seizure.

Anderson blacked out for less than a minute, but his collapse caught everyone around him by surprise. Paramedics who were on duty for the race rushed to him. As he came to, they checked his pulse and blood pressure and then loaded him into an ambu-lance. At Fairview Southdale Hospital vari-ous tests, including brain imaging, found no cause. The physicians on duty talked about "anomalous seizures" that can occur when no underlying disease is present. In most cases patients return to their routines and never experience another attack.

Watching the doctors struggle to find an explanation for her husband's collapse, Julie Anderson had to wonder if she might know the answer. Jeff had consumed even more than his usual amount of alcohol the night before. When she got the chance, Julie pulled one of the doctors aside and quietly told him that her husband had drunk himself to sleep late the night before. She asked if that recent consumption, or perhaps his long-term habit, might have caused him to suddenly black out. "Wasn't it possible?" she said in a near whisper. "Couldn't drinking have something to do with it?"

Faced with an alert, engaged patient who looked to be at the peak of health and who obviously functioned at a very high level, no one at the hospital seemed impressed by the fact that his wife thought he drank too much. Julie would try again, with a neurologist who handled her husband's aftercare, but with the same result. None of the tests, including blood work that would have shown telltale liver problems, indicated Jeffrey Anderson was anything but healthy. Besides, all you had to do was look at the man — smiling, happy, and fit — and you could tell that he was in control of his life.

Jeff Anderson's buoyant confidence reassured

potential clients who came to him because his successes were widely publicized. Many appeared with complaints about priests who were known offenders and with a modest amount of work their accusations could be verified by documents or witnesses. A notable exception arose when two women who would be known as Jane Z. Doe and Jane G. Doe contacted Anderson in 1992. The women told stories of being abused by a priest named Gerald O'Keefe who had been the rector at the Cathedral of St. Paul. O'Keefe had since moved to Iowa where he was bishop of Davenport. The women, who said they were not acquainted, described events that were so similar that they seemed to corroborate each other. They each said the abuse occurred when they were between the ages of nine and twelve.

Anderson didn't think much about the fact that his two Jane Does saw the same psychiatrist. They both gave him permission to consult with her, and when he spoke to Diane Humenansky she said she believed both women. However, in a public statement Bishop O'Keefe denied the womens' claims and said, "I will fight these accusations until a judge or jury publicly declares that I am innocent. I am not interested in settlement. I am interested in restoring my good name." O'Keefe's denial was firmly stated, but when he repeated it during his deposition Anderson wasn't persuaded. With two victims offering similar stories he believed he was on solid ground. Then, in June 1993, local reporters rang the phone to say they had been called to a press conference by the archdiocese. There, O'Keefe's attorney Patrick Schiltz, the same lawyer Anderson had surprised with a hot-off-the-press copy of the Minnesota delayed discovery bill, announced that one of Anderson's clients had recanted her story.

As Patrick Schiltz told reporters, one of the Jane Does had come to him and said she wanted to drop her claim. She blamed her psychiatrist for steering her to name O'Keefe as an abuser when she wasn't truly certain of her memory. While the other Doe reaffirmed her claim, without a second victim her case would be difficult if not impossible to continue. At his press conference Schiltz was scathing in his criticism of Anderson, describing him as "the real villain" in the case. Weeks later he would back off this charge, describing Anderson as an important "pioneer" and shifted his ire to therapists and other lawyers who had created a "cottage industry of victimology who almost have an interest in seeing victims stay in that state."

The collapse of the case bewildered Anderson. He had believed both women and nothing that arose in the course of investigating the case led him to suspect a problem. However, in a matter of months several of

Dr. Humenansky's patients would file a lawsuit against her alleging she committed malpractice as she helped them remember episodes of sexual abuse. Years would pass before the resolution of the charges and Anderson would wind up advocating for one patient who said she had been mistreated by the psychiatrist. Before it was all over, insurers would pay millions of dollars in various lawsuits and Humenansky's license would be suspended by state authorities. Anderson would become more intent in his review of the claims made by potential plaintiffs and more aggressive in probing for problems in their presentation and background. However, there was no way for him to ever guarantee the truthfulness of a client, and he ultimately had to accept that he had to believe them, and in that belief dwelled risk.

Coming after years of humiliating scandal and costly settlements, the outcome of the O'Keefe cases came as a big relief to defenders of the Church. "We could give in to the temptation here and say, 'Ha, ha, see there,' but that's a luxury we can't afford," confessed Archbishop John Roach. "We don't want this to color in any way our responses to victims of abuse." Roach could also find reason for restraint in the words of O'Keefe's lawyer. Patrick Schiltz reminded the public that "we continue to see very few out-and-out false charges, where absolutely nothing happened."

He also worried, aloud, about the flood of abuse claims nationwide producing pushback on a grand scale.

"As the pendulum swings, we are going from a time when victims weren't believed to a time when they won't be believed again," said Schiltz. "Things are going so far there will be a backlash."

In fact, backlash sentiments had already been expressed. In February parents and alumni of the All-American Boys Chorus of Costa Mesa, California, rallied to support Fr. Richard T. Coughlin after he had been suspended in the wake of abuse allegations from five victims. Eventually Church leaders would find the charges credible enough to defrock him and pay more than $3 million in settlement. But at the time his defenders said, among other things, "He is a scapegoat for unhappy boys later in life."

In other cases around the country parishioners held vigils and mass meetings to show their support for priests who had been suspended after allegations they deemed incredible or malicious. In Palos Heights, Illinois, twelve hundred supporters of Fr. Patrick O'Leary protested in vain when he was removed from Incarnation Church because he was deemed by superiors to be "at risk of sexual misconduct." In Boston, hundreds of letter writers accused the *Globe* newspaper of "anti-Catholicism" in its treatment of the James Porter case and Cardinal Law.

In an appeal to the intellectual elite, Fr. Richard John Neuhaus spelled out a pro-Church defense in an article called "When Shepherds Go Astray." A convert who became a priest, Neuhaus had founded *First Things,* a magazine that became a leading voice for conservative politics and religion. Published in the January 1993 issue of the journal, "When Shepherds Go Astray" included his description of the crisis as an expression of anti-Catholicism and feminism run amok. As Neuhaus saw it, the clergy abuse issue reflected a "mass hysteria" about sexual abuse evidenced in the McMartin day care case. It was also, he complained, the product of the "changing definition of sexual harassment and even rape promoted by some feminists." Under these new definitions "the most innocent (as it used to be thought) erotic allusions . . . become a matter of criminal law." The scandal was further inflated, he wrote, by a press that viewed Catholics as "threatening, if not as the declared enemy."

Neuhaus also took a swipe at Andrew Greeley, who had called the sex abuse issue the most serious crisis in the Church since the Reformation. Lumping Greeley in with Oprah and Geraldo, Neuhaus called his estimates of the abuse problem "hype [that] does not bear close examination."

While others might blame celibacy or sexual hypocrisy within the institution, Neuhaus found the roots of the abuse problem in the sexual revolution of the 1960s, "gay activism," and in homosexuality in certain corners of the Church itself, which had taken on "a distinctly lavender hue." The vast majority of clergy offenders were not committing crimes against little children, but against adolescents, he argued, as if this made the offenses a matter of sexual preference, not an abuse of trust. He applauded the Church for attempting to "put its house in order" by cracking down on homosexuality.

Altogether, Neuhaus spelled out a defense of the Church that would echo through the coming decades. He said that the abuse cases showed not that the Church was corrupt, but that it needed to "mend the culture [of the modern world] after the devastations wrought by the sexual revolution." After noting a growing sense of skepticism over "whether some of the acts were committed at all" Neuhaus concluded that, contrary to the alarms sounded by Greeley and others, the abuse scandal was not the worst crisis since the Reformation. Indeed, he said, it was not "even the greatest crisis of the last ten years."

Months after Neuhaus offered his argument, Pope John Paul II met with a group of American bishops and called attention to both the injuries suffered by victims and the damage inflicted upon the Church. Seven years after the case of Gilbert Gauthe first focused attention on the problem, the Pope finally addressed it directly. In a letter that followed the meeting John Paul II acknowledged the abuse perpetrated by priests, called it evil, and expressed his concern for how much his brother bishops and the faithful "are suffering because of certain cases of scandal given by members of the clergy."

It was the *scandal,* not the rape and molestation of children, that was the main problem, according to the Pope. Indeed, he didn't mention the pain, suffering, and loss of faith among victims, nor did he use words like "abuse" or "rape." Instead he referred to "certain offenses" and "sins" and said that the bishops had two responsibilities in the face of the crisis: to deal with problem priests and their victims, and to address the damage done to society when the Church is swept by scandal.

In selecting the blandest words available to refer to the acts committed by abusive priests, the Pope occupied one extreme in an ongoing struggle over the terms used to discuss sexual victimization. In many jurisdictions, legal authorities had come to define any unwanted sexual activity carried out by an adult with a child as "rape." However, others, including some defense lawyers and Church leaders, would use words like "molestation" or "fondling," which tended to soften a reader's or listener's impression of what had occurred. The conflict over terms would continue, with parties on all sides communicating their perspectives, and priorities, with their differing choices.

By any measure, John Paul II's sentiments were focused primarily on the welfare of the Church. The problem of clergy abuse was, in his mind, a product of America, a society that "needs much prayer — lest it lose its soul." Prayer was the primary remedy recommended by John Paul II, but he also suggested temperance on the part of the mass media. "Evil can indeed be sensational," he wrote, "but the *sensationalism* surrounding it is always dangerous for morality." This point was echoed in repeated complaints by priests and bishops who said the media and plaintiffs' lawyers were exaggerating claims, stirring public animosity, and singling out Catholicism in a bigoted way.

Anyone who missed the Pope's point could turn to his spokesman Joaquín Navarro-Valls for clarification. "One would have to ask if the real culprit is not a society that is irresponsibly permissive, hyper-inflated with sexuality and capable of creating circumstances that induce even people who have received a sound moral formation to commit grave immoral acts."

The media came in for more papal scolding

when John Paul II visited Denver in August 1993. At outdoor services for an international youth conference the Pope made his first public remarks on sexual abuse by clergy, acknowledging "the pain of the suffering and scandal caused by the sins of some ministers of the altar." In the same speech he also denounced abortion and euthanasia as a "slaughtering of the innocents."

In Denver the Pope was met by huge, adoring crowds of fervent Catholics who had come to Colorado from around the world. His criticism of the American media prompted much applause, as did his attacks on alcohol, drugs, pornography, and "the moral evil which flows from personal choices." At various points he was interrupted by cheers of "John Paul II, we love you" and, as usual, he responded by offering his love in return. In all, the visit was a triumph of inspiration for believers and a demonstration of John Paul II's persistent popularity. It also obscured the few signs of caution, if not dissent, expressed by American Church leaders. As Jason Berry would report, Cleveland bishop Anthony Michael Pilla actually rejected the idea of holding the Pope's youth rally in his diocese out of concern that a visiting youth might be sexually abused.

The Pope's visit also confirmed the thinking expressed by John Neuhaus as he had linked the abuse crisis to social ills outside

338

the Church and argued that the institution itself, though damaged by scandal, was poised to lead the world back to traditional morality. In fact, as the political scientist James Kurtz explained just prior to the Pope's visit, in the Vatican's view the big problem facing the Church was not abusive priests but American individualism.

Interpreting Rome for Americans, Kurtz noted that the title "pontiff" meant "bridge builder" and he described the Vatican as a religious state led by a figure who believed he provides a personal connection between the earthly world and the divine. Kurtz wrote that America represented to the Church an "idolatry of self" growing out of excessive freedom and uncontrolled capitalism. In the century to come, he suggested, the Vatican's former partner in the battle against Marxism might become its main opponent in the struggle over morality.

In this context, the very highest Church officials were not likely to regard the sexual crimes of priests as a product of their own failure to follow Church law, or the clerical culture they inhabited. From the Vatican's perspective, the scandal was a North American phenomenon rooted in individualism. It was significant, from this point of view, that the United States was a mostly Protestant place and that it was the center of both mass media and materialism. It was noteworthy, too, that no one was suing the Church for clergy abuse in the mainly Catholic countries of Western Europe. Under this analysis, Neuhaus was right. The abuse scandal wasn't a big deal, and the Vatican could expect America's bishops to resolve it in time.

15.
PUSHBACK

Joseph Bernardin was in New York when the rumor finally caught up to him. The date was Wednesday, November 10, 1993, and the cardinal had given the annual Thomas Merton lecture at Columbia University. After the talk, he stayed overnight at the Madison Avenue mansion of the archbishop of New York. It was the archbishop, John O'Connor, who told him that an American cardinal was about to be accused of sexual abuse.

O'Connor and Bernardin were very different people. The cardinal of New York was a tall, thin, blue-eyed man of Irish descent who was theologically conservative and comfortable taking strong public stands on issues like abortion. Long a military chaplain, he was known to be one of John Paul II's favorites and was widely credited with maintaining the antiabortion movement in America. He was appointed to his post in New York even though his name didn't appear on a list of candidates sent to Rome by the American bishops.

Bernardin was the brown-eyed son of Italian immigrants and a theological liberal who had recently joined the Dalai Lama in a call for women's rights. For much of the 1970s he was considered the most powerful figure in Catholic America and leader of a liberalizing movement that sought to put the Church at the center of political discussions. In 1982 his peace activism landed on him on the cover to *Time* magazine. In 1983 he gained more fame by calling for a Consistent Ethic of Life that joined mostly left-wing politics to antiabortion sentiment in a way that alienated many conservatives.

All the attention heaped on Bernardin in the early 1980s obscured the fact that his side in the struggle for the future of the institution was losing to the conservatives led by the new Pope. By the early 1990s, Bernardin's influence had waned while O'Connor and other pro-Vatican bishops gained power. But as different as they were, both men were devout, ambitious, and accomplished. They both loved the Church and feared for its reputation. And they enjoyed the bond that came with membership in one of the world's most exclusive bodies in the world, the 180-member College of Cardinals.

Upon appointment, cardinals receive the heavy gold rings that identify them as

"Princes of the Church," and they are required to swear that they will not bring scandal upon the institution. Once elevated, they serve as the pontiff's chief advisers and bear the responsibility of representing his views in major cities that are centers of culture, finance, politics, and media. Upon the Pope's death they select a successor, who typically comes from their number. Given their status and power, an abuse allegation against one of them would reverberate around the world.

As of 1993 America claimed eight active cardinals. If the rumor were true, the odds were better than one in four that the accused was in the room as O'Connor and Bernardin spoke of it. Both men had expressed their worries about the abuse crisis in open forums, dwelling on the damage being done to victims and their Church. Earlier in the year, for example, O'Connor had told seminarians in Rome that "real horrifying damage" had been done to victims but that the press's pursuit of the story had been "merciless" where the Church was concerned.

In his later recollection of his discussion with O'Connor, Bernardin offered scant detail, except to say that his fellow cardinal reported that the source of the story was "uncertain" and the content frustratingly vague. These factors, Bernardin would write, "made it seem unworthy and yet ominous at the same time."

The "unworthy" part echoed Bernardin's automatic assumption that an ordained Catholic man was celibate until proven otherwise. (In fact the opposite was more likely true.) "Ominous" referred to the personal threat — were Bernardin or O'Connor the target? — signaled by the rumor. Any priest accused of abuse confronted a daunting challenge to defend himself. Having dismissed more than twenty accused clergy, Bernardin understood this reality better than most.

Bernardin got a sense of the storm to come when he returned to his office in Chicago on Thursday, November 11. Phone calls from friends around the world brought the news that *he* was the subject of the rumors. While aides scrambled to gather more information Bernardin, who told them the accusations were unfounded, thought for a moment about how Christ had been falsely accused before his crucifixion. As he later wrote, he asked himself, "Was this what the Lord was preparing me for, to face false allegations about something that I knew never took place?"

Soon the cardinal's staff delivered more details. His accuser had been a seminarian in Cincinnati when Bernardin served there as archbishop from 1972 to 1982. His attorney was expected to file papers on Friday. More pieces of the puzzle were offered by a TV reporter who called to say she had heard the allegations recited over the telephone. The accuser's name was Steven, said Mary Ann Ahern, and he claimed to have pictures.

By the end of the day, the world would know that a man named Steven Cook was saying that Bernardin pressured him into a sex act when he was a high school sophomore. Cook was a recovering drug addict who was suffering from AIDS. Bernardin would say he could not recall the man, but somehow he knew that Cook had previously filed a complaint against a Cincinnati priest named Ellis Harsham. Now Bernardin guessed that Cook was unhappy with the response he had gotten from Cincinnati's current archbishop, Daniel Pilarczyk, and had decided to expand his complaint. This decision had brought a caravan of television news trucks to the curb on Superior Street, directly beneath the window of Bernardin's office. Reporters from all the major networks had come to report on the lawsuit and hear the cardinal's response. He didn't speak to them but issued a brief statement including this simple declaration:

"I have never abused anyone in all my life, anywhere, anytime, anyplace."

The lawsuit was reported on the 10 P.M. local news programs Thursday night. Bernardin would not speak to the press until the next afternoon, after the suit against him was actually filed. In the morning the cardinal met with advisers and, following the policies he had put in place, notified the diocesan review board of the allegations. He then spent an hour alone, which ended when he called a close friend for support. At 1 P.M. Bernardin walked into a small, wood-paneled auditorium at Church headquarters where he was met by seventy reporters and photographers and a bank of television cameras. Dressed in simple clerical black, with a gold chain crossing his chest and his cardinal's ring on his right hand, he walked to a bouquet of microphones affixed to a podium as photographers fired their cameras.

For the ensuing hour, Bernardin stood before the press and steadfastly repeated that he was innocent of the charges, which had left him "flabbergasted" and "saddened." He said he had no recollections of Steven Cook, and was most concerned about the effect the suit would have on the faith of Chicago's Catholics. "I am not really concerned about myself," he said. "I know that I am innocent. I'm more concerned about my people, the people whom I love, the people whom I shepherd."

When a reporter asked, "Are you sexually active?" Bernardin paused for a moment and said, "I am sixty-five years old, and I can tell you that all my life I have lived a chaste and celibate life."

Although most would take Bernardin's declaration at face value, experts on celibacy knew it was open to interpretation. When they felt free to speak plainly, few clerics said they believed that "chaste" and "celibate" meant a life lived entirely without any sexual experience. Most made exceptions for the occasional lapse, as long as they confessed and resumed their commitment to the ideal. On rare occasions, high Church officials even addressed the topic in a public way. At about the time when Bernardin faced accusations, a correspondent of the British Broadcasting Corporation asked Cardinal Jose Sanchez, then Prefect of the Vatican Congregation for the Clergy, about the findings of Richard Sipe and others who said that at any given time between 45 and 50 percent of Catholic priests were sexually active. His response: "I have no reason to doubt the accuracy of those figures."

Sipe, who had continued his research and writing after publication of *Secret World,* was deeply disturbed by the sexual hypocrisy he discovered in the Church, especially when it involved men he knew and admired. One high-ranking Jesuit told Sipe that a priest who "has sex a couple of times a year" qualified as celibate, even if his version of chastity and celibacy produced a host of offspring. Indeed, Sipe had never met someone who had actually lived a "chaste and celibate life" in a literal way. To him, Bernardin's claim was yet another example of the way men who demanded so much of others when it came to sexual morality, used self-deception and even lies to protect themselves.

No matter what anyone thought of Bernardin's description of his own sexual experience, the spectacle of a Roman Catholic cardinal answering such questions was something no one in the room could have imagined a decade earlier. It was an almost surreal occurrence even to those who devoted themselves to the cause of abuse victims and overcoming church cover-ups. Also, of all the major figures in the American church, Bernardin may have been the most popular with victims because he had met the problem of abuse more directly than most other bishops and seemed genuinely affected by their experiences.

As one of the main advocates for victims, Barbara Blaine heard from many members of SNAP who remained loyal Catholics and were shaken by the idea that a favorite leader of the Church had been accused. Blaine, who had enrolled in law school, had recently moved out of the Catholic Worker House on the South Side and into a tiny apartment where her walk-in closet became SNAP headquarters. She was hard-pressed to answer every person who called to talk about Bernardin and somewhat shocked, herself, by the news. As the case progressed she would be won over by the cardinal's openness. "He has set a perfect example of how to respond to allegations," she told one reporter.

"I didn't know him at the time," recalled Blaine, years later. "But he had a good reputation with people like the Catholic Workers because he had made very significant gestures to deal with homelessness." Blaine would support any victims who came forward with a credible claim and Cook's complaint contained specific details that merited a proper investigation. Nevertheless, she feared that a case brought against a man who was so well-regarded by so many people could end badly for the small movement that had been coalescing around the cause of abuse victims and the conflicts over Catholic sexual morality.

Indeed, Bernardin represented the friendlier face of Catholicism for those who questioned the Church's stands on sexual morality and the status of women. Although he never broke directly with Rome on any essential issue, the cardinal was most receptive to hearing opposing views. And he never expressed the Church's antiabortion and antigay views in an aggressive way. Indeed, he frustrated many antiabortion activists who considered him to be soft on the issue and viewed him as a weak ally, at best. Indeed, as the charges against Bernardin became known, some of his supporters imagined that archconservatives were somehow behind it all.

The notion that conservatives lurked behind the charge against Bernardin got some support when a priest named Charles Fiore told a Chicago radio station that he believed the accusations. Fiore, who made his comments even before the lawsuit was filed with the court in Cincinnati, was outspoken on the issue of clergy sex abuse, and upset over priests who would violate young people. His analysis of the problem pinned much of the blame on homosexuality in the priesthood. An ultraconservative, Fiore had been ousted by the Dominican order and allied himself with a traditionalist movement. Bernardin would eventually claim that Fiore had spoken with Steven Cook before he filed his lawsuit and encouraged him to add Bernardin, whom he once called "an evil man," to the suit. Fiore disputed this claim.

As an ancient, secretive, and opaque institution infused with mystery, the Church was an ideal focus for anyone who feared conspiracies and hidden agendas. Historically, the Church was rife with intrigue, power plays, and even mysterious deaths. Those inclined to assume that the hierarchy kept innumerable sordid secrets could point to this record and wonder how anyone could believe anything uttered by a pope or a bishop. In modern times this view found further encouragement from the evidence that emerged from scandals like the sex abuse cases. Every time a lawsuit forced the disgorgement of documents or a high-level cover-up was revealed, people like Fiore could feel affirmed in their belief that the Church was corrupted by secrets. As the old saying goes, even paranoids have enemies. In this case, even extreme critics of the Church could find disturbing stories to prove one point or another.

In the Bernardin case, the Vatican indulged in immediate hyperbole, with the Holy See's official radio station declaring Cook's suit "Filthy, worthy only of disdain." The station also observed that "accusations of this kind" are, at times, aimed at American priests "in order to receive compensation money." In Minneapolis, Archbishop John Roach, who had dealt with dozens of verified claims against priests, observed that "There is something rotten about all of this." In Baltimore, Archbishop William Keeler criticized members of the press, whom he claimed valued being first with a scoop above "accurate reporting."

The case also renewed the battle over memory. By sheer coincidence, about a hundred and thirty members of the Midwest chapter of the False Memory Syndrome Foundation met in the Chicago area on the day after Steven Cook's complaint was lodged. Outside the Des Plaines community center where they had gathered, a handful of picketers protested that the FMSF was "an advocacy group for perpetrators." Inside, people who had been accused of committing sexual abuse heard a psychologist from Tucson compare the ongoing wave of abuse cases to a witch hunt.

"We did this same thing four hundred and five hundred years ago," said Dr. Paul Simpson. "It's the same, in as much as the accused only have one of two options. It's either you're guilty or you're in denial." Simpson insisted "there is no solid, scientific, qualitative evidence" to support the idea that traumatic memories may be repressed, and criticized hypnosis and other therapeutic techniques used by some psychotherapists whose patients claimed to have suddenly remembered incidents in the past.

Hypnosis was a factor in Steven Cook's claim. A longtime drug abuser, Cook had gotten sober after being arrested and had relied on counseling to steady his life. In sessions with a therapist who used hypnosis he talked about his high school years and experiences with Fr. Ellis Harsham. He described using drugs and alcohol with the priest, who showed him pornography and, according to the complaint, "repeatedly and continually sexually abused" him "at St. Gregory's Seminary and in other locations." Cook also

claimed to recall being brought to the archbishop's quarters by Harsham, where he was
then sexually abused by Bernardin.

Coincidentally, Cook's suit had been filed
as the CNN news network prepared to air a
special report on the clergy abuse scandal
and he gave correspondent Bonnie Anderson
an exclusive interview. In bits of this interview
broadcast on the day the case became public,
he described how Bernardin had allegedly
raped him when he was a high school student
and he recounted the effects of the trauma
inflicted by Harsham and Bernardin. "It shatters your world," he said. "It shatters your
soul. It shatters your life." Cook followed
these comments by answering a few of the
questions posed by reporters who tracked
him down in Philadelphia. Although he then
stopped talking, the press continued to call
and staked out his home.

As often happened when charges are made
public, others contacted attorneys and reporters to say they had been abused. Several men
made claims against Harsham, and within a
year Church officials would find the evidence
sufficient to place him on administrative
leave. In the case of Bernardin, no further
public claims emerged. Instead, reporters
found court records showing that in 1984
Cook had spoken about being abused by
"priests," which gave the cardinal's supporters an opening to challenge the idea that his

recollections of Bernardin were recent. As the press dug deeper into Cook's claim, the nature of memory became a pressing issue. Ten days after the news broke a piece in the *Chicago Tribune* compared Cook's testimony to the "spectral evidence" of the Salem witch trials of the seventeenth century.

The witch trial comparison was amplified by *Time* magazine, which featured a long cover story reassessing Freudian psychology accompanied by a sidebar titled "Repressed Memory Therapy: Lies of the Mind." The piece presented instances where people felt that therapists had led them to make false accusations and made a forceful case against the existence of ritual abuse. However, it also included unsubstantiated claims that accusations of incest had reached "epidemic proportions." If such an epidemic existed, it had not been identified by lawyers, therapists, or public health experts.

Time made no mention of any falsely accused priests and attorneys on all sides of the Catholic scandal said that false claims were almost nonexistent in clergy cases. ("The vast majority of those accused of this stuff are guilty," said Patrick J. Schiltz.) However, all the publicity devoted to the issue of memory inevitably affected perceptions of the Bernardin and Cook case. As skeptical reporters dug into Steven Cook's past to reveal him as a troubled man, Cardinal Bernardin took the high road, saying "my heart goes out to" Cook and announcing, "I have a great desire to meet him. I want to pray with him and comfort him." An editorial in *The Wall Street Journal* titled "Trial By Accusation" leveraged the Bernardin case to complain that rape and sexual abuse "have been politically anointed and given special weight" and to argue that legal "mills" were turning out abuse claims because they were "financially rewarding."

With deft construction, the *Journal* and others used Cook and Bernardin to propel a broader argument about gender politics. Greed was cited as a motivator for many of the complainants and their lawyers came in for their share of criticism for clogging the courts with suits that lacked real merit. The individuals who alleged crimes were painted as maladapted whiners.

These arguments were fueled by the same energy that motivated a larger conservative response to decades of social change. Spelled out most clearly by writer Charles Krauthammer in a 1993 essay called "Defining Deviancy Up," this thesis revolved around the central complaint that normal behavior had been erroneously transformed into something objectionable if not illegal. The terrible result, in Krauthammer's mind, was that people became "exquisitely oversensitized" to child abuse and sexual "behavior that had long rbeen viewed as normal" had been redefined as abusive. To Krauthammer and his allies, all the concern for people (mainly women and children) who were being exploited was overblown and unreasonable standards were being applied to the behavior of bosses, authorities, and men in general. The resulting decline in respect for powerful institutions like the Church, and their leaders, was something to grieve and, if possible, repair.

Two months after the claim was made against Bernardin, the press in Chicago reported that Cook's own lawyer, Stephen Rubino, had doubts about his memories. In a letter Rubino sent to Church officials, which was subsequently filed with the court, he wrote, "I am gravely concerned with his inability to remember some of the specifics of his visit when he was a junior in high school to the private quarters of Cardinal Bernardin."

Three months after the claim, Bernardin's lawyers uncovered problems with the therapist Cook was seeing when he recalled the alleged abuse. It turned out that Michele Moul was not licensed and had graduated from an unaccredited psychology program. The cardinal's lawyers said they would challenge her methods, arguing they did not meet the standards required by the courts. If they prevailed, which was likely, Cook's claim would be dismissed.

The reports on Cook's case, and mounting editorial support for the cardinal, would have made many observers doubt the conflict would ever get before a judge. Watching from afar, other victims of abusive priests shuddered at the prospect of the most high-profile claim falling apart and damaging their effort to be recognized and change the way the Church responded to claims. And then, it did.

On February 28, 1994, one hundred and eight days after news of his claim against Bernardin echoed around the world, Steven Cook withdrew his suit explaining to the court that he could "no longer be sure that his memories of abuse by the cardinal are true or accurate." In interviews Cook said, "If I knew at the time I filed the lawsuit what I know now, I would never have sued Cardinal Bernardin."

Cook's announcement took the pressure off Bernardin. However, he did not withdraw the charges he had leveled against Ellis Harsham. And contrary to press reports on his decision, Cook did not actually "recant" his claim. Rather, he said that he was no longer certain of his memory.

"I filed the lawsuit against Cardinal Bernardin because I had vivid memories of abuse which I believed to be true," Cook said. Before deciding to sue, added Cook, he had taken two polygraph exams to test his memory. However, the confidence he felt after passing those tests faded as the weeks passed. "I now realize," he explained, "that the memories which arose during and after hypnosis are unreliable."

An hour after Cook spoke, Bernardin walked into a hastily called press conference in the same room where he first talked publicly about the case. Those who attended would be forgiven if they thought that Cook had fully recanted as the cardinal beamed and declared, "Our justice system has publicly affirmed my innocence. Truth has prevailed." Sounding a bit like a prosecutor he added that "no deal" was offered to Cook and he had acted "voluntarily, without pressure of any kind."

In this moment Bernardin's transformation from "accused" to "vindicated" was completed. "The travesty was that I, a man of sixty-five years, who has been a priest for forty-two years and a bishop for twenty-eight years, was publicly humiliated before the world," he said. "An innocent man. That's a travesty."

Bernardin spoke about the pain he had experienced during the uproar over the accusation, and then denied that he was angry at the man who had called him a rapist. "I harbor no ill feelings toward Steven Cook," he declared. "I have compassion for him. I have prayed for him every day, and I will continue to do so."

After Cook and Bernardin had delivered the news, editorial writers around the country praised the cardinal, criticized Cook's therapist, and called on the press to treat abuse claims with more skepticism. *New York Times* columnist Anthony Lewis covered this ground in a piece titled "Savaging the Great." The *Las Vegas Review Journal* decried an "epidemic of amnesia" and the *Chicago Tribune* trumpeted the headline, "The Cross Is Lifted."

In May 1994, Northwestern University hosted a symposium titled "Guilt by Allegation: Lessons from the Cardinal Bernardin Case." It was attended by journalists and lawyers, including Jeffrey Anderson, who considered the Bernardin affair a setback for the great majority of claimants who lodged legitimate complaints. At the end of the day, a poll of the three hundred participants found them evenly divided on whether the press had handled the case well. Bernardin's popularity rebounded and in December 1994 he arranged to meet his accuser. Bernardin flew to Philadelphia and went by car to the local Catholic seminary, where he sat down with Cook and his partner. Cook, who was obviously very ill, apologized. Bernardin forgave him.

The record of this encounter between the cardinal and Cook comes from Bernardin himself and appears in *The Gift of Peace,* a book he published after Cook died in September 1995. In it Bernardin writes that Cook still seemed confused about whether the cardinal had in fact abused him. He then reports:

> I looked directly at Steven, seated a few inches away from me. "You know," I said, "that I never abused you."
> "I know," he answered. "Can you tell me that again?"
> I looked directly into his eyes. "I have never abused you. You know that, don't you?"
> Steven nodded. "Yes," he replied.

Cook died in September 1995, before Bernardin's book was published and the world received the cardinal's full account of their conversation. Stricken with pancreatic cancer, Bernardin died in November 1996, leaving behind his version of events, which depicted Cook as a psychologically wounded and confused man who was influenced by an incompetent therapist and a vindictive priest to file false charges he eventually disavowed. In Chicago, the *Tribune* responded to the cardinal's death with a recounting of the reconciliation of accused and accuser and declared Bernardin "a hero for all time."

Bernardin's friends and admirers, including church critics such as Andrew Greeley and

Eugene Kennedy, would continue to promote him as a heroic figure, but many victims of clergy abuse and their supporters would never shake their doubts about him. They focused on the fact that Cook was paid by the Diocese of Cincinnati to settle his suit against Ellis Harsham and saw in this an arrangement that also covered Cardinal Bernardin.

In time journalist Jason Berry would reveal additional elements of the Bernardin case, and note that Archbishop Pilarczyk's initial rejection of Cook's complaints led to the explosive charges he then leveled against Bernardin. In a book titled *Vows of Silence,* coauthored with Gerald Renner, Berry revealed that Jeffrey Anderson had refused to take up the cause of a young man who said Cardinal Bernardin had abused him at a seminary in Minnesota. Eventually this man found a lawyer and accepted $120,000 to drop his complaint. As part of those arrangements, he retracted his charges, but later he told a reporter for *The Boston Globe* that the retraction was "false."

While Bernardin's most ardent supporters considered him practically a martyred saint, skeptics would never let go of the idea that the truth was buried with him. Some archconservative Catholics placed him at the center of a community of sexually active gay clergy and published their views in books and

Internet postings that were largely ignored outside of their circle. On the other end of the spiritual spectrum, Richard Sipe conducted extensive interviews with many clergy who knew Bernardin well and some who claimed to be his sexual partners. At a 2003 conference of clergy abuse survivors he noted, bluntly, "Bernardin was sexually active. He had homosexual activity with some priests. There is a homosexual cabal within the Catholic priesthood. A great deal of power and money is involved in this group."

After the Bernardin affair, the bishops of the Catholic Church in America seemed to stop dealing directly with the overall problem of clergy abuse. Although a paper published by their conference at the end of 1994 recommended prevention strategies and ways to respond to accusations, it was never approved by the group as a whole. Studies recommended by this committee were never undertaken and the bishops even rejected the group's request for information on the number of active cases in U.S. dioceses and the amount of money paid to settle claims to date. These ideas "just didn't fly" because "the climate was different," one bishop explained at the time.

Across the country, bishops mounted a disciplined and well-funded campaign to lobby against efforts to give more victims access to the courts by easing statutes of limitation. They also opposed legislative and legal efforts to recognize repressed memory or delayed discovery of harm related to abuse. In most locales bishops encouraged victims to seek a Church-based resolution that typically included counseling at Church expense and, in some instances, a payment of a few thousand dollars.

When claimants declined settlement and pressed forward in civil suits the Church often responded with aggressive tactics, including counterclaims that parents failed to protect their children from abusive priests. In some cases private detectives were dispatched to investigate the sexual behavior of people who said they had been abused, and families who filed suits found that their garbage had been picked over. Depositions conducted by Church lawyers became battlegrounds as they pressed people who said they were abused as minors with questions that suggested that they had encouraged, invited, and enjoyed sexual activity with priests. In a case in Pennsylvania, Church officials actually filed a lawsuit against a victim's parents alleging they neglected their child by allowing him to interact with an abusive priest. This claim was thrown out of court, but not before the family had to retain counsel and fight it.

For people who had, in fact, been abused as children or adolescents, these questions could revive feelings of guilt and self-hatred that they had worked hard to overcome. In truth, children and adolescents often respond physically and emotionally when they are drawn into sex by adults. The ensuing confusion adds to the trauma they experience and victims may require psychotherapy to sort out their feelings and assign proper blame to their perpetrators. Intense questioning by a skilled attorney could and sometimes did reopen old wounds.

Hardball techniques were employed by the Church even as top-ranking clergymen expressed public sorrow and regret for the crimes of guilty priests. In New York, where Cardinal O'Connor said "it's long since time to get on our knees, beat our breast, to ask God's forgiveness," lawyers for the archdiocese mounted a fierce defense of a priest named Daniel Calabrese, who was previously convicted of abusing a minor. The Church said the boy who was the plaintiff in the civil suit "willingly consented" to sex with the priest and claimed that its personnel records enjoyed First Amendment protection from discovery. In another case the New York Archdiocese refused to settle claims against a priest who had already pleaded guilty to a variety of sodomy and sexual abuse charges.

Lawyers for the Church could feel supported in their tough tactics by the outcome in the Bernardin case and by a spate of legal rulings that went their way. In Minnesota, the state supreme court overruled the court of appeals to bar a sex abuse claim against Richard Kemp, a junior high school guidance counselor. In this case a man named Mark Blackowiak said that he didn't realize the effect of the abuse, which took place in the 1970–71 school year, until twenty years had passed. The case was complicated by the fact the Blackowiak had confronted the counselor when he ran into him in the company of a young boy. In the claimant's own words he had "freaked out" about the boy's safety. This encounter had occurred in 1981.

The court didn't consider whether Blackowiak had been abused as a boy, nor did it decide whether he had been harmed. It only deliberated on the statute of limitations bill that Jeffrey Anderson had helped to push through the state legislature and on the concept of delayed discovery of harm. While Blackowiak said he didn't understand the extent of the harm done to him until 1991, the court found that a "reasonable person" would have recognized he had been the victim of a crime — and therefore injured — long before. This finding led the justices to rule that the suit fell outside the six-year time limit.

In her written decision, Justice Mary Jeanne Coyne focused directly on the passage in the law that gave a victim a six-year window for filing suit after he or she "was aware or should have been aware that the sexual abuse caused his damages." As the authors of the bill later explained, they meant that the clock started ticking after a victim understood that his depression, addiction, or other problems were the product of the abuse. Legislators chose this standard after hearing testimony that persuaded them that victims of sex crimes often deny the connection between their experience and later troubles and needed special consideration. The court of appeals had interpreted the statute to provide for this dynamic.

Judge Coyne, who had come to the court with a background in corporate law, declared that a victim's understanding of psychological cause and effect "is simply not relevant." Citing an insurance case called *Fireman's Fund Ins. Co. v. Hill,* Coyne wrote that the key question is "the time at which the complainant knew or should have known that he/she was sexually abused." Blackowiak may not have known that a sexual assault had caused him trouble later in life, but he did know he was assaulted, and that was good enough for Coyne.

The ruling, which included a dismissive reference to "repressed memories," provoked a sharp dissent from Sandra Gardebring, a recently appointed justice who was more than twenty years younger than Coyne. Gardebring argued that Minnesota lawmakers had clearly intended the law to allow for people to sue once they grasped the ways that shame, sexual confusion, guilt, and other products of sexual abuse affected them much later in life. "The statute at issue here does not turn on the legal determination of 'injury by sexual abuse,' " she wrote in her opinion, "it turns on the victim's *knowledge* of the link between the two." According to this view, sexual abuse can have a long-term, corrosive effect that may not be evident until it has eaten a hole in a victim's life.

Gardebring's argument was couched in the politesse of the court. But attorneys who understood the vernacular saw real passion in her phrasing, especially the observation that her colleagues could only reach their conclusion "by consistently misreading the statute." Remarkably, it was the defense lawyer who represented the man accused of raping Blackowiak who put the decision in terms the public could grasp. Philip Villaume said, "It's a major victory not only for my client, but for the insurance industry, for professional people. It's obviously a major blow to victims who have been abused."

Victims of abusive priests understood the effect of *Blackowiak v. Kemp* immediately. They had been using the civil court system to hold the Church accountable and to discover the whole truth of what had happened to them as children, including cover-ups and transfers of perpetrators. Most individuals could mount this kind of effort only with the help of lawyers who were willing to gamble that the outcome would include a judgment that would pay them for the effort. The ruling would bar many of them from the courtrooms of Minnesota and those in other states where judges looked to this precedent.

Blackowiak's lawyer considered the decision part of the "backlash" against abuse claimants inspired by the Bernardin case and false memory activists. James Wall, editor of *The Christian Century* magazine, called this "the Bernardin factor." More backlash came from other states where judges denied delayed discovery arguments and legislatures stopped passing laws that accommodated the nature of childhood abuse.

In practical terms, the backlash stalled the movement represented by SNAP, and froze many of the claims brought by attorneys like Jeffrey Anderson. Anderson found himself in constant conflict with his partners, who began to chafe at the expense of cases that might not go anywhere. He poured thousands of hours and tens of thousands of dollars into these claims, most of which were dismissed on statute of limitations issues. With losses piling up, he pledged his home and every other asset he possessed to maintain his firm's line of credit but still bumped up against the bank's $3 million limit. The mood in the firm became tense and divided, similar to a home where a couple is on the verge of divorce.

"My partners said it was over and I had to stop," recalled Anderson. "I thought I was doing the right thing for the right reason and that somehow it was going to work out." However, the Bernardin case had halted the momentum of Anderson's cause. And while he refused to quit and insisted he was a happy warrior, much of what he said and did betrayed this claim. He continued to drink heavily, on the road and at home, and the conflicts with his wife grew more intense.

As Julie Anderson pressed harder to get her husband to stop drinking, he talked about the demands of his work, which he equated with a sacred calling, and insisted he was managing well. In his most sober moments Jeff Anderson did not actually believe his own claims and sometime he feared that his wife would leave him. But he never voiced either his doubts or his worries. Instead he would try to focus conversations on what Julie was doing wrong. He often criticized her for making too much of an effort to look pretty when they went out together and attracting attention. This complaint, from a man whose party antics sometimes ended with his pants around his ankles, struck his wife as particularly ridiculous.

Ridiculous as he might seem to his wife, Jeff Anderson talked rings around her. Only once in their early years together did she actually prevail in a showdown over booze. In this case the family was vacationing and at a distance Julie heard her husband tell three-year-old Darrow to "go get me a beer." With teeth clenched she asked to have a word with him. When they were alone, she told him that he would never again ask one of their sons to fetch him a drink. He agreed.

With her husband refusing to stop drinking, or see a counselor, Julie started attending group therapy on her own. The other women in the group would listen to her describe her life caring for three small boys with little help from a husband who was absent much of the time and often drunk when he was at home.

"Are you kidding?" they would ask. "Why are you putting up with this?"

Struggling to answer, she would say that for all his flaws, her husband was the most impressive man she had ever met and she just wasn't ready to give up on him. She held to this view, but she also began to develop the belief that keeping her marriage and family together would require her to be braver, more assertive, and more confident. Becoming a mother had motivated her to stand more firmly for what she believed was right and build up her own strengths. In the process she could become a fuller partner in her marriage, a better example for her children, and gain a level of self-respect she would value more each day.

16.
"WOULD A BISHOP LIE?"

More than 125,000 people turned out to shiver and cheer and cry and laugh when John Paul II said Mass in Central Park on a cold October Saturday in 1995. Dressed in gold vestments and beaming a crinkly smile, the seventy-five-year-old pontiff sent ripples of emotion through the crowd with every word and gesture. Even the trembling of his hand was greeted as something warm and familiar. He was loved as a grandfatherly figure, although the great majority of American Catholics said that his views had little bearing on their personal morality.

The disconnect between acceptance of the man and his ideas had much to do with the content of those ideas. Throughout his papacy John Paul II had pushed an aggressively traditional Catholic morality and a dim view of the modern society, especially American society. More recently he had talked about "a culture of death" represented by the United States and a "culture of life" offered by the

Church. In 1995, during a five-day tour of America, he linked abortion rights to violence of all kinds and implored crowds to "Stand up for marriage and family life."

In a diverse, pluralistic nation moving toward gay rights and gay marriage, the Pope's pronouncements sounded like a call from a distant and less tolerant time. However, his personal popularity was unrivaled. In New York, as elsewhere, he electrified crowds and outshone every luminary who stood near him. His appeal was subjected to regular analyses, which invariably concluded that as a former stage actor, John Paul II wore his office better than any man in modern times. His charisma invited people to project their fondest sentiments upon him, and his personal triumphs over assassination attempts and many illnesses made him a symbol of fortitude and courage. No matter what they thought about his message, people liked the man.

The ultimate weapon in the Vatican's public relations arsenal, a papal visit could highlight his views, announce the opening of a new dialogue, or punctuate the end of one. After John Paul II's tour of America, Cardinal Joseph Ratzinger made sure that everyone understood the Pope was determined to close debate with liberal-leaning Catholics. In a public letter he invoked the power assumed by Pius IX when his troops were in retreat and announced that John Paul II's opposition to ordination for women was "infallible" doctrine that must be accepted by the faithful. Those who were disturbed by this news were encouraged to ask the Holy Spirit for help in accepting that while women would never gain the special status accorded men, they were nevertheless equal.

In early 1995 an historian of religion at Pennsylvania State University surveyed the Catholic landscape and declared that the abuse crisis had "reached its height in 1992–93" and was receding. Philip Jenkins wrote that well-meaning but misguided Catholic "culprits" like Richard Sipe, Jason Berry, and Andrew Greeley had contributed to "the often outrageous exaggeration" of the problem because they truly believed their Church needed reforming. However, thanks to the resolution of the charges against Cardinal Bernardin, the notion that an historic problem afflicted the Church was passing into "oblivion."

The Bernardin case, publicity about false memories, and legal decisions that barred many claims from victims *had* pushed the clergy abuse issue to the bottom of the public agenda. The number of articles about the issue published in major media would plummet from a high of 535 in 1991 to a low of 101 in 1996.

In this same time period, many of the

people who had worked hardest in the cause of victims shifted focus. Jeanne Miller, founder of VOCALink-up ended her activism to take up a career in the law. Barbara Blaine began working with the Church as a member of a committee appointed by Cardinal Bernardin to deal with clergy abuse issues in a quiet and deliberate way. Jason Berry turned his attention to writing about politics and producing a book about jazz funerals in New Orleans. Richard Sipe accepted chairmanship of the Interfaith Sexual Trauma Institute, which was founded by Abbot Timothy Kelly at his alma mater, St. John's of Minnesota.

Sipe still hoped that the Church could reform its own culture in ways that would reduce, if not eliminate the problem of clergy abuse. Believing that even the critics could be brought into the process he approached attorney Jeffrey Anderson. At dinner in a Minneapolis restaurant he laid out the goals of the institute and explained how together, all the parties in the crisis might resolve it. Sipe suggested that Anderson participate and perhaps donate money to the ISTI budget. Anderson listened without interrupting and recognized Sipe's sincerity. He also believed him to be naive. When the pitch ended he said, "But Richard, the Church is the enemy."

By "Church" Anderson didn't mean all Catholic people but rather the institution represented by orders, dioceses, priests, bishops, cardinals, and the pope. These organizations and men were, to his mind, irredeemably corrupt and incapable of contributing to reform or reconciliation with abuse victims. While others considered the Bernardin case and concluded that the scandals were ending and Catholicism would return to its pre-1984 status, Anderson was certain the quiet would be momentary. He believed that the abuse of power that had been exposed had inspired a movement that was nowhere near its end. And while he couldn't predict when or where the next point of conflict would be reached, he had no doubt about its inevitability.

As the public furor related to Bernardin receded and the sense of crisis in the Church seemed to abate, Pope John Paul II's stature rose. He began 1995 as *Time* magazine's "man of the year." The honor acknowledged, as the editors wrote, both his popularity and his "rectitude or recklessness as his detractors would have it" in pursuit of sexual moral absolutes. Having made a single public mention of sexual abuse by clergy, he would not utter a word about it again for a year. Instead he would continue to travel the world, lecturing industrialized nations on their social evils and calling people to the comfort of the Church. Only the best-informed American observers would have a basis for challenging the idea, expressed by Philip Jenkins and others, that clergy abuse had been an American problem and that it was under control. Few knew that a second crisis was brewing in Ireland where, as early as 1986, bishops had suddenly decided they needed to buy insurance policies to protect themselves from liability in civil cases brought by victims. Indeed, in this most conservative Catholic country, the Church had also formed a special committee to deal with claims of abuse that hadn't yet been made.

The first major reports of a sex abuse scandal in the Church in Ireland came in 1994 when a priest named Brendan Smyth surrendered to authorities in Northern Ireland. Smyth had assaulted dozens of children in Belfast and in the Republic of Ireland, where he had been resisting extradition. His case was the first of many that were subsequently revealed by the national press, most notably *The Irish Times* and the Irish network TV program *Prime Time.* In 1995, a month before the Pope departed Rome for America, the program revealed that a young man named Andrew Madden had received the equivalent of $50,000 to settle his complaint against Fr. Ivan Payne, who had sexually assaulted him over the course of four years. The abuse had begun in 1977, when Madden was an eleven-year-old altar boy.

Madden, who was not quite thirty, had

been a suicidal alcoholic for much of his adult life. The rapes he had suffered as a boy had left him so depressed and dispirited that he was unable to establish stable relationships, complete schooling, or even maintain a steady job. He had been in and out of hospitals and outpatient psychotherapy and seen little of his family since his teens. He had nevertheless developed the determination to hold Payne accountable and won the settlement, which Payne paid with a loan from the Church.

Although church lawyers in America typically pressed victims to keep cases secret in exchange for payments, Madden was not asked to sign a confidentiality agreement. Certain that Payne had victimized other boys, he made his claim public in the summer of 1995. As so often happens, the publicity prompted others to report that they too had been abused by priests. By the end of the year further complaints been lodged against Payne and against two other Irish clerics.

Ireland was not the only country outside North America suffering from a clergy abuse scandal. Weeks before his trip to the United States, John Paul II accepted the resignation of Austria's highest Church official, Cardinal Hans Hermann Groer, who had been accused of sexual abuse by several different men who had been his students. Groer's case, which involved the abuse of underage boys, had been widely publicized and thousands of Austrians left the Church in the wake of the scandal. In the same period two bishops in Germany were under investigation for covering up abuses committed there.

Compared with the hundreds of cases in the United States, the handful made public in Europe seemed unremarkable, and they did little to undermine the notion that a mainly American problem had been placed in proper perspective and resolved. As far as most people knew, the Church was moving past the sex crime scandal. What no one outside the Church bureaucracy knew was that the Vatican was under pressure to resolve many cases that remained secret. Often these problems were reported directly to the Pope during the one-on-one, "ad limina" visits that all bishops were required to attend at least once every five years.

The routine of the ad limina meetings made it possible for the Pope to be more fully informed of conditions in the worldwide Church than anyone else. He required these contacts because he held direct authority over all of the bishops of the Church. The Pope also represented the court of last resort for anyone appealing for action against a priest who had committed crimes or for priests seeking to retain their faculties after an accusation had been made. Rome was generally sympathetic to the rights of priests. Bishops who requested a canonical investigation of one accused of sexual abuse could expect that years would pass before anything substantive occurred.

Of course requests for canonical trials and reports on criminal priests were not publicized by the Church. Thus, no one outside the Church bureaucracy knew that in July of 1996 Milwaukee Archbishop Rembert Weakland wrote to Ratzinger asking for help with two priests who were the subjects of sworn statements accusing them of sexually abusing minors. One, Lawrence Murphy, had long worked at a residential school for the deaf where he had sexually assaulted many boys. Weakland said that he had become aware of these cases within the past year and was turning to Ratzinger because the offenses were "under your jurisdiction."

Transferred from Hulbert Field in Florida to an isolated airstrip in the Portuguese Azores, Thomas Doyle no longer had easy access to old friends in the Church and other sources who kept him informed on what might be happening behind chancery doors. He found his new assignment pleasant enough. His home was a little two-bedroom house atop a hill that overlooked the flightline. Fellowship was available at local Alcoholic Anonymous meetings and the other officers on the island welcomed him warmly. With some help he began a food program for the poor that operated out of an unused wing of the base hospital and he organized volunteers to repair homes in poor neighborhoods. Engaged as he was, he missed being, as he termed it, "in the know" and he remained concerned about how the Church responded, or rather failed to respond, to abuse victims.

A few reporters who had interviewed Doyle during the height of the abuse scandal kept in touch by phone; so did Richard Sipe and Ray Mouton and a handful of lawyers who continued to press abuse claims. Dallas-based attorney Sylvia Demarest, who had visited Doyle in Florida, called regularly to keep him informed about a case she was working with a famous litigator named Windle Turley. Turley, who once thought he'd become a preacher, had recently won a $105 million verdict against General Motors for a faulty truck design that contributed to three hundred accident deaths. In 1993 he and Demarest teamed up to represent several young men who said a priest named Rudolph "Rudy" Kos had raped and molested them when they were as young as nine. By the time the case neared trial, the number of plaintiffs had reached eleven and included the parents of a victim named Jay Lemberger, who had committed suicide by shooting himself at age twenty-one. Rudy Kos had conducted the funeral.

Working for the better part of three years, Turley and Demarest conducted more than 150 depositions as they prepared their case. Although high courts in other states such as Minnesota, California, and New York were limiting victims' access to the judicial system, the two Texas lawyers worked as if they were certain of a trial. The effort was a demonstration of virtues Demarest cherished most — persistence and the ability to delay gratification — that she had acquired very early in life.

Like Raymond Mouton and Minos Simon, Demarest was a Cajun with roots that grew deep into Louisiana's past. Her family settled in watery Cameron Parish, on the Gulf shore, before the Civil War. Demarest was born in the summer of 1944 to parents who spoke patois French. She picked cotton as a child and learned the concept of negligence on the day when herbicides used at a neighbor's farm killed the entire Demarest crop. Observing that "there are people with power and people without power" she did everything she was told she couldn't do, including going to college and then law school at the University of Texas.

After passing the bar exam, Demarest took legal aid jobs and spent much of a decade suing various institutions on behalf of the poor. Next, in private practice, she took on cases ranging from medical negligence to sexual harassment. Her first clergy abuse client was a young man who was fourteen when he was sexually assaulted by a priest who had invited him to the military base where he was serving and got him drunk. The boy was discovered running naked around the base housing complex. He was brought home by a second priest who promised to explain what happened to his parents, but in fact said nothing.

At the start of the Kos case, Demarest and Turley consulted with Jeff Anderson, who gave them a quick survey course on the record-keeping practices of the Church and suggested the sources they might pursue to discover what the officers of the diocese knew and when they knew it. Anderson also urged Turley and Demarest to cooperate with reporters who might want to publicize the case. In his experience, media reports often prompted calls from witnesses and other victims whose statements propelled the discovery process. The Dallas attorneys had the same experience after the press reported on the suit. As Demarest would later recall, a host of key witnesses called her out of the blue to say their complaints to bishops about Kos and other priests had been ignored.

As they investigated, the lawyers learned that Fr. Kos had been married and divorced and had obtained an annulment in order to become a priest. When church officials considered his candidacy for the priesthood they heard from his ex-wife, who told them that Kos "was gay and was attracted to boys." The lawyers also learned that Kos's brother informed the Church that Rudy had molested him when they were both children. Despite these warning signs, Kos was ordained and placed in parishes where, from the very start of his ministry, people reported him keeping minors in his room overnight. After many complaints the diocese consulted a social worker who determined Kos was a "classic, textbook pedophile." Kos orally and anally raped or molested boys as young as nine, often giving them drugs or alcohol to make them compliant. He had a foot fetish, which moved him to masturbate with boys' feet, and many of his victims said they had been abused by the priest hundreds of times.

In an effort to put Kos in some context, Demarest and Turley turned to Doyle and Sipe, who provided expert witness statements and promised to testify if needed. Based on what they heard from these insiders, Demarest and Turley believed they saw a broad conspiracy throughout the Church in America and targeted the national bishops' conference as well as the local diocese. They commissioned Doyle to write a report that laid out the responsibilities assumed by various bishops of the Church and showed how higher authorities, including the national bishops' conference, might be liable for the damage done to his victims. Doyle was most definitive when it came to questions about standard Church practices regarding priests who abuse minors and claims that the problem was something new and not well understood. He wrote:

The sexual abuse of adults, adolescents and children by the Catholic clergy is not an issue that only began to happen in 1984. It has always been a serious problem for the Church. This is evidenced by the fact that there is on record Church legislation going back to the fourth century concerning priests who sexually abuse people but especially children. This legislation was first codified in 1917 and revised in 1983.

In modern times, Doyle noted, bishops have known that clergy who abused minors were committing criminal acts and went to great lengths to protect them and keep their crimes secret. When complaints arose, the subjects were transferred and victims were persuaded to stay quiet. "Evidence from cases across the country indicates there has been a conscious and organized cover-up of this problem," added Doyle. "There is little evidence that I know of that Church officials followed State reporting statutes and reported incidents of child abuse to civil authorities."

Richard Sipe had come to view sexual secrecy as the main problem of the clergy, and believed it governed behavior throughout Catholicism. Much of what he wrote was based on his own research, which was leading him to ever-more-painful conclusions about the institution that had served as the foundation for much of his life. As he would recall it, "priest by priest, person by person, student by student, consult by consult, text by text" he had found further evidence that the Church was rife with sexual blackmail and cover-ups that were both the cause and the product of great suffering. Then an attorney from Arkansas named Morgan "Chip" Welch travelled to Sipe's home in Maryland to ask him to testify in court for the first time.

Welch and Sipe sat at a big round oak table that had been made at St. John's Abbey. Sipe was moved by Welch's story of a young girl who had been assaulted by a priest, but he was reluctant to appear in court and issue opinions. Then his wife and research partner Marianne asked him if he didn't have a duty to help the victim in the case. Sipe chose to testify. The victim won more than $1 million. Sipe's abbey-built oak table became the place where dozens of attorneys (including Sylvia Demarest) and reporters and victims sat to ask and receive similar help. In the process, Sipe would also continue a painful personal reassessment of Catholicism and the institutional Church he once gave his life to. Sometimes this experience made him feel depressed, if not despairing. But he found that once he started working for victims and their supporters, he could not turn away any of them.

For his report to Demarest, Sipe used his own data and also cited a recent survey of Spanish priests that found that more than a quarter of them had "acted-out sexually with minors" and an American study that found a similar number of Franciscan friars at one Catholic school "had inappropriate sexual contact with minor students." In the United States, the national bishops' conference set guidelines for the selection and training of priests and for responses to abuse claims. In Sipe's view this group should have warned the public about dangerous priests and had failed to meet its obligations to keep certain men out of ministry.

Turley and Demarest hoped that the Doyle and Sipe reports would allow them to sue national Church agencies but in pretrial rulings Judge Anne Ashby found the responsibility for Kos stopped with the Diocese of Dallas. However, this was one of the few rulings that went against the plaintiffs. At other key junctures Ashby threw out a First Amendment defense raised by the Church, and she accepted delayed discovery of harm arguments that helped the plaintiffs get around the statute of limitations.

The essential arguments in the case were clear to Demarest long before the jury was even selected. She saw Kos as "a sexual predator with a long history of preying on little boys before he ever became a Catholic priest." Warnings about his behavior had been ignored by higher-ups who failed to investigate despite repeated complaints. On the other side of the case, Randal Mathis, who would represent the diocese, settled on a strategy that would paint Kos as a brilliant deceiver who victimized his bosses as well as the boys he abused. "Kos is a serious, serious sociopath," he said before the trial began in May 1997, "and he's good at fooling people."

The proceedings were held in a small courtroom in the George S. Allen Courthouse on Commerce Street, directly opposite the austere plaza that memorializes the assassination of President John F. Kennedy, which occurred a block away in 1963. From the start, no one contested Rudolph Kos's sociopathy. The sides also agreed that he had committed the acts described by the plaintiffs, including the rape of a preteen boy who had become unconscious after the priest gave him alcohol. Providing his victims with drugs and drink were part of Kos's routine. He also brought boys on vacation trips and kept them overnight in his bed. During trial, two young men testified that Kos had abused them hundreds of times when they were minors.

Details of the abuse were offered without much objection from the defense and a bishop named Michael Sheehan even apologized on the witness stand for what had happened, saying:

> I thought he was a good man and would be a good priest. He deceived us. I'm deeply saddened by what Rudy Kos did to his victims. I apologize to the victims and their families.

Sheehan's statement reflected the dilemma experienced by many bishops in abuse cases. They felt pastoral desires to comfort faithful Catholics who had been betrayed, but also believed they should defend Church coffers and protect its special status under the Constitution. This second priority — defending the Church — put them in the position of deferring to attorneys. The lawyer for the Dallas diocese chose not to emphasize these arguments but instead focused on the efforts made by the Church as it followed its due process and was ill-served by experts. "The diocese relied in a number of instances — and now wish it hadn't — on the advice of doctors that turned out to be very, very wrong," he said. "We as a diocese have egg on our faces today. We're embarrassed, upset, regretful. This diocese wasn't negligent. It was fooled with the help of a lot of other people."

For nine weeks the jury heard often sordid testimony about Kos's sexual behavior and complex descriptions of the canon law procedure for disciplining priests. Witnesses representing the diocese spoke about how they felt limited by the content of the complaints they received and constrained from taking action. Demarest would call two pivotal witnesses. Bishop Charles Grahmann steadfastly defended the way he and his predecessors responded to complaints dating back ten years or more. As Windle Turley pressed him to acknowledge that "red flags" of warning had been waving the bishop said, "They were yellow flags." Turley replied, "Unless you're colorblind. How are your eyes? Do you see well?"

The second key witness for the plaintiffs was Thomas Doyle, who took the stand wearing a white collar and a black suit. Doyle thought to himself "bring 'em on" as he faced a courtroom packed with clergy — he called them the "Dallas Sanhedrin" — and contradicted much of the testimony offered by Church officials. He said that the bishops had possessed the authority, under Church procedures, to move suspected abusers out of ministry quickly. As he addressed Church procedures, Doyle spoke as a canon law expert. When asked to assess the clerical culture, he spoke as a still-active priest with broad experience. His most powerful contribution came when Demarest referred to a bishop's testimony in the trial and asked, "Would a bishop lie?" Doyle replied, "I know a bishop would lie, and he did."

The judge prepared a forty-three-page questionnaire for the jurors to consider as they reviewed the case. Altogether the answers would determine, among other facts, whether Kos and the diocese had harmed the plaintiffs in ways that affected their lives in an ongoing basis. They were asked to consider whether the Church had committed fraud, concealed information, and conducted a conspiracy to hide crimes committed by Kos. Finally, they were to weigh whether years of abuse by Kos was the "proximate cause" of Jay Lemberger's suicide. Once all these issues were resolved the jury could determine compensation for the victims and, if they found "gross negligence" by the diocese, they could award punitive damages.

After Judge Ashby gave the jury their charge and they departed, she asked the plaintiffs and defendants to wait a moment before leaving the courtroom. She took off her black robe and told the court reporter to stop making a record. She then came off the bench, took a seat in the jury box, and began to speak, not as a judge, but as a person who had been deeply affected by the proceedings. The only record of what she said was published by *The Dallas Morning News* and its reporter, Brooks Egerton. In her account she wrote that the judge addressed both parties and said:

> If anything like this can ever be positive, then let there be healing and let there be hope . . . everybody in this courtroom has been grieving. . . . You've been horrified. You've been hurt. You've been miserable. I've been so close to your tragedy it just breaks my heart.

As Ashby spoke, the young men who brought the lawsuit leaned forward in their front-row seats so they could catch every word. "Each and every one of you is a valuable member of this community," said Ashby as she addressed the plaintiffs. "I know that your Church and your God is very, very important to you. Don't give it up." Turning to the defendants she said, "You're never going to be the same again, but you're going to get through this. The Church has many wonderful things ahead of it." When she finished talking Ashby volunteered to answer questions from anyone in the courtroom. One lone woman raised her voice to praise the judge for her conduct in the case and then the crowd in attendance burst into applause.

Unprecedented in the experience of any of the lawyers present, Ashby's monolog left defense attorney Randal Mathis stunned, red-faced, and at a loss for words. Demarest and Turley were quietly thrilled by Ashby's remarks but they were also sensitive to the possibility that the judge might rule on future motions. They restrained themselves when asked to comment. Turley allowed that what she had done was "unusual" but he insisted it was not "improper."

More unusual jurisprudence came when the jury reported it had reached a verdict. Their notice to the judge had included a message they wanted read aloud. She agreed to the request, but wanted their findings announced first. As Ashby looked down on the packed courtroom she saw the young men whom she had counseled and about sixty of their friends and family gathered around them. Conspicuously absent from the courtroom were the bishops of Dallas. Only a single monsignor sat with defense attorneys as Ashby announced that the jurors had found for the plaintiffs and awarded actual and punitive damages of $119.6 million to be shared by about a dozen victims.

The number reached by the jury was so large that some in the courtroom had trouble grasping it. As the shock passed, Ashby called the courtroom to order and said that she had agreed to read the jury's message. Its most important passage began with a declaration that the Church, in considering abuse claims, should recognize that "the child is of the utmost importance." The jurors also called for the Dallas Diocese to adopt stricter rules and practices regarding clergy conduct and added a plea. "Please admit your guilt," they said, "and allow these young men to get on with their lives." As Ashby fell silent, the plaintiffs, their families, and friends stood as one and applauded for a full thirty seconds.

If required to pay the plaintiffs nearly $120 million, the Diocese of Dallas might go bankrupt. With this in mind defense attorney Mathis promised appeals that he would take all the way to the United States Supreme Court. However, such an appeal would have put the Church in danger of adverse rulings which, issued from a federal courthouse, might establish the kind of precedents that the Church as a whole wanted to avoid. Appeal would also keep Rudy Kos in the news for as long as the process required. The diocese was already suffering withering attacks even from conservatives like William F. Buckley, a Catholic, who suggested the Church "Crank up the polygraph, FBI style, and then ask the postulant: 'Have you ever, with sexual motive, fondled a boy?' "

Faced with such image problems the Church negotiated a settlement that required a far lower payment — $23.4 million — but also a formal apology. Rudy Kos learned of the agreement while serving a fifteen-year prison sentence he received after being convicted on criminal charges. In a prison interview he told a reporter that he too was a victim and that given the chance he would ask his victims for forgiveness. "If I offended you, you know, tell me, give me your forgiveness, let me make it up to you, let me do something," he pleaded. "That is the way it is with all sin."

17.
OLIVER O'GRADY

The Kos verdict showed that some judges and some juries were willing to set aside the statute of limitations and punish a priest whose crimes were proven and a diocese that failed to protect children. False memory, the Bernardin affair, and the Pope's moral vision had not been considerations for the court in Dallas. Instead, the jury weighed the documentary evidence and witness testimony as they would in any fraud and negligence case. In the end they denied the Church special protections under the First Amendment and found it responsible for one of its priests in the same way any corporation would be responsible for an employee.

For lawyers representing Catholic institutions, the Kos decision represented a terrible outcome in a case that should have been settled but might now embolden other plaintiffs. For Jeffrey Anderson it felt like an affirmation of his commitment to a cause that had come to consume his career.

Anderson had long been convinced that men with sexual problems sought shelter in the Church. As priests, they gained the trust of others and the power to abuse them. Even when they were found out, the Church protected them in ways no other institution would. At the core of this problem was the very tool the Church employed to solve it: an ancient view of sex that was impossible to fulfill and filled believers with guilt and shame. Catholic sexual prohibitions, and the feelings they engendered in priests who failed to comply, made it impossible for them to deal with their sexuality forthrightly. As long as the Church fostered sexual shame in so many people, it would never escape its crisis.

Shame was something Anderson understood at a gut level, although he wouldn't have admitted it to anyone. In the years after Bernardin and Blackowiak, which shut down many of his cases, he promised to control his drinking but always failed. At the office his colleagues pressed him to account for the debt he ran up in his travels around the country. He insisted his work was going to pay off and kept on spending. At home he was alternately repentant, ashamed, and resentful. Unable to sleep, on most nights he kept pouring until he fell asleep.

Through more than a decade of drinking, Anderson managed to hide his problem from almost every colleague, client, and consultant. The one exception was an attorney in Illinois who brought him into a case against the Diocese of Belleville, which was just east of St. Louis. As Anderson would recall, he once flew into St. Louis, spent the night drinking, and overslept a morning deposition. He arrived "late and smelling like a goat." The local attorney, Diane Spier, said nothing at the time but telephoned after Anderson was back in Minnesota. "She asked me if I didn't think I had a problem with drinking," said Anderson. "I told her I appreciated her concern but 'No, I didn't have a real problem.' The call didn't make me think I might be an alcoholic but it did horrify me. For a minute she put the mirror up. I put it down real quick and made sure I was more careful."

The worst for Anderson came on a trip to Reno where he met up with Tom Doyle, who was sober and was trying hard to stay that way. During the day, the two men worked together with clients. At night Anderson went out alone and gambled and drank. He slept through his departing flight and woke up, still too drunk to drive to the airport. His body was bruised and scraped, but he had no memory of an accident or fight. When he finally got sober and returned home, he found a $5,000 casino charge on his credit card and had no idea how it got there.

Through even the worst of his addiction,

Anderson managed his cases well enough. At the office he seemed to be focused and engaged. However, he had to pour enormous amounts of energy into covering up his problems and explaining his absences, especially to his wife. As he lived with the fear of being found out, Anderson believed he knew how the priests and bishops he pursued in lawsuits thought and felt. At depositions he saw something familiar in their eyes. It was the fear of men with secrets.

Anderson feared most the loss of his wife and family. Finally convinced that this could happen, he decided that the party set for his fiftieth birthday — August 7, 1997 — would be his last drunk. Telling no one but Julie, he downed blue martinis until he couldn't speak or even stand up. In the morning he called a therapist who saw him immediately and told him, "You have a chance to fix everything before it really gets broken." He recommended outpatient treatment for thirty straight days. Before signing up, Anderson called his old friend Grant Hall, who had been sober for more than a decade. The two met for lunch.

"I know I'm an alcoholic," said Anderson. "And I'm ready to do something about it."

Hall brought Anderson to his "home" meeting of Alcoholics Anonymous, which was held on Sundays at a county social services building in the St. Paul suburb of White Bear

Lake. The next day Anderson began outpatient rehabilitation. He went every day for thirty days and never slipped. In that time he accepted that he was an addict who, as the first of the Twelve Steps says, was "powerless over alcohol." He worked on the rest of the steps, from seeking the help of a "higher power" to making amends to others in a halting way. And even after he left the day program, he did not drink.

On any given day, AA in the St. Paul area offered morning, afternoon, and evening meetings. At these sessions, where people pray, testify, and encourage each other, Anderson struggled with the steps that are hardest for most people — the ones about God, and his own failings. His "moral inventory" included a long list of lies, deceptions, and betrayals. He had broken drug laws and traffic laws, his own moral code, and the rules of golf. Perhaps the only virtue he could claim was that he didn't hold others to a standard higher than his own, unless, as in the case of priests and their bishops, they set themselves above others.

Sobriety didn't make Anderson's life easier. Without the anesthesia of drink, problems that were once ignored became real, and feelings that had been denied became sharp, painful, almost unbearable. Instead of peace, recovery brought demands that he face up to his own ego and a long history of failures in his personal relationships. The work was difficult and full of the bitter taste that comes when a man must incorporate all the dark elements of human nature — pride, hypocrisy, self-indulgence, etc. — into his self-concept.

It was in this time that Anderson, who harbored serious doubts about the existence of a supernatural God, developed a strong moral code organized around what he called "rigorous honesty." Certain that his sobriety depended on telling the truth, he became open about everything in his life and used candor as an antidote to his long-standing habit of secrecy and deception. In AA meetings, with friends, and with Julie he shared his past sins and insights into his own flaws. Among these were a lack of grandiosity, impulsivity, and a tendency to be oblivious to the feelings of others and his effect on them. Although he felt a great deal of grief about these things, he eventually understood that acknowledging these problems helped him to understand others, including the churchmen he confronted in his work. Sexually abusive priests and bishops who covered for them were tragically flawed individuals who couldn't find a way out of the trouble they had created. Anderson, who had tried and failed so often in his own life, could relate to their pain. He didn't approve of anything they had done, but he could imagine the inner conflict, shame, and desperation they surely felt.

Although recovery was almost a full-time job, Anderson still represented hundreds of clients who claimed clergy abuse in jurisdictions across the country. In one especially complicated case, two brothers in California called him to ask if he would represent them in a claim involving a priest who was a friend of the family. James and John Howard explained that they had been abused by Fr. Oliver O'Grady after the priest had been the subject of a report to the police and Church officials in Stockton, California, had promised to keep him away from children. Instead they had moved O'Grady to the parish where the Howard family worshipped, and he would be allowed to work alone. Although O'Grady had been convicted in a criminal trial for his crimes against the Howards, they wanted to take the diocese to court to win release of Church documents on O'Grady and compensation for their pain and suffering.

Anderson, who couldn't have found Stockton on the map when the Howards called, took the case and arranged for his old friend in Orange County, Joe Dunn, to serve as cocounsel. He then flew to the Northern California city to track down police detective Jerald Cranston, who had handled the criminal complaint against O'Grady. Cranston told him the investigation had produced enough evidence to support a prosecution, but it ended when Church officials promised to move O'Grady to a post where he would not work with children. The detective was shocked to learn of O'Grady's subsequent crimes, and agreed to testify about the arrangement that had ended his investigation.

The detective's recollection, added to documents that emerged in discovery and facts recalled by other witnesses, gave Anderson a firm basis to push for punitive damages. However, as he presented motions in the San Joaquin County court he found the judge consistently resisting his efforts. Frustrated and fearing his case was in danger, he asked Dunn for advice. Dunn recommended a switch in co-counsel. "Bring in Larry Drivon," said Dunn. Anderson didn't recognize the name, but he wrote down the number Dunn gave him, hung up the phone, and immediately dialed.

On the other end of the line Laurence Drivon spoke in a deep, slow voice, which sounded even slower juxtaposed with Anderson's excited description of his situation. "I have a case going to trial in two months. I'm in front of this judge and getting *hometowned* and I need your help. It's a clergy abuse case and it involves a cover-up by the bishop."

"Did the bishop know?" asked Drivon.

"Yes. The bishop knew and I can prove it, Larry."

"Well, sure, then. I'll help ya."

Unbeknownst to Anderson, Drivon was a local legend in Northern California who had learned much of what he knew while working with Melvin Belli of San Francisco. Belli had famously represented Jack Ruby in the killing of Lee Harvey Oswald and raised a Jolly Roger flag outside his office whenever he won a case. Under his tutelage, Drivon had learned to reserve his compassion for his clients and pursue defendants as aggressively as possible. When he met Anderson he felt like he was in the presence of a kindred spirit "who had everyone below Jesus in his sights."

The evidence in the O'Grady case included a confession the priest had written to a family in 1975 and testimony from higher-ups who confirmed that bishops had been informed, repeatedly, that O'Grady might be a pedophile. One of the bishops in question was Roger Mahony, who had left Stockton in 1985 to become archbishop and then cardinal of Los Angeles.

Mahony had been in charge when local police investigated a child abuse report against O'Grady in 1984. Stockton was a small diocese with about eighty priests. He knew O'Grady, who still spoke with the brogue of his native Ireland. Four years earlier he had heard complaints about

O'Grady's relationship with John and James Howard's mother. (Mahony thought the issue was serious enough to order O'Grady to stay away from her.) In the 1984 episode, the police report said that O'Grady had told a county health worker "he had contact of a sexual nature [with a child] approximately two weeks ago, and other past behaviors of a similar nature." The final entry in the police file on the case noted that Church lawyers had assured officials that "the suspect will be sent to counseling through the Church." A psychiatrist who evaluated him informed the diocese that, "Father O'Grady reveals a severe defect in maturation. Not only in the matter of sex, but more importantly in the matter of social relationships, and shows a serious psychological depression." The psychiatrist also questioned whether his patient was "truly called" to be a priest.

After O'Grady was evaluated and found to be suffering a "severe defect" Mahony assigned him to a new parish in the tiny rural community of San Andreas, far from where he had gotten into trouble, and placed no restrictions on his activities. Arriving just before Christmas, O'Grady installed a playpen in the Church rectory. Here, and in a later assignment at a parish eighty miles south in Turlock, he continued to molest children. Turlock was where he insinuated himself into the Howard family.

Since the damning facts were available to defense lawyers before the case got near to a courtroom, Drivon and Anderson expected the other side to offer an acceptable settlement. Their clients' main condition required that the record of the case remain open. No confidentiality agreements. No sealed documents. The defense wouldn't agree, and the two sides proceeded to select a jury. In questioning potential jurors through a process called voir dire, Drivon and Anderson didn't ask whether the men or women called to the courthouse liked trial lawyers or the notion of people filing lawsuits. (Drivon told Anderson that Stockton was so politically conservative he should assume that everyone hated plaintiffs' lawyers as a matter of principle.) The two lawyers did manage to exclude people who attended Catholic services on a daily basis, and those who believed, as a matter of faith, that men wearing collars always told the truth. However, several Catholics were part of the panel.

Jeff Anderson arrived in Stockton in the middle of June 1998, a few days before the trial. He had spent months preparing the case and doing very little else. His plan for trial included a sequence of fifteen witnesses — starting with Nancy Sloan-Ferguson, who first reported O'Grady as an abuser — and hundreds of pages of documents. He anticipated calling O'Grady and using him to testify against higher Church officials.

With less than a year of sobriety, drink still called to Anderson every day and he depended on AA meetings to get through most nights. In the past his spare time on the road would have been spent at bars and clubs where he would have instantly made friends who would consider him one of the most entertaining men they ever met. In Stockton, Larry Drivon introduced him to an alcoholic lawyer who had achieved more than a decade of sobriety.

This new friend, who identified himself only as "Robert" to preserve his anonymity, made himself available day and night. He brought Anderson to his home group, which had been running in Stockton for roughly fifty years, and made sure he could get to a meeting every single day of the week. At these sessions Anderson encountered farmhands, businessmen, clerks, and doctors. A few of the regulars seemed to be fellows who lived on the street. When Anderson stood to introduce himself — "I'm Jeff. I'm an alcoholic." — he got the same chanted welcome ("Hi, Jeff") he would have received at any AA meeting in the world. When he stood to "share," which meant talking about how he had hurt himself and others and now struggled to stay sober, Anderson did his best to speak directly and plainly and without trying to charm or entertain. During coffee breaks and in post-meeting chats, he made a conscious effort to stay focused on the steps, the slogans, and lessons at the core of AA.

After meetings and long talks with Robert, Anderson would eventually have to face his hotel room and the battle for sleep. Without chemical assistance, his racing mind flashed through images and thoughts like a strobe light firing in a darkened room. When the show inside his head got to be too much, he would flick on the bedside lamp and spend some time with the files and legal pads that he had arranged on the second bed in the room. During these sessions, Anderson absorbed the case so well that he could recall every detail and event better than he could recall the story of his own life.

All the study came in handy at trial where Anderson and Drivon shared the job of presenting their own evidence and witnesses and cross-examining those brought by defense attorneys. The details of O'Grady's offenses were more disturbing than the crimes reported in most other clergy abuse cases. A true sexual deviant, O'Grady's victims were both male and female and age didn't seem to matter to him. Scars had been found in the vagina of a two-year-old girl left in his care. He also had sex with at least two adult women who were mothers of his child victims.

As the details accrued, and the faces of the jurors betrayed their shock, defense attorneys offered higher amounts to settle. Anderson's new AA friend and fellow lawyer was stunned when he heard that an offer of $5 million had been rejected.

"What would it take?" he asked.

"There's not enough money in the fucking world," answered Anderson.

Profane as it was, Anderson's response to the settlement offer reflected the feeling in the courtroom as a series of witnesses recounted the many times they had warned the diocese about O'Grady. When she took the stand, thirty-three-year-old Nancy Sloan-Ferguson described how O'Grady had molested her when she was eleven. She held up the confession O'Grady had written in 1976 and recounted how, ten years later, she had spoken to diocesan officials about the danger O'Grady posed to children.

"I told them I was a rape crisis counselor, that I was concerned about the possibility that O'Grady was continuing to abuse children. I told them a pedophile was somebody who was sexually excited by children, that they had an incredibly high likelihood of repeat offending and that they needed to continue to monitor."

Although higher-ups said they did not understand the threat O'Grady posed, Drivon turned to items in the priest's personnel file that contradicted this claim. In a letter from 1980, a father complained that O'Grady took his two-year-old son out alone for long drives in a car. Another note from 1984 reported that O'Grady had admitted to feeling sexually attracted to children. Soon after this paper was placed in the file it was followed by a notice from a social worker assigned to see O'Grady. He said he was reporting the priest to child protective services. A monsignor who testified about the file said he didn't ask why the social worker was calling authorities but added, "I suspected it had to do with the acting out of urges toward a boy."

As they presented documents and testimony Drivon and Anderson taped big sheets of paper on the wall beside the jury where they wrote a time line and noted key moments in the case. Every time a witness made a point, they returned to the wall to point out connections between the testimony and events. All along the lawyers tried to show that O'Grady's superiors were partly responsible for his crimes. Repeated and documented complaints and suspicions, especially those related to pedophilia, should have made any supervisor take notice. This would be doubly true for leaders of an organization devoted to the care of a trusting community.

Drivon and Anderson suffered a setback when O'Grady, handcuffed and dressed in a prison jumpsuit, came to court from nearby

Mule Creek State Prison, where he was serving time for his criminal convictions. In the judge's chambers he listened as he was ordered to take the stand but then announced that he would not answer any questions. He invited the court to hold him in contempt and confine him, a penalty that would be meaningless since he was already in prison. Anderson and Drivon had expected O'Grady to implicate Cardinal Mahony in covering up his career as a child molester. Instead, he went back to Mule Creek without offering a word of testimony. Later, Anderson would find out that O'Grady had been promised compensation from the Church upon his release from prison, and further severance payments in retirement. Church officials denied that this money was intended to buy his silence.

Despite losing O'Grady as a witness Drivon and Anderson believed they had made their points well before they called the highest-ranking witness in the trial, Roger Mahony. As far as anyone on either side of the case knew, no cardinal had ever been sworn to testify in an American courtroom. In decades past, Mahony might have been excused on the basis of some First Amendment argument or out of respect for his position. However, the legal system had moved so far away from this kind of privilege that the defense didn't even ask for it. Instead, Mahony's attorneys

411

claimed he was too busy to attend and that the court should rely on his pretrial depositions. When the archdiocese said he was in Texas and couldn't travel to Stockton in time, Anderson hired a private jet for him to use. The defense then agreed to get him to the court on time.

Mahony appeared dressed in a deep black suit, black shirt, and stiff white collar. Well over six feet tall, with hair turning silvery gray, he towered over Anderson as he moved to the witness stand. Trained in social work and gifted in both communication and organization, Mahony had begun his life as a priest in farm fields and on street corners advocating for the poor. He became a bishop before he was forty. By 1998, as cardinal in Los Angeles, he was chief manager of a huge and ethnically diverse archdiocese. He moved in elite circles and counted the rich and famous as friends. A recent book had described him as the only American with a chance to become the Pope upon John Paul II's death.

With thirty-five years of public speaking experience Mahony had the skill to address the court in any number of ways. He chose to speak in a soft, low voice that was barely audible. "I was not informed that this priest had admitted to molesting a child," he said, referring to the police investigation of 1984. "That was not the information I was given. I was operating under the assumption that an allegation had been made, been thoroughly investigated, and dismissed."

Drivon and Anderson struggled against Mahony's explanation, noting that he had been bishop in one of the smallest dioceses in the country and supervised fewer than one hundred priests. Mahony himself had asked for the psychiatric evaluation that found O'Grady was seriously troubled. But he had reassigned O'Grady to San Andreas *before* it was completed. Why couldn't he have waited until after O'Grady was evaluated? And why didn't he take him out of ministry when the doctor issued his warning?

The way Mahony recalled it, the psychiatrist hadn't been alarmed. He had merely "found some difficulties that were all treatable." He trusted that O'Grady could continue in his work while he received some counseling.

Persistent questioning failed to move Mahony off his position and by lunchtime he had made a thorough and consistent claim that he had never been fully informed that O'Grady was a threat to children. Moreover, he insisted that his ignorance was easy to understand. He had been a busy man and left problems like O'Grady to others. The judge called a recess for lunch and a confident Mahony left the witness chair and strode into the hallway outside the courtroom. There he

413

was surrounded by reporters. In this moment he broke one of the basic rules for witnesses in trials: he answered questions. Worse yet, he answered questions with lawyers for the other side standing nearby.

With microphones pushed in his face Mahony quietly repeated the points he had made on the stand and added that "when we placed [O'Grady] in the parish we did everything we humanly could have done to make sure there was no problem there."

It wouldn't take legal training for someone to consider Mahony's claim and ask whether it was wise to send a suspect priest out to a distant parish if he knew extraordinary efforts were required to prevent him from molesting children. This was precisely the question Anderson asked when the judge reconvened the case and Mahony resumed his testimony.

"At the time, Cardinal, did you talk to the police?"

"No."

"You could have."

"Well, I'm not sure I could have."

"What was restraining you?"

With the cardinal on the defensive, Anderson pressed him for several minutes, forcing him to admit that during the time when he did "everything we could humanly do" he failed to speak to those who complained about O'Grady and didn't send him for treat-

414

ment with the Paracletes or some other specialist. He failed, even, to open O'Grady's personnel file and review it.

Jeff Anderson delivered the plaintiffs' closing argument, which included a reference to O'Grady as a "wolf in shepherd's clothing." He asked the jury to award his clients a total of $60 million, including $52 million in punitive damages. It was a home-run swing, but Anderson believed the Church had given him a fat pitch to hit. This kind of penalty was required, he said, because the diocese had neglected to control O'Grady, and allowed him to molest untold numbers of child victims. He asked the jurors to consider those children in their deliberations.

"A child feels some kind of special pain," he said. "A child has no past and has no future, he just lives in the present and lives it whole-heartedly. When he suffers, he suffers with his whole being."

The final argument for the diocese came from John Cotter, a defense specialist who practiced mainly in the state capitol of Sacramento. Cotter couldn't argue that O'Grady was innocent or that his client, the diocese, was blameless. A criminal trial had already established O'Grady was a sexual predator and the sum total of the evidence presented at the trial showed that Church officials failed, repeatedly, to determine what O'Grady was up to and protect the public.

With no other option, Cotter told the jury that the diocese of Stockton "has gotten the message, and it's not going to happen again," Cotter said. A big penalty would only harm everyday Catholics and an institution that served the community well. "I'm asking you," said Cotter, "not to interfere with that."

A week later, the jury finished work and ordered the defendant to pay the Howard brothers $29 million, which was almost half the amount their attorneys recommended. The jury award, which called for more per person than the Kos case, proved that that outcome was not a fluke. Lawyers who brought timely abuse cases with solid evidence of serious crimes could get into court and win enormous sums. This was a defining moment in the clergy abuse crisis.

While his clients embraced, Jeff Anderson stood for a moment in shocked silence. (He was alone at the moment when the verdict was issued because, to Anderson's amazement, Drivon was travelling to attend an annual art sale he never missed.) Then the two young men hugged him, as well. Afterward they discussed the appeal that would inevitably come and how they might handle negotiations over a final settlement. Ultimately the brothers would accept a total of $7.5 million.

In the past, win or lose, Jeffrey Anderson would have started drinking before sunset and reach oblivion sometime after midnight.

In Stockton he decided it would be best for him to get home as soon as possible. A red-eye flight from San Francisco would put him into Minneapolis before 8 A.M., but it wouldn't depart San Francisco until about eleven o'clock. Anderson decided to just drive to the airport and wait. The main problem was there would be the many bars available in the concourse. His AA friend Robert volunteered a solution.

"Just call me when you get there," he said. "We'll talk for as long as it takes."

It took more than five hours, as Anderson sat at a pay phone in an airport waiting area and kept the receiver pressed to his ear. In that time the two men discussed everything from the law, to family, to their childhoods, and their hopes for the future. Both men dwelled on regrets. Anyone with a shred of self-awareness has them. Drunks carry them like masons hauling bricks up a ladder. Talking lightens the load, and in the end the conversation was so reassuring and cathartic that when he was called to board, Anderson knew he could fly without ordering a drink. He made it home sober.

The size of the O'Grady verdict and a cardinal's appearance as a witness made the Stockton case national news. All the publicity inspired other victims of O'Grady to contact attorneys and soon more claims were filed.

The wildfire dynamic was the same wherever a major case was tried in the courts or revealed in the press. It happened in the Gauthe case in Louisiana, in the Adamson case in Minnesota, and with Porter and Kos. Typically the original plaintiffs' attorneys would hear from victims of the same priest abuser, or their families. But almost as often, the publicity would prompt complaints about other priests.

And then there were the charges that arose in other dioceses as men, women, and children were motivated by press accounts datelined from some distant city to bring allegations against a priest in their local diocese. In San Antonio, the Catholic archdiocese was forced to arrange bank financing to obtain $4 million that would be paid to the families of seven boys who had been molested by a local priest. In Boston the archdiocese quietly paid millions of dollars — one report said the figure was as high as $10 million — to settle a dozen lawsuits filed by victims of a priest named John Geoghan. Other settlements were made by the Church in Bridgeport, Connecticut, and Portland, Maine, and dozens of new claims were filed around the country. However, the most startling development in the period after O'Grady arose in Palm Beach, Florida, where a sudden scandal drove a bishop from office.

Joseph Keith Symons was little known

outside of the Palm Beach area. His one previous brush with notoriety came in 1991 when he allowed the ABC television network to film an exorcism conducted in his diocese. The broadcast stirred controversy. When contacted by the press Symons confirmed that he had authorized the filming. "The Devil really exists," said Symons. "He is powerful and actively at work in the world." The bishop said the broadcast would "counteract diabolical activities around us."

When he suddenly retired in the middle of 1998, Bishop Symons issued a single-page public statement to the press confessing that he had molested five boys and noting that he had submitted his resignation to Pope John Paul II, who had accepted it. The head of the St. Petersburg diocese who took over Symons's administrative responsibilities offered a most concise version of the institutional church response to such cases when he observed, "The old theory was 'Make a good confession and sin no more,' " said Bishop Robert N. Lynch. "We never realized it was a disease."

By using words such "sin" and "disease," the bishop avoided expressing any feelings or mentioning that whenever a grown man had sex with minors he committed a serious crime. It was left to Symons's brother to vent emotions about the scandal. James Symons, who lived in a tiny house along the railroad tracks that cut through the town of Largo, Florida, told a reporter, "I'm glad our mother is dead." Reflecting on the brother he thought he knew well he described him as "damn sick" and asked, "How does he sit in a confessional, sit there and listen to others, with this on his mind?"

18.
BY OTHER MEANS

Arthur Budzinski, Robert Bolger, and Gary Smith had each been sexually assaulted by Father Lawrence Murphy when they were boys at St. John's School for the Deaf, near Milwaukee. For nearly two decades they had tried to use the convoluted system of Church justice to hold him responsible. Finally fed up with delays and diversions, they decide to drive to Murphy's summer home on a lake in the small town of Boulder Junction. It's the first day of the summer of 1997. The trip takes more than four hours. Arthur films the expedition, creating a record that will later be presented in court.

In tiny Boulder Junction the men look for a spot on the road where two Texas license plates — both read 1IRISH — have been nailed up to mark a dirt road that leads off the pavement. As the car makes the turn they also see a cluster of white-painted wooden arrows on a post. The arrows bear family names. MURPHY is written on one in black letters.

Father Murphy had been a fixture at the St. John's school for almost thirty-five years, serving first as assistant director and then director. As the three men knew, in that time he had used his authority and his status to access, abuse, and silence as many as two hundred boys. He approached some in the beds at night and others when they came to him for confession. When reported to a bishop by a fellow priest, he talked his way out of trouble by insisting that his efforts at sex education had been misunderstood.

When they were young adults, the Church and court system had offered Smith, Bolger, and Budzinski no real hearing for their complaints. Exasperated, the men had distributed homemade "wanted" posters showing Murphy's face, outside the cathedral in Milwaukee. Smith had gotten a lawyer and threatened to sue Murphy and the archdiocese. A nun summoned Smith to a meeting where he was paid $2,000 in exchange for his signature on a document recanting the claims, apologizing for "false" allegations, and promising to never make such accusations again. Not understanding the contents of the letter, he had signed.

The letter had prevented Smith from confronting Murphy in court, but it didn't bar him from doing so man-to-man. When the car stops at Murphy's small, white-painted cottage, the video shows an older woman standing outside holding a lawn chair. The men know her. She is known to them as "Sister Grace." As Bolger signs to her, she replies, also in sign, telling him to wait while she goes inside. Bolger gestures with quick and powerful movements. "He's been molesting boys for twenty-five years. How dare you live here with him?"

Sister Grace returns with an older man who is balding and a bit stooped. Father Murphy greets Bolger in sign and the two immediately begin to argue.

"We came here for sex," signs Bolger, ". . . you are a molester!"

Murphy, looking old and tired, tries to argue with him.

The confrontation lasts less than five minutes, but it's long enough for the men to force an apology out of their abuser. They also get an opportunity to shout, in sign, "You go to prison now!"

As Murphy escapes inside, Sister Grace stays behind to persuade Bolger that he's wrong about Murphy. "Bullshit!" he responds. She wants to talk to him about being a Catholic. He dismisses her, signing out the words, "I'm not talking about religion! I'm talking about child molestation!"

Before the video ends, the men remind Sister Grace that Murphy had molested boys at the cottage where she is living. As the elderly nun continues to defend Murphy, an exasperated Bolger cuts her off. "Oh forget it!" he signs, "I'm out of here!"

Just like their "wanted" poster, the home-made video about Lawrence Murphy and the sexual abuse of deaf boys would eventually become known around the world. But in the late 1990s, the video was nothing more than a cathartic inspiration for Smith, Bolger, and Budzinski because they had been assaulted by a priest in the state of Wisconsin. There, the state supreme court had decided that higher Church officials and organizations could not be sued for negligent supervision of personnel, even one who had assaulted scores of disabled boys who were entrusted to his care and would have great difficulty reporting the crimes to anyone who didn't know sign language.

At about the time when the filmmaking trio made their trip, a fourth victim, Terrance Kohut, wrote Murphy a long letter that recalled how he had enrolled at St. John's school after his father's suicide only to be abused countless times. He wrote:

I was numb with grief and fear and looked to you for some kind of comfort and security. You were all I had. No one at home signed. I could not communicate

424

with them. I turned to you and what did you do? You molested me, that's what. You took advantage of a lost little boy . . . Do you know that you really ruined my life? I could never trust men because I thought maybe they would molest me as you did. Do you remember that first time? I came to confession and you asked if I had been masturbating. Then you told me to pull down my pants. I will always feel the horror of that moment.

Often, while he was being abused, Kohut gazed at a crucifix on the wall, hoping for a divine intervention that never came. He wrote:

Can you imagine that? Can you? Jesus on the cross on the wall saw you coming every night to molest us. He must have been shocked and grieved every time. I hope he cried like we did, because we were innocent children, pure Christians, good altar boys, and cute lambs. I hope Jesus is very furious at you and will send you to hell very soon.

An elementary school teacher with a master's degree, Kohut had devoted much of his life to recovering from the abuse, which burdened him with shame, anxiety, and fear that grew worse as he kept the past secret out of feelings of guilt. Like many victims who are abused by trusted adults over long periods of times, he needed years to sort out his feelings and conclude that his assailant was wholly responsible for what had happened to him. In the meantime, Kohut struggled in relationships and, due to anxiety attacks, lost jobs and almost lost his marriage. In his letter, which he also sent to Archbishop Weakland and Pope John Paul II, he recalled the day when another boy walked to a local police station to report that Murphy had abused him and the priest persuaded officers that the child was mentally retarded and could not be believed. Kohut noted that Murphy had arranged for other priests, even one at another school, to molest St. John students. He described one young man who was so tormented by abuse that he spent years in a psychiatric hospital. Another of Murphy's victims had killed himself, he wrote. None of this suffering was ever considered by civil authorities thanks to a series of judicial rulings that barred them from filing suits.

The rulings that closed the courtroom doors to most clergy abuse victims in Wisconsin enforced a strict standard for the statute of limitations and gave higher Church authorities shelter under the First Amendment's provisions for freedom of religion. In one case the court said these protections "prevented state courts from determining what made one competent to serve as Catholic priest since such determination would require interpretation of Church canons, policies, and practices." In another important case brought by Jeffrey Anderson on behalf of seven men and women, the court denied clergy abuse victims the same leeway under the statute of limitations laws enjoyed by people who were abused by family members or psychotherapists. About a year after the decision, one of Anderson's clients committed suicide.

Eventually well over one hundred suicides would be connected to clergy abuse. A few shamed priests would be among the dead, and in one extraordinary case in Hudson, Wisconsin, a court would find that Fr. Ryan Erickson almost certainly murdered a man named Daniel O'Connell, who knew Erickson had abused children.

As a Wisconsin judge would ultimately find, O'Connell had decided to expose Erickson to the police. The priest learned of his intention and drove to O'Connell's funeral home, where he killed him with a gunshot to the head. James Ellison, who was working at the funeral home, ran in to see what happened and was also killed by the priest. Erickson fled and was not immediately connected to the killing by police.

Days after killing him, Erickson presided over O'Connell's funeral. Police investigated for about a year before they interviewed

Erickson and seized his computer. The next day, Erickson hanged himself from a church fire escape.

Records that emerged in the case showed that Erickson had long been the subject of abuse complaints but his superiors had permitted him to stay in ministry. When they learned this, the O'Connell and Ellison families retained Jeffrey Anderson to sue every bishop in the United States, demanding they disclose the names of accused offenders so communities could be warned in the way Hudson was not. The bishop of Wilmington, Delaware, did release a list, but all the others resisted and the court would not require them to comply with the request.

The tragedy in Hudson was actually exceeded in rural Kansas, where five young men who had accused the same priest of molesting them when they were altar boys killed themselves. Fortunately the overwhelming majority of abuse victims never reached the desperate point of self-destruction. A much larger number found more productive outlets for their responses to abuse. Thousands joined groups like SNAP, which offered them self-help meetings, one-on-one peer counseling, and opportunities to be public advocates for legal reforms. Many victims told their stories to reporters, who presented them in print and broadcast media. The stories found a receptive audience in a world where sexual ethics had evolved to the point where deception, the abuse of power, and betrayal of trust were regarded as important sources of harm.

Western societies were becoming more sensitive to the ways that position and power came into play in cases of sexual misconduct. This trend had begun in the 1970s as courts recognized that employees who were disciplined or denied benefits and advancement because they turned away sexual advances were victims of real discrimination. In the ensuing decades, courts found that employers could be held liable for the behavior of managers and workers and legislatures created new penalties for sexual harassment or discrimination based on gender or sexual orientation. While different branches of government brought legal changes, highly publicized events involving the more general abuse of power and the hypocrisy of men in leadership positions encouraged people to look askance at anyone who claimed great authority. From Watergate to Iran Contra to sex assaults committed by priests, the crimes of the powerful and their subsequent cover-up schemes gave ordinary people reasons to look everywhere for hypocrisy and self-dealing and to believe that reports of scandal were based in facts.

In this context, Jason Berry found himself receptive to shocking stories of sexual abuse and drug use by the Rev. Marcial Maciel Degollado, founder and leader of a religious order called Legionaries of Christ. Little known in America, the legionaries operated mainly in Latin America and Europe but maintained their worldwide headquarters in Hartford, Connecticut. In America they would enjoy the greatest protection from interference under the cover of the Constitution. However, those who considered themselves Maciel's victims felt free to bring their stories to Berry. The first had contacted him in 1993. That was when he began the long process of learning about Maciel, his order, and its place within the Church.

With hundreds of priests in service and hundreds more in training, the legionaries operated schools, seminaries, media, medical missions, and many other ministries. Maciel also founded a group for laypeople called Regnum Christi that claimed tens of thousands of members. Both organizations embraced intensely conservative Catholicism and supported the authority of the Pope. John Paul II ordained sixty of the order's priests in 1991 and invited Maciel to accompany him on visits to North America.

Working with a *Hartford Courant* staff reporter named Gerald Renner, Berry coauthored a series of articles exposing the complaints against Maciel, which included charges that he sexually abused boys as young as twelve. The allegations were made by a man who had been a priest and president of the Legionaries in America. Juan Vaca said he had first reported Maciel to higher Church authorities in 1978. The complaints went as far as the Vatican, but were apparently ignored.

The assignment for the *Courant* set Berry off on a reporter's odyssey that continued into the next decade and beyond. Much of what he discovered would appear in a book he coauthored with Renner titled *Vows of Silence* and a subsequent documentary film he produced based on the book. (A second book by Berry, *Render Unto Rome,* would explore the issues even more deeply.) Altogether, Berry's reporting would reveal Rev. Maciel to be a morphine-addicted man of the cloth who fathered between three and six children, stood accused of multiple counts of pedophilia, and had sexual relations with at least twenty seminarians. Maciel got away with it, in Berry's estimation, because he enjoyed support at the highest levels in the Vatican and sent large amounts of money to Rome. Much of this money was delivered as cash in envelopes handed directly to individuals in the Church bureaucracy.

Remarkably, Berry's reporting on Maciel caused barely a ripple in the American media. In part this was because the tale was incredibly complex and involved an institution that was little known in the United States. But

431

Berry also noticed that, in general, people were no longer shocked by reports on criminal behavior by Catholic clerics. By the end of the 1990s the phrase "pedophile priest" had appeared thousands of times in major newspapers and thousands more in smaller print outlets and on TV and radio broadcasts across America. Documentary filmmakers had addressed the subject in Canada, Ireland, and America and priest abusers were becoming a target for comedians. Denis Leary mocked them and the Church to a merciless degree in a national cable TV broadcast. But five years after Sinéad O'Connor was met by a blast of criticism when she tore up a picture of the Pope, Leary provoked no outrage.

Depending on one's perspective, Americans had either folded the problem of abusive priests into their overall concept of the Catholic Church, or they had become inured to the outrage. Fr. Thomas Doyle feared that as big cases like the ones in Dallas and Stockton were resolved, laypeople and clergy were becoming complacent about the problem. Fr. Doyle had continued to consult on abuse cases as he was transferred from the Azores to Tinker Air Force Base in Oklahoma and then to Ramstein Air Base in Germany. Each year brought him greater numbers of cases. Indeed, he would eventually deal with almost two hundred American dioceses. For the most part his involvement in a case was meant to signal to the Church that he was ready to testify and this threat often encouraged them to settle.

In trips back to the United States Doyle made a point of visiting with Richard Sipe, who had moved to La Jolla, California. The two renegades would walk along the water and talk about cases, men they knew in the Church, and their shared disillusionment. Doyle's temper was hotter that Sipe's, and he would often vent his frustration. "The Catholic Church is basically a crooked institution," he would say. "You know it. I know it. How is it that everybody else doesn't get it?"

Sipe understood the ambivalence of Catholics who could not reach a firm conclusion about the Church because he had long wavered in his own relationship to it. Born into the faith and seasoned in both the seminary and the priesthood, he had worked within the Catholic world most of his life. Though he was pained by the facts he had uncovered in his research, he had maintained his emotional attachment to the Church until he learned that his old order at St. John's had covered up abuse cases while he was chairing its sexual trauma institute. This realization, and the spiritual example he saw in Doyle and Jeffrey Anderson, converted Sipe to a new kind of spirituality. He saw in their example, as members of AA, a faith in action that seemed more selfless and sustaining. (Anderson's honesty about his past, which Sipe called "radical," was particularly inspiring to him.) To understand it better he stopped drinking and began attending meetings even though he was not technically an alcoholic. In the fellowship of sobriety he found a community and a unique and intriguing combination of self-determination and group support.

More solid in his sobriety with every passing year, Doyle would talk about himself as "a good AA guy." He would say, "I'm going to take care of my resentments so I'll be sober today and sober tomorrow." However, experience had taught him that this struggle, to contain his emotions, would require regular attention. The problem of abusive priests was broad and deep and the quiet resolution of hundreds of lawsuits had allowed the Church to escape making the kind of reforms needed to protect children. Instead of opening itself to change, it seemed to be perfecting the practice of quiet diversion and delay.

As Fr. Doyle knew, the Church was now facing challenges on sex abuse in countries other than America and in arenas beyond the courts. The summer of 1998 had found John Paul II in Austria where he tried to stem the defections from the Church caused by the abuse scandal that brought down Cardinal Groer. The percentage of Catholics in the country was in the middle of a long, steady decline. Hundreds of thousands of Austrian Catholics had signed petitions opposing the Church on matters of sexual morality and the country was the center of an Internet-based organization formed to promote the power of laypeople within the institution. But while he told Austrians "Don't leave the Church!" the Pope did not mention Groer, or the disillusionment of ordinary believers. At the historic Heldenplatz, where Hitler had announced Germany's annexation of Austria, the Pope appeared draped in bright green vestments and wearing a tall white and gold miter. He warned against "premature or inadequate involvement of public opinion" in matters of faith and morals. In other words, the crisis in Catholicism was a matter of too much talk among ordinary Catholics.

Standing in the vast square among 50,000 people, one Catholic priest felt deeply disappointed in the Pope. Rev. Eduard Fischer was one of the many men who had said that Cardinal Groer had molested them when they were young. In response, Fischer's bishop had disciplined him in the way that bishops refused to discipline priests accused of sex crimes. He immediately dismissed Fischer from his parish position. A faithful priest devoted to Christianity, Fischer considered his own experience, and what he heard at the Heldenplatz, and said, "The Pope is visiting a burning house, but instead of speaking about the fire, he talks about the lovely flowers in front of it."

Bad as things were for the Roman authorities in Austria, they were worse in Ireland, where an intensely traditional Catholic society was rapidly throwing off its old attitude of obedience. Here the media played a far bigger role than the courts as a series of print and television reports revealed both individual cases of minors being abused by priests and the systemic maltreatment of Irish children in schools and institutions operated by Catholic orders.

The process began in 1993 when the Sisters of Our Lady of Charity in Drumcondra sold land near their convent to developers as property values began to rise across Ireland. The run-up in real estate prices heralded the arrival of the Celtic Tiger, an economic boom that transformed the country from one of the poorest in Europe to one of the richest. It occurred thanks mainly to policies that encouraged foreign countries to build manufacturing and operation facilities that took advantage of a well-educated but underemployed workforce. By the mid-1990s, 40 percent of the computer software used in Europe would come from Ireland and a country that long sent young people abroad to find work became a net labor importer. Farmers and other large landholders became rich overnight as builders in need of sites for industry, housing, and retail centers snapped up properties at record prices.

After their land deal was made, the nuns in Drumcondra discovered that more than a hundred women had been buried on the land they had sold. The bodies were dug up and cremated. Local reporters, curious about how a cemetery could become a development, discovered that the women had lived and worked in servitude at one of twenty so-called Magdelene laundries. They had been placed by families or various authorities because they were pregnant out of wedlock, accused of prostitution, or orphaned. Locked in at night and required to work without pay for twelve hours per day, these outcasts often remained at the laundries for years, even decades. More than 30,000 women had been relegated to these institutions over the years. Their plight had been known, but never recognized, as shame and respect for the Church silenced families, authorities, and the women themselves.

Stories published in local papers led to a public outcry and a play and a film about the Magdelene laundries. It also prepared the Irish public for a searing, three-part television documentary — *States of Fear* — that revealed generations of abuse and the Dickensian conditions in a Church-run system of residential schools and reformatories for poor and troubled children. Filmmaker Mary Raftery documented sexual abuse, malnutrition, beatings, and neglect on a systemic scale. The nation was so appalled that Taoiseach (prime minister) Bertie Ahern addressed the parliament after the last episode of the series was aired. He promised the government would appoint a Commission to Inquire Into Child Abuse that would scour the country to document the extent of the mistreatment of children. "The government wishes to make a sincere and long overdue apology to the victims of childhood abuse," said Ahern, "for our collective failure to intervene, to detect their pain, to come to their rescue."

As Raftery's documentary series prompted an official inquiry and opened a national conversation on child abuse and Irish Catholic culture, the stories of individuals who had been abused by priests also came into view. In 1995 the Irish media revealed Andrew Madden's settlement over abuse perpetrated by a priest named Ivan Payne. The abuse Madden experienced beginning when he was twelve likely shocked the Irish public, but much of the outrage around the case came as Archbishop Desmond Connell declared that Church funds had "not been used in any way" to resolve the case. As viewers of the TV program *Prime Time* had heard, the settlement had been paid with Church funds lent directly to Payne. The bishop had looked into the TV camera and lied. As usual, the deceptions intended to deflect scandal were considered, by many, to be worse for the institution than the crimes committed by an individual inside it.

Soon after the Madden case became known, a priest named Sean Fortune was arrested and charged with twenty-two counts of sexual abuse of minors. In January 1996 authorities added forty-four new charges. Attempting to respond to critics, the Irish bishops issued what they called a Framework Document that seemed to set a standard for a prompt response to claims of abuse, including reports to civil authorities. But while the framework called for all bishops to adopt its policies, this never happened.

The bishops didn't act because Archbishop Luciano Storero, the Vatican's ambassador to Ireland, intervened. In a secret letter sent to every diocese he ordered the country's bishops to ignore their own plan, especially the part about reporting claims to the police. Storero noted that canon law gave accused priests options that might well thwart the kind of quick action the bishops hoped to take. He also expressed "moral" reservations about mandatory reporting to police. Besides, wrote Storero, the Vatican had commenced "a global study" of abuse policies and "will not be remiss in establishing some concrete directives with regard to these policies."

439

■ ■ ■ ■

Like everyone else in Ireland, the young man whose charges led to the arrest of Sean Fortune had no idea that the country's bishops were caught between their own need to respond to a growing number of complaints about criminal priests and the power of the Holy See. Colm O'Gorman knew only that he wanted to stop Fr. Fortune from raping other boys in and around his parish in Wexford. When his complaint was followed by accusations from six other young men, O'Gorman agreed to be identified in the press and quickly became the public face of the issue.

O'Gorman's choice was brave in many ways. First, it required him to be honest with his entire family, including a very traditional Irish father, about his identity as a gay man. Second, he had to risk living "out" in a place where, as he told his father, "There are people who would cheerfully kill me for being gay." Finally there was the matter of challenging the Church in a country where Catholicism was practically universal and the institution was thoroughly entwined with the government and social organizations. Ninety percent of Irish elementary schools and half of the country's high schools were run by the Church. The influence of the Church had kept divorce illegal until 1995 and abortion remained so. Medical care was dominated by Catholic-run hospitals and even when the Church didn't own or operate a clinic its practices were ruled by a religious ethos. In one famous case, women had to fight to receive a new cancer drug at a state-run hospital because officials opposed a protocol that required doctors to prescribe birth control to patients they were providing with the medicine.

Despite the fear he felt in challenging the Church, O'Gorman described in detail the schemes Fr. Fortune used to get him away from his parents so that he could rape and molest him time and time again. In *Beyond Belief,* a book he wrote, O'Gorman described how, at age fourteen, he was awakened and anally raped by Fr. Fortune on a night when he had previously fought him off for the first time. He wrote:

I don't know how long I'd been asleep but I awoke to find myself forced over onto my stomach. I felt a searing pain as he forced himself inside me. His weight knocked the breath out of me and I couldn't speak. I was terrified. He didn't say a word to me. He treated me like an object. I wasn't human.

The brutal rape, which occurred when

O'Gorman's parents sent him on an overnight visit with Fr. Fortune, marked the end of the boy's resistance. He became submissive with the priest and in every aspect of his life. Schoolyard bullies became his tormentors and, perversely, the abusive priest became a kind of refuge.

The journalists who reported O'Gorman's story also pursued the usual questions about who knew what about Sean Fortune and when they knew it. For O'Gorman, the publicity brought empathy and affirmation. For the Church, it led to revelations of coverups that mirrored the actions of bishops in America who had ignored reports of abuse and sought a geographical cure for problem priests by moving them to new posts. The bishop of the Diocese of Ferns, Brendan Comiskey, who was Fortune's supervisor, left for America and inpatient treatment for alcoholism.

Following the pattern set in America, one well-publicized case prompted additional victims to come forward. More Irish priests were arrested and charged with abuse as Colm O'Gorman contacted an attorney to explore filing a civil suit against the Church in Ireland and the Vatican. At the same time he worked with prosecutors preparing to try Sean Fortune. In early March 1999, Fr. Fortune offered to plead guilty to minor charges but not to the rapes he had committed. When consulted, O'Gorman said he objected to any plea deal. Having learned the power of taking a public stand he told the lead counsel for the State:

I would be vehemently opposed to the dropping of any charge, and I would be very vocal in my opposition.

The trial of Sean Fortune began with the forty-five-year-old priest hobbling into the courtroom in Wexford on crutches. Fortune was dressed in clerical black and wearing a white collar and dark glasses with perfectly circular lenses. He demanded to be addressed as "Father" and asked to sit down during the recitation of the sixty-six crimes he was charged with committing against eight minors. Before this task was completed, Fortune began wobbling in his seat and then talking gibberish. When the priest's attorney asked for a delay so that doctors might judge whether he was fit to stand trial, the judge granted it. Days before he was to return to court, Fortune downed a lethal combination of drugs and alcohol. A housekeeper found him dead in his bed. At his funeral, Bishop Comiskey prayed that he would receive God's mercy.

Months after presiding at Sean Fortune's funeral, Comiskey joined the rest of Ireland's bishops in Rome where they met with Pope

John Paul II. Prepared to discuss the state of the Church in Ireland, the Pope noted the wealth brought about by the roaring Celtic Tiger but left out any mention of the nuns who capitalized on the boom by selling off their cemetery. Instead he concluded that the "exaggerated materialism, which sometimes accompanies increased material prosperity, has brought in its wake a declining sense of God's presence and of the transcendent meaning of human life." Some had begun to believe, added the Pope, "that the Church no longer has anything of relevance to say to the men and women of our day."

Though well-briefed on the extent of the clergy sex abuse problem in Ireland, the Pope chose to touch on it lightly. He stressed that given the "suffering of priests due to the pressures of the surrounding culture and the terrible scandal given by some of their brother priests, it is essential to invite them to draw strength from a deeper insight into their priestly identity and mission." John Paul II expressed solidarity with the bishops on this matter and asked they pray with him for the guilty. For their victims he recommended the "God of all comfort" and nothing else.

Denied a verdict in Fortune's criminal trial, Colm O'Gorman did include the Pope in a lawsuit that also named the Diocese of Ferns. As the Church paid €300,000 and issued a formal apology to avoid a trial, O'Gorman's suit provided an opening for the BBC to assemble a dramatic documentary that revealed that Church officials first learned of Fortune's crimes in 1982. The papal ambassador in Dublin and Bishop Comiskey had both failed to act as they heard complaints throughout Fortune's career. Besides his sexual crimes Fortune was known for embezzlement, manipulating elderly Catholics to give him their life savings, and concocting fake education and job schemes that cost donors millions of dollars.

As a sexual offender, Fortune used group "retreats" to isolate boys, get them drunk, and conduct orgies augmented with graphic pornographic movies. Reporter Sarah MacDonald also uncovered what she called a "pedophile ring" involving two priests and the principal of a seminary in Wexford. To put the response, or lack of one, in perspective she travelled to Germany to interview Tom Doyle. Fr. Doyle wore a black sweater but no collar for the interview. It was conducted in a small parish church that happened to sit across the street from Doyle's home. As a thank-you Doyle gave the accommodating pastor a bottle of Johnnie Walker Black whiskey.

In the BBC film *Suing the Pope,* which was aired across Ireland, Doyle decried the "arrogant, you know, self-satisfied attitude" of

445

Catholic bishops in the face of horrendous criminal behavior by priests. ". . . in many cases they've known. That's why these lawsuits have happened . . . that's why it has cost the Catholic Church in the United States alone over a billion dollars over a ten-year period. That's a lot of dollars." Fr. Doyle suggested that the Vatican, and perhaps the Pope, knew about Fortune all along and recommended the state prosecute "any leader or anyone who harbors a criminal."

While Doyle provided an insider's perspective, Fortune's surviving victims and the relatives of men who had committed suicide after he raped them offered heartrending testimony using terms such as "torture" and "anal rape." Many echoed the anger of O'Gorman, who talked about "bastards like Brendan Comiskey, hiding in his nice palace in Summerhill, behind his alcoholism and his regret and his, you know, his inability to understand or to do anything about it. It's not good enough; it's not good enough. It's not good enough anymore. People have died. People are dying. People are hurting."

Shocking as the abuse stories were, viewers may have been most startled by Sarah MacDonald's pursuit of Bishop Comiskey. The film ends with MacDonald and her camera crew staking out a church like detectives waiting for a drug deal to take place. When Comiskey arrives to say Mass they run to confront him as he gets out of a car. It was the type of scene that American viewers of programs like *60 Minutes* would have found familiar, but for an Irish public accustomed to seeing bishops treated with the utmost respect it was a television landmark. As she approaches, microphone in hand, Mac-Donald, who is a small woman with curly brown hair, calls out to the bishop who responds, at first, with as much charm as he can muster.

"Bishop Comiskey!" shouts MacDonald.

"We will survive, how are you?" answers Comiskey.

"I'm fine, thanks. Sarah MacDonald, BBC television."

"Sarah, how are you?"

"Very well, thank you. I've just come to ask you just a question about Sean Fortune . . ."

"I'm going to have Mass at half past six."

"We just wanted to know why didn't you stop Sean Fortune abusing young boys? Bishop Comiskey?"

"I-I-I moved. When it was brought to my attention I moved him out of the parish and sent him on treatment for two years."

"Not for six years. Not for six years, you didn't move him out of the parish. Why didn't you stop him?"

"Thank you very much."

It was the kind of thank-you an overly polite hospital patient might offer after a spinal tap.

Comiskey scuttled into the church. In the final minute of the film MacDonald reminds viewers that "Dr. Brendan Comiskey remains the Bishop of Ferns. Since Fr. Sean Fortune's suicide, six of his victims have begun legal action. So far, the Church's only response has been to deny liability and plead diplomatic immunity. Colm O'Gorman is suing the bishop, the Papal Nuncio, and the Pope."

In a nation of fewer than 4 million citizens, a documentary that presented so many victims in so many locales was felt quite personally by the people who saw it. If a viewer didn't know one of the men or women presented directly, it would be safe to assume that just a few degrees of separation stood between them. Certainly every Irish man and woman recognized the places where the abuse occurred and the bishops in charge of the criminal priests. The Irish government responded to the broadcast, and subsequent citizen uproar, by establishing a commission to investigate the Ferns Diocese and its handling of abuse cases. Bishop Comiskey promptly resigned. In the meantime, documentarian Mary Raftery completed a series on child sexual abuse by priests in the Archdiocese of Dublin. *Cardinal Secrets* was broadcast on the Irish national TV network RTE. Again the government promised an investigation.

By the end of 2002, three separate commissions had embarked on investigations of child abuse in the small country of Ireland. Inspired, in every case, by outspoken citizens and widely viewed media accounts, these commissions worked with the authority of the government and the power to obtain documents and witness testimony. Never before had civilian officials challenged the Church in such a direct and sweeping way. Never before had Irish society confronted long-simmering suspicions about the Church and its regard of children.

It was that status of children that concerned Colm O'Gorman most. As he would later note, Irish tradition held that "If you are a child, you do as you are told no matter what it is. Be good and everything will be okay. If things are not okay it's because you are bad." As O'Gorman saw it, abuse and neglect of children at the hands of families and the Church were endemic. "We are a brutalized society," he said, "where twenty-seven percent of men and women report they were abused as children."

Old-fashioned Irish Catholicism — rigid, punishing, controlling — formed the foundation of beliefs about children and had enabled centuries of abuse and neglect. "What's happened after *States of Fear* and *Suing the Pope* won't fix five hundred years of casual brutality," added O'Gorman. "But the films and the fact that the problem was no longer

449

anonymous started people talking and thinking differently about the Church, families and children, and the casual level of brutality that had been acceptable for a long time."

Remarkably, the economic rise of Ireland also played a significant role in the nation's sudden reconsideration of long-standing attitudes about authority and power. The money that built up the middle class allowed for greater access to higher education, more travel abroad, and an expansion of the mass media. These factors, as well as a spike in immigration, brought new ideas into the country and emboldened politicians such as Bertie Ahern to violate a long-standing taboo against criticizing the Church. Individuals including Andrew Madden and Colm O'Gorman were inspired to speak publicly about not just child abuse but also rights for homosexuals, lesbians, and women.

Perhaps the most powerful agent of change where the Irish Catholic Church was concerned was the example of America. For centuries Ireland had sent clerics and nuns to the States, where they seeded Catholic communities with an especially pious and sexually repressive brand of Catholicism. But during the Tiger years, the Internet and greater direct contact with the international community had reversed the flow. As both Madden and O'Gorman would eventually reveal, their actions were guided in large part by the example of the Americans who challenged the Church in St. Paul, Boston, Dallas, and Stockton. And even in 2002, as they watched the Church in Ireland reel under the weight of scandal, they understood that a much bigger drama was unfolding simultaneously on the other side of the Atlantic.

19.
PAPER CHASE

Michael Rezendes was always a document guy. In early 2001 he had mined records at courthouses and government offices to help expose shoddy practices by a major national construction company. With this proof, Rezendes and others on the Spotlight Team of *The Boston Globe* showed how executives misled consumers, skirted environmental regulations, and strong-armed people who stood up to them. Of course the story started with people who had bad experiences with the builder and wanted to talk about it, but the paperwork was the proof the *Globe* needed to proceed.

A decades-old institution, the Spotlight Team was one of the top investigative groups in American journalism and a plum assignment for Rezendes, who had worked for the *San Jose Mercury News* and *The Washington Post* before returning to his native city in 1989. Having grown up with the paper, he had always wanted a job in the *Globe* newsroom and even in his twelfth year there he felt real pride in his work. People all over New England depended on the paper to keep them informed and, occasionally, serve as a check on the powerful. It also functioned as a court of last resort for people with problems no one else would or could address.

Since documents made Rezendes's pulse race a little, he took notice when a confidential source visited the *Globe* in the summer of 2001 armed with a stack of files. The man, who said he had been the victim of a pedophile priest, spent three hours briefing the Spotlight Team on cases he knew firsthand, using the press clippings, affidavits, depositions, and court transcripts he brought to back up his recollections. As he told it, the Porter case of 1992 was just the tip of the iceberg. The Archdiocese of Boston had a much bigger problem involving dozens of priests, including some who were well-known public figures. The source then handed over records of the Rudy Kos trial. Study the way the Church behaved in Dallas, he said, and look for the same pattern here.

In the years since the Porter case, the *Globe* had reported the problem of priests who abused minors on a case-by-case basis, noting occasional complaints and lawsuits. When an accused priest named John Geoghan was defrocked in 1998, the report ran on the front page. But almost all the other stories about the issue were tucked inside the paper, where they didn't stir up readers. Then, in March 2001, the weekly Boston *Phoenix* ran a big article about Geoghan by writer Kristen Lombardi, who revealed him to be a true pedophile with many victims and complaints dating back to 1980. The priest stood accused of sexually assaulting hundreds of children of varying ages. His alleged crimes included many instances of oral rape of children as young as seven. The first complaints about him were made in 1973, and though they continued his superiors kept him in ministry until 1993.

Lombardi quoted Tom Doyle saying, "Geoghan is what you'd call a predator." Richard Sipe told the paper, "He is well known in the circles of those who treat priest pedophiles. He is notorious because he has been treated by so many people, at nearly every psychiatric hospital in the country." Sipe meant that Geoghan was known at nearly every one of the facilities that treated sex-offender priests, and this was true. In fact, Sipe had seen Geoghan with his own eyes inside Seton hospital in Maryland.

An alternative weekly in the muckraking tradition of New York's *Village Voice,* the *Phoenix* was not, like the *Globe,* New England's paper of record. Instead it was the place for edgier reporting that often broke new ground but without the authority of one of the country's most respected dailies. It was a little mosquito boat of a paper that could ask, as it did, how Geoghan "managed to get away with it" and tweak Boston's Cardinal Bernard Law with the suggestion that the abuse problem might force his retirement. The *Globe* was more like a battleship that required time and care to steer in the proper direction, but once its guns were trained on a target it could do enormous damage. If the *Globe* ever sought Law's retirement, it would likely happen.

Michael Rezendes would recall that his editors were careful in their relationship with the Church. The *Globe* and the archdiocese were among just a handful of leading institutions in the city. Founded by members of the Protestant elite, the paper was sometimes criticized for being anti-Catholic. Because of this record, editors would have to have very good reasons for picking a fight with the Church. The reasons multiplied as more complaints were lodged in the courts and the *Phoenix* published its story. Finally, in July 2001, a new top editor named Martin Baron arrived and he decided that the ship would change course.

The four journalists assigned to the investigation — Rezendes, Walter Robinson, Matthew Carroll, and Sacha Pfeiffer — were born Catholics. Two had attended parochial schools. All four would need help understanding how the Church they thought they knew as a compassionate and moral institution could protect abusive priests.

As he combed the Kos file Rezendes was captivated by Richard Sipe's report, which was both generous to good priests and searing in its review of the secrecy, sexual shame, and power relationships that dominated the clerical culture. Rezendes called him for advice. Sipe returned the message the reporter left, catching him on his cell phone as he drove to Fenway Park for a Red Sox game.

In the days before state law required hands-free cell phone use in cars, Rezendes habitually grabbed the phone when it chirped. Wedging it between his shoulder and ear he spoke to Sipe about his project and listened with rapt attention as this soft-spoken former priest and psychiatric expert recalled his encounter with John Geoghan the psychiatric patient and explained, in terms laypeople rarely hear, how clergy become paralyzed by their fear of sexual scandal. Rezendes had never heard someone give such a thorough review of priests, power, and Catholic dogma and concluded on the spot that Sipe would become one of the Spotlight Team's guides through the history, culture, theology, and psychology of the abuse crisis. Without checking with his bosses Rezendes told Sipe the *Globe* would fly him to Boston and put him up in a good hotel for a few days if he would answer the team's questions. Within days, Sipe was aboard a flight landing at Logan Airport.

In Boston, Sipe helped Rezendes and the others on the team to see beyond collars and cassocks to recognize priests and their superiors as men who embody all that was good and evil about human beings. They experience the same emotions as everyone else, were motivated by the same desires, and were capable of the very best and worst actions. And like everyone else, they mostly muddled through life, making compromises and balancing the generous and self-sacrificing Christian values they promised to uphold with self-interest and ambition.

For journalists who were raised Catholic, Sipe's insights came as an antidote to whatever lessons they absorbed as children who were taught that priests were possessed of supernatural powers and were deserving of special respect. In fact, Catholic priests could and did commit rape, murder, and theft and often got away with their crimes because others assumed them to be especially good men. Indeed, the Constitution and the institutional strengths of the Church and the Vatican state provided them with protections others did not enjoy.

The *Globe* journalists were not without their own powers, however. The same First Amendment that sheltered religion also

457

protected the freedom of the press, which gave reporters more rights than ordinary citizens as they pursued their work. Rezendes, Pfeiffer, Robinson, and Carroll also enjoyed the backing of New England's most powerful media outlet, including its attorneys. They were informed by the growing utility of the Internet, which exceeded the highly developed human network of the Catholic Church in its ability to transmit information. And they felt a calling to their profession similar to a religious impulse. Reporters were just as susceptible to corruption as anyone else, but newspaper pay was so low, and the work was so demanding that those who worked long enough and hard enough to rise to a place on the Spotlight Team were the ones who still believed it was their job to check the power of important institutions.

As they interviewed Geoghan's victims and found men and women who had been abused by other priests, the *Globe* reporters discovered that more than thirty Boston diocese priests had been subjects of abuse complaints and that many of these cases had been resolved by cash payments from the Church. They also figured out that priests assigned to long sick leaves were often being sent to places like St. Luke's after charges from sexual abuse victims. By tracking their assignments and finding the gaps, they were able to make educated guesses about which clergymen were trouble. As they dug, the reporters kept returning to Sipe to ask him if what they were being told could be true. He informed them that yes, it was common for a bishop or cardinal to move a sex offender priest from parish to parish; and yes, the Church often sought advice from doctors and therapists who really were not qualified. In Geoghan's case, the Archdiocese of Boston relied on one doctor who was a general practitioner and described himself as the priest's "longtime friend" and another who was a psychiatrist with no special education in sexual deviance. Both wrote evaluations that failed to protect the public but did allow Cardinal Bernard Law to say that he had consulted experts who cleared Geoghan for duty.

Law became the key target in the *Globe*'s investigation because, as Rezendes would recall, "We did not discover clergy sex abuse. Our story was about the institutional cover-up." Court files on lawsuits settled by the Church seemed a logical place to start looking for documentary evidence. In midsummer a *Globe* staffer named Kathleen Burge reported that Law had admitted that he knew, as early as 1984, that Father Geoghan had been accused of molesting seven boys. Burge's report, which was published on the inside of the paper, also noted that Law's lawyers had asked Superior Court Judge

James McHugh to seal the records.

Although some readers may have been struck by Law's admission, the Spotlight Team found the archdiocese's request for secrecy more intriguing. With a little work they discovered that judges across the state, but especially in Boston, routinely sealed records in suits involving the Church to spare it negative publicity. One local attorney, Mitchell Garabedian, had filed more than eighty abuse-related suits. In order to get around the law protecting charities he had named individuals, including Law, as defendants. However, almost all of the documents, depositions, and other evidence in Garabedian's cases — thousands of pages — remained sealed. Garabedian believed that some key evidence remained in about a dozen related suits where the Church had failed to obtain confidentiality rulings.

Through the summer and fall of 2001, Rezendes conducted a kind of courtship of Garabedian. He visited the lawyer's office — a space piled with papers and empty coffee cups where Garabedian worked alone — and telephoned him frequently. Rezendes earned the lawyer's trust but Garabedian was subject to confidentiality orders and couldn't share what he knew directly. He eventually told Rezendes that he had included some key information in files for other cases that were not restricted. Hoping to save a bit of time

Rezendes said, "Why don't you just give me copies?" Garabedian said Rezendes would have to get them himself, at the courthouse, but he told him that he had put the most important documents into fourteen different case files not covered by secrecy orders.

"I had already asked for those," recalled Rezendes years later. "The documents he said had been placed there were all gone. They were empty files."

An appalled Garabedian couldn't explain why the case files had been stripped, but he wasn't going to risk angering a judge by giving the stuff to the newspaper. The solution would be a lawsuit filed by the *Globe*'s attorneys. This challenge would be heard by a judge named Constance Sweeney, a no-nonsense Catholic woman with short brown hair who peered at lawyers over eyeglasses perched at the end of her nose. In more than fifteen years on the bench, Sweeney had overseen several high-profile trials and once approved a TV station's petition for police videotape showing the line-ups used as a witness was asked to identify a murder suspect.

Sweeney's ruling on Garabedian's files was kind to her fellow judges, noting that their secrecy rules had the "unintended effect of impeding the access of the public and the press to certain aspects of the case." As in the murder case, she favored disclosure, and ordered that the documents be released after a thirty-day period, during which names could be blotted out to protect the privacy of victims and others. Referring to Church claims that the documents were shielded by the First Amendment she wrote that the Constitution "does not automatically free them from the legal duties imposed on the rest of society." A second woman jurist, appeals court judge Cynthia Cohen, upheld Sweeney and the documents were set to be made public in January 2002.

Although the *Globe*'s lawyers won the ruling, the documents would be available to anyone who asked for them. The prospect of another paper, or TV station, getting the story at the same time was unsettling. But as the reporters and their editors worried over how to be first with the news, they got some help from Mike Rezendes's new friend, Mitch Garabedian. Late in December Garabedian mentioned that Judge Sweeney's order opening the records of suits against the cardinal applied to future cases as well as those on file. He intended to deposit new copies of them at the clerk of courts' office on the first Friday in January. Once again Rezendes asked for copies. Once again Garabedian said no. However, he did agree to make his visit to the courthouse at 4:15 P.M. Rezendes and his colleague Matt Carroll could stake out the place and get first shot at the papers.

Garabedian was good to his word. At about

4:20 P.M. the reporters appeared at the superior court clerk's office and saw the papers on a rolling cart. The staff woman who heard their request said she couldn't hand over the documents because they were subject to the waiting period the judge had imposed when she ruled on the old cases. Hardly equipped to make a legal argument with someone who wasn't empowered to rule anyway, the two journalists appealed to a supervisor. Neither woman seemed to know that the *Globe* had prevailed in the court of appeals. However, they told Rezendes and Carroll that they could have the ruling faxed from the *Globe* to the clerk of courts and see a judge who was on duty for eventualities like this one.

Judge Viera Volterra occupied chambers several floors above the clerk's office. The elevator in the old building creaked slowly in response to the call button and the two reporters felt like it wasn't actually moving as it carried them up. The judge made them sit quietly in the jury box as he considered their request and the files they wanted, which were on his desk. "These are very sensitive documents," he noted as he leafed through psychiatric records, depositions, and internal documents from the Church. "Where is the editorial responsibility in publishing these?"

Rezendes wouldn't recall exactly what he said, only that, "In my most earnest voice I defended journalism's role. Other than that, I was sweating and begging." As he ran out of things to say, a clerk appeared with the fax from the *Globe.* Judge Volterra took it in hand, studied it, and said, "Yep, that's it. You can have it."

Returning by elevator to the floor where they could find a copying machine, the reporters were met by a court employee who had just locked the door to the room where it was kept. "I can't open the door," she said, adjusting her winter coat. "I'm meeting my daughter in Kenmore Square."

With a little more begging, Rezendes and Carroll persuaded her to stay late so they could copy the files. The men caught their breath in a taxi that took them from the courthouse to their office. Working through the night and the next day, the team produced the first article on the scandal, which appeared on the front page of the Sunday paper. For generations the front page of the Sunday *Globe* had been the most important media space in New England and despite the decline of newspapers it retained this status. More than one million people saw the headline "Church Allowed Abuse by Priest for Years" and the facts laid out in the article shocked the six-state region.

Geoghan was the main focus of that first report, which explained that the Church knew that more than a hundred victims had complained about him and that they were as young as four when the abuse began. The priest had apparently abused seven boys in one extended family and when the aunt of these victims wrote Law's predecessor, he asked her to "love the sinner and pray for him." The documents provided proof that Cardinal Law was warned about Geoghan and nevertheless transferred him into parishes where he would have access to children. It also foreshadowed an avalanche of future scandal as the records for eighty-four lawsuits became public later in the month.

In the week that followed the original article, the *Globe* published a dozen more. Cardinal Law, who at first refused to answer questions, publicly apologized to victims "particularly those who were abused in assignments which I made." Seventy years old, Law was a solidly built man with white hair and bright blue eyes. His face flushed red as he spent an hour answering questions at a press conference that was broadcast live on television. He promised a "zero tolerance" policy for priests who abused minors and said that "no one who is guilty of sexually abusing a minor" was serving in a parish.

The public reaction surprised Rezendes and others at the *Globe*. Although he expected picketing by Catholics incensed over the Sunday article, Monday brought only a trickle of reader responses and most of those were positive. By midweek a phone line set up to receive reader calls was jammed. Many callers wanted to discuss how they too had been abused by a priest. Among those who were accused were many of the priests who had been identified by the reporters as they did their early research.

Days after Law made his dramatic pledge of zero tolerance and promised that no abusers remained in ministry, a local priest named Kelvin Igubita was arrested on charges of raping a girl who did housekeeping for him. On the day when the arrest was reported, *Globe* columnist Derrick Jackson issued the first call for Cardinal Law's resignation. "The only way he can restore the Church's credibility on abuse," wrote Jackson, "is to leave his altar open for a successor who has both eyes wide open."

The scandal revealed in the first set of *Globe* articles was amplified as Geoghan faced a jury in a criminal trial and the national media turned its attention to the Archdiocese of Boston. For weeks on end, almost every day brought a new revelation. By February the diocese itself had identified six more priests who were the subject of sexual abuse complaints and suspended them from ministry. The Massachusetts attorney general called for Law to reveal all past allegations against priests and attendance at vigils for victims, held outside Law's office, grew to more than a hundred people. Cardinal Law flew to Rome to consult with Vatican officials and upon his return on February 8 told reporters that eighty priests in his diocese faced charges of abuse. He rejected calls for his resignation and the Vatican spokesman Joaquín Navarro-Valls confined his statements to a blunt assessment of gay clergy. "People with these inclinations," he said, "just cannot be ordained."

American churchmen in Rome talked of fellow bishops "in hysteria" who compared the cascading scandal to the French revolution, when the besieged Church became more secretive. Long-standing tradition and practice called for superiors to protect the institution and individual priests by hiding cases from civil authorities. In late summer of 2001, the cardinal who headed the Vatican office that supervises clergy actually praised a French bishop for hiding sex crimes admitted by one of his priests. In a letter to Bishop Pierre Pican, Cardinal Darío Castrillón Hoyos wrote:

I congratulate you for not denouncing a priest to the civil administration. You have acted well and I am pleased to have colleagues in the episcopate who, in the eyes of history and all other bishops in the world, preferred prison to denouncing his son and priest.

The priest in question, Rev. Rene Bissey, was arrested in 1998 and convicted of raping and molesting eleven minors. During Bissey's trial, Bishop Pican admitted that although Bissey had confessed to his crimes, he had kept quiet for two years and allowed the priest to continue in ministry. In a separate trial Pican was found guilty of failing to report sexual abuse. It was after this conviction that Cardinal Hoyos wrote to praise him. Years after the fact, with his own reputation in tatters, Hoyos would say that he had consulted with John Paul II before writing to Pican and "The Holy Father authorized me to send this letter to all bishops in the world and publish it on the Internet."

Cardinal Law couldn't count on letters of support from officials in Rome. Instead, he returned to Boston intent on demonstrating he could manage through the crisis. He called on local leaders for advice and named a panel to prevent abuse in the archdiocese that included professor David Finklehor and other experts. He also began visiting parishes to show his concern. But even as he tried to be a pastor, he came across as someone who still didn't put victims first. At a church in the suburb of Dedham, for example, he spoke most eloquently about his own trials. "I personally have these past weeks experienced closeness to Jesus on the cross in a way I never have before in my life," said Law. Days later the cardinal's face appeared on the cover of *Newsweek* next to a headline reading, "Sex, Shame and the Catholic Church."

The scandal in Boston was especially appalling to an unofficial defender of the faith named William Donohue, who generally agitated on behalf of the institutional Church as head of the Catholic League for Religious and Civil Rights. For ten years Donohue had delivered outraged complaints about everything from sex education to media portrayals of Catholicism, all with the intention of calling out what he saw as religious bigotry. Just about everything Donohue said was voiced in fighting terms, and much of what he did was intended to incite others. In other words, the job was a perfect fit for his personality.

Born in 1947, the same year as Jeff Anderson, Donohue came to his cause from a staunch Irish Catholic childhood dominated by his old-fashioned grandmother. Raised mainly without his father's presence in suburban Long Island, he had led a very Catholic life except for a divorce from a wife with whom he had two children. In taking leadership of the league, he once explained, he gave himself permission to make the kind of points bishops couldn't because of their pastoral roles. In his words he was "the pit bull, the feisty Irish guy." Sometimes he chomped down on a deserving target. Just as often, he came off as frivolous and his outrage seemed manufactured. But in viewing the bishops and sexual abuse he could only say, "I am not here to defend the indefensible."

With public opinion so united against the Church, the archdiocese needed just ninety days from the publication of the *Globe*'s first big article on John Geoghan to agree to a settlement with Mitchell Garabedian's clients that would include payments totaling as much as $30 million. However, other victims who had long-standing suits, and the one hundred or so men and women who brought complaints since January 1, were not covered by this arrangement. Attorney Roderick MacLeish represented many of these people, including several who had been abused by a priest named Paul Shanley. At the start of the Boston crisis, Shanley's name was noted among many others suspected of abusing minors. On Monday, April 8, 2002, thanks to MacLeish, he became as notorious as John Geoghan.

Roderick MacLeish's first clergy abuse case involved a man who had been repeatedly raped by a priest starting when he was nine years old. He buried his bloody underwear to keep anyone from finding out. The pain expressed by this client, and more than a hundred others, drove MacLeish to pursue the release of church documents that would reveal who knew what, when, and how they had responded.

When a judge finally forced the archdiocese to give MacLeish what he wanted, he combed through the pages, identified key passages, and then created a presentation that he could project onto a screen set up in the ballroom of the Sheraton Boston Hotel. On April 8, 2002, the members of the press who came to the early afternoon meeting saw MacLeish, wearing a wireless microphone, pace the floor as he described the importance of documents that flashed on the screen. The pages showed how Church officials discussed Shanley as a "sick person" but feared confronting him. Cardinal Law's predecessor didn't react at all when a Catholic layperson told him he had heard Shanley say "that he can think of no sexual act that causes psychic damage — 'not even incest or bestiality.' "

MacLeish, who had once praised the Boston Archdiocese for its handling of abuse cases, spoke with disdain and anger. At one moment he shouted, "We were lied to! We were deceived!" At another he looked at a photo on the screen that showed the cardinal shaking hands with Fr. Shanley, and said, "We believe that photograph was taken shortly after Cardinal Law had received [a letter] indicating that Paul Shanley was engaging in deviant behavior."

By the time MacLeish was finished, he had shown that for decades high Church officials, including Law, knew of complaints against Shanley — twenty-six in all — and continued to promote him, and recommend him for postings in California and New York. Noting that the first warning about Shanley was raised in 1967, MacLeish concluded, "All of the suffering that has taken place at the hands of Paul Shanley — a serial child molester for four decades, three of them in Boston — none of it had to happen."

A highly visible priest who often claimed runaways and other street kids as part of his ministry, Shanley had exploited these same youngsters, engaging them in sex at a secluded cabin he kept in a wooded area close to the city. One of MacLeish's clients, Arthur Austin, appeared at the press conference to talk about his case. Calling out to Cardinal Law, Austin said:

> You are a liar; your own documents condemn you. You are a criminal, a murderer of children; you degrade the office you hold in the Church; you are an affront to Jesus Christ; and I call on Almighty God to bear witness to the foulness and treachery of your behavior, the evil you have nurtured and condoned, and the minds, hearts, and souls you have destroyed.

Austin's words echoed Bernard Law calling

down "God's power" on the Boston press during the 1992 scandal involving Fr. Porter. They also reflected the growing assertiveness of victims and their supporters. In the Boston area, old classmates and friends began talking to each other and discovering they had similar experiences with abusive priests. In his book *Our Fathers* the writer David France would document how many communities were divided by the abuse issue and neighbors sometimes argued bitterly. One victim, Olan Horne, told France how he dealt with co-workers who suggested he had engaged in consensual sex with Fr. Joseph Birmingham. After recalling he was eleven years old when he was raped, Horne explained how the priest beat him, seized him by the back of the head, and forced his penis into his mouth. Horne then said:

. . . and then this guy puts me on the floor with his knee on my back, you know, the guy's ejaculating all over my back, he's beating the shit out of me because I'm trying to get away but I'm still like, "Fuck you!"

That's a blow job? Hell no, that ain't no blow job. That's rape. You need me to fill you in on any other sexual points? You want to hear some more? You tough enough, because I can go places you've never been.

While victims coped with challenges from coworkers and even family members, several different groups formed to support them and to press the hierarchy to share power. The leaders of these organizations were earnest Catholics who believed in the Christian message but doubted the ability of men like Law to deliver it to the world. Terence McKiernan, for example, was a forty-nine-year-old parishioner at Our Lady of Help who had returned to the Church when his children were born. Early in the scandal he began wearing a homemade button that said "Law Must Go" and he became an activist after meeting the parents of a child who had been abused by a priest when he was six. McKiernan's daughter was six.

As one of the earliest members of a lay organization called Voice of the Faithful, McKiernan attended meetings that grew from twenty-five to one thousand people in early 2002. On his own he began collecting and cataloging reports on accused priests in Boston and across the nation. An editor by profession, McKiernan soon became the unofficial archivist of the movement to confront clergy abuse. He obtained data from other groups around the country and established a Web site called BishopAccountability.org where anyone in the world could search for information.

As time passed, Boston-based groups like

Voice of the Faithful, which pressed for structural reforms in the management of the Church, would never gain the visibility of SNAP. The power in the Church would remain in the hands of the ordained and they would not share it simply because thousands of people in one diocese or another demanded they do so. McKiernan's project, however, would grow to become an international resource offering hundreds of thousands of pages of documents that could be searched by lawyers, academics, lawmakers, prosecutors, journalists and victims looking for connections, patterns, and evidence.

On a national level, the Church documents published by the *Globe* gave reporters around the country hints on how to investigate local dioceses and these efforts produced a stream of scandals similar to Boston's. In Milwaukee, for example, the press reported that Archbishop Rembert Weakland kept a priest named William Effinger in ministry for more than a decade after he confessed to being a sex offender. In Philadelphia, fifty sexual abuse claims against priests were reported, and in Los Angeles the press reported that during one two-week period half a dozen priests had been dismissed. In 2001 the diocese had promised in a court proceeding to get rid of all priests who confessed or were found to have committed sexual abuse. The pledge was part of a $5.2 million settlement of a complaint against Fr. Michael Harris by a young man named Ryan DiMaria. Harris, a charismatic Catholic high school principal known as "Father Hollywood" denied the claim. The first complaints about Harris had been lodged in the 1970s. In the weeks after the settlement, DiMaria's lawyers Kathy Freberg and John Manly signed up more than one hundred new clients who said they were abused by priests in Southern California.

Southern California also became the site of one of the few truly entertaining moments of the sex abuse crisis. On the afternoon of Thursday April 4 a talk radio duo on KFI-AM began reading from confidential e-mails sent to and from Cardinal Mahony. John Kobylt and Ken Chiampou had recently embarrassed a judge accused of child abuse by reading his diary aloud. This time they held in their hands more than sixty messages discussing everything from public relations to how the diocese might respond to inquiries from local law enforcement investigators looking into possible criminal activity by priests and their superiors.

Altogether, the e-mails showed Mahony was deeply involved in planning responses to official inquiries and still hoped to protect his priests while controlling the flow of information released to the public. This attitude stood in contrast to his declaration, a year before, that "We want every single thing to be out, open and dealt with, period."

In one of the leaked e-mails Mahony wrote that the diocese might warn those who may be subject to criminal investigation. "They should probably have some heads-up lest the PD comes knocking at their doors without notice," he explained. In another Mahony suggested his aides delay releasing the names of suspected abusers in the hopes that public interest would wane. In a third he expressed concern about facing "charges of cover-up, concealing criminals, etc., etc." A fourth revealed that he was relieved that he would be traveling and unable to conduct the funeral of an accused priest who was dying. "It may be best if someone else were to handle his funeral anyway," wrote the cardinal, "given his past difficulties."

As the hosts of the *John and Ken Show* gleefully announced they possessed these e-mails and began reading them over the air, an attorney for the archdiocese called the radio station and insisted they stop because a court had issued a cease-and-desist order. Although their ratings were at stake, Ken and John suspended the narration until their attorneys got a judge to rule that the e-mails could be broadcast. The following day they set up their microphones in front of the almost-complete new Los Angeles cathedral and worked through all the e-mails. The decision to broadcast from the cathedral site further tweaked the cardinal, since its construction, at a cost of $180 million, was a point of conflict between him and critics who thought the cost was more than excessive and called it the "Rog Mahal."

The e-mail spectacle was embarrassing for the cardinal but also illustrated the effects of the scandal on the standing of the institutional Church. The person who leaked the confidential messages was most likely a Church insider. This meant that someone close to the cardinal had lost confidence in him and felt that the *John and Ken Show* could play a necessary role in policing the Roman Catholic Church. A leak like this one also showed that the respect and even fear that traditionally shielded the Church from criticism was evaporating. This change had already occurred in the media as investigative reporters, columnists, and editorial writers swarmed around chanceries, courthouses, parishes, and law offices to exploit every morsel of scandal. Gone was the discretion and cozy cooperation that had marked relations between the press and the pulpit. It had been replaced by mutual suspicion and outrage.

In Los Angeles the adversarial dynamic was led by columnist Steven Lopez of the *Los Angeles Times,* who used his opinion pieces to repeatedly point out the contradictions between the cardinal's promises of openness and his many refusals to release the names of suspect priests and documents related to cases. With jokes and rhymes Lopez mocked the cardinal even as he called on him to be more forthcoming. Writers in other cities around the country made similar demands of local bishops, making a sport out of holding prelates to the standard of honesty and compassion for the suffering set by Christ himself.

With so many local and national press outlets pursuing the abuse story, and victims feeling inspired to seek help, the leaders of Survivors Network of those Abused by Priests responded to hundreds of inquiries per day. The SNAP activists were not employed by their movement. They each worked full-time jobs and because of this they gave up mealtimes and sleep to respond to the calls. Barbara Blaine, who then worked in the Cook County courts as an advocate for children, found that the voice mail on her SNAP phone filled to capacity every fifteen minutes. By her estimate hundreds, if not thousands of callers could not reach her because of the limited capacity of the phone system.

Blaine, David Clohessy, Peter Isely, and other SNAP leaders became national media figures as journalists sought them out to provide perspective on the long-running scandal. Clohessy told the *Los Angeles Times*, "I never thought I'd see this day. We've been crying from the rooftops for someone to notice what's going on for so long."

In fact, seventeen years had passed since Barbara Blaine organized the group at the Catholic Worker House in Chicago. SNAP now had more than three thousand members and had active leaders in every corner of the country. Like the others, the Milwaukee-based Isely made SNAP the equivalent of a full-time job. Unlike the others, he was a psychotherapist with a graduate degree from Harvard Divinity School. Along with his expertise in theology and psychology, Isely was informed by his profoundly devout upbringing and the education he received at the seminary where he was abused. In the ten years he had devoted to activism he had become deeply involved with bishops and priests in Wisconsin, pressing them to find a constructive way to deal with sexual abuse.

In Isely's own case, and others he observed, the Church had defended its treasury and reputation by spending "tens of millions of dollars on the highest-priced lawyers from across the country and hiring the best public relations firm to fight us." In Wisconsin this struggle had produced a stalemate, with courts barring most lawsuits and legislators deadlocked over proposals to revamp the laws so that claims could proceed. For years Isely had met with Church officials, including Archbishop Rembert Weakland, hoping to establish a voluntary system that would help victims and restore public confidence in the Church. By 2002 he had come to believe that the structure of the institution required insiders to act. "Where are the good priests?" he said. "When they turn in one of their own, they'll start to make me a believer."

Not one priest in Milwaukee came forward to report an abusive colleague, but something even more startling occurred in the month of May 2002: Archbishop Rembert Weakland suddenly resigned and revealed that he had carried on a long affair with a male lover who had received a $450,000 payment. Paul Marcoux was an adult when the relationship began in 1979, but had complained that he had been the victim of date rape. In exchange for the money he had agreed to stay silent, and keep confidential the letters Weakland had written him over the years. However, in the wake of the Boston scandal, Marcoux broke this promise and told the story to ABC news. Working with Jason Berry as a consultant, ABC reporter Brian Ross broke the story, in which he pointed out that the archbishop had "urged the Catholic Church to open up about its growing sex abuse crisis" even as he conducted a secret affair. The point was clear: A prelate who had called for less sexual secrecy had, in fact, been hiding a sexual relationship. Weakland didn't respond to ABC's request for an interview but after the piece aired he said, "I never abused anyone" and then resigned. On the same day, a priest in New York and another in Maryland were arrested for sexually abusing children under the age of thirteen.

As the Church reeled, bishops prepared for one of their regular twice-yearly conferences. It would be held in Dallas and the main topic — perhaps the only topic — would be the abuse crisis. Institutional insiders and their supporters were deeply divided over how to respond. The president of the bishops' organization, Wilton Gregory of Illinois, struck a humble tone as he accepted criticism of the Church and wrote, in a February 2002 op-ed piece in the newspaper *USA Today,* "The law rightly makes it clear that sexual abuse of minors is a crime. We have all been enlightened. We continue to learn from our experiences and, hopefully, even more from our mistakes." While Gregory reminded the public that Church institutions provided social services to 11 million people and health care to more than 77 million patients, he dwelled mainly on the crisis at hand. He wrote, "The United States' 350 bishops and 47,000 priests share in the shame and humiliation felt by our laity."

Bishop Gregory focused on the responsibilities of the Church. Others began to parse the scandals. Historian Philip Jenkins wrote in the March 3, 2002, Pittsburgh *Post-Gazette* that "the 'pedophile priest' scandal is nothing like as sinister as it has been painted." Having missed on his declaration that the abuse crisis was ending, Jenkins opted to cast it as something other than a criminal sexual scandal involving children. He noted that most victims were teenagers and therefore most priest offenders were behaving more like irresponsible gay men than true pedophiles. He also argued that all denominations had their "share" of abuse cases and "The fact that Cardinal Law's regime in Boston seems to have blundered time and again does not mean that this is standard practice for all Catholic dioceses, still less that the Church is engaged in some kind of conspiracy of silence to hide dangerous perverts."

Professor Jenkins was correct about victims and their age, but he didn't seem to realize that this was a difference without a distinction for most people. Sex between adults and minors of any age was illegal and men who committed these crimes time after time with multiple adolescents abused them and the trust of the community. No matter the age of their victims, they came across as out-of-control predators. As for other religions suffering their share of scandal, the best informed experts on clergy abuse saw no parallels in other faiths. Sociologist Anson Shupe told the *Globe:*

There are absolutely no Protestant equivalents [to the Catholic crisis]. If I could find some spectacular cases, that would help my career, but I can't. You don't have rapacious serial predators, and the Protestant establishment doesn't tolerate it the way the Catholic establishment has.

When he was asked to comment, Richard Sipe, who had begun to work as an expert witness for plaintiffs in abuse cases, seconded Shupe. "All the researchers I know say there is nothing comparable in the other churches," he said. "And we have no evidence that it is as prevalent in other professional populations, such as doctors and lawyers." Sipe was correct, however — very little work has been done on the rates of abuse in different professions or faiths. Incidents of sexual abuse have been noted among Protestants, Jews, and Buddhist clergy but no widespread scandal had emerged in any faith other than Catholicism.

Jenkins was further off base with his claims about the practices of Catholic dioceses. In every major case where lawyers forced the Church to divulge documents, they showed that bishops followed roughly the same practices to avoid scandal. Priest offenders were sent to new postings, laypeople were discouraged from speaking publicly about their offenses, and settlement payments came with demands for confidentiality agreements. Sometimes bishops sent problem priests to different states and foreign countries, without informing locals of their history. Similar practices had been seen in Ireland and would emerge around the world.

The global nature of the scandal was apparent to anyone who cared to look. In the midst of the American meltdown, the Church in Ireland signed an agreement with the state establishing a $110 million fund to compensate victims of abuse in Irish institutions like the Magdelene laundries. (Inquiries into the problem of sexually abusive parish priests were continuing.) In the meantime, scandals were brewing in Australia, France, Belgium, Italy, and Chile. Just before Easter Pope John Paul II accepted the resignation of his friend, Polish Archbishop Julius Paetz, who had been accused of using a secret tunnel exiting his palace at Poznan to access young seminarians for sexual purposes. Paetz consistently denied the accusations and there were no official findings.

Against this background the Pope summoned America's cardinals, and Archbishop Gregory, to Rome for a conference on the scandal. Having reached the age of eighty-one, Karol Józef Wojtyla had been pontiff for more than two decades and a priest for more than fifty. His shaking body and rigid-looking face betrayed that he suffered from Parkinson's disease and the side effects associated with common treatments. He was increasingly dependent on other Church officials and at least one of his greatest admirers in America, writer Peggy Noonan, feared they were serving him poorly. Writing in *The Wall Street Journal* as the American cardinals arrived in Rome, she noted that the crisis was not a media creation but the fault of cardinals and bishops who were "excusers or enablers of sex abusers." If the Pope wanted to make a start on getting control of the "calamity," added Noonan, he should consider plucking the red cap off Cardinal Law's head when he knelt to kiss his ring.

No hats were plucked in Rome. Instead, the Pope, who considered every one of the American cardinals a loyalist, continued to support them. He did describe clergy abuse of minors as a crime and express "solidarity and concern" for victims and their families. However, he still spoke in the oblique manner that left room for evading full responsibility. He said he regretted the way that "the Church leaders are perceived" but said little about the way they had acted. And he reiterated the idea that sexual offenses committed by priests represented a problem in "society as a whole." As for any solutions, the Pope once again stressed the supernatural, urging the cardinals to be concerned "above all else, with the spiritual good of souls."

On his flight home, Archbishop Gregory let a reporter for *The New York Times* sit with him for an interview. As the paper reported the next day, Gregory felt the American bishops were not yet united in their response to the scandals. One major point of disagreement involved accusations of abuse that were many years old. Some Church officials felt they should be regarded with the same seriousness as recent allegations. Others wanted to be able to deal more leniently in cases where priests had an otherwise clean record. The differences would be hashed out in Dallas.

Gregory spoke with the urgency of a chief battling a windblown forest fire that was sending dangerous embers across the countryside. More than three hundred new lawsuits had been filed in five months and prosecutors had convened grand juries to investigate the Church in Los Angeles, Cleveland, Cincinnati, Philadelphia, and on Long Island. Jeff Anderson had filed a federal racketeering lawsuit against three dioceses, and several states were considering legislation to extend statutes of limitation in clergy abuse cases. Across the board, the Church stood to lose money, members, and moral standing. In a handful of cases the effects of the crisis were even more serious. Two American priests accused of abuse had committed suicide since the scandal flared at the start of 2002. A third was shot and wounded by a young man who said he was victimized by him when he was a minor.

Viewed from any angle, the Catholic landscape was devastated. When asked to assess the situation from the perspective of a man who warned of just this outcome, Fr. Tom Doyle offered a typically sardonic analysis. "The Church in America is a dinosaur with a head the size of an ant, and the head thinks it's in charge. The bishops need to understand just how precarious their situation is."

20.
CATHOLIC GUILT

Before she walked down the aisle, Barbara Blaine handed her cell phone to David Clohessy and told him he would have to respond to any calls from the press or victims looking for SNAP's help. Blaine may have allowed her activism to take over her life, but she wasn't going to let it disturb her wedding. This much she had promised to her fiancé Howard Rubin.

Rubin and Blaine had met at DePaul University, where she had returned to school in her thirties to study law. He was director of the legal aid clinic that connected students with poor clients who might otherwise be defenseless in court proceedings. A first date at a hockey game had grown into a solid partnership. Neither of them could have guessed that the date they chose to be married at a former chapel on the DePaul campus would fall smack in the middle of the frenzied crisis begun by the Boston scandal.

The original plan, or at least Howard Rubin's hope, had involved a honeymoon in Italy. A compromise took the couple to New Mexico, where he was delighted to discover that his wife's cell phone couldn't receive calls at their bed-and-breakfast. She did her best to set aside work, but whenever they went out driving she turned on her phone and searched for spots where she got a signal. Hilltops were best, and Rubin did allow for stops so Blaine could respond to the most urgent calls, especially those from other SNAP leaders who were preparing to meet with the bishops at their upcoming national conference in Dallas.

By the second Monday in June 2002, there was hardly a city in America where there hadn't been a scandal of note. For all practical purposes, every one of the two hundred and eighty-five bishops who came to Dallas had dealt with complaints of priest abuse or been required to take some sort of position. Most had offered generalities like "zero tolerance" but since God was in the details, real answers awaited their conference.

The details would prove elusive. Well before the conference, the bishops invited members of SNAP to meet with them, but then publicly withdrew the invitation because SNAP was a party to a class-action suit brought against them by Jeff Anderson. When the victims group removed itself from the suit, the bishops welcomed them back. This push-pull process made the Catholic leaders seem more like bosses negotiating with a union than pastors tending a flock. However, one bishop did manage to act decisively days before the conference opened: accused of abuse by three former altar boys, Bishop J. Kendrick Williams of Kentucky resigned. (Williams denied the allegations but the claims would eventually be resolved as part of a $25 million settlement. Williams was not prosecuted.)

Amid the preconference chaos, the producers of the TV news program *60 Minutes II,* put together a one-hour report titled "Tale of Shame," which recounted the key points in the twenty years of scandal going back to Gilbert Gauthe. More than 7 million households tuned into *60 Minutes II,* to hear a woman who was raped as a girl by a priest recall him saying, "It's okay. God knows about this" as he covered her mouth with his hand. The witness accounts in "Tale of Shame" were heartrending but the most trenchant statement came from the reporter, Ed Bradley, who said, "Perhaps the most shocking thing about these scandals is how long they've been going on."

On Wednesday, June 12, big TV satellite trucks idled on the street outside the Dallas Fairmont Hotel, throwing extra heat into the ninety-degree morning. Picketers of various sorts stood on the sidewalk holding carefully lettered signs. Some of the placards, like those held by the members of a group called Our Lady's Warriors, demanded the bishops remain steadfast in defense of their authority and dogma. Others wanted the world to know that the bishops inside were, in their view, part of the problem. One man in khaki pants and a button-down shirt held a sign above his head announcing "The Bishops Have Sinned."

Beyond the demonstrators, private security officers and local police guarded the entrance to the hotel and walked the hallways. Catholicism, like other big powerful organizations, can provoke violence from both rational enemies and disturbed individuals. Pope John Paul II had been subject to attacks from would-be assassins of both types. Church leaders were always concerned about security. But the scandals, and a tragedy that took place the day before, had cast an even greater sense of danger over the Dallas meeting. In rural Missouri an elderly man had taken a rifle into a Benedictine abbey where he killed two priests, wounded two others, and then committed suicide. No link to sexual abuse had been established, and in the end the shooting was found to be unrelated, but in Dallas it made the bishops and their guards extra nervous.

Besides the Catholic activists, the meeting

of the American bishops attracted correspondents from the nation's major networks and newspapers, and many from overseas. The estimated 750 journalists came expecting, if not substance, spectacle. They knew that at the very least, the conference would be confronted by victims of abuse who had, during more than a decade of campaigning, become comfortable with conflict. Between them David Clohessy, Barbara Blaine, and Peter Isely had given more than a thousand interviews and spent hundreds of hours in front of television cameras. They also knew more about how the Church as a whole had responded to sex abuse claims than almost any member of the clergy.

Blaine, having come to Dallas after her honeymoon, struggled a bit in her first encounter with the press in Dallas. Taken aback by the dozens of microphones thrust in her face and by the way that some of the journalists jostled in front of her, Blaine felt for a moment like the teenager she was when Chet Warren abused her. She felt overwhelmed by the idea that so many people wanted to hear what she had to say about the Church and its failure to protect children. In her hand Blaine clutched a sheaf of papers given to her by David Clohessy. He had scoured press accounts from the previous decades to come up with quotes from bishops who had promised to act after previous scandals. She read some of these quotes and quickly gained confidence.

Besides recalling broken promises, Blaine and other victims pushed for a tougher policy than the bishops were considering. A draft made by a committee of bishops, which had already been sent to the Vatican, called for defrocking priests who confessed or were otherwise proven to have molested even one minor. However, the committee would enforce this policy only in future cases. Bishops would have discretion when dealing with priests who committed a single crime in the past. This exception was unacceptable to victims who likened it to giving murderers or bank robbers one free crime as long as they weren't caught a second time.

This objection, and others, emerged in a closed-door session held Wednesday afternoon in a conference room guarded by security agents. Twenty-five male and female victims sat in a circle with four cardinals and a handful of bishops. (Boston cardinal Bernard Law, who avoided press by flying to Dallas in a private jet, was conspicuously absent.) As she took a chair, one member of SNAP, Helen Daly, opened a laptop computer and began typing as the people in the circle introduced themselves. Unbeknownst to all, she was making a verbatim transcript of the session. As Daly's record showed, survivors from Boston were among the first to speak and they were blunt.

"I was abused by two priests. I am here to bring up the abuse of adult women as well," announced the first.

"I was raped by a Catholic priest," said a woman who formerly was a nun. "My order and his order tried to gag me, so I left."

"I'm here to support my son," said a middle-aged father, "who was sodomized and raped by Fr. James Hanley."

From this beginning the group spent about an hour reviewing the toll of abuse carried out by Catholic priests and the effects of inaction by their superiors. The parents of Eric Patterson, one of the five abused boys who committed suicide in Kansas, told the story of how their son had killed himself. Peter Isely held up a photo of himself when he was a boy. Standing beside him in the photo was the priest who molested him. "I'm here to try to help you guys out," he said. "We've been trying to help you guys out for fourteen years."

In fact the clerics said they wanted help devising their policies, but they seemed unable to respond forthrightly. One victim asked, "Can you change this proposal so that all known offenders have their collar removed now?" Cardinal Theodore McCarrick of Washington, D.C., answered, "We can't speak today on that. That's something to speak to the whole conference."

"Would you support that?"

Cardinal McCarrick answered, "I can't say it at the present time. We all feel that anyone who had done what you have indicated has been done to you should not be a priest anymore."

Another victim noted that his abuser had confessed his guilt but remained a priest. "He's still getting a pension check. He is still called father. He is still a priest. Do you think that someone who had pleaded guilty should still be a priest?"

Philadelphia Cardinal Anthony Bevilacqua dodged the question, but Cardinal Mahony of Los Angeles rose to it. "I have a couple of people like that. They have disappeared on us. I can't follow the canon system while finding the guy."

"Are you saying you have no known men [abusers] in your diocese?" asked Isely.

"I've got several in the process of being laicized," answered Mahony. "We need this process very, very desperately. I am not keeping these people as priests."

Isely respected Mahony's commitment as an individual in charge of one archdiocese, but he wanted a stronger system to govern not just priests but the actions of bishops. "The Church fights like hell to keep divorced Catholics from receiving Communion," he noted, "but I don't see that fight about thousands of people who have been devastated. There is no accountability in this draft for bishops who have knowingly transferred [priest abusers]. We need accountability for future actions and past actions."

Although many victims cried and tears welled in the eyes of a cardinal or two, most of the session was conducted in a calm way. Bishop Bevilacqua caught an angry response when he complained about false claims, but this brief exchange marked the only flash of anger in the session. At the meeting's end Barbara Blaine, social worker/attorney/activist/victim/Catholic, tried to sum things up in a way that would promote progress. She asked the bishops to stop fighting so hard against claims made by adults who were abused as children. "The impact of the abuse forces us to deny that it happened and by the time we realize it, we've come to adulthood and you know that. Please settle the suits and stop playing hardball," she said.

Blaine also challenged the hierarchy to come out of their defensive crouch and greet victims as partners and not adversaries. "We're offering a gift because we're naming this evil and putting light on it and you bring light to us. It's a really healing experience to know your concern, to meet with you face-to-face and to hear that your hearts and minds are good. By being so distant and not seeing each other face-to-face, it's been easy to see each other as the enemy."

■ ■ ■ ■

In June 2002, America's Catholics were more aligned with SNAP and other victims than with their bishops. This truth was revealed in a poll conducted at the start of the month by the public opinion center at Quinnipiac University, which found that 80 percent wanted priests defrocked after one incident of abuse. Nearly as many, 70 percent, said that bishops who transferred accused priests to keep them in service should resign their positions.

By the end of the bishops' meeting, conference president Archbishop Wilton Gregory spoke like a leader who understood he had failed. In a sober and confessional public statement he connected the Catholic abuse scandal to a larger child protection movement that was a positive force for good around the world. In contrast to this movement, he admitted, "We are the ones, whether through ignorance or lack of vigilance or, God forbid, with knowledge, who allowed priest abusers to remain in ministry and reassigned them to communities where they continued to abuse. We are the ones who chose not to report the criminal actions of priests to the authorities, because the law did not require this. We are the ones who worried more about the possibility of scandal than bringing about the kind of openness that helps prevent abuse. And we are the ones who, at times, responded to victims and their families as adversaries and not as suffering members of the Church."

The policies approved by the bishops called for immediate suspension of any priest accused of abuse — past, present, and future. Until cleared, they would not be able to dress, function, or speak as Catholic priests. Bishops pledged to report all allegations to civil authorities, cooperate fully with investigations, provide full reports to parishes receiving new priests, and to conduct background checks on church personnel involved with children. The policy statement, formally known as the Charter for the Protection of Children and Young People, was brief and left much open to interpretation. This vagueness became evident in the critique Tom Doyle wrote in response to all the reporters who called him at Ramstein Air Base. Doyle pointed out three dozen issues raised by the document that was intended to be a response to the crisis. Most pointedly, Doyle noted, "The bishops did not address the issue of their own responsibility for the cover-up."

Nevertheless, as David Clohessy said, the charter was the most ambitious Church response in the long history of the crisis and though they wondered about how the bishops might put their words into action, activists in

Dallas gave them high marks. Special praise was offered for the creation of a national review board to oversee its new commitments. Former Oklahoma governor Frank Keating agreed to lead the group, which would also include former White House Chief of Staff Leon Panetta and the Washington attorney Robert S. Bennett, who had helped to defend President Clinton against impeachment. Keating was an outspoken person who was raised Catholic and educated mainly in Catholic schools. A former federal agent and prosecutor, he was just the person to lend credibility to the bishops' crisis response. Keating thought that many of the problems the bishops faced were self-inflicted and he considered payments made in exchange for confidential agreements "hush money." He believed that bishops may have acted criminally in covering up crimes and he intended to "apply some good, old-fashioned Catholic guilt" to protect children and restore the integrity of the Church.

Keating's call for some Catholic guilt to be heaped upon the bishops showed how the Church leaders could be confronted with the same principles they typically used against others. Guilt, most especially sexual guilt sown in childhood, was the tool clerics had deployed for centuries to control the lives of the faithful. However, the Church had also identified itself with other moral imperatives including the defense of the weak and the vulnerable. Child abuse and the protection of sexual offenders could never be reconciled with this commitment, which meant that bishops were forever vulnerable to anyone wishing to hold them to their own standard.

They were also made vulnerable by the structure of the Church itself. Highly developed and widely dispersed, Catholic institutions enjoyed autonomy in most matters outside essential doctrines. At the same time, they communicated with each other and with Rome through a formal and outdated system that depended upon carefully crafted letters and personal visits. In the Internet age, this system could not maintain an effective flow of information. Indeed, plaintiffs' lawyers and critics of the Church ran circles around the bishops by using confidential communities on the Internet to share information and strategies. They also pursued so many separate initiatives, like insurgents conducting attacks on a traditional army, that bishops were often caught off-guard.

The power of information technology was evident in the fall of 2002 when rumors that the important parts of the charter had been changed spread from the Vatican to America. A group of American bishops meeting in Rome had neutered the panels that were supposed to oversee claims in every diocese, making them merely "advisory." Also, the

Congregation for the Doctrine of the Faith had asserted its power, requiring that evidence of complaints be shipped to the Vatican, where it would conduct secret hearings and make decisions on the fate of suspect priests. Gone was the transparency promised in Dallas. Gone was the power-sharing envisioned by laypeople in the United States. Nevertheless, the bishops adopted the revised charter when they gathered in Washington for their autumn meeting. Afterward, TV commentator Bill O'Reilly, a conservative and a Catholic, asked rhetorically, "Isn't it true that there is no moral leadership in the American Catholic Church right now?"

If the leaders of the Church in America felt besieged, and they did, no one felt it more than Boston's Cardinal Law. The documents ordered into public view by the courts had proven that, in Judge Sweeney's opinion, priests who had committed crimes against young people "may well have been assigned to parishes, youth groups, and the like, even though the cardinal or other archdiocese personnel knew" they were suspect. As prosecutors prepared to compel his testimony before a grand jury, Bernard Law finally concluded that he no longer possessed the credibility to serve. He flew to Rome and on Friday, December 13, submitted his resignation to the Pope. John Paul II accepted it immediately and Law became the former cardinal archbishop of Boston.

At the height of the furor over Boston, Jeff Anderson and Larry Drivon took a rented Lincoln Continental on a road trip to meet a potential client named Manuel "Manny" Vega in Oxnard, California. It was Easter Day, 2002. A police officer and marine veteran, Vega had been abused when he was an altar boy by a Mexican priest serving in California. He didn't recognize how much the abuse affected him until he received police training on handling sexual abuse complaints and began to suffer psychological symptoms. By then he was past the age of twenty-six, which was the state cutoff for filing claims related to abuse in childhood.

Vega had told Anderson and Drivon that he knew of others who had been abused by the same priest. When the lawyers got to the conference room Vega had rented for the meeting, half a dozen of these men were present. In tearful group settings, and individual interviews with the lawyers, the men described similar patterns of grooming and then different levels of abuse, including anal and oral rape. At the end of the day, Anderson promised "something will be done."

As they left Vega, Anderson got behind the wheel of the Lincoln and headed down a two-lane highway. The two lawyers cussed and complained to each other and then Drivon wondered aloud, "What if we could get the law changed?"

The idea ran through Anderson like an electric shock. He was so excited by it that he jerked the steering wheel and the tires on the right side of the car veered onto the gravel shoulder. For the next couple of hours the two men drove and talked about Anderson's experience with the legislature in Minnesota and the intricacies of California politics. Drivon was working for a task force set up to investigate the infamous Enron bankruptcy and its effect on California. The panel had been established by Senator Joe Dunn — who had been elected in 1998 — after working with Anderson on previous abuse cases.

With a call to Dunn, Anderson and Drivon devised a strategy for getting legislation drafted to create a one-year window allowing any victim to file a claim without concern for the statute of limitations. With Vega's help, they won support from the Hispanic caucus in the state legislature, which was led by a representative named Marta Escudia. After hearings on the bill, where Vega, David Clohessy, and other victims testified, it passed in the senate with no opposition. On the assembly side of the capitol Drivon and Anderson turned to a Los Angeles lawyer named Raymond Boucher for help. A prominent trial attorney with some experience with abuse cases, he was best known in Sacramento for helping Democratic candidates raise money, exploit issues, and win campaigns. Energetic and focused, Boucher spoke with an accent that revealed his roots in working-class Massachusetts, where he grew up a devout Catholic and Red Sox fan. He enjoyed playing insider politics and often helped Dunn, a relative newcomer to Sacramento, negotiate with more established figures on the assembly side of the capitol.

Ultimately the bill passed unanimously in both houses and Gov. Graham "Gray" Davis signed the bill into law on July 13. It would take effect January 1, 2003. Anderson had not waited but instead filed suits ahead of the law's approval. In Minnesota his law partners challenged his judgment, noting that in many of these cases he had already failed. They considered the expenses related to these claims, and protested more loudly than ever. This conflict reached a crisis point as they demanded that he get out of all the California cases. Anderson summoned his partners into an office where he said, "I have to do this. You don't believe in it. I want a divorce." The partnership would be dissolved in six months, but disputes over future revenues would continue for years.

In the history of the abuse crisis, no single act would have greater effect than the opening of the California window. In 2002, the twelve dioceses of California faced more than a thousand potential plaintiffs in lawsuits alleging abuse by hundreds of priests. The state was also home to more than a dozen attorneys with the expertise, experience, and resources to pursue multiple cases in every jurisdiction in California. Most of these attorneys had turned to Jeffrey Anderson for guidance and he had taught them much of what he knew. He would remain a presence, as either co-counsel or consultant, in hundreds of cases.

If precedent had been established in prior cases like the O'Grady trial in Stockton or the DiMaria settlement in Los Angeles, the Church and its insurance companies faced liabilities that might exceed $1 billion. The money did provide a kind of incentive for victims and lawyers, but it wasn't their sole motivation. The people who had been abused wanted the Church to recognize their injuries, take responsibility, and implement reforms. The same desires inspired the majority of the prominent lawyers and activists who took up this cause because they too were Catholics and they believed what the Church said about justice.

21.
THE OPEN WINDOW

There were more than a few things about Emery Worldwide that appealed to Patrick Wall. For one, the air freight business required order and organization and Wall's previous experience as a Benedictine monk and Catholic priest made him familiar with both. Emery also took advantage of Wall's work ethic, sending him out as a salesman to knock on doors and win new business. But most of all, Wall appreciated the paychecks Emery gave him. Considering the struggle he had endured looking for a job in the midst of a recession with nothing on his résumé but his assignments as a Catholic priest, Emery's money was a godsend. It also came with generous benefits, which a man with family needed.

At five foot ten and two hundred thirty-five pounds, Wall had played college football and he looked like one of the Emery guys who had worked himself up from a freight-handler's position to an office job. His bright blue eyes, fair skin, and short-cropped blond hair also made him look far younger than his thirty-seven years. Then there was the way he talked. Raised on a farm in tiny Lake City, Minnesota, Wall never sounded unpleasant or judgmental or pushy. He could listen to a client tell the same joke at every meeting, and chuckle every time he heard it.

When Wall was dating, a few women guessed he had once been a priest. One even asked him to hear her confession. (He declined.) But after he married in 2001 and settled in at Emery he began to feel like a real civilian. The only things that called him back to his clerical past were the occasional reports he read about clergy abuse. He felt deep sadness for the victims, anger toward the institutional Church, and a twinge of guilt because more than most priests, he had been part of the system of cover-up.

Wall had been educated at St. John's, the same monastery in Minnesota that produced Richard Sipe. There he had adapted to the rules and endured the silence and tried to block from memory the strange stories that made him think something was not quite right about the place. In one, a senior priest informed him that a classmate had suffered a nervous breakdown and left the grounds in the middle of a winter night. The young man was on a highway off-ramp raving about how he "must see God right away." Students picked him up in their car and delivered him to a hospital. Wall learned later that his classmate had been stark naked when he was found. He never asked his superiors why they left this detail out of their reporting, or what had happened to the fellow.

Brother Patrick got his first experience cleaning up after an abuse case before he finished his education, when he was suddenly asked to take charge of a dormitory where a supervisor had abused a student. Wall managed to calm down the seventy boys in the dorm and the storm over his predecessor passed. This success led to assignments in parishes where priests had been chased out by scandal. One was St. Mary's of Stillwater, where three victims had accused a priest of abuse and Wall lived within sight of Jeff Anderson's home. Another was in St. Paul, where he discovered that the pastor was having a sexual relationship with a nun and $100,000 in parish money had been placed in secret checking accounts that only they could access.

Through his service as a fixer for parishes, Wall became a spokesman for a Church sex abuse response team and used denial, diversion, and his calming personality to minimize the effects of scandal. As a member of this team, Wall first heard the term "monk's disease" to describe the idea that isolation and celibacy increased the likelihood that a

509

monk would abuse minors. He was stunned by the number of sex abuse claims made against priests and brothers from St. John's. On one day, nine different men accused the same monk of having abused them when they were at the seminary.

In local communities Wall discovered more about the varied dynamics of a priest's life than he could have ever learned as a regular pastor or in some administrative post for the Benedictines. Besides the sexual crimes and the financial shenanigans, Wall came to understand the strange power that still came with the Roman collar.

When properly outfitted Wall could walk into a bank or an executive's office and get immediate attention in ways that ordinary people did not. "I didn't have to show ID or have my name on the account at the bank," he explained. "All I had to do was say I'm Father so-and-so, the new priest at St. Whoever's, and I got access to the money." The collar also put him, a twenty-something fellow with little life experience, on an equal footing with the most powerful people in a community. This authority, and the obvious ways it could be abused, became a subject of conversation in his regular visits with his spiritual adviser, an elderly Dominican nun who was stunned by his stories. With her help, Wall realized he couldn't continue to work in an institution run by men who preached a morality it couldn't maintain. He quit the priesthood and traveled to the West Coast in hopes of beginning life anew.

In the fall of 2001, Wall took special note of an article that attorney John Manly had published on the op-ed page of the *Los Angeles Times*. Catholic born and educated, Manly called out the Church for its hardball legal tactics, including a countersuit the Archdiocese of Portland filed against a victim. "The only way the Church can deal with this issue," wrote Manly, "is to stop denying it, admit fault, minister to victims and expel perpetrators from the clergy."

Six months later, Wall happened to stop at an Emery client's office and noticed that Manly occupied space in the same building. Without thinking much about it, he went to Manly's suite and asked to see him. Years of practice had taught Manly to avoid cold calls and he didn't see Wall. But he did look at the note Wall left, explaining that he was a former priest and monk from St. John's and he wanted to talk. Manly, who had been relying on Richard Sipe for years, called him to ask if he knew anything about Wall. With a few telephone calls Sipe learned that Patrick Wall was considered by the Benedictines to be strong-willed and unmanageable. Manly called Wall to ask when he could come for a meeting.

Manly and Wall were the same age and alike

in many ways. Manly had lots of Catholic education. He had graduated from the local Mater Dei high school and attended retreats conducted by Donald Maguire, a conservative Jesuit priest famous for his close relationship with Mother Theresa of Calcutta. An outgoing, talkative storyteller who sometimes let his anger flare into view, Manly appreciated Wall's steady presence. By October the former priest had quit Emery and was working in Manly's small firm, interviewing prospective clients and poring over documents, including records of priest assignments. On evenings and weekends he worked long hours reviewing statements made by people who had contacted Manly to say they had been abused by priests.

The news reports on the "window" brought hundreds of calls to Manly's office and to Wall's surprise he immediately fell into a grinding routine that kept him working ten-hour days, six days per week. Much of this time was consumed with interviewing potential clients who came with a range of tragic stories about priests who harassed, molested, and raped them. Male and female, they recalled incidents that occurred when they were as young as six and as old as sixteen. Ryan DiMaria, the victim who claimed to have been abused by Father Hollywood, soon joined the team, fresh from law school.

With Manly relieving the tension with pretend tirades and off-color jokes, the men waded through testimony to determine whether claims would hold up in court and to identify priests who seemed to be repeat offenders. Wall was especially helpful using printed Catholic directories to track priests' assignments and match their presence in a parish with claims made by victims. He was also able to decipher Church documents and place current events in context. As Wall told Manly, the Church has been aware of the problem of sexual abuse by clergy for about a thousand years. The evidence of this concern included *The Book of Gomorrah,* written by St. Peter Damien in response to fears that priests were soliciting sex from parishioners. Produced in the year 1048, the book warns of the destruction that could be wrought by the abuse of children. Damien pointedly quotes the Bible's admonition that, "Whoever scandalizes one of these little ones, it were better to have a millstone hung around his neck and to be drowned in the depths of the sea."

Manly often reflected on millstones and the deep blue sea as he pursued priest abusers and their supervisors. When initial settlement talks with Church officials in Los Angeles and Orange counties stalled, he began approaching every case with the intention of going to trial. Manly scheduled depositions with priests, vicars, bishops, and others in the Church bureaucracy and filed discovery requests for all sorts of documents. Church lawyers understood the risks that arose whenever they let a plaintiff's attorney into a room with a bishop. In the DiMaria case a bishop named Norman McFarland actually testified in a deposition that a girl of fifteen could pose a sexual dilemma. "She may be very precocious or adult looking and everything else, and there would be a temptation there," he explained.

Across California dozens of attorneys also began building cases for clients who came to them seeking to make complaints while the window was open. Among them was Raymond Boucher in Los Angeles, who developed an archive of hundreds of video depositions of men and women who described how priests manipulated or coerced them into sexual acts when they were children and adolescents. The variety of sex acts described by victims was practically infinite, but certain elements in these crimes appeared again and again. In almost every case the victims were from extremely devout families and they revered the Church. Many were lonely and isolated. Offenders poured their time, money, and energy into building trust with these youngsters and with their families.

Telling these tales typically prompted a return to the fear, anxiety, and trauma that victims experienced as children. Some found themselves contemplating suicide after their meetings with lawyers. One of Boucher's clients acted on these feelings and killed herself. All of the attorneys who listened and made notes on the legal aspects of what they heard struggled to maintain professional distance in client interviews. For Boucher, who knew and respected Roger Mahony, evidence showing the cardinal transferred priests and protected them from claims of abusing minors came as a personal shock and a disappointment. Jason Berry would recall that Boucher was "furious" about Mahony and said as much during an interview.

A lifelong Catholic, Boucher was frustrated by Church officials and their lawyers, who felt they were under attack by hostile people who were determined to drain the Church of its resources. "I tried to tell them that this was not revenge, it was a reckoning," recalled Boucher. "But they acted like they were the ones being victimized, like all anyone was after was their money."

The money was a factor, on all sides, because payments to victims would compensate them in real terms for their pain, suffering, and for the losses associated with depression, post-traumatic stress, and other disorders that make it difficult for people to secure an education, establish relationships, and build careers. In many jurisdictions juries had estimated these losses in excess of $1 million per person. With this figure in mind, Boucher and the other plaintiffs' attorneys put substantial effort into tracking down every insurance policy and Church asset that might be used to pay damages to victims. Meanwhile, the Church and its insurers looked for ways to manage the litigation to preserve the institution and prevent bankruptcies.

Although bankruptcy could seem a reasonable option, it was risky for those who feared the release of secret documents on thousands of priests. Federal judges who oversee the bankruptcy process enjoy broad powers to compel institutions to turn over paperwork to anyone who might be a creditor. Every single plaintiff suing for abuse would have standing as an individual creditor and demand volumes of confidential materials to aid his or her pursuit of damages.

Both sides were aware of the possibility that the evidence might show that Cardinal Mahony and the Vatican were negligent in supervising priests and may have actively protected criminals. Jeffrey Anderson had long believed that the Pope and the Roman bureaucracy were responsible for the abuse crisis and should bear responsibility for the past crimes of priests and bishops and for reforms to safeguard the future.

Church officials, despite the Pope's claim

to ultimate authority, insisted the responsibility for priests stopped with bishops. In the spring of 2002 Anderson found a case that might let him defeat this claim. It involved an Irish priest who was sent to America after confessing to abusing a child in his home country. When he was sent to America, Andrew Ronan remained a member of his order, which was based in Italy. The international element of the case strengthened Anderson's assertion that Ronan, like all priests, was under the Vatican's control.

In *John V. Doe v. Holy See* Anderson sought to make those who set the rules for clergy responsible for their conduct. To make the charges stick, he had to show that his case qualified under a law that allows for sovereign states to be sued in American courts under special circumstances. One of these exceptions permits suits against employees of a foreign power who harm another person, thereby committing what's legally called a "tort." Another exception allows for suits to proceed if a sovereign state involved in substantial business activity committed a commercial fraud. Here, Anderson believed, he could show that Ronan was ultimately an employee of the international Church and that the same Church, led by officials of the Holy See, had committed fraud as they sought to protect institutional assets. (Although the paperwork was filed on April 1, and defense attorneys scoffed at Anderson's premise, it was no joke. In the years to come Anderson would beat back efforts to dismiss the case and eventually the U.S. Supreme Court would reject the Holy See's claim of sovereign immunity and allow the case to proceed.)

In Southern California, the names of more than two hundred and fifty accused priests emerged from the documentation released in the early stages of trials. This roughly doubled the number of clergy facing claims by more than a thousand victims. In Northern California, Anderson pressed a handful of cases to trial with co-counsels Larry Drivon, Rick Simons, and Joseph George, suing separate dioceses in San Francisco, Oakland, Sacramento, and Fresno. In each jurisdiction the attorneys got mixed results that eventually led to general settlements for large groups of plaintiffs. In Southern California the big dioceses of Los Angeles, Orange County, and San Diego marshaled greater resources to defend against greater numbers of complaints that put much more valuable assets at risk.

As he took up the job of defending the Archdiocese of Los Angeles, attorney Michael Hennigan believed his charge was to help "save the Church" from its worst crisis since the Reformation. One of his first calls on the case was to the prominent Catholic layman

William Clark, who had been President Reagan's national security adviser. (In this capacity he would have had access to every secret element of America's Cold War relationship with the Vatican.) As Hennigan would recall it, Clark spoke first in spiritual terms, suggesting that God may be using the crisis to make the Church "a smaller, humbler institution than we have become." He then told Hennigan that the Pope and his closest aides "haven't made up their minds yet" on the question of whether clergy abuse was an "American problem or a global one."

Others Hennigan contacted in the early stages of his work shaped his perspective on the nature, causes, and proper response to the claims made against priests. In his own mind Hennigan separated acts committed against prepubescent children from those perpetrated against adolescents. Even though both were illegal, and represented violations of trust, he could understand why "a typical male might find a seventeen-year-old attractive." Hennigan also concluded that while the priest scandal "needed addressing," other major institutions had similar problems that just weren't receiving the same media attention.

The media was a major player in the crisis and in Los Angeles it was led by *Los Angeles Times* columnist Steve Lopez, who repeatedly criticized Cardinal Mahony for his changing statements on the crisis and refusing to report all claims against priests. To help turn around public opinion, Hennigan brought in a high-powered consulting firm called Sitrick and Company, which had previously guided both the Enron Corporation and Orange County through bankruptcies. He then focused on the civil complaints made in various courts and the demands of grand juries seated in both Ventura and Los Angeles counties. In all these proceedings, which numbered more than a dozen, Hennigan would have to negotiate requests for testimony from Church officials and respond to demands for documents.

At the height of the Boston scandal Cardinal Mahony had said of the records, "We want every single thing out, open and dealt with, period." But in the calmer season that followed he retreated from this stand. Under Hennigan's guidance the archdiocese withheld papers requested by civil lawyers and prosecutors.

Sought by the press to comment on this change, Richard Sipe was blunt. "What's happening is that the bishops, who say they want transparency, are exposing themselves as liars." Michael Hennigan insisted the cardinal had the right to discuss sensitive subjects with priests without fear of losing his privacy.

One of the city's best-known litigators,

Hennigan was a tall man with bright blue eyes and white hair. His face was weathered by days spent in the Western sun "relaxing" while competing on horseback in rodeo events. In state and federal court Hennigan had represented both plaintiffs and defendants in cases worth hundreds of millions of dollars and involving high-profile parties including movie studios, major banks, and investment firms. Hennigan had also pioneered the use of technology to manage the flow of documents in complex cases. When other lawyers were still carting files around in wheeling briefcases, Hennigan was able to access tens of thousands of searchable pages on his laptop computer.

Throughout his career Hennigan had dealt almost exclusively in matters where the stakes involved money and reputation. In the church cases he encountered, for the first time, clients responsible for disturbing and personally damaging crimes and courtroom opponents who had suffered deep psychological and spiritual harm. The sincerity of the plaintiffs was demonstrated before Easter, 2003, when Manuel Vega conducted an eight-day vigil and fast on the sidewalk in front of the cathedral. Palm Sunday crowds attending Mass at the cathedral offered him a mixed reaction. Some expressed their gratitude. One complained that he "mocked the house of God." But Vega would persist for eight days, sitting and standing in sunshine, darkness, wind, and rain beneath a banner that read. "Innocence is a child's right. Sexual abuse is not." One night the cardinal visited Vega and gave him rosary beads. When Steve Lopez then asked Vega to compare the cardinal to a figure from the life of Christ, Vega said, "Judas."

Michael Hennigan was moved by Vega's story, but as much as he empathized with victims, he recognized the archdiocese and Cardinal Mahony "as my clients" and he believed his duty was "to protect them and bring the cases to a close." In order to accomplish these tasks, Hennigan resisted demands that Mahony submit to depositions and fought requests for documents. Other lawyers followed similar strategies as they represented the Church against claims from coast to coast. On a national level this behavior so distressed Frank Keating that he told a journalist that the Church was behaving like "la Cosa Nostra." A week later the former governor of Oklahoma resigned his position as head of the national panel of laypeople formed a year before to investigate the abuse crisis. Keating was supposed to lend his credibility to this effort. Instead he affirmed the worst fears of its critics. "To resist grand jury subpoenas, to suppress the names of offending clerics, to deny, to obfuscate, to explain away; that is the model of a criminal organization," he said upon his resignation, "not my church."

Cardinal Mahony couldn't resist criticizing Keating publicly, calling him "off the wall." But otherwise Mahony stayed quiet as Hennigan began working on a massive settlement that would resolve most of the Los Angeles claims. The courts and plaintiffs cooperated by consolidating about five hundred suits and empowering Raymond Boucher to negotiate the terms of a proposed settlement with Hennigan. (Anderson was excluded as opposing attorneys fought to prevent him from being admitted to the bar in Southern California.) This process would take years. In that time a similar settlement was negotiated in suburban Orange County, where some cases dated to a time when the region was still part of the Archdiocese of Los Angeles.

Boucher and Hennigan labored to find common ground and to grant concessions where they could. Boucher would recall that he agreed to "a modified request for documents" in exchange for a promise that Hennigan would not use the Los Angeles cases to ask a court to declare the "window" legislation unconstitutional. (Both men held to the agreement, technically, though Hennigan did try and failed to have the statute overturned in San Diego.) No such arrangement was reached in other jurisdictions, which is why, in the fall of 2004, Cardinal Mahony found himself seated in front of more than a dozen attorneys in a conference room on the twenty-sixth floor of a Los Angeles office building. Besides the lawyers, the deposition was attended by Richard Sipe and Patrick Wall.

Videotaped for posterity, Mahony's second-ever deposition (the first occurred in the O'Grady case) began with a display of attorney wrestling interrupted occasionally by testimony from the witness. For twenty minutes almost every question posed by the plaintiffs, who were led by John Manly, was greeted by an objection from the defense team led by Hennigan and a lawyer named Donald Woods. A snippet from the official transcript illustrates the tenor of the day. The passage begins after Manly asks the cardinal if he ever forgot the very first incident of sexual abuse reported to him as a bishop, in 1981:

MR. WOODS: I'm going to object. Irrelevant to the subject matter. There's no difference whether he forgot or didn't forget at some point in time. I'll let him answer.

MR. MANLY: Do you want to have a running objection to every question under all bases so you don't have to object to every question?

MR. WOODS: I'll take it, but I need to voice the objections anyhow.

MR. MANLY: Because I think what you intend to do is what you did in the last deposition, which is object to every single question to delay the proceedings.

MR. WOODS: If you'd ask standard questions. I mean . . . "How do you feel about it?" those, those aren't the type of questions you should be asking here.

MR. MANLY: Don, you know what, we've all worked very hard to get here. And I would ask that you behave courteously, as I am, not be nasty, not be insulting, because we're going to get this done a lot faster and get His Eminence out of here.

MR. HENNIGAN: We're going to quote a line from a movie some time ago, "If you think you're being courteous, you must be from New York City."

MR. MANLY: Well, I'm certainly not from Hancock Park.

Hancock Park is, of course, an old-money neighborhood of Los Angeles, and it was home to Michael Hennigan and much of the region's business and legal elite. By invoking it, Manly called attention to his opponent's rarified social connections. New York City, as Hennigan deployed it, represented bad manners and worse, something foreign to Los Angeles. Neither were part of the subject at hand, but then again, Donald Woods's objection to questions about how the cardinal might "feel" was plucked out of thin air as well. No one had used the word "feel" or "feelings" or "emotions," and Woods was clearly straining to find a reason to interrupt the flow of Manly's questions.

The flare-up actually calmed the opposing counsels a bit and they did manage to conduct an extensive deposition in which Mahony described how he handled complaints against priests, including the one involving Oliver O'Grady, and recounted his own evolving awareness of the sexual abuse problem among clergy. Perhaps the most important revelation of the day was Mahony's acknowledgment that he had dealt with two serious abuse cases prior to the complaints against O'Grady. This testimony contradicted what he told Jeff Anderson during the O'Grady proceedings. Memos that Mahony had written on these two cases provided proof of his involvement, but he insisted that the discrepancies in his testimony were due to memory lapses.

Mahony, who wore black and a white Roman collar, used the words "don't recall" more than seventy times during his deposition and in several moments he launched into longer explanations for these lapses. "We had many events in the Archdiocese of Los Angeles, and I was very preoccupied," he answered at one point. "We had the visit of the Holy Father. We had the earthquakes. We had riots. We had everything. And I simply did not remember everything that happened many years ago in Stockton." Manly reacted incredulously when Mahony said he didn't remember police investigations of complaints against priests, and that during the first five years of his priesthood he was unaware of the possibility that some men broke their vows of celibacy.

However, the most telling response of the day was a single-word answer Mahony offered when Manly asked, "If if it had come to your attention that Father O'Grady told your Vicar General that he had sexual urges towards a nine-year-old or a ten-year-old or an eleven-year-old, is that cause to remove him from ministry?"

"No," replied the cardinal.

For John Manly and the other attorneys pressing cases, the Mahony deposition would help establish the evolution of his approach to complaints against priests. However, no one could have predicted the greater impact it would have when the video was made public by the courts. Filmmaker Amy Berg put the footage to use in a startling documentary she had already begun to develop. Beginning in the U.S., Berg tracked O'Grady's crimes by interviewing his victims and their families. She then traveled to Ireland, where Manly had engaged a private detective to find O'Grady, who had settled there after his release from prison in California.

Ian Withers was an old-fashioned shoe leather investigator who operated out of a small compound of houses in rural Antrim, Northern Ireland. The place was hidden down a leafy lane and guarded by a herd of dairy cows. From this base he pursued cases all over the world. Much of his work was paid for by British newspaper editors who didn't want to know everything about how he gathered information. A short, stout man with gray hair, Withers cultivated an air of mystery and insisted that his activities helped protect the public from the power of institutions that sought to hide their misdeeds. The way he saw it, every time he pushed the limits of the law to get some bit of secret information, he blazed a trail for others to follow.

In the O'Grady case, Withers and his men started with the basic public documents, including the priest's birth certificate, which led them to his hometown where the family still maintained a home. Records "found" in trash set out for collection yielded an address at a house on Dublin Road in the Thurles in County North Tipperary. When a stakeout revealed O'Grady was present, Withers's men served him with a subpoena requiring him to be deposed by John Manly and lawyers for the diocese of Stockton. O'Grady responded without the help of a lawyer, drafting a letter denying the charges and attaching a drawing of a child's rectum and his own erect penis with a notation indicating that based on the size of the two body parts, he could not have raped someone younger than twelve.

Despite the argument he made in his illustrated letter, O'Grady agreed to be questioned and Manly flew to Ireland with Patrick Wall. They drove to a countryside hotel near Cork where they were joined by opposing counsel. The lawyers for the diocese had collected documents, including some they found in Ireland, and handed copies to Manly and Wall as they entered the room. In the cache was a letter, dated 1971, that showed Church officials were aware of the priest's criminal impulses as he was sent to serve in America.

O'Grady arrived dressed in a white shirt that hung loosely on his shoulders, a black tie, and a gray cardigan. He came without an attorney and when told that none of the lawyers present would offer him any legal assistance he acknowledged this fact and agreed to proceed anyway. With Manly gently prompting, he described having sex with his nine-year-old sister when he was twelve and explained how this experience and a sexual relationship he had as a teen with a local priest shaped him.

"To me, it was not a very pleasant experience on some occasions, but it was a very normal thing," said O'Grady. "No one ever talked about it."

Sent to America in 1971, O'Grady began abusing prepubescent boys and girls almost immediately. At times, said O'Grady, he would pause before acting and wonder, "Do I really want to do this?" However, he added, "On the other side there were urges in me to be sexual with him and this was an opportunity."

Most damaging for the Church was O'Grady's insistence that he confessed his crimes to then bishop of Stockton, Merlin Guilfoyle, in 1976, and wrote out a detailed apology to the mother of one victim. Neither Guilfoyle nor his successor, Roger Mahony, acted to protect children in the parishes where O'Grady served until 1984. When Manly asked O'Grady, "If you were the bishop of Stockton, would you have appointed you as the pastor?" O'Grady answered, "No, I would not."

Anyone watching the deposition video could see that O'Grady enjoyed the attention and wanted to explain himself. Fifty-nine years old at the time, he looked physically fit and very much at ease. His wispy gray hair was combed across the top of his head to cover some of his baldness and he smiled frequently as he discussed his attraction to men, women, and children as young as six. O'Grady confessed to cross-dressing while he was a priest in California, and noted that he poured enormous amounts of time into reading about his sexual urges and even formed a self-help group for sex addicts who met in the basement of his church in San Andreas.

As they listened, both Wall and Manly felt a strange combination of disgust and fascination. O'Grady was obviously intelligent enough to carry on a spirited conversation about complex topics and he was quite charming. At the same time, he talked about his seduction of adults and assaults upon children without showing any signs of true remorse. He said words like "sorry" and "regret," but his eyes shone with delight.

During breaks in the deposition, which occurred over two full days, Manly and Wall went outside to walk by a stream that ran through the grounds of the hotel. As he stood watching the water flow, as it had for all of time, Manly tried to detach from what he heard from O'Grady, but he couldn't. He tried black humor — "This guy's the Lucky Charms leprechaun from hell" — but Wall could see that his partner and friend was struggling to contain his anger. Wall considered O'Grady to be more like the character Hannibal Lecter from *Silence of the Lambs* and he believed the deposition was a once-in-history opportunity for study.

"Let's find out what makes these guys tick," he told Manly. "Let's get him to tell us how he feels, how he thinks, what he does."

Back in the wood-paneled hotel meeting room, Manly pushed O'Grady to explain his methods. The former priest talked about how he slowly established relationships with child victims, whom he called "friends," and disguised his intentions. Sometimes he slipped his hand up a dress in a way that seemed accidental. In other cases he began with rubbing a child's shoulder and progressed to undressing him. O'Grady clearly enjoyed discussing his seduction of children, but he was careful to avoid describing incidents in Ireland, where no statute of limitations could protect him, or those that he might still be prosecuted for in California.

Knowing that they might never get another chance to debrief a sexual predator at such length, Wall flashed on a question that might animate O'Grady. Leaning in to whisper into Manly's ear he said, "Give him a name. A hypothetical. Call her Sally."

Manly turned to O'Grady and asked, "How you would greet that little girl you were grooming? Just use the name Sally."

A change came over O'Grady as his face

warmed into a smile and he pretended to look down at a child. "Hi, Sally, how you doing?" he said. "Come here. I want to give you a hug. You're a sweetheart, you know that? You're very special to me. I like you a lot."

It was a persuasive rendering, one that evoked O'Grady's seminary days when he performed on stage in drag and his superiors noted he was "a natural for the part" of a woman. When he finished he looked up at Manly as if he expected applause.

O'Grady clearly wanted to be understood, and he wanted to shift blame, wherever possible. "I would have liked somebody in the diocese or somebody to have intervened as early as possible in helping me confront this situation as a very, very serious one," he told the interviewers. "And help to educate me to the very serious nature of the problem that I had and was causing."

For two full days, O'Grady answered every question. Fifteen hours of videotape were produced and this record was the key factor in the $3 million settlement the diocese decided to pay to Manly's client. It also provided a guide to lawyers pursuing many other cases and an essential element for the documentary film produced by Amy Berg. Armed with the deposition, and interviews with many of O'Grady's victims and their families, Berg went to Ireland where detective Withers had again located O'Grady. He was staying in a hostel in Dublin called the Avalon, where a bed cost less than $20 per night. Publicity had chased him out of the village where he had been living and his real name did not appear on the hostel's register. Nevertheless, O'Grady was accommodating. Confident that he could make himself understood, he cooperated fully, submitting to interviews and allowing Berg to film him walking the streets of Dublin and peering over a fence to see children at play.

A prize-winner at the 2006 Los Angeles Film Festival, Berg's film *Deliver Us from Evil* featured clips from video depositions of American Church leaders, including Cardinal Mahony, to deliver a wrenching portrait of a voracious sexual predator loosed on society by supervisors who should have known better. The film was nominated for an Academy Award and stirred controversy around the world. In Ireland, O'Grady agreed to be interviewed by the local press and announced that he would voluntarily place his own name on a sex offender register, since officials had failed to do so. "I take precautions to make sure I do not come in contact with children," he told one Irish newspaper. "I often see children on buses and then it dawns on me, 'Cripes, I'm on a bus with kids,' but I'm not a threat."

Irish public opinion about Berg's film ranged from gratitude among advocates for abused children to alarm among those who considered O'Grady a danger. At the time when the film was released, the country was reeling from the details of widespread abuse in the report of the government commission established to investigate cases in the diocese of Ferns, which counted just 100,000 in its population. (There Bishop Brendan Comiskey had failed to protect children from Fr. Sean Fortune.) In Ferns the government found more than one hundred claims of abuse against more than twenty priests. The incidents reported by victims ranged from forced oral sex to molestation carried out in the confessional and on an altar. According to *The Ferns Report,* the local bishop who preceded Comiskey had ordained men who were clearly unfit to serve because of their sexual problems and he had ignored the criminal aspects of complaints for decades.

In response to *The Ferns Report,* several Irish parliamentarians called for the government to severe its relationship with the Church. This impulse was tempered by the fact that the Ferns bishop, Brendan Comiskey, had already resigned in disgrace and so had the archbishop of Dublin, Desmond Connell. The Vatican had sent the diplomat Diarmuid Martin to replace him while the Irish government appointed another commission to find out what had gone on in Dublin.

The government's shift, from reflexive

deference to aggressive investigations and public reports, was a sign that the nation's leaders were catching up with ordinary citizens. For several years Ireland's traditionally devout Catholics had been withdrawing their support for the Church. Attendance at Masses that once overflowed with believers had declined precipitously. Traditionally, 90 percent of Irish went to church every Sunday. By 2005 this number had declined to 62 percent. In a couple of years attendance would drop to 42 percent. Some of this phenomenon was credited to the cultural change brought about by Ireland's sudden wealth, but the scandal was also a key factor, as it gave people a kind of permission to challenge Church authority.

The decline of the Irish Catholic Church coincided with the rise of state interest in child welfare — a child protection amendment was proposed for the constitution — and the development of new agencies devoted to preventing abuse and caring for victims. One in Four, which was founded by Colm O'Gorman, grew quickly to offer a range of services including psychotherapy and education. In the same period the government's Commission to Inquire into Child Abuse was created in response to Mary Raftery's film *States of Fear.* The commission had become a fixture in Irish politics, conducting hearings on child abuse in religious and state institutions. Fifteen hundred men and women who said they were abused in these institutions came forward to testify, and a job that was intended to last a year stretched on indefinitely.

Painful as it was, the commission's work contributed to a national reconsideration of children. Beginning in 2006, a group led by Trinity College professor Sheila Greene designed and conducted massive surveys as well as field research to determine the physical and emotional condition of kids and their families. Greene had been studying related issues for twenty-five years and knew that in Ireland more than 80 percent of children older than eighteen months were disciplined physically and that old ideas about children as the property of parents exerted a continuing influence on family life. In the clergy abuse scandal Greene saw the effects of an Irish preference for privacy and a reluctance to question institutions. "The Church got away with it because it was ours," she believed. "It was knitted into our lives and looking at it was like looking at ourselves. It wasn't until the suppression and repression of the truth was lifted that it lost its grip."

22.
A RECKONING

On the evening of April 2, 2005, five clerics — one young, four old — knelt around John Paul II's bed in a small room lit by a single candle. Long suffering from Parkinson's disease and apparent cognitive impairment, Karol Wotyla had withdrawn from public view a month earlier. He was being treated for a urinary infection that his body couldn't seem to overcome.

In the Pope's absence, Cardinal Joseph Ratzinger had celebrated the Easter vigil mass at St. Peter's. The Vatican secretary of state Cardinal Angelo Sodano officiated at Easter services on the big public square outside the basilica. On that day John Paul II, whose infection now raged as sepsis throughout his body, stood in a ceremonial window of the apostolic palace. He was unable to speak.

In the Pope's bedroom, his longtime secretary Stanislaw Dziwisz said a Mass at 8 P.M. When he finished he knelt with the others. At 9:38 John Paul II stopped breathing. Rising to stand, Dziwisz switched on a light and began to sing the early Christian hymn known as the *Te Deum*. The other men who had been kneeling in the shadowy room stood and sang along.

Te Deum laudamus
te Dominum confitemur
Te aeternum Patrem
omnis terra venerator

Translated, *Te Deum* begins with "Thee of God we praise" and in its entirety it is a cry of praise and a plea for mercy. In the Pope's apartment, the words were sung by men who had long anticipated the death of their friend and leader. Some cried. All surely reflected on the task that lay ahead for the Church — the selection of a successor.

As the third-longest reigning the Pope in history, John Paul II had led the Roman Catholic Church for twenty-six of his eighty-five years. His loyal biographer George Weigel, who never mentioned the abuse scandal in a thousand pages about the Pope's life, called him "not the man of the Catholic 20th century," but "the man of the century, period." Jason Berry offered a different assessment. Noting John Paul II's papacy was "riddled with paradoxes," Berry described him as "one of history's great Popes" but also noted, "His response to the worst crisis of the modern Church was passive to a fault."

The problem of sexually abusive priests was known to the hierarchy long before John Paul II became the pope and it raged as a true scandal through two decades of his reign. In all that time, he addressed it publicly fewer than a dozen times. In many of these statements he seemed most concerned about the welfare of the Church and said little about the victims of abusive clergy.

Near the end of his life John Paul II did acknowledge the betrayals of priests who raped and molested minors as crimes. But to the very last he described the crisis as a product of the larger society and not the culture of clerics. And he said that Christian witness and hope juxtaposed with the secular "culture of the material and the ephemeral" was the best way to deal with the scandal.

If not for the clergy abuse scandal, Bernard Law or perhaps Roger Mahony would have been considered candidates to succeed John Paul II. But in the wake of all the controversy, no American would be trusted with such a position. Instead the College of Cardinals quickly affirmed the candidate most Vatican watchers had considered the inevitable heir since the mid-1980s, when he was known as the "Pope's pit bull." Joseph Ratzinger, who became Benedict XVI after his rapid election, had been involved in abuse cases for twenty years as head of the Congregation for the Doctrine of the Faith. As of 2001, management of these cases had been consolidated in Ratzinger's office. Before and after this consolidation the Vatican acted hesitatingly and indecisively, showing more concern for the institution of the Church than it did for victims of abusive priests.

Considering Ratzinger's response to the sexual abuse crisis, Jason Berry went so far as to declare, in a commentary published by the *Los Angeles Times,* that Benedict "cannot credibly lecture us on moral law." As Exhibit A he pointed to Ratzinger's handling of the more than twenty allegations of abuse against the infamous leader of the Legionaries of Christ, Marcial Maciel. As Berry wrote, when he was not yet the Pope, Ratzinger had stopped an investigation of Maciel under pressure from secretary of state Sodano. The probe was resumed just prior to John Paul II's death because, Berry suggested, Ratzinger didn't want to look soft on crime as the College of Cardinals considered him to be the next pontiff. Berry warned that the Church "cannot presume to remain above the law if it persists in shielding child molesters."

Ratzinger's supporters would argue that his shift on the issue of abuse, from defensiveness to assertive policing of his fellow clergy, was already under way before he became the Pope. On Good Friday 2005, before John

Paul II's death, then Cardinal Ratzinger had performed the Stations of the Cross, which recall the day of Christ's crucifixion, at the Roman Colosseum. At station IX, where the celebrant quotes Christ saying, "Do not weep for me; weep instead for yourselves," Ratzinger reportedly added some commentary. "How much filth there is in the Church, and even among those who, in the Priesthood, ought to belong entirely to him! How much pride, how much self-complacency!"

According to the newspaper *La Stampa* Ratzinger subsequently encountered a monsignor on the streets of Rome who criticized him for being so outspoken. As the paper reported, Ratzinger replied, "You weren't born yesterday, you understand what I'm talking about, you know what it means. We priests. We priests!"

Six weeks after Joseph Ratzinger became Benedict XVI, the running total for payments made to abuse victims in America exceeded $1 billion. This line was crossed when the diocese of Covington, Kentucky, created a $120 million fund to settle claims against its priests. Reporters who knew about the 1985 report written by Thomas Doyle, Michael Peterson, and Ray Mouton called Doyle for comment. He said, "Nobody believed us. I remember one archbishop telling me, 'My feeling about this, Tom, is no one's ever going to sue the Catholic Church.' "

By 2005, Doyle had come to make a decent living by conducting research and testifying in court on behalf of people who sued the Church. He hadn't leaped into this job, he had been pushed. The process began in 2003 as the U.S. military invaded Iraq and Doyle began to shuttle between duties in the Middle East and his post at Ramstein Air Base. In Germany his superiors asked if he could streamline his normal ministry to make more time available for counseling soldiers who passed through on their way to and from the war. Doyle cut back on saying daily Masses, which gave him more time to spend with fighting men. He also moved his office from the chapel compound to a space in squadron headquarters, so he would be more visible and accessible to combat soldiers and airmen.

Besides his ministry to the fighters, Doyle was known, even at Ramstein, for his work on the clergy abuse issue back in the United States. During one flare-up in the scandal he conducted a forum at the base where he presented his views and asked for questions. The meeting was held in a chapel that was filled to overflowing. As Doyle recalled it, he tried to give an even-handed account but was challenged by a civilian teacher at a base school who said she believed victims who claimed they were unable to speak up for many years were involved in "a scam." She was followed immediately by another civilian woman who, Doyle recalled, "said that she had been abused at her family's ranch in rural Idaho and when she said something, her mother rejected it all, and rejected her. She didn't talk to anyone about it but the horses on that ranch, until she was an adult."

Overall, Doyle felt supported at the forum but he also detected an undercurrent of disapproval among more conservative Catholics on the base. He heard grumbling about his informal style and rumors of gossip about his priorities. Committed to the service people who needed his counsel, Doyle was giving them more time and energy than he gave to performing ordinary duties like providing sacraments on a daily basis. Finally, a woman who considered herself to be a volunteer watchdog for the faith faxed a complaint to Doyle's boss. She said that by conducting fewer Masses Doyle was neglecting his most important duty.

The fax went to Edwin O'Brien, the archbishop of the military diocese. As Doyle would recall, "O'Brien had been looking for a way to get rid of me for at least four years prior to this." Doyle said that the bishop had objected to public statements he had made about clergy abuse but "he didn't have the ammunition on either occasion to make a move." At one point in their conflict an aide to O'Brien threatened Doyle with excommunication because he was in "schism" with the Church. "I responded that I knew what schism was and I didn't qualify. But what really enraged him was when I told him to go ahead and excommunicate me because it meant nothing to me anyway."

Ultimately O'Brien withdrew Doyle's endorsement, which meant he could not function in the military as a priest. The Air Force kept Doyle on for a while in the role of a substance abuse counselor. He was the only Catholic clergyman in the service with credentials for this work, but eventually his superiors could not justify keeping a chaplain who could do no chaplaining. Having reached the rank of major, Doyle had been looking forward to the possibility of retiring with twenty years of service, but he was discharged just six months shy of the twenty-year mark. He believed it was payback for all his outspoken agitation on behalf of sexual abuse victims, but he fought the urge to lash out at the hierarchy over his personal problems. "I'm a good AA guy," he told friends. "I'll be sober today and sober tomorrow."

Sobriety remained the foundation of Doyle's life and when he returned to Washington, D.C., he found support in several Alcoholics Anonymous meetings. At some of these he ran into prominent Washington figures who trusted the group's promise of anonymity and were never betrayed. But for the most part the meetings were filled with a cross-section of everyday Americans, from secretaries and custodians to doctors and lawyers. Doyle loved these men and women. On more than one occasion Doyle found himself listening to the wisdom of a homeless man or a lifelong drunk who had lost almost everything — family, career, friends — and thought, "There's more wisdom in one of these guys than in all those fuckers in Rome."

Besides the AA fellowship, Doyle found inspiration in writings of theologians like John Shelby Spong, the former Episcopal bishop of Newark who advocated a modern view of Christianity that was less rules-bound and more inclusive. By the time he was done with active ministry Doyle was also finished with the fear that he might face the wrath of God for his straying from Catholic orthodoxy. He took comfort in the camaraderie he found within the movement that had grown up around the abuse issue. Attorneys such as Jeff Anderson, a fellow alcoholic in recovery, became his colleagues and friends. At SNAP conferences and other gatherings Doyle sometimes attended local AA meetings with Anderson. Doyle also set to work on a book he would publish with Richard Sipe and Patrick Wall.

Sex, Priests, and Secret Codes would trace the Roman Catholic struggle to control sex back to the year 309 and document more than ten centuries of crimes committed by priests against children. In conducting research for this book, and for later projects, the three men targeted the Servants of the Paraclete, who had established the first treatment program for priest sex offenders. Founded by a priest named Gerald Fitzgerald, the center in Jemez Springs, New Mexico, first admitted priests who molested and raped minors in the early 1950s. Fitzgerald, who originally intended to treat alcoholism, reluctantly agreed to deal with these men but from the start he held out little hope that they could change. In fact, he became the first whistleblower of the modern crisis when he began warning bishops, and even the Pope, about the men guilty of "tampering with the virtue of the young."

The line about tampering was in a letter Fitzgerald sent to the bishop of Reno, Robert Dwyer, in 1952. In it he urged that priests who abused be defrocked and cast out because "leaving them on duty or wandering from diocese to diocese is contributing to scandal or at least to the approximate danger of scandal." Of course "scandal" was, and continued to be, the preferred euphemism for sexual abuse and despite Fitzgerald's many warnings to his superiors, they did let hundreds of these men wander about as priests.

Fitzgerald's letter to Dwyer was found in a box of documents that the Paracletes had sent to an attorney in Santa Fe named Stephen Tinkler, who had sued them on behalf of people abused as children by men the order had sent into local communities while they were in treatment. It was discovered when Doyle, Patrick Wall, and Richard Sipe went to New Mexico to conduct research for their book. As they read Fitzgerald's papers the three men found a kindred spirit who doubted that priests who abused children could ever be allowed to return to ministry. Among the more compelling finds were letters noting that Fitzgerald intended to discuss the issue of clergy abuse with Pope Pius XII in 1957 and his plan to house offender priests, whom he called "vipers," on an isolated island. Fitzgerald actually paid a $5,000 deposit on an island that was for sale in the Caribbean, but he never completed the purchase. As his papers showed, Fitzgerald became more alarmed the longer he served. After discussing the problem with Pope Paul VI he followed up with a letter that said, in part:

Personally I am not sanguine of the return of priests to active duty who have been addicted to abnormal practices, especially sins with the young. However, the needs of the Church must be taken into consideration and an activation of priests who have seemingly recovered in this field may be considered but is only recommended where careful guidance and supervision is possible. Where there is indication of incorrigibility, because of the tremendous scandal given, I would most earnestly recommend total laicization.

Along with this correspondence, Sipe, Wall, and Doyle found photos of Fitzgerald with the Pope and documentation showing that high-ranking officials from many dioceses, including the Archdiocese of Los Angeles, had sent sexually abusive priests to New Mexico for treatment long before the current crisis erupted. Altogether, the Fitzgerald documents contradicted Catholic leaders who said the Church was ill-informed on the problem and only came to understand it in the 1980s or 1990s. Fitzgerald's repeated warnings were delivered to responsible men at every level, including the Vatican, in the 1950s and 1960s. When Los Angeles attorney Anthony DeMarco persuaded a judge to release them, they became key documents in future lawsuits.

Because they did research that produced results, Doyle, Wall, and Sipe were often quoted in the press and invited to conferences around the world, where they offered insider perspectives on the Church and its problems. The three former priests approached the subject with varying types of expertise. As the most academic and psychological of the three, Sipe was the intellectual leader who knew more about the spiritual, historic, and mental health aspects of Catholicism. Doyle possessed a canon law degree, had experience with the many layers of the hierarchy, and knew the details of the modern crisis better than anyone. Wall understood how the Church responded institutionally to trouble in a parish, because he had been one of its troubleshooters. He also had a gift for on-the-ground investigations.

Part pastor, part jock, and part Emery freight salesman, Wall could talk to anyone. Victims of abuse were comforted by the fact that he understood their faith but shared their critique of the Church system. His uncanny ability to make people feel comfortable was especially valuable as he travelled rural Alaska, often by small plane, meeting native people who had been abused as children by Jesuit missionaries. Wall wound up in Alaska at the invitation of a local attorney named Ken Roosa, who represented several native Alaskans who had been abused by a locally famous Jesuit priest, Rev. James Poole. A non-Catholic, Roosa had first consulted Richard Sipe to help him understand the Church and its bureaucracy. When Sipe met with five of Roosa's clients in the small village of Bethel, a high-ranking official of the Jesuit order arrived to offer them settlements of $10,000 apiece. To Sipe, this man's presence signaled that the Jesuits were deeply concerned, which meant the problem was probably bigger than Roosa knew. He urged Roosa to reject the offers and call in Wall and Manly for backup.

Wall would travel north many times, racking up frequent flier miles on Alaska Airlines and learning to tolerate stomach-churning flights with the bush pilots who brought him to villages that could not be reached by any highway or scheduled commercial flights. Moving from one isolated village to another, he listened to men and women talk about Jesuit missionaries who had raped and molested them. Some of the women had given birth to fair-haired children. Every one of the victims expressed profound grief and anger. Entire communities were outraged by testimony offered by a former Jesuit leader of the order who minimized the harm done and said the Alaskans "were fairly loose on sexual matters." (His words, uttered in a deposition, were made public by Manly.) In the same time period a spokesman for the Jesuit province of Oregon, which included Alaska, explained that priests in the wilderness of the north endured "a Third World existence. The priests are out in the middle of nowhere. They don't have a lot of supervision. We did the best we could."

Among the Jesuits in Alaska, three abusers stood out. Two — Rev. George Endal and a former monk named Joseph Lundowski — traveled the state together from the 1940s to the 1980s. Lundowski, who was called "Brother," became notorious for molesting dozens of boys as young as six. Endal was also accused by multiple victims. In one village, 80 percent of the men in one generation said they had been sexually abused by Lundowski, Endal, or both of them.

During the time when Lundowski and Endal were moving from assignment to assignment, Fr. James E. Poole's voice boomed across the tundra on the power of KNOM radio, a station he helped to found. Named Alaska's "hippest DJ" by *People* magazine, Poole was attracted to young girls and eventually admitted in a deposition to molesting many of them. As an adult, a native woman named Rachel Mike accused Poole of getting her pregnant when she was fourteen. She also claimed he encouraged her to get an abortion and blame the pregnancy on her father, who went to jail. The Jesuit order settled Mike's claim and others and apologized to victims, but Poole never admitted wrongdoing in her case and has never been convicted of a crime. When another victim complained to Poole's direct supervisor, a bishop named Michael Kaniecki wrote a letter indicating he had "tried to cover all bases, yet not admit anything" to anyone who knew of the complaint.

Kaniecki's letter, Poole's confession, and volumes of additional evidence led eventually to a $50 million settlement for more than a hundred victims of Jesuits. A few years later, the order would settle a larger suit involving five hundred victims across the Pacific Northwest for $166 million. In the same states, local dioceses faced hundreds of separate lawsuits involving allegations against their own priests. Most would pay settlements in excess of $10 million. The dioceses of Spokane and Fairbanks would declare bankruptcy.

Keeping track of the thousands of lawsuits filed in hundreds of cities would have been impossible for any one person, and as the crisis continued no one was able to describe, with real certainty, how many victims and priests were involved and how much money had been paid out. David Clohessy and Barbara Blaine of SNAP traveled widely to meet with victims and the membership of their organization exceeded four thousand, but they didn't keep records that would describe the actual scope of the scandal. Far more people called for counsel and never signed up to participate in the organization.

Perhaps the best running account of the national and global crisis was maintained by

Terry McKiernan in Boston, whose Bishop Accountability.org Web site became a repository for thousands of articles, depositions, and court rulings. Lawyer Sylvia Demarest and others donated their case files, and McKiernan busily scanned and indexed their contents so they could be searched online. Other databases, including AbuseTracker, which was begun by the Poynter Institute for journalism, were folded into BishopAccountability, which would eventually employ both McKiernan and fellow activist Ann Barrett Doyle. The site made legal concepts and news instantly available so that individuals and small groups could act in hundreds of places at once. It also reinforced the idea that the Church was not suffering from the sins of a few bad actors but was afflicted, systemically, with a kind of moral disease.

For dioceses and religious orders challenged in the courts, the volume of claims and the unpredictable nature of juries posed an existential threat. Bishops who were required to respond in these cases were also responsible to serve Catholics as pastors, which required answering their concerns without losing credibility. Almost all conducted their own studies, sending researchers to comb through files and produce reports on the history of abuse allegations in their communities. Though intended to settle controversy, many of these reports prompted journalists and critics to conduct their own analyses, which often uncovered more cases not previously revealed by Church authorities. In Los Angeles, for example, BishopAccountability .org quickly found more than two dozen accused priests not counted in the archdiocese's official report on the issue of clergy abuse, which was called *Report to the People of God.*

On a national level, American bishops commissioned a similar accounting by professors at John Jay College of Criminal Justice in New York who asked dioceses to disclose cases going back to 1950. Their report suggested that about 4 percent of priests had been accused of sexual crimes. They also noted that abuse complaints had risen steadily until the 1980s and then declined. The vast majority of victims were boys between the ages of eleven and fourteen.

Because it was based on self-reporting by Church officials, the John Jay study — titled *The Nature and Scope of the Problem of Sexual Abuse of Minors by Catholic Priests and Deacons in the United States* — arrived with limited authority. SNAP leaders immediately said the estimate for the number of offenders was too small and, as a self-survey, the study was seriously flawed. In fact, in several dioceses a case-by-case check of claims against priests revealed that as many as 10 percent had been accused of sexual abuse by a minor. (By 2012 the American bishops would count more than 6,100 accused priests among those who have served since 1950, a figure that represented 5.6 percent.)

The John Jay authors didn't attempt to name a cause for the crisis, but others used their findings to make arguments that fit their pre-conceived notions. William Donohue of the Catholic League said the study "vindicates what we have been saying for the past two years. The report notes that the scandal began in the late 1960s and trailed off considerably after 1984. This coincides with the onset of the sexual revolution and its waning after AIDS was discovered in 1981."

In Milwaukee, Rembert Weakland's successor Timothy Dolan interpreted the report to mean that gay men should be watched more closely in seminaries because "there would be added temptations to the fruitful living of one's chastity." Bishop Wilton Gregory, head of the bishops' conference, used the report to declare an end to the crisis. "I assure you that known offenders are not in ministry. The terrible history recorded here today is history."

The record was a matter of history, but despite periodic claims that it was over, the crisis would grind on. As bishops across the country plotted their own courses through lawsuits, most tried to avoid liability by taking cover behind statutes of limitation and other legal and technical defenses. Among these were the claims that priests were independent contractors not under direct supervision by bishops and that they were protected by the First Amendment. A few sought to negotiate settlements that would resolve large numbers of cases with a single signature. In Orange County, California, Bishop Tod Brown agreed to a court-managed settlement process overseen by Judge Owen Kwong, who sat in Superior Court in Los Angeles. Kwong, known as an expert in settlement, said, "I have no authority to do anything on my own. I'm not the slayer of bad people and I can't punish you for not settling. I work for the government and I only do fair deals. That means I have a purpose for everything I do. Even the chitchat has a purpose."

Kwong worked in a massive building where courtrooms lined hallways that stretched the length of a city block. In his chambers, which were behind one of these courtrooms, he labored at a desk piled high with papers and files. Few judges would speak as bluntly as Kwong, who said from the start that the struggle would revolve around money. "Settlement conferences are dirty business," he said. "And this was a settlement conference for what was basically a personal injury case. It was not that complicated." Kwong was right. The money would be a major factor. But victims bringing the suit also pressed for access to Church documents that held the truth about what had happened to them.

In most cases, including this one, Kwong studied briefs and developed a view about an equitable financial settlement before he ever met directly with attorneys. In the summer of 2004 he greeted the parties, including insurance companies, by saying, "Gentlemen, I've got this case settled. I'm only waiting for you to catch up with me." Kwong's mathematical model for the settlement, which he plotted on a single sheet of paper, was based on what he believed was fair payment to each of the people who said they had been abused by Orange County priests. The final agreement would depend on how many individuals were included. This process was complicated by the fact that the victims were represented by several different attorneys and they had trouble reaching agreement. At least one argued that the victims each deserved $2 million.

Kwong's goal was to reach a settlement that included as many plaintiffs as possible, which would take pressure off the courts and deliver prompt justice. As he watched the attorneys for the victims debate proposals, he signaled his impatience with blunt declarations. Raymond Boucher would recall the judge snapping, "You fucked up, Ray," when it appeared that lawyers representing half the cases had rejected a proposed agreement. Boucher also recalled that the attorneys on his side finally came together and Kwong reached the point where he would agree to propose a deal of $99,950,000 to the diocese. Boucher and the others insisted the figure be $100 million and that the diocese release all records of priests who faced abuse claims. The victims and their attorneys knew that in these records would lie both an accounting of their cases and clues to incidents not yet made public. Both of these demands were agreed to by the diocese and its insurers. The settlement, a full $100 million, was announced in early January 2005.

Although he was not much involved in the actual negotiations, the leader of the diocese got credit from victims who praised his willingness to release documents and his candor about the damage done to those who were abused. Bishop Tod Brown conducted a service of thanksgiving at the Orange County cathedral on the night the agreement was announced. For the first time, members of SNAP were invited into the sanctuary to distribute literature and participate in a Mass. Afterward, at a reception where he spoke privately with victims, Brown was startled when a few of them met him with an embrace. He said, "I wondered why I didn't anticipate being embraced. I finally came to realize why I hadn't. It's because I was unworthy."

By the end of the Orange County scandal, Bishop Tod Brown had earned the admiration of lawyers on all sides of the conflict and the respect of local SNAP leaders. As Brown moved on to other issues, his neighbor and seminary classmate Cardinal Roger Mahony sank into a protracted struggle with the 570 people who had charged more than 220 Los Angeles priests with sexual abuse. Represented by Michael Hennigan, Mahony refused to hand over many of the sensitive documents victims sought, and rejected Raymond Boucher's prediction that the Church would have to pay $1 billion to get out of the tangle of crimes committed by priests. Mahony was also imperiled by an ongoing criminal investigation that put him in danger of indictment and prosecution.

Perhaps the most threatening case, where Mahony was concerned, involved a priest named Michael Baker. In the summer of 2002 one of Baker's victims, Matthew Severson, contacted Jeffrey Anderson and said that he had been raped by Baker multiple times and that when he and his family complained Mahony had promised to remove him from ministry. Anderson called an attorney for the diocese who refused to discuss Baker at all.

In a deposition he gave to Anderson, Mahony recalled that in 1986 Baker had admitted to the cardinal that he had molested two or three boys. At that time Mahony could not have been ignorant of the seriousness of Baker's problem. The press had revealed the Gauthe scandal in Louisiana and the national bishops' conference had begun to confront the issue of clergy abuse as an organization. Even so, Mahony did not remove Baker from the priesthood. Instead he sent him for treatment, allowed him to return to the ministry, and transferred him to nine different parishes where he allegedly abused, at a minimum, twenty-three more young people. None of the parishes were notified of Baker's past problems and, according to Baker, Mahony had said, "No, no, no" when he was asked if the police should be contacted about his offenses. Baker's escape from the law was not an exception. As the *Los Angeles Times* and other news organizations reported, other priests who had committed sex crimes had evaded prosecution, and some had even fled the country without facing the authorities, while Mahony was head of the archdiocese.

As Mahony resisted handing over documents to officials conducting criminal probes, he also stood fast against providing them to victims of abuse. This stance prolonged negotiations on a mass settlement for years. Victims grew angrier as time passed and expressed themselves with rallies and protests at Mahony's new cathedral. In 2003, victims paraded inside with a six-by-eight-foot cross plastered with photos of children who had been abused. In 2005 a man who said he had been abused by two brothers at a Catholic school handcuffed himself to the cathedra — or bishop's chair — as Mahony conducted Mass. James C. Robertson had bought the handcuffs at a yard sale with this protest in mind. He watched in silence as Mahony calmly finished the Mass. When it was over, a few of the two thousand worshippers came to speak to Robertson. Some snapped pictures. One man told him, "Don't you dare scratch that throne." As they exited the cathedral people discovered about two hundred SNAP members conducting a protest. Some of the SNAP protesters had stretched yellow crime scene tape around the building.

The victims of abuse had been frustrated by the ways Mahony and his attorneys had resisted efforts to obtain full access to files on priests identified in lawsuits. Insisting the Church was protected by the First Amendment, Michael Hennigan had provided a limited accounting on these priests. He had also fought Boucher's $1 billion estimate of the final cost for settling the five-hundred-plus cases that became part of a global negotiation. However, Hennigan and Boucher were not opponents at all times. When insurance companies filed a separate lawsuit against the archdiocese, complaining about the lack of documentation they had received, Boucher said they were trying to avoid paying their fair share of the money due to victims.

The money was always a big issue for victims, who believed the Church should be punished and they should be compensated for their pain and suffering. But it was not any more important than the documents. Individual claimants wanted to understand fully who knew what, and when, about the crimes committed against them. Activists and plaintiffs' lawyers believed they would find, in the files, previously unknown perpetrators as well as communications proving that liability extended all the way to Rome. In time the phrase "exposure, disclosure, and then closure" would become a kind of mantra, signifying that what plaintiffs wanted was for children to be protected and for the truth to be known.

Raymond Boucher felt he bore the primary responsibility for moving both the defendants and the courts toward the release of the documents. To accomplish this he put a substantial effort into building a relationship with Cardinal Mahony, whom he met with in private several times. Boucher gave Mahony copies of the video statements made by his clients and he confirmed that the cardinal had watched many of them and that they had moved him to tears. But while he recognized

Mahony "as a person with real empathy" he also considered the cardinal to be a "chameleon" who was able "to rationalize and convince himself that he was not a part of it."

Still a Catholic, Boucher had long believed he had been born to serve some higher purpose. As a high schooler he had experienced something of a miracle when, during a fight, he was struck by a 22-caliber gunshot. The incident occurred outdoors in the dead of winter and Boucher was wearing a big down parka. The bullet hit a double seam in the coat and was slowed so much that it barely penetrated his skin. Boucher and some friends went to a drugstore and bought tweezers and antiseptic. The other boys removed the lead from Boucher's back, cleaned him up, and Boucher wore the coat for the rest of the season.

In surviving, Boucher later said, he became far more alert to the possibilities of life. He was ambitious enough to come to California as a young man and rise quickly to become an insider in Democratic politics. Like Jeff Anderson and Larry Drivon and Roderick MacLeish, he was a driven and highly energetic man who seemed capable of accomplishing much more than the average person. He studied the life of Martin Luther King Jr. and wrote poetry about racism and war. One of his favorite sayings was, "Life's short, eat dessert first." At many meals, he did exactly that.

Life had taught Boucher that "really good people can still do really bad things" and for that reason he believed that big institutions required others to keep them in check. In the clergy abuse crisis the courts and the press had been activated to check the power of the Church and an unstoppable process had begun.

"I told Hennigan, 'This isn't revenge, it's a reckoning,' " recalled Boucher. "And I said that I can have hundreds of people at the cathedral tomorrow hanging him in effigy if that's what it takes." On occasion Boucher leaked items to the press to shame the archdiocese, but if called by a judge to compromise so that talks wouldn't break down, he tried to compromise.

In the end, the struggle over documents, particularly priest personnel files, proved frustrating to Boucher and his colleagues. Although attorneys for victims were certain the dossiers showed that Mahony kept priests in ministry after he had been informed of their crimes, the documents remained locked away. Boucher felt like the battle had consumed his life for several years and that for all concerned, including himself, he needed a deal. Estimates of the archdiocese's wealth ranged as high as $4 billion, but most of this was tied up in real estate. Beginning with the value of insurance policies, the attorneys then worked toward a number that could be reached without forcing the sale of parish properties or the bankruptcy of the institution. In July 2007 the pressure of delivering opening statements in a trial that was slated for a Monday morning produced an agreement on Saturday. The Church and insurers would create a $660 million fund to settle 570 claims against more than 220 priests. This figure pushed the aggregate of money paid by Church entities in California to the $1 billion mark.

Big as it was, the Los Angeles settlement did not spark any criticism among the faithful. Some even suggested that the Church got off easy, considering the lifelong effects of child abuse. Victims were also generally positive about the deal, telling reporters that the average payout — more than $1 million — was a potent symbol. However, parts of the settlement governing the documents sought by victims disappointed many. It created a review process, to be overseen by a judge, that was supposed to lead to the release of files. Instead of producing a flow of information this system cut it to a trickle. Years would pass with few documents reaching the public as lawyers for the Church contested requests and each page was analyzed. Five years after the settlement, the clergy personnel files remained secret. Cardinal Mahony was retired, and Raymond Boucher struggled to repair the parts of his life that had been broken under the weight of the big case.

Unbeknownst to any of his co-counsel and clients, or even Boucher himself, the marriage that had anchored his life was falling apart during the last stages of the settlement negotiation. Days after the settlement was announced and Boucher made the rounds of TV news programs, his wife left him. The divorce and subsequent battle over assets shocked Boucher and the people around him. It would continue into the year 2012.

Boucher was not the only lawyer in the clergy cases to reach a point of personal crisis in the aftermath of a big victory. In New England, Roderick MacLeish entered psychotherapy for post-traumatic stress disorder related to abuse he had suffered in childhood and the demands of his work. In therapy he realized that his work for clergy victims had been inspired and driven by his own experiences as a boy. MacLeish also divorced but, unlike Boucher, he quit the practice of law entirely. He traveled to Great Britain to visit the boarding school where he was abused but discovered no records were available. He eventually settled in New Hampshire, where he took a teaching job at tiny Plymouth State University. In 2010 he told a reporter for *The*

Boston Globe, "I need to be peaceful, I need to be nonadversarial. I fell pretty far, but I am in a good place now."

The demands of representing abuse victims against the Church also took a toll on John Manly, whose practice drew hundreds of cases from Alaska to San Diego and additional ones in the East and Midwest. Once an altar boy, Manly had given the priesthood serious thought before attending a two-week spiritual retreat that helped him decide against it. He remained devout through college, where he also became a staunch member of the right-wing group called Young Americans for Freedom. He went to Central America as part of a study mission for young conservatives. When he married his wife Jill in 1999 he was still so committed to the Church that he asked her to convert to Catholicism. She did.

Loyalty to conservative institutions made sense to Manly until he began investigating abuse cases. The abuse and cover-up he discovered among powerful men he once respected led him to first question and then abandon most of the assumptions that guided his life. One by one, he changed his political, religious, and spiritual views.

On an intellectual level, Manly accepted the facts in clergy cases and understood how power might corrupt leaders. But emotionally, he was unable to manage the disillusionment he felt about the Church. A frequent guest on local talk radio shows, he often made pointed statements about corruption in the Church. He did the same in interviews with print reporters, telling the *Los Angeles Times,* "I think the institutional Catholic Church — from Rome all the way to Orange County — is absolutely and completely corrupt."

As assertive as he seemed on the outside, Manly often struggled to maintain his composure. He failed when he publicly accused opposing attorneys of delaying a deposition in the hope that "the witness will die" before he could testify fully. The outburst earned Manly an official rebuke from the court and he was forced to pay a fine. It also led him to seek psychotherapy and, finally, a weeklong stay at a therapeutic center where he began to confront his abuse of alcohol and his suicidal feelings. At the center, Manly wound up in a group that included a man who reminded him of priests he had known. (To make matters worse, the fellow had complained about Manly's swearing.) For most of the week Manly found himself obsessing over the man and growing angrier and angrier about his presence. At one point he broke the rules, got in his car, and drove to a spot where he could use his cell phone to call his wife.

"Go back," she told him after he calmed

down. "Go back and do what you have to do."

When he returned to the group, Manly decided to confront the staff and the man he believed was a priest. "He's a fucking priest!" shouted Manly. "I didn't come here to be lectured by some fucking priest on the language I use or anything else."

The therapist leading the group interrupted Manly and asked, "Do you know him? Do you know anything about him?"

"I know he's probably a priest."

"Do you know how much power you are giving him?"

In an instant, Manly understood the effects of his own rage. For years he had used this anger to power his work, but it had also hurt his family, colleagues, clients, and himself. The outburst in court and the loose-cannon comments to the press were also the product of this feeling, which came from a limited understanding of the cause he served. He later said, "I had to get to the place where I could deal with the perpetrators and the bishops as wounded people who had gone on to hurt other people, not just monsters who had to be slain." Beginning the transition from rage to understanding saved Manly's marriage and, perhaps, his life. The ultimate destination remained years in the future, but the nature of the abuse scandal, which continued to evolve, would provide him hundreds

of opportunities to practice advocacy with
less anger.

23.
"DON'T TRUST ME"

Most addicts in recovery say that before they let go of drink or drugs, they worried about who they might be without them. Many *do* discover they are different, but *not* in the ways they expect. Jeff Anderson, for example, still worked long hours and when a trial was nearing he labored through the night over arguments drawn on yellow legal pads. But he no longer needed to take big personal risks — in his car or in his marriage — in order to feel alive, or connected to the world. As his wife Julie would say, "He didn't need extreme experiences in order to feel real."

Which isn't to say that Anderson stopped pushing limits. With Joseph Ratzinger's ascent to the papal throne, he saw a greater opportunity to connect the crimes of priests with fraud and conspiracy at the very highest levels of the Church. Before he became the Pope, Ratzinger and the men he supervised directed Rome's response to claims of abuse against priests all over the world. They were the ones who needed years to investigate priests who were subject to multiple complaints. Their signatures were on the documents. In U.S. District Court in Portland, Oregon, Anderson's suit on behalf of men making claims against Fr. Andrew Ronan would be amended to include Benedict XVI by name. At the same time Anderson began discussing with other lawyers the possibility of suing Vatican officials in some international legal forum, like the World Criminal Court at the Hague.

The irony of a recovered drug and alcohol addict with a truly sinful past becoming the Church's main legal tormentor was not lost on Anderson. Enriched by settlements, he bought an old bank building in downtown St. Paul and renovated it with an ecclesiastical flair that included marble floors, stained glass windows, an old confessional, and ornately carved moldings that looked like they had been ripped out of a gothic cathedral. His own massive desk and chair, made of heavy carved oak, could have come from a bishop's palace. Anderson added lawyers and administrative staff to his firm and encouraged them to be as aggressive as criminal prosecutors. He also set about digitizing millions of pages of documents to make them useful for future cases and he made all of it available to colleagues around the world.

Although no one at the Vatican uttered his

name in public, Anderson was, by 2006, the man most identified with the decades-long campaign to hold the institution accountable for clergy sex abuse. Not bound by the demands of dignity necessary for the Pope and leading cardinals, William Donohue of the Catholic League identified Anderson as an enemy, calling him a "radical who hates the Catholic Church." In the summer of 2006, when a judge in Oregon allowed Anderson's case against the Pope to proceed, Donohue told the press, "What's really going on here is an attempt to fleece the Vatican by a multimillionaire with an agenda — it has nothing to do with justice. Look for Anderson to lose in the Supreme Court."

In addition to predicting Anderson's failure, Donohue tried to make him a subject of controversy, noting he was a former student radical and explaining that one of Anderson's children had been abused by a psychotherapist who was formerly a priest. In this event Donohue saw the motive for the attorney's work. Never mind the fact that the incident in question occurred long after Anderson had focused on clergy abuse or that he considered the man a therapist and no longer a priest. Donohue found the association strong enough to declare, "Hate, mixed with greed, makes a sick stew."

Such attacks — personal and insinuating — were Donohue's stock in trade. When he argued with the gay Catholic writer Andrew Sullivan, he would make sure to recall that a decade in the past Sullivan, who was HIV positive, had taken out a personal ad seeking unprotected sex. This fact was presented as if it disqualified Sullivan's suggestion that the police get more involved in clergy abuse cases. "It just doesn't get much sicker than this," wrote Donohue. He also dismissed another opponent, writer Mark Silk, because "Silk is not a Catholic — he is a Jew." And between 2002 and 2012 Jason Berry would evolve, in Donohue's view, from a "loyal son of the Church" into a "liar" who practiced "Church-bashing."

Donohue's use of language — his opponents were "well greased" and "goose-stepping" — reflected his personality and his perspective. When Philadelphia district attorney Lynne Abraham investigated abuse claims in 2002 he declared she had begun a "witch hunt" and was guilty of "anti-Catholic bigotry." Although Abraham found broad evidence of abuse by clergy, the statute of limitations prevented her from prosecuting them. This decision was announced in 2005 and provided an occasion for Donohue to mock the DA — "how disappointing it must be" — and accuse her of wasting taxpayer money with her investigation.

By 2005 Donohue had decided that it was the Church that was being victimized in the abuse crisis and he was convinced "that the Catholic Church had better learn to play hardball with those who are out to destroy it." His Web site declared, "The time has come for the Catholic Church to put the vultures in their place." While he waited for bishops to answer his call, Donohue built a war chest of more than $25 million to support his actions on behalf of the Church. Out of this he accepted a salary and benefits package that eventually reached $370,000 in 2008. As the chief of an organization that reported employing just two people and annual expenses of less than $2.7 million, this figure made him one of the best-paid executives in the nonprofit sector of the economy. In comparison, the median salary for charities with comparable budgets in the Northeast, the region with the highest pay in the country, was $120,000.

What did the Catholic League get for its money? Donohue was often quoted in the press, drawing attention to a point of view that might otherwise be passed over. However, his most inflammatory statements about the abuse crisis rarely received attention beyond his own Web site and the online echo chamber of like-minded activists. He also suffered from the demands of an agenda that took him in a dozen different directions as he engaged in battles over anything that might be deemed "anti-Catholic." Films, TV shows, art works, and even a holiday greeting card sent by President Bush all raised Donohue's ire. (The card bothered him because it omitted any reference to Christmas.) As a consequence of all this scattered activity, Donohue could only attack clergy abuse victims, advocates, and their lawyers in a sporadic way. While he occasionally popped up on a TV talk show to defend the Church, the media terrain was mainly occupied by his opposition. One comprehensive database shows that between 1995 and 2005, Donohue appeared in major newspapers about 650 times. During the same period SNAP was noted in more than 2,200 articles.

While William Donohue was involved in many other issues — most notably the defense of actor/director Mel Gibson after a drunken, anti-Semitic tirade — Jeff Anderson worked on clergy abuse to the exclusion of all else. He spent much of the summer of 2006 preparing to bring his first suit against a Latin American prelate. So wealthy that he never needed to work again, Anderson poured millions of dollars into cases that were unlikely to produce any fees, but might push the institutional Church toward meaningful reform and lay the groundwork for future legal advances. In his mind, sexual abuse continued to be a problem for the Church because of its basic theology and hierarchical structure. As long as Catholicism cultivated sexual shame and kept true power away from women and other laypeople, it would suffer from the abuse of power expressed in terms of sexual crimes.

In September 2006, Anderson flew to Mexico to conduct a press conference about a lawsuit he had filed against Cardinal Roger Mahony of Los Angeles and Cardinal Norberto Rivera Carrera of Mexico City. Anderson's clients included Joaquin Aguilar Mendez and others who alleged they had been raped, as boys, by a Mexican priest named Nicolas Aguilar Rivera (no relation to the cardinal) who had been sent to Los Angeles. In California the priest allegedly abused about two dozen boys in the 1980s. Wanted by the police, who were investigating a complaint from a boy in Los Angeles, Aguilar Rivera went back to Mexico in 1998 when Church officials permitted him to remain in the ministry.

After the priest fled, Mahony wrote to his counterpart in Tehuacán, Bishop Norberto Rivera, saying, "It is almost impossible to determine precisely the number of young altar boys he has sexually molested, but the number is large . . . This priest must be arrested and returned to Los Angeles to suffer the consequences of his immoral actions." Bishop Rivera responded by providing some information about the missing priest, but said

"You will understand that I'm not in a position to find him, much less force him to return and appear in court."

In an echo of the blame-shifting Anderson saw in his first case in Minnesota, where Bishops Watters and Roach tussled over who-knew-what-when, Rivera wrote to Mahony in 1988, claiming that in "the letter of presentation of January 27, 1987, I included an identification photograph, and in the confidential letter of March 23 of the same year, I provided a summary of the priest's homosexual problems." To be precise, Rivera's January 27 letter said that "due to family and health reasons" Aguilar Rivera requested posting in Los Angeles. In that letter, the bishop reassured Mahony, telling him, "don't have any concerns" about accepting him.

Mahony answered on March 30, 1988, "I would like to tell you that I have not received any letter from you dated March 23, 1987, nor any other information concerning 'the homosexual problems of the priest' . . . We have here in the Archdiocese of Los Angeles a clear plan of action: We do not admit priests with any homosexual problems."

Upon his return to his home state the Mexican priest, who could not be found by his bishop, was later accused of sexually assaulting Joaquin Aguilar Mendez, who was then thirteen, and several other boys. He was eventually arrested, tried, and convicted on a single misdemeanor abuse charge, but served no prison time. Mendez and others who were identified only as "Juan Does" turned to the civil courts only after years of efforts to obtain help from the Church failed. When Anderson filed his suit, Fr. Aguilar Rivera remained a priest and a free man. Norberto Rivera, elevated to cardinal of Mexico City, was on record saying the Church in Mexico did not have an abuse problem.

When Anderson arrived in Mexico he was accompanied by a small group. Among them were attorney Michael Finnegan from Anderson's own office, SNAP director David Clohessy, and a Mexican journalist named Sanjuana Martinez. The group also included a lawyer named Vance Owen, who was associated with Raymond Boucher in Los Angeles. A U.S. citizen who was born in Guadalajara and was experienced with the Mexican justice system, Owen had arranged for the Americans to be met by a security team. At the airport they whisked the group into a pair of vans and brought them to the hotel where they would conduct a press conference the following day. Their purpose was to publicize the case, alert other victims, and promote a national conversation about the Church.

The next day, more than a dozen reporters, photographers, and TV technicians gathered around Anderson and Owen in a hotel meeting room. Anderson distributed copies of his complaint against the two cardinals and their archdioceses and then spoke about his clients and their allegations against Fr. Aguilar Rivera. After about an hour, Vance Owen turned toward Anderson and told him to wrap up the press conference immediately. The urgency in Owen's voice caught Anderson by surprise. At first he resisted the suggestion and kept talking. Then he looked up and saw about a dozen men with suits entering the room. Two came directly to the podium, and as the crowd began to stir they spoke in slightly accented English, demanding to see Anderson's travel papers.

Taken aback, Anderson turned toward Owen, who advised him to cooperate with the men, who claimed they were Mexican immigration officials. The private security detail Owen had hired remained in the meeting room and they tried to protect the Americans. Anderson agreed to go back to his room, where he showed two of the men his travel documents that admitted him to the country legally. When Anderson and the men returned to the hotel lobby he found others in his group were being questioned. The reporters, who had begun to leave, returned to see what was happening.

As the men in suits began to pressure the Americans to come with them, Sanjuana Martinez told Anderson, "Make them show you some identification." Others telephoned the American embassy and Mexico City police. One of the intruders flashed open his wallet to reveal some kind of identification card. Another grabbed Michael Finnegan's arm. Finnegan, a tall and muscular former minor league ballplayer, twisted out of the man's grasp. As Anderson would recall, the crowd grew noisier and more intense, closing around the Americans to prevent their departure. He turned to Vance and said, "You're my lawyers down here. What do I do? He said, 'Pray to God.' " Anderson glanced around to see the private security team departing.

Smaller than every other man in the room, Anderson nevertheless stood his ground as the self-proclaimed immigration agents tried to push him, Finnegan, and Clohessy to the door and the vans that waited outside. Suddenly about a dozen police cars arrived outside and twice as many uniformed officers poured into the hotel. As the police came rushing in, trailed by U.S. embassy officials, the men in suits tried to leave. Outside they found their vehicles were blocked. A senior police official, who took charge of the scene, told Anderson the men were kidnappers and his group was in danger. The police drove them to Mexico City's international airport. American embassy officials escorted them inside, and remained with them until they reached the security checkpoint.

On the flight home, Anderson told Clohessy, "It's too bad they didn't get you and kill you. This movement needs a martyr." Clohessy didn't laugh. Weeks later Anderson, Finnegan, and Clohessy received letters from the Mexican government banning them from entering the country for five years. The letter claimed that they had declared they were tourists when they entered Mexico and violated the terms of entry by conducting business. Anderson said he had, in fact, noted on his entry form that he intended to work while in the country.

Anderson's lawsuit against the two cardinals would proceed in Los Angeles, where both Thomas Doyle and Richard Sipe offered affidavits as experts. Doyle described the Church system of authority, with the Pope as the ultimate executive, judge, and legislator. Sipe described how the stilted communication between the churchmen contained disguised references to abuse. Cardinal Rivera had actually admitted that his own references to the offending priest's "family and health reasons" was code for sexual abuse, which he was certain Cardinal Mahony, and any bishop, would understand.

Pretrial motions and legal maneuvering slowed the Aguilar Rivera suit to a crawl, but Anderson and his co-counsel Anthony De-Marco kept pursuing it despite receiving no payments for their time or expenses. In 2011, a federal judge would find they had sufficient grounds to proceed under the Alien Tort Claims Act, which allows for individuals to sue foreign entities in America if they have inadequate access to justice abroad. The ruling marked the first time a clergy abuse claim was found, by a judge, to revolve around a plausible allegation of a crime against humanity, which was covered by the tort claims act.

The crisis that was supposed to be a matter of "history" blazed on, despite efforts by Church leaders to declare it dead. The fire found fuel outside of North America as civil authorities from Australia, South America, and Europe received new civil and criminal complaints. And where the crisis had been most intense — the United States and Ireland — more scandal emerged in government investigations and ongoing litigation. This dynamic was at once the product of the Church's vast interests in these countries where dioceses were confronted one by one, and a result of the slow-moving pace kept by courts. Indeed, as Church lawyers defended their clients with motions and requests for delays, they dragged out the process in a way that forced the institution to be tormented by years of publicity and new claims.

Some of the most extreme examples of unexpected legal consequences involved the Archdiocese of Milwaukee, which had been largely protected from financial losses by favorable court decisions on the statute of limitations. The problem for the diocese, however, was that it might be vulnerable to suits filed in other states. This hazard became serious when Rev. Siegfried Widera was arrested in California on more than thirty charges of sexual crimes. As Church records later revealed, Widera had been convicted in the 1970s of committing a sex crime against a minor in Wisconsin. When he was assigned to new parishes, this history was never mentioned. After more complaints about Widera molesting children, the Milwaukee Diocese sent him to Orange County with a warning that his record included "a moral problem having to do with a boy in school" and that he had suffered a "repetition" which required him to leave the state for "legal reasons." The Church in California accepted him anyway, and Widera resumed abusing minors. He was defrocked in 1986, but was subject to no legal action.

Widera was finally charged by California authorities when the "window" opened in 2002. He fled, and for a brief time he was among the most-wanted fugitives in North America. Eventually tracked to Mexico, where he had reportedly been acting as a priest, Widera was trapped in a third-story hotel room by local police. He leaped from a balcony and died from the injuries he suffered when he hit the ground. His death ended criminal proceedings but not civil suits naming both the Milwaukee and Orange County Dioceses. Eventually the Milwaukee Church would pay much of a $17 million settlement.

The Widera settlement came with a release of documents that revealed complaints filed by additional victims against Widera and others. More victims would come forward, requiring more payouts that dwarfed the value of counseling the Church had offered to Catholics in Wisconsin whose claims against clergy were barred by the state's courts. Each time a settlement was reached, reporters gave victims in Wisconsin a chance to speak, which prolonged the public relations nightmare for the Church. In 2009, for example, SNAP leader Peter Isely used the occasion of a settlement to challenge the credibility of Archbishop Timothy Dolan. Isely reported that he had asked Dolan about the diocese's negotiations with various victims and said, "He never mentioned this case. How many other secret negotiations of sex abuse cases has Dolan got the archdiocese in?"

Isely had a deep understanding of the region's heavily Catholic culture and how it influenced politics, the law, and local media. And he probably knew more about the experience of Wisconsin's clergy abuse victims than anyone in the state. Much of what he saw, including a countersuit filed to force one victim to pay the diocese's legal costs, appalled Isely, but he remained a practicing Catholic and hoped the institution could change. "I think the Christian story is true," he would explain. However, he interpreted the tale in a modern way. He didn't consider God to be an otherworldly power in the sky, but rather a force for healing the human spirit. He saw miracles in the psychological recovery of victims who "say that a part of them died because of what happened to them and then come alive when they speak the truth."

When Dolan took over in Milwaukee, Isely began working with him on a process to reconcile victims and the Church. At the start of this work, the state legislature was considering a new law that might open the courts to victims of clergy abuse in childhood. Isely believed that when the proposed law was not enacted, Dolan began taking tougher stands and the negotiation boiled down to offers from the Church which could be accepted or rejected. When the archbishop offered a settlement fund of less than $4 million for seventy-five victims, Isely rejected it and the process ended. Isely kept, as a souvenir, a letter from Dolan that contained a friendly negotiator-to-negotiator warning. "Don't trust me," wrote Dolan.

With the reconciliation process over, Isely spent more time meeting with victims and investigating cases. In one, he tracked down a priest named Franklyn Becker who was first charged with abuse of a minor in the 1960s and was the subject of complaints throughout his career. He was diagnosed with a sexual disorder in 1983 but remained in active ministry until 1993. Curious about the man, Isely went to see him in the small city of Mayville, Wisconsin, and knocked on the door of his home. Becker invited him to visit. Isely would later recall the encounter this way:

He lived in a house in a subdivision overlooking a playground. The place was immaculate, like a rectory, and there were stuffed animals on his couch. When I asked him about a priest who was accused in some cases that had been settled but disappeared, he turned toward this little octagonal cabinet and opened it like he was opening some sort of tabernacle. He took out these meticulous photo albums and showed me pictures of himself and the priest in a play dressed up like women with coconut bras.

He also showed me a picture of an eight- or nine-year-old boy sitting on his bed. He kept it with a ticket stub from a movie they went to together. He said the kid grew up to be a race car driver.

According to Isely, Becker was relaxed in their conversation and quite content to speak with someone who knew as much as he did about the way the Church operated and understood the priesthood. Isely was so well known in Milwaukee Catholic circles that he often heard from disaffected priests who supported victims of abuse, and even received documents from insiders. The most shocking of these were in a packet of handwritten letters between priests in a Wisconsin parish who wrote openly about their attraction to adolescent boys and described their sex lives in graphic detail. As SNAP leader, Isely also heard from victims who called from all over the state. Eventually he was contacted by the men who had been abused by Rev. Lawrence Murphy at the St. John's School for the Deaf.

In the time since he had been the subject of leafleting around the school by alumni who printed up a fake "wanted" poster, Murphy had confessed to his superiors and was evaluated in 1993 by a sexual disorders specialist. She estimated he had victimized at least two hundred minors and noted that he believed that his crimes were really "sex education" and that by abusing boys he had "fixed the problem" of "rampant homosexuality" among them. The evaluator noted that Murphy was unable to acknowledge the harm he had done and that he was not likely to cooperate with treatment.

When Rembert Weakland asked then Cardinal Ratzinger to defrock Murphy, he received no reply until 1996 when the cardinal's second in command wrote to instruct him to begin a secret Church trial. Murphy then wrote directly to Ratzinger, who told Weakland that the trial should be cancelled because the accused was sick and repentant and the particular crimes in question occurred beyond the canon law statute of limitations. Murphy remained a priest until he died in 1998. For years his victims searched for a way to sue Church authorities for both monetary damages and access to documents related to their cases. They were turned away by lawyers who saw no path around the statute of limitations. Then Isely introduced several of the men to Jeff Anderson and his associate Michael Finnegan, who believed they had found the route.

While digging through the papers that had been released in the settlement covering Rev. Siegfried Widera, Finnegan had begun to wonder if higher-ups could be subject to complaints of fraud, which enjoyed some leeway under the Wisconsin statute of limitation. Finnegan and Anderson represented two men — identified only as John Doe 1 and John Doe 2 — who said that as boys they had been sexually violated by Widera after he had been convicted of criminally abusing a child. Widera's conviction, they would argue, put the Milwaukee hierarchy on notice and their failure to keep the priest out of ministries that brought him into contact with children constituted a fraud against Catholics who relied on them to assure the conduct of clerics. A similar claim of fraud was made by Anderson and Finnegan on behalf of a man named Charles Linneman, who said he was abused by Franklyn Becker.

The fraud argument was a bit of a long shot, but not so improbable that the attorneys were surprised when the Wisconsin Supreme Court overturned a lower court that had denied the plaintiffs a trial. The decision wouldn't allow every person who had been abused by a priest to sue, but it signaled to those who had been harmed by known offenders — like Rev. Murphy — that the courthouse door had been cracked open. The archdiocese responded to the news with restraint, noting that these cases would require much work before any legal resolution might be found. In the meantime the Church would support victims spiritually. "The tragedy of clergy sexual abuse of children and, perhaps even more, the failure in the past of some within the Church to deal decisively with it long ago, will always be an ugly stain on our history. We renew our apology to all victims/survivors and repeat our sincere effort to support their personal recovery."

24.
A ROLLING CATASTROPHE

The new Pope didn't play hardball. Instead, he abandoned the perspective he held in 2002, when he complained about the "constant presence of these news items" as if the crisis had been a matter of public relations, not crime. In its place he adopted a more open approach to victims and a sterner response to known abusers.

As he traveled to America for the first time, in 2008, Benedict XVI said he was "deeply ashamed" of clerical abuse. In Washington he met privately with a handful of victims chosen by the Archdiocese of Boston. The encounter took place at the same apostolic embassy where, decades earlier, Pio Laghi had ordered Tom Doyle to investigate the abuse case that began the crisis. One participant, Bernie McDaid, said he told the Pope, "You have to fix this." Like the others, McDaid was grateful for the encounter but not overawed. Asked what he thought about the potential effect of the meeting he said things will get better, "If everyone wants change."

Most things did not change with Benedict's rise. For example, he continued to focus on homosexuality in the priesthood, and soon the Vatican issued rules banning even chaste men who have "deeply rooted" homosexual identities from the priesthood. However, he did take one notable step to signal toughness on the abuse issue, forcing Legionaries of Christ founder Marcial Maciel into retirement and "a reserved life of prayer and penitence."

In disciplining Maciel, Benedict XVI affirmed Jason Berry's reporting on the once-great priest and boosted the reception that awaited a documentary that the writer produced and directed based on the book *Vows of Silence,* which he cowrote with Gerald Renner. In 2008 the film was named best TV documentary at the International Documentary Film Festival of Mexico City. The film's success contributed to growing concern about clergy abuse across Latin America. Berry would feel gratified, but this satisfaction was soon overwhelmed by the death of his daughter Ariel.

Born with Down's syndrome and diagnosed early in life with a degenerative heart disorder, Ariel had lived for years on borrowed time. Her father had often visited the St. Jude Shrine at Our Lady of Guadalupe church to pray for her, lighting candles and thanking

God for his daughter's health. Ariel enjoyed going to his neighborhood church, Mater Dolorosa, and when she died at Christmastime the family thought it natural to have her funeral there. Berry was overwhelmed by the number of people who attended, which included many of the people he had come to know in almost twenty-five years of writing about clergy abuse. Researchers and abuse survivors were among the people who traveled to New Orleans for the Mass. More than a few fellow journalists, who had drawn insights from Berry's work, also paid their respects.

Ariel was seventeen years old when she died. When she was eight, Berry explored his relationship with her in a piece titled, "Why I Am Still a Catholic." He wrote:

> Through my child I sensed a glimmer of light beyond the sky, a force that can blast you to the knees, something I had only vaguely thought about before . . . a force outside the self that *simply comes,* a spirit that upsets all one's reading and embattled purpose with the sudden mystery of sheer love.

Catholicism, as he felt it, would help Berry through the years immediately after Ariel's death. In this time he contributed many articles on the Church crisis to the *National*

Catholic Reporter but he also allowed himself to explore new territory. He published a play — *Earl Long in Purgatory* — about Louisiana's infamous governor, and he wrote extensively about New Orleans' struggle to recover from Hurricane Katrina. He added 120 new pages to his 1986 book *Up from the Cradle of Jazz,* which was reissued in 2009. He covered the massive oil spill that occurred in the Gulf of Mexico after a drilling rig working for British Petroleum caught fire, exploded, and sank.

As the twenty-fifth anniversary of the Gauthe case arrived in 2009, Berry was drawn back into the big story of his career as he embarked on an investigation of the Church's finances, which would end with the publication of his third major work on the Church, *Render Unto Rome.* The book would reveal how secrecy and special status allowed the institution to evade the scrutiny endured by others and, as in the abuse crisis, enabled both criminal and immoral behavior. It also affirmed the role of money in the pursuit of the institution's goals and the resolution of its problems.

Historically, the Church protected its assets, along with its moral power, by deflecting abuse complaints and conspiring with secular authorities to cover up crimes against children. In May 2009 this pattern was revealed in stark terms by the final report of the Irish commission that had been formed to investigate child abuse at church-run schools and reformatories. Headed by a high court justice named Sean Ryan, the panel reported shocking levels of rape, beatings, physical neglect, and emotional abuse by clergymen, nuns, and lay staff charged with caring for thirty thousand children. Their findings drew on testimony from more than a thousand people. The authors said that at institutions housing boys, which were run mainly by Christian Brothers, molestation and rape were "endemic." At girls' schools, run mainly by the Sisters of Mercy, students were more likely to be subjected to humiliation and denigration but "ritualized" physical abuse was also practiced.

The so-called Ryan Report counted eight hundred abusers in two hundred locales. It outraged the Irish press — *The Irish Times* called it "the map of Irish hell" — and thousands signed a solidarity document dedicated to victims. Money entered the conversation immediately as officials in the Irish government noted that fourteen thousand victims had filed claims and called on the Church to fund an estimated $1.5 billion in settlement costs. The Sisters of Mercy offered about $200 million in cash and property, which could be added to nearly $50 million paid to victims in 2001. Tom Doyle, who had begun to visit Ireland to consult with victims, urged them to use civil institutions to get justice from the orders. "They must be forced by a power greater than themselves," said Doyle, "and that's the courts and the Irish government, to make sure the compensation comes, even to the point of forcibly divesting them of properties."

Months after the Ryan Report, investigators completed a separate probe of the Archdiocese of Dublin. Although focused only on the local diocese, this document counted more than one hundred priest abusers. The commission also found that local authorities, including the police, had aided the cover-up of crimes committed by priests and that abusers who were notorious to authorities were permitted to continue in ministry for years. One priest admitted to molesting a different boy every two weeks for about twenty-five years.

Four Irish bishops resigned in the immediate aftermath of the Dublin report and Pope Benedict XVI summoned the remaining bishops to the Vatican, where he described the abuse committed by Irish priests as "heinous crimes" and told the prelates they had damaged the trust of their flocks. The Pope followed this crisis management session with a letter to Irish Catholics that began with the observation that, "I can only share in the dismay and the sense of betrayal that so many of you have experienced on learning of these sinful and criminal acts and the way

597

Church authorities in Ireland dealt with them." In the four thousand words that followed Benedict did not blame the evils of secular society for the scandal, nor did he mention homosexuality or anti-Catholic bigotry. Instead he pointed to the dangers of excessive regard for priests and "misplaced concern for the reputation of the Church."

It was an historic turn in the Vatican's response to clerical sex abuse, consistent with the Pope's avowed intention to deal with it more directly and decisively. However, anyone who hoped that this turn would end the crisis would be disappointed. Instead of receding, the tide of scandal flooded into Munich, where Church officials admitted that when Benedict was the city's archbishop a priest suspected of pedophilia was quietly transferred to a parish where he then abused children. Local church officials said that Benedict, then Ratzinger, knew nothing of the case, which was one of two hundred recently revealed in Germany.

While no documents emerged to connect the Pope to mishandled cases in Germany, Jeff Anderson named him as a defendant in a lawsuit filed on behalf of deaf men who claimed they had been victims of Fr. Lawrence Murphy, whom Ratzinger had failed to discipline. Ratzinger's role was highlighted in Anderson's filings, which noted that as head of the Congregation for the Doctrine of the

Faith the cardinal failed to respond to allegations against Murphy and allowed the priest to retain his status for years, until he died. Correspondence proving this course of events, which had emerged from the legal discovery process, was placed in the public record and widely reported in the media.

The St. John's plaintiffs eventually came together at meetings where Anderson, speaking through a sign language interpreter, gave them updates and individuals compared their experiences. At one of these sessions, in a hotel outside Milwaukee, more than a hundred victims and their families gathered to listen as men described lifelong struggles with anxiety, fear, failed relationships, and self-blame.

A sixty-year-old man with graying hair and a white moustache, Terrance Kohut stood in the middle of the crowd and used sign language to recall for the group how he and his wife had suffered because he had been abused. "I kept it to myself," he signed, putting his fist up to his mouth. "I kept it hidden until I couldn't keep it hidden, and then I told my wife." Burdened by panic attacks and anxiety, Kohut saw psychologists who helped him explore what had happened. "I finally blew and wrote a seven-page letter. I poured it out. I let Fr. Murphy have it. I said, 'You destroyed my life.' I got no answer."

Following Church procedure, Kohut had

gone to then Archbishop Weakland with his complaints and he submitted to questioning by canon lawyers. He also wrote to Cardinal Angelo Sodano in Rome, asking him to bring his complaints about Murphy to the attention of the Pope. As Kohut recalled, Father Murphy also wrote to the Vatican "and they were so soft about it with him." To illustrate the point, Kohut used one of his hands to pet the other, as if he was petting a small animal. "They didn't treat me soft about it."

Murphy would die before Kohut got satisfaction. Then his wife saw an article about Anderson in *People* magazine. The piece, titled "Serving Rome," described Anderson's first filing against the Pope and was accompanied by photos of him and his family. As Pamela Kohut would recall it, "I saw. I said, 'Yes! 'Yes! That's it. I want Jeff to sue the Vatican for me.' "

Revealed in March 2010 on the front page of *The New York Times,* the case of the deaf victims and Fr. Murphy presented an unusually manipulative abuser who got away with his crimes. The *Times* report was written by Laurie Goodstein, who had covered the abuse crisis since 1994. It was accompanied by documents, published online, detailing Murphy's history as an abuser, his confession, and a long and ultimately ineffective effort to discipline him. Days after the report, SNAP leaders Barbara Blaine, Peter Isely, Barbara

Dorris, and John Pilmaier flew to Rome to conduct a street-corner press conference near the Vatican. Rome police, who said the group needed a permit for their activity, took them into custody and held them for three hours before releasing them. In the meantime an elderly Roman cardinal named José Saraiva Martins complained to reporters of a "conspiracy" against the Church, although he didn't name the conspirators or their purpose. However, he did defend the secrecy practiced by the Church in abuse cases. "We should not be too scandalized if some bishops knew about it but kept it secret," he said. "This is what happens in every family. You don't wash your dirty laundry in public."

The cardinal's defensive impulse was shared by many, but only the activist William Donohue expressed it a comprehensive way. He argued that the majority of clergy abuse victims were males at or just beyond the age of puberty and therefore the scandal was a "homosexual crisis" and not a "pedophilia" crisis. And instead of trying to hold the Church accountable for crimes, said Donohue, the victims movement wanted to "weaken its moral authority. Why? Because of issues like abortion, gay marriage, and women's ordination. That's what's really driving them mad, and that's why they are on the hunt."

Many, if not most of the people challenging

the Church on sex abuse were persuaded that the Church was wrong about women and gays, but it would have been difficult to say the same number supported abortion rights. It would also be hard to determine whether they began their activism with these convictions, or developed them through an analysis of the Church's problems. As scholars like Richard Sipe argued, Catholic thinking about gender, sex, and reproduction provided the inspiration for its response to abuse claims and untangling the two would be impossible. This was something Donohue and Sipe would agree upon, even if they found little common ground elsewhere.

Within the ranks of bishops, many in Europe and America defended the Pope. Sounding a bit like William Donohue, Bishop David Zubik of Oakland complained, "What gives me the ache is not only the hunger and thirst to rush to judgment without an honest look at the facts, but the absolute hatred . . . and disrespect for who we are and especially for what we believe." In Rome, the official preacher to the papal household, Rev. Raniero Cantalamessa, compared criticism of the Pope to the historic persecution of the Jewish people. Cantalamessa quoted an anonymous "Jewish friend" who, he said, wrote that "The use of stereotypes, the passing from personal responsibility and guilt to a collective guilt remind me of the more shameful aspects of anti-Semitism."

The comment drew immediate objections from Jewish leaders and a Vatican official rushed to disassociate the Pope from Cantalamessa's view. This statement was followed by orders from the Vatican requiring all allegations of abuse against priests to be reported to civil authorities, wherever they occurred. Twenty-six years into the crisis, this declaration marked the first time that such a policy was imposed on the worldwide Church. After it was issued, Benedict went to Malta where he met with eight men who alleged they had been abused as children, and was moved to tears by the encounter.

Benedict himself struggled to maintain the less-defended and remorseful pose he had begun to practice. He spoke of a Church under "attack" but acknowledged that repentance was necessary. He begged for the forgiveness of God and those who had been abused and he repeatedly promised to deal decisively with perpetrators. In what became a season of apology, the Pope also took control of the Legionaries of Christ and began their reorganization. He accepted half a dozen resignations from bishops around the world and announced that the Vatican would conduct its own investigation of the scandal in Ireland.

These responses, measured and somewhat

contrite, continued as reports of clergy abuse came pouring into Rome from around the world. In Brazil, a national television network aired what it claimed was video of an elderly priest having sex with a young man of nineteen. The younger man had reportedly been involved with the priest since he was twelve. This priest and two others were suspended from their duties in the northern district of Alagosa while claims against them were being investigated. In Africa the bishop of Johannesburg used his Easter message to say that sexual abuse by priests was just as common in Africa as it was in more developed regions but it had not yet received attention. (Soon investigators would link Irish-born priests to child sexual abuse across the African continent.) In Belgium the archbishop of Bruges resigned when it was revealed he had sexually abused his nephew.

Coming in rapid succession, the revelations appalled even some of the more ardent supporters of the Church. Writer Peggy Noonan, who had all but deified John Paul II in her book *John Paul the Great,* decried "a rolling catastrophe" that "has lowered the standing, reputation and authority of the Church."

Worse, for the Pope himself, were the documents that showed that when he was in charge of the Vatican office responsible for such complaints, he was well informed about extreme cases but did not respond to them with any urgency. This claim was at the heart of Jeffrey Anderson's efforts to sue the Vatican in Wisconsin and as this case made progress through the courts the Vatican considered it a serious threat. In response, the Holy See hired a little-known attorney named Jeffrey Lena to represent it and its officials, not only in Wisconsin but in every American jurisdiction where they were named as defendants.

Lena was born in 1958 and grew up in the social tumult of 1960s Berkeley. His social worker mother and public school teacher father raised him with New Deal politics and Catholic faith. Lena was also influenced by the heritage of his father's family, which had emigrated to Petaluma, California, from Florence. Before entering law school he studied history, and he enjoyed considering major events from a variety of perspectives that produced a nuanced understanding of people, places, and their time.

A law school exchange program brought Lena to Italy where he became fluent in the language. Between 1997 and 2005 he spent long periods teaching in Italy's three major law schools — in Trento, Milan, and Turin — and developed both an appreciation for and deep understanding of the European justice system. In this time he found a mentor in Franzo Grande Stevens, who was chief counsel to Gianni Agnelli, president of Fiat. In the

Italian model, a lawyer acted less like a public advocate and more as an adviser and assistant who handled sensitive issues with discretion. Lena, who considered American lawyers the equivalent of "hired guns" and U.S. law firms "corporate machines" preferred the Italian way, which encouraged long-term relationships conducted on a human scale.

An American who was well connected to prominent Italian lawyers and legal academics, Lena was a natural choice for the Holy See and it became, for all intents and purposes, his sole client. While the Pope sought reconciliation and confessed the Church's sins, Lena squared off against Jeff Anderson in Oregon and Wisconsin. In both jurisdictions he would argue that as a sovereign, the Holy See should not be sued for the offenses of local clerics. Beyond this point he would insist that priests were not under the direct control of Vatican officials, and that responsibility for them rested with local bishops.

In Rome, Lena studied the Church to find out how the men who ran the institution thought and acted. He came to believe that their basic principles, which revolved around faith and forgiveness, had made it difficult for them to respond as others might. "They believed in the power of prayer and the capacity of people to reform themselves," he explained. "They ignored the power of sex." With Ronan, Church leaders also valued the man's status as a priest, which "is not just something you are hired to do. It's a matter of consecration, which puts a mark on the soul." These facts persuaded Lena that his client was both morally and legally innocent and he set to work on a defense.

Lena worked out his legal perspective in his small office and at a cabin he and his sons built deep in a redwood forest north of the San Francisco Bay area. He gathered information, and rendered his advice during long visits to Rome, where he soaked up local culture and reveled in the cuisine. As Lena saw it, religious orders and dioceses were like independent corporations and the Holy See was "factually innocent" because its relationship to these entities was religious, not bureaucratic. "Jeff Anderson is trying to make it seem like this is an employment issue," he said, adding that the "Holy See does have employees but they all work for the Curia [its bureaucracy] not in churches around the world."

In the Oregon case of *John V. Doe v. Holy See,* the federal district court judge hearing the case rejected Jeff Anderson's fraud argument but let it proceed as a tort case. When the Ninth Circuit Court of Appeals upheld this ruling, Lena asked the Supreme Court to throw out the claim. He sought support for his petition from the United States government, which had ongoing relations with the Holy See. In March 2010 the parties went to Washington to discuss the case with solicitor general Elena Kagan and State Department lawyer Harold Koh.

Kagan and Koh sat with aides on one side of a big table in a meeting room at the Department of Justice while the two sides presented their perspectives. Lena insisted that the Holy See was not responsible for individual priests and that no sovereign, not matter how small, should be hauled into an American court without more compelling reasons. Citing the 1976 Foreign Sovereign Immunity Act, he insisted that like any state of any size his client could not be forced into a courtroom on the basis of such limited evidence and claims.

On the same day Jeffrey Anderson appeared in front of Kagan and Koh with his co-counsel Marci Hamilton. A constitutional scholar who had clerked for Supreme Court justice Sandra Day O'Connor, Hamilton was questioned by government officials for two hours. They pressed her to admit that the Supreme Court should hear Lena's appeal. Noting that *John V. Doe* was being considered under state statute, Hamilton repeatedly told the government lawyers "the high court never takes cases in order to interpret state laws and they shouldn't do it now."

Ultimately Kagan and Koh made a choice that Hamilton considered "political" and urged the Supreme Court to take up the case. Following the rule Hamilton cited, the court declined Jeffrey Lena's petition and allowed the suit to continue. This decision marked the biggest victory to date in Jeff Anderson's decades-long effort to force the Vatican to disclose documents. The first batch of papers, which Lena made public in the summer of 2011, suggested that the Holy See was not informed of the perpetrator priest's criminal tendencies until after John V. Doe was abused and therefore could not be held responsible. However, this evidence came at the start of the discovery process and Anderson immediately requested a more thorough record be produced. Both sides expected this fact-finding phase of the case to continue for years.

In the meantime, Lena seemed to prevail in Wisconsin, where Anderson dropped a lawsuit naming the Holy See as a party responsible for Rev. Lawrence Murphy's abuse of students at St. John's School for the Deaf. Anderson's decision was made as he received 30,000 pages of documents on Murphy, including papers from Rome, in a separate proceeding before a federal bankruptcy judge. The diocese had sought shelter in bankruptcy court, filing for protection as Anderson was about to begin deposing bishops. A few years prior to the bankruptcy filing the finances of the diocese were rearranged and more than $50 million was placed in a trust for cemeteries. Additional funds were moved from the archdiocese to individual parishes.

These moves, made before Archbishop Timothy Dolan was transferred to New York City, seemed to leave little for victims of abuse to claim, though the Church denied it had moved assets to shield them from victims. However, bankruptcy proceedings can yield unexpected results. The judge in this case allowed Anderson to search out three hundred additional clients whose abuse claims made them creditors. Two hundred others joined the action as clients of other lawyers. Together they alleged more than 8,000 incidents of abuse. Judge Susan Kelley established a process for discovery and depositions. Anderson deposed Archbishop Weakland and a longtime vicar general and auxiliary bishop, Richard Sklba, to determine if these actions were part of a deliberate effort to evade responsibility for claims. After reviewing the depositions, the judge allowed the fraud claims to go forward.

The pressure placed on the Church by civil claims in the United States was matched by criminal investigations and suits around the world. Police in Brussels, where a cardinal had already been questioned by authorities, raided a bishop's palace, interrogated Church officials, and confiscated their cell phones. In their search for documents they even opened a burial vault. All this was done as a government commission completed a report that found abuse cases throughout the Belgian Church involving more than 320 male victims and more than 160 female victims. The investigation found thirteen suicides among the victims.

Weeks after the Belgian report was issued, Jeff Anderson, John Manly, and Patrick Wall arrived in Brussels to meet with attorneys and victims who were just beginning to organize themselves for legal action. With the Belgian lawyers Anderson urged them to "be willing to take the hits and lose cases" in order to gather information and devise strategies for future successes. In the nearby university town of Leuven, Anderson spoke to about fifty abuse victims, some of whom formed the nucleus of a new SNAP chapter.

The meeting, which was held at a community center called Seniorama, was one part political rally, one part twelve-step meeting, and one part legal seminar. Outside the small meeting room a light rain fell on a narrow street. Inside middle-aged men and women cried as they told stories of childhood abuse and adult struggles with depression and dysfunction while Anderson sat in the middle of the crowd, listening to a translator and nodding. When it was his time to speak he stuck to generalities and answered questions the best he could. Many in the crowd were skeptical about him and SNAP, and they questioned his motivations. The session reminded him of the early days of the movement in America, when the terms of the campaign were not yet defined and victims moved warily around each other and the advocates who sought to help them.

Anderson received a warmer welcome when he flew from Belgium to London, where he negotiated the creation of a partnership with a British firm that would soon begin filing claims against Catholic institutions across the United Kingdom. In each country the courts permitted different kinds of actions and placed varying limits on discovery and the penalties that might be imposed if a plaintiff prevailed. But locals welcomed Anderson's expertise in the affairs of the Church and he also brought Tom Doyle and Patrick Wall into cases as investigators and counselors. They would prove especially helpful in Ireland where male victims found them to be good listeners.

The Irish scandal never seemed to abate. In the summer of 2011 a third report, on the Diocese of Cloyne, found that between 1996 and 2009 it had failed to report charges against sixteen priests. The furious political response to this report included a march through the streets of Dublin that ended at the seat of Irish Catholicism, St. Mary's Pro-Cathedral, on Marlborough Street. There, more than a thousand people tied children's shoes to an iron fence. The shoes represented child victims of abuse at the hands of priests. When a bishop appeared to speak with the protesters he was met with a furious response from men and women who called Irish clerics "child-abusing terrorists" and the Church "the largest pedophile ring in the world." Anger flared in the Irish parliament and Prime Minister Enda Kenny condemned "the dysfunction, disconnection, elitism, and the narcissism that dominate the culture of the Vatican to this day."

Normally mild mannered, Kenny excoriated the Church, noting that cover-ups had been practiced "three years ago, not three decades ago." He added, "The rape and torture of children were downplayed, or 'managed,' to uphold instead the primacy of the institution — its power, its standing and its reputation." Instead of dealing with abuse directly "the Vatican's response was to parse and analyze it with the gimlet eye of a canon lawyer." After Kenny's statement the Holy See summoned its ambassador to Dublin home for consultation. In turn, Ireland closed, permanently, its embassy at the Vatican.

As the relationship between the Irish state and the Catholic Church soured, members of the hierarchy came under intense scrutiny. Eventually the BBC would implicate the highest-ranking churchman in the country, Cardinal Sean Brady, in a cover-up that had allowed Fr. Brendan Smyth to stay in ministry and gain access to his victim Andrew Madden. The TV network report showed that Brady had interviewed two boys whom Smyth had assaulted before he abused Madden, but did not report him to the police. One of the two, Brendan Boland, said he had reported to Brady that Smyth was continuing to abuse five other boys and girls. None of this information was reported to police or the families of the children, and in some cases the assaults continued into the 1980s.

The mere fact that the BBC would pursue, produce, and broadcast such an aggressive investigation of Cardinal Brady — and the Irish public would voice no real objections — showed how much had changed in the country. As the religious affairs correspondent of *The Irish Times,* Patsy McGarry, noted, "The obsequiousness of the Irish state toward the Vatican is gone. The deference is gone."

Deference toward the Church was gone, too, in many parts of America. In staunchly Catholic Philadelphia, for example, 2011 found four clergymen, including a monsignor, indicted on criminal charges related to sexual abuse of children or child endangerment. The grand jury that indicted the men also reported that Church officials allowed dozens of accused abusers to remain at work. At first Cardinal Justin Rigali insisted none of these men remained in ministry. Weeks later he announced that twenty-one had been discovered in active service and suspended.

In time, the Philadelphia scandal would produce damning evidence of a cover-up conspiracy practiced by high-level Church figures. Charged with the criminal endangerment of children, Msgr. William J. Lynn revealed that then Cardinal Bevilacqua ordered the destruction of a 1994 memo that listed the names of thirty-five priests suspected of sexual abuse. As Lynn's defense attorneys revealed, one copy of the memo was preserved by a Church official named James Molloy, who kept it in a safe along with contemporary notes about the cardinal's order. Molloy's papers were obtained by Lynn's lawyers weeks before their client's trial, when the eighty-eight-year-old Bevilacqua died of cancer. In ten appearances before Philadelphia grand juries, where he was sworn to tell the truth, Bevilacqua had denied playing a substantial role in abuse cases. He expired on the day after a judge ruled he was competent to testify at Lynn's trial.

In the spring of 2012, Lynn was tried in criminal court on charges of child endangerment and conspiracy. The trial lasted for three months. In the end, Lynn was convicted of child endangerment and acquitted of the conspiracy charge. When she sentenced him to serve three to six years in prison, the judge said that Lynn had enabled "monsters in clerical garb." The conviction marked the first time a supervisor of priests, and a higher Church authority, was convicted of a crime related to the abuse crises. Days later the press reported that the Philadelphia diocese was suffering a $17 million budget deficit and was shuttering parishes and schools to help close the gap. The diocese also put a beach-front villa in New Jersey up for sale. It was listed at $6.2 million.

While local civil officials pursued clerics in various jurisdictions, the International Criminal Court at The Hague in the Netherlands considered a request for an investigation into the Holy See's involvement in crimes against humanity. The complaint, filed by members of SNAP, named Pope Benedict and other high officials as potential participants in a conspiracy to allow the rape and torture of children around the world. Among them was the same William Levada who decades before had encouraged Thomas Doyle, Michael Peterson, and Raymond Mouton in their effort to help the Church avert a protracted crisis, and then withdrew his support for them. Joseph Ratzinger's replacement as head of the Congregation for the Doctrine of the Faith, Levada was the highest-ranking American at the Vatican.

Pamela Spees of the New York–based Center for Constitutional Rights authored the complaint to the court. Her named complainants included victims from Africa, Europe, and North America. According to the complaint, Wilfried Fesselmann was abused by a priest in Essen, Germany. The priest was allegedly transferred with the consent of then Archbishop Joseph Ratzinger. The complaint also claimed that Benjamin Kitobo of the Congo was thirteen when he was first assaulted by a priest who continued to abuse him for four more years. Finally, the complaint cited the case of Megan Peterson, who at age fourteen was raped by a priest visiting her diocese in northern Minnesota.

A client of Jeff Anderson's, Peterson had recently settled her lawsuit against the Diocese of Crookston for $750,000. She accompanied Spees and Barbara Blaine to The Hague and to a series of press conferences conducted in cities across Europe. Suicidal during her high school years, Peterson had been hospitalized more than twenty times for psychiatric care and she continued to need counseling. "It tears your soul right out of you," she explained. "And the thing is, it's still happening. It happened to me just a few years ago. And the priest who abuses me is still active. These are not just crimes of the past. Who is to say that in a few more years my generation won't come forward and say it happened to us?"

For their part, many Church authorities suggested that the incidence of clergy abuse had declined. In 2011 a Church-funded study by professors of criminology at John Jay College said that the majority of known offenses occurred before 1990 and the perpetrators were mainly men trained and ordained in the 1960s and 1970s. The John Jay report, which followed up a similar study issued in 2004, said that the majority of victims were males and that offenses against young children were unusual. (It estimated that 80 percent of victims were boys older then eleven or twelve.) The report also noted that homosexuality was not a major factor in the phenomenon, but that the influence of the 1960s sexual revolution may have been.

Not surprisingly, the John Jay paper brought protests. Critics noted the fact that the men ultimately responsible for the handling of the crisis had paid for the study, which a reasonable person might suspect influenced its outcome. They also pointed to its scientific deficiencies. The researchers had relied almost entirely on the Church's own data on clergy sexual abuse, even though bishops had been consistently inaccurate in their accounting, erring always on the side of reporting fewer problems than they had. No accounting was solicited from victims, or their supporters. But while sober analysis was applied to the methods of the report, critics generally adopted a mocking tone as they considered its conclusion that "the sixties" were a causative factor.

In an open letter to New York Cardinal Timothy Dolan, Constitutional scholar Marci Hamilton solicited funds to "apply the tried and true research methods followed by the John Jay team to definitively link" a series of 1960s events to the trouble in the Church. The factors she proposed to assess included:

Alfred Hitchcock's *Psycho* was released. My educated guess is that most seminarians and priests started out the sixties scared stiff. *Star Trek* aired on television for the first time. Once *Star Trek . . .* made it eminently plausible that extra-terrestrials exist — and can be more rational than humans — what man of God would not be concerned? The first Super Bowl. The beginning of the end of Western civilization. Neil Armstrong walks on the moon. As you may know, the Church once persecuted Galileo for saying that the earth was not the center of the universe . . .

With enough money from them, Hamilton promised, she could examine these phenomena and "add significant cover for you and your fellow bishops who even today do not call the police when you learn of abuse by your employees."

On the other side of the debate, William Donohue felt comfortable with the way the report blamed liberal social trends, but complained that the numbers pointed to homosexuality as a cause of the crisis although the authors refused to acknowledge it. "The attempt to skirt the obvious," he said, "is not only disingenuous, it is bad social science."

Although nearly all the research on the topic showing no connection between homosexuality and abuse, Donohue stood comfortably alone in his position. However, he was disturbed by the way the world seemed to be moving when it came to homosexuality. As gay marriage became legal in more countries and across the United States, Donohue acknowledged "the battle over homosexuality has been lost. Young people just don't see anything wrong with it." But while the Church held no appeal for millions of children from Catholic families, he noted that its orthodoxy drew a strong commitment from a devoted few. Perhaps the Church was becoming the remnant that Joseph Ratzinger imagined during the 1960s, he said. "And if you don't like what you find there, you can become a Protestant."

In America, elements of the Church did

begin to behave like an endangered sect, lurching away from the mainstream by reviving old objections to making contraception readily available and adopting a newly aggressive attitude toward sexual abuse claimants. The former cardinal of New York, Timothy Egan, publicly withdrew an apology he had made to victims ten years earlier. "I never should have said that," and added, "I don't think we did anything wrong." Egan also denied that any priests had ever sexually assaulted a child in his former Diocese of Bridgeport, Connecticut, where, in fact, as many as ninety people had come forward with claims of sexual abuse by priests.

Although Egan's comments prompted outrage among abuse victims, they were more disturbed by the aggressive conduct of Church lawyers in Missouri who targeted SNAP and its leaders with subpoenas. The attorneys, who represented priests accused of sexual attacks, demanded SNAP turn over documents accumulated over twenty-three years and provide testimony that could reveal the identities of rape victims and the content of conversations with journalists around the world. The officers of SNAP resisted the request, insisting it went beyond any reasonable definition of the proper discovery process in a civil suit. Five lawyers questioned David Clohessy during a six-hour deposition in which they focused primarily on SNAP's finances, activities, and network of contacts. Noting that SNAP was not involved in any of the cases the Church lawyers were defending, Clohessy refused to answer many questions and his organization resisted turning over documents.

When they targeted the abuse survivors group, the Church's lawyers forced SNAP to incur legal costs that quickly threatened its solvency. After *The New York Times* and *St. Louis Post-Dispatch* published editorials criticizing this tactic, public donations to the organization surged, and several prominent attorneys agreed to volunteer their services. On the other side of the conflict, Cardinal Timothy Dolan of New York took to the Internet to call attention to advocate Bill Donohue's criticism of SNAP and Clohessy, whom he suggested had become a "con man driven by revenge." In directing readers to Donohue, Dolan put them in touch with the main get-tough voice for the Church, an activist whose inflammatory rhetoric included calling advocates for victims "rapacious" and repeatedly called on bishops to play legal "hardball." Donohue still believed the Church faced a war with moral enemies, although at times he was able to see they believed they were guided by certain higher principles. Considering Jeffrey Anderson in 2011, Donohue said he knew he was not in it "just for the money."

Indeed, Anderson continued to intensify his pursuit of the Church on abuse claims because he believed his clients were worthy and that Catholicism as represented by the hierarchy was hopelessly corrupt. Fully American in his view of human nature, he saw in the Church a system devoid of the checks and balances that would prevent abuses. As long as the men who ran the Church believed they possessed the exclusive power to discern right and wrong, Anderson believed his work would continue. Toward that end, he planned for successors to maintain his firm and its mission after his death.

Michael Finnegan, Anderson's young associate, seemed positioned to lead the campaign in the future and he was deeply involved in a 2012 jury trial that ended with the Church threatened by a new wave of abuse claims. Finnegan and Anderson argued that bishops in the Diocese of Green Bay, Wisconsin, had defrauded the public when they allowed a priest who was plagued by complaints of sexual improprieties with children to continue in ministry and eventually assault two boys. Todd and Troy Merryfield had been unable to sue for damages because a state statute of limitations said too much time had passed between the moment when they knew they had been harmed and their decision to go to court. Noting that fraud stops the statute clock from ticking,

Anderson and Finnegan got into court on a fraud claim.

In the records presented to the court, Fr. John Patrick Feeney's superiors didn't use the kind of smoking gun language that would scream "we knowingly loosed a criminal on the community." Instead his bishop seemed exasperated, scrawling, "Father Feeney Please!" at the top of one letter of complaint and writing, "If I hear any more about the swimming in the nude and encouraging boys to do it I'll suspend you."

In court, Anderson argued that as the evidence of Feeney's criminal sexual compulsions accrued, the bishop neglected the danger he posed. And it was this neglect of duty, juxtaposed with the bishop's role as pastor to the Catholic people of Green Bay, Anderson contended, that met the legal definition of fraud. In his closing argument Anderson said, "They knew he had sexually molested and they knew he posed a danger and a risk to children and thus they deceived the Merryfields and the community." The jurors agreed, finding in the Merryfields' favor and awarding them $700,000. Approximately six weeks later, however, the judge granted a new trial to the diocese of Green Bay on the ground that a juror was biased.

The Appleton case was followed closely by the community of lawyers dealing with claims of clergy abuse. But by 2012 such claims against priests had become so routine that they rarely became national news. In California, John Manly and Vincent Finaldi conducted a ten-week trial on behalf of an airline pilot named Travis Trotter, who said Fr. Kelly abused him when he was an altar boy. Well connected to local business people, government officials, and even judges, Kelly appeared in the courtroom with dozens of supporters who sat stony-faced to show their commitment. Officials of the diocese of Stockton announced their conviction that Kelly was innocent and, in a move consistent with the more assertive strategy urged by William Donohue, paid a team of experienced attorneys to represent him and the diocese.

The support for Kelly held until the first phase of the trial ended with the jury finding him liable. At that moment Kelly suddenly fled to Ireland. In the next part of the trial, which would determine the financial responsibilities of the diocese, Manly and Finaldi presented evidence that, in their view, showed that Bishop Stephen Blaire knew of complaints about Kelly before he abused their client. With Blaire and retired Cardinal Roger Mahony about to testify, the diocese offered Trotter $3.75 million to settle his claim. He accepted. Bishop Blaire and Cardinal Mahony were spared from testifying.

In Mahony's case, the Stockton settlement

kept him out of the press and in the quiet of his retirement. However, his long-running association with the sexual abuse crisis was not over. In Los Angeles he remained a central figure in an ongoing struggle over documents related to abuse cases. Manly said that he thought the leaders of the Church in Los Angeles were trying to wear down his clients, hoping they would simply stop asking for the papers that Mahony had agreed to release. A spokesman for the archdiocese, Tod Tamberg, said, "We agreed to a process to release the documents. We didn't just agree to dump them out the window."

Technically speaking, the lawyers who fought disclosure of the documents complied with the text of the settlement agreement, even if they thwarted its spirit. In this legalism, they followed the example of Vatican authorities, who often stressed the letter of Church law as if they were prosecutors and not pastors.

On the day when Fr. Kelly fled America to escape the consequences of his sexual abuse of a child, William Levada's Congregation for the Doctrine of the Faith moved to discipline and publicly humiliate an organization that represented 80 percent of America's Catholic nuns. As three bishops were named to police the Leadership Conference of Women Religious, the Vatican declared that the nuns had promoted "radical feminist" ideas such as the ordination of women. Rome also scolded the sisters for taking positions that "disagree with or challenge the bishops, who are the Church's authentic teachers of faith and morals."

Anyone who followed Church affairs knew that the male hierarchy wanted nuns to talk more about the evils of abortion, contraception, and sex outside marriage and less about the claims to equality pressed by gays and women. This was an old problem for the men who ran the Church. For decades religious women had focused more on direct service to the young, the sick, the old, and the poor while sometimes critiquing the prerogatives assumed by ordained men. A layperson consulting a sister with questions of sexual morality would be more likely to hear a nun say "follow your conscience" than "follow the Pope."

Reaction to the Vatican's move against the nuns was swift and almost entirely negative. (An exception was the Catholic League, which complained, "Church Bashers Rally for Nuns.") Tens of thousands of laypeople signed petitions protesting the notice from Levada's office and sent nuns donations to indicate their support. Public statements, by Catholic and non-Catholic commentators, ran heavily against the churchmen, with most observers noting that the sisters did most of the gritty, dangerous, and thankless work of the Church and represented the essence of Christian love. In more than fifty cities laypeople took to the street to protest the Vatican's action.

Seemingly inspired by the support they received from ordinary Catholics, the nuns did not back down. On June 1, 2012, they issued their response, which noted that Rome had acted upon "unsubstantiated accusations" and relied on "a flawed process that lacked transparency." They accused the men who run the Church of causing "greater polarization" and announced that they would take the debate to the hierarchy in the Vatican. "Following the discussions in Rome, the conference will gather its members both in regional meetings and in its August assembly to determine its response to the CDF report."

Ultimately the conflict over the loyalty of American nuns, who sought to serve the larger society, would depend on the same factor that governed the way the institutional Church had managed the sexual abuse crisis: Pope Benedict XVI's view of the world outside the Church. Despite the passing of communism, the flowering of democracy, and continually rising levels of well-being, he saw the West as a failing civilization drenched in error and in need of his authority and leadership. As evidence he cited the West's low birthrate (due to contraception and abortion) and what he considered to be the absence of morality in industrialized societies on both sides of the Atlantic.

Social science experts would reach opposite conclusions, finding a steady increase in the physical and mental health of people in America and across the European continent. For children the picture was even brighter. Awareness and advocacy had led to a gradual decline in child abuse and neglect while the spread of information about psychology improved the ways all types of caregivers — parents, day care workers, teachers and others — treated children. Eventually researchers at Cambridge University would consolidate the data and report that the West exceeded other regions in nine out of ten measures of well-being. They found that people with the highest levels of peace and contentment — the Scandinavians — were also the least religious on Earth.

In America, despite periodic spikes in media attention for conservative Churches, religious institutions have been losing support for decades. Between 1957 and 2007 the number of people claiming no religious affiliation rose from 3 percent to 17 percent. In the same time, the number of people attending church each week dropped to an estimated 25 percent, and those saying they *never* go to church almost doubled to 22 percent. Belief in the Bible as the inerrant and literal truth declined by about a third in the last three decades.

When American Catholics were considered apart from other Christians, similar data emerged. Between 1987 and 2011 weekly attendance at Mass declined from 44 percent to 31 percent. The number of Catholics who said they went to church less than once per month rose from 26 percent to 47 percent. During this same time, respect for the Pope's authority and the authority of bishops and priests dropped lower and lower. By 2011, a solid majority of American Catholics believed that individuals, and not the Church, should have final say on sexual morality. And like other actively religious Americans, Catholics expressed greater tolerance for others. Today, a solid majority say that religions other than their own can offer a true path to God and half would actually vote for an atheist politician.

Altogether, the best data show a slow, steady decline in traditional religious beliefs and practices even as Americans continue to describe themselves as generally "spiritual." This trend is matched by long-term studies showing inexorable increases in well-being — as measured by health, access to education, and economic conditions — for Americans in every demographic group. (Well-being is highest in the Northeast, the region where formal religion is weakest. It is lowest in the

South, where religiosity is strongest.) These were the fruits of the society judged by Vatican officials to be so much in need of prayer to save its soul.

As the leaders of the Church who have failed in their response to a crisis of child abuse within their ranks deliver lectures on morality, the dissonance announces a tragedy in three parts. The first element of this tragedy can be seen in the eyes of those who have been sexually violated by Catholic priests, bishops, and nuns. No matter what point an individual may have reached in his pursuit of recovery, he or she will forever live with betrayal experienced in childhood and will grieve over many types of loss. The time, relationships, faith, and community stolen from them cannot be restored.

The second aspect of the great Catholic tragedy can be seen in the Church itself. The hierarchy's defensive response to the crisis has demoralized and divided the Catholic community. This process has emptied churches, forced the closing of schools, and required once vibrant independent parishes to merge with their neighbors. It has also handicapped those who do the good work of the Church, especially those who are priests and nuns. When they go into the world they are associated, in the public mind, with a level of disgrace that makes it all the harder for them to serve.

Finally comes the tragedy suffered by the larger society the Church hopes to save. Historically, Catholicism and the rest of Christianity have made more vital contributions to humanity than can be counted. Much of the morality, conscience, and selfless social perspective felt and practiced by people in all walks of life can be traced to the Church. Entire traditions of service, charity, community, and sacrifice were born in the faith and they were being lost as the institution met its current crisis with angry inflexibility. In failing to grow out of its monarchical structure and into a more humane perspective, the Church impoverishes the world as well as itself. In its crisis, the Church could have seized the opportunity to make itself more relevant and real in service to all. Instead it has turned inward.

In the meantime, the Church in America will inevitably face new civil claims based on fraud, which will drain it of resources and credibility. SNAP and similar organizations are becoming active in parts of Asia, Africa, and Latin America where clerical abuse has not been addressed, and human rights lawyers promise a continuing effort to hold the Vatican accountable in international courts. Plagued by their own intrigues — Pope Benedict XVI's butler was arrested in 2012 after embarrassing private letters were leaked to the press — Church officials in Rome showed no evidence that they were capable of ending the era of scandal.

POSTSCRIPT

With sad predictability, the scandal-without-end that first afflicted the Catholic Church in the Gilbert Gauthe case of 1983 actually reached another low point in early 2013, as this book neared publication.

On January 31, the Archdiocese of Los Angeles made public more than 12,000 pages of documents related to priest sex abuse cases, including files that showed Cardinal Roger Mahony's direct involvement in efforts to shield priest child abusers from prosecution. The papers showed that despite his many claims to the contrary, in depositions and other settings, the cardinal had been deeply involved in the archdiocese's response to claims against priests.

"Sounds good — please proceed!" wrote Mahony, in script, on one note suggesting that a psychiatrist who was also a lawyer treat a sexual predator because attorney-client privilege would preclude the doctor from making a report to police. In another document Mahony directed that Father Peter Garcia, who admitted raping Mexican-American children, remain out of state because "we might very well have some type of legal action filed in both the criminal and civil sectors."

Mahony, who had retired in 2011 but remained active in Church affairs, was in Rome at the time of the documents' release. His successor, Archbishop José Gomez, announced that Mahony would be relieved of his duties and that Santa Barbara Bishop William Curry, vicar general under the old regime, would step down from his post. "I find these files to be brutal and painful reading," said Gomez. "The behavior described in these files is terribly sad and evil." Mahony bristled defensively, offering reporters copies of a letter to Gomez in which he wrote, ". . . when I retired as the active Archbishop, I handed over to you an archdiocese that was second to none in protecting children and youth."

Six years had passed since the archdiocese had agreed to make the files public, but attorneys for the Church had used legal maneuvers to delay actually issuing it. The court finally stopped allowing the Church more time under pressure mainly from Jeffrey Anderson's co-counsel, Anthony DeMarco. Joined in the pursuit of the papers by the *Los Angeles Times* and the Associated Press, De-

Marco had persuaded Judge Emilie Elias that members of the Church and the general public, were entitled to the records.

On the day when the Church acted, news outlets across the country cited excerpts that revived the most gruesome cases of assaults on children and the schemes used to cover up crimes. Police and prosecutors announced they would search the pages for evidence of crimes. In the meantime a federal bankruptcy judge in Milwaukee seemed ready to make public priest files held by the Church in Wisconsin. In that case, Judge Susan V. Kelley, had found that then Archbishop Timothy Dolan had improperly transferred $55 million to a cemetery trust fund. Agreeing with Anderson, Kelley ordered that the money be made available to creditors including abuse victims. The Archdiocese of Milwaukee planned to appeal, but once again the actions of Church leaders had amplified public revulsion and extended, rather than ended, the crisis.

As Catholics in America absorbed the developments in Los Angeles and Wisconsin, an historic announcement was made in Rome. For the first time in six hundred years a pope resigned. Benedict XVI had been at the center of the abuse crisis since the 1980s, when he ran the Congregation for the Doctrine of the Faith (previously The Inquisition). He cited weariness and the Church's need for a strong and vigorous leader among the reasons for his abdication. Virtually every news story published on the day his decision was announced mentioned the abuse scandal, and more than a few noted it as the heaviest of his burdens and one that would be shouldered by his successor.

ACKNOWLEDGMENTS

The tragic truth about sexual abuse in the Catholic Church would have remained secret but for the courage of victims who spoke up and pursued justice for themselves and others. Scott Gastal, who was among the very first to speak out when he was still in elementary school, stands as a hero in this pursuit. He is joined in the ranks of truth-tellers by Greg Lyman, and a host of others who generously helped me. Among them were Megan Peterson, Phil Saviano, Arthur Budzinski, Peter Isely, John Pilmaier, Terrance Kohut, Colm O'Gorman, Aidan Doyle, and Andrew Madden. Many of these strong people became activists who powered a vast social movement. O'Gorman founded a child advocacy group called One in Four before becoming director of Amnesty International of Ireland. Kohut has been honored by the deaf community of America for his work on behalf of men who were abused as boys at the St. John's School for the Deaf.

Because the court system was often the field of battle in the fight for the truth, attorneys became essential figures in the story told here. They also became valued guides and informants as I sought both understanding and an accurate accounting of events. Among the many officers of the court who helped me, I owe thanks to Raymond Boucher, Theodore Collins, Tony DeMarco, Sylvia Demarest, Larry Drivon, Vincent Finaldi, Michael Finnegan, Marci Hamilton, Michael Hennigan, Tom Krauel, Jeffrey Lena, Roderick MacLeish, Tahira Merritt, Raymond Mouton, Pamela Spees, and Mark Wendorf. Judge Owen Kwong offered much assistance, despite the great demands on his time.

Among the national advocates in the cause of victims, I received invaluable help and insights from Barbara Blaine, whose life has been lived in service to those in need of a strong voice. Her colleagues Barbara Dorris and David Clohessy deserve my gratitude, as do Terrence McKiernan and Ann Barrett-Doyle. As archivists who safeguard and share vast amounts of information and literature on the Church crisis, Ann and Terry are much in demand and responded to my requests with unending generosity.

Many people supplied both documentation and recollections of key events. Psychologist Susan Phipps-Yonas, witness Jay Klein, and former activist Jeanne Miller all generously offered their time and input. I also received outspoken and direct answers to my questions from William Donohue of the Catholic League, who is never uncertain in his positions. Minnesota legislator Ember Reichgott-Junge helped me with the intricacies of politics and law in her state.

Catholicism's era of scandal unfolded before the eyes of several talented journalists who have chronicled the various stages of the crisis. One, Jason Berry, was there at the beginning and has stayed with the story even beyond the many moments when it was supposed to have ended. In practicing his craft Jason became a part of the history he reported. Recognizing this fact, he agreed to share his personal experience along with many of his records. Without this material and the light shed by Jason's books I would not have been able to write my account.

Patsy McGarry of *The Irish Times* helped me understand the story of the Church and abuse in Ireland and Michael Rezendes of *The Boston Globe* filled in elements of the story not reported by the paper's Spotlight Team, who earned a Pulitzer Prize for their work. The book written by the *Globe*'s investigative team, *Betrayal: The Crisis in the Catholic Church,* was one of my essential sources. I also depended on *A Gospel of Shame: Children, Sexual Abuse, and the Catholic*

Church by Frank Bruni and Elinor Burkett, and David France's *Our Fathers: The Secret Life of the Catholic Church in an Age of Scandal.*

A trio of experts helped me understand the workings of the Church. Richard Sipe, author of the very first comprehensive consideration of the clergy's sexual culture — *A Secret World: Sexuality and the Search for Celibacy* — offered the frank and friendly inputs of a former priest who became a psychotherapist and social scientist. Another former priest, Patrick Wall, answered every question I could ask about his personal experience as a Benedictine monk and an investigator. And the Rev. Thomas Doyle, Dominican priest and U.S. Air Force major (retired), translated the mysteries of clerical culture into plain terms.

Tom Doyle, Richard Sipe, and Patrick Wall were also extremely forthcoming when it came to their personal experiences, with faith and human frailty, and it is in this aspect of my work that I was fortunate to encounter some radically honest people. In particular, John Manly explained how work on abuse cases affected him as an attorney and as a human being. Few professionals would possess the grace and generous spirit required to be so candid.

Remarkably, just about every person I encountered as I gathered the story told in these pages spoke with great candor about experiences and issues rarely discussed in private, let alone for the purpose of making a public record. Their openness is proof of the progress we have made in the struggle against the misplaced shame that keeps people from living honestly. First among them were Jeffrey and Julie Anderson, who shared their stories as individuals, and as a couple, in the hope that they might inspire others. Through hard experience, the Andersons learned the danger inherent in secrecy and the refuge provided by the truth.

My ultimate thanks go to those who supported me, personally, as I worked on a task that demanded much time, attention, and emotional commitment. My publisher Thomas Dunne is witty, wise, steadfast, and demanding when he needs to be. My editor Peter Joseph is both a gifted critic and ally, and wherever a bit of grace may appear in my text you can be sure he is present too. My lifelong collaborators Amy, Elizabeth, and Toni deserve more gratitude than can be offered here. I can only hope to support them as they have supported me.

BIBLIOGRAPHY

Joseph Cardinal Bernardin, *The Gift of Peace,* Chicago: Loyola Press, 1997.

Jason Berry, *Render Unto Rome: The Secret Life of Money in the Catholic Church.* New York: Crown Publishing Group, 2011.

Jason Berry, *Lead Us Not Into Temptation: Catholic Priests and the Sexual Abuse of Children.* New York, Doubleday, 1992.

Jason Berry and Gerald Renner, *Vows of Silence: The Abuse of Power in the Papacy of John Paul II,* New York: Free Press, 2004.

Angela Bonavoglia, *Good Catholic Girls,* New York: HarperCollins, 2005.

The Investigative Staff of *The Boston Globe, Betrayal: The Crisis in the Catholic Church,* Boston: Little, Brown, 2002.

Daniel Brown, Alan W. Scheflin, & D. Corydon Hammond, *Memory: Trauma, Treatment, and the Law,* New York: W.W. Norton & Company, Inc., 1998.

Frank Bruni, and Elinor Burkett, *A Gospel of*

Shame: Children, Sexual Abuse, and the Catholic Church, New York: HarperCollins Publishers Inc., 2002.

Nicholas P. Cafardi, *Before Dallas: The U.S. Bishops' Response to Clergy Sexual Abuse of Children,* New York: Paulist Press, 2008.

Betty Clermont, *The Neo-Catholics: Implementing Christian Nationalism in America,* Atlanta, GA: Clarity Press, Inc., 2009.

Paul E. Dinter, *The Other Side of the Altar: One Man's Life in the Catholic Priesthood,* New York: Farrar, Straus and Giroux, 2003.

Bill Donohue, *Secular Sabotage: How Liberals Are Destroying Religion and Culture in America,* New York: Faith Words, 2009.

Matthew Fox, *The Pope's War: Why Ratzinger's Secret Crusade Has Imperiled the Church and How It Can Be Saved,* New York: Sterling Ethos, 2011.

David France, *Our Fathers: The Secret Life of the Catholic Church in an Age of Scandal,* New York: Broadway Books, 2004.

Eric Frattini and Dick Clusterpp, *The Entity: Five Centuries of Secret Vatican Espionage,* New York: St. Martin's Press, 2008.

Jennifer J. Freyd, *Betrayal Trauma: The Logic of Forgetting Childhood Abuse,* Cambridge, Massachusetts, 1996.

Andrew M. Greeley, *The Catholic Myth: The Behavior and Beliefs of American Catholics,* New York: Charles Scribner's Sons, 1990.

Marci A. Hamilton, *God vs. the Gavel: Religion and the Rule of Law,* New York: Cambridge University Press, 2005.

Robert Kee, *Ireland: A History,* Boston: Little, Brown and Company, 1980.

Thomas Keneally, *The Great Shame,* New York: Doubleday, 1998.

Eugene Kennedy, *This Man Bernardin,* Chicago, IL: Loyola Press, 1996.

Timothy D. Lytton, *Holding Bishops Accountable: How Lawsuits Helped the Catholic Church Confront Clergy Sexual Abuse,* Cambridge, MA: Harvard University Press, 2008.

William Lobdell, *Losing My Religion: How I Lost My Faith Reporting on Religion in America — and Found Unexpected Peace,* New York: HarperCollins Publishers, 2009.

Philip F. Lawler, *The Faithful Departed: The Collapse of Boston's Catholic Culture,* New York: Encounter Books, 2008.

Andrew Madden, *Altar Boy: A Story of Life After Abuse,* Ireland: Penguin, 2003.

Peggy Noonan, *John Paul The Great: Remembering a Spiritual Father,* New York: Penguin Books, 2005.

John Julius Norwich, *Absolute Monarchs: A History of the Papacy,* New York: Random House, 2011.

Colm O'Gorman, *Beyond Belief,* London: Hodder & Stoughton, 2010.

Leon J. Podles, *Sacrilege: Sexual Abuse in the Catholic Church,* Baltimore, MD: Crossland Press, 2008.

David Price, *Altar Boy Altered Life: A True Story of Sexual Abuse,* Indianapolis, IN: Dog Ear Publishing, 2008.

Joseph Cardinal Ratzinger with Vittorio Messori, *The Ratzinger Report,* San Francisco: Ignatius, 1985.

Thomas J. Reese, *Inside the Vatican: The Politics and Organization of the Catholic Church,* Cambridge, MA: Harvard University Press, 1996.

Joe Rigert, *An Irish Tragedy: How Sex Abuse by Irish Priests Helped Cripple the Catholic Church,* Baltimore, MD: Crossland Press, 2008.

Bishop Geoffrey Robinson, *Confronting Power and Sex in the Catholic Church: Reclaiming the Spirit of Jesus,* Collegeville, MN: Liturgical Press, 2008.

Geoffrey Robertson QC, *The Case of the Pope: Vatican Accountability for Human Rights Abuse,* London: Penguin Books, 2010.

Peter Seewald, *Benedict XVI Light of the World: The Pope, the Church, and the Signs of the Times,* San Francisco: Ignatius Press, 2010.

Anson Shupe, *Wolves in the Fold: Religious Leadership and Abuses of Power,* New

Brunswick, NJ: Rutgers University Press, 1998.

A. W. Richard Sipe, *A Secret World: Sexuality and the Search for Celibacy,* New York: Brunner/Mazel, 1990.

A. W. Richard Sipe, Thomas P. Doyle, & Patrick J. Wall, *Sex, Priests, and Secret Codes: The Catholic Church's 2,000-Year Paper Trail of Sexual Abuse,* Los Angeles: Volt Press, 2006.

A. W. Richard Sipe, *The Serpent and the Dove: Celibacy in Literature and Life,* Westport, CT: Praeger, 2007

Hilary Stiles, *Assault on Innocence: For the First Time . . . The Untold Story of Pedophilia,* Albuquerque, NM: B & K Publishers, Inc., 1987.

Rembert G. Weakland, OSB, *A Pilgrim in Pilgrim Church: Memoirs of a Catholic Archbishop,* Grand Rapids, MI: William B. Eerdman's Publishing Company, 2009.

George Weigel, *God's Choice: Pope Benedict XVI and the Future of the Catholic Church,* New York: HarperCollins Publishers Inc., 2005.

George Weigel, *The Courage to Be Catholic: Crisis, Reform, and the Future of the Church,* New York: Basic Books, 2002.

George Weigel, *Witness to Hope: The Biography of Pope John Paul II,* New York: HarperCollins Publishers Inc., 1999.

Garry Wills, *Papal Sins: Structures of Deceit,* New York: Doubleday, 2000.

David Yallop, *The Power and the Glory: Inside the Dark Heart of John Paul II's Vatican,* New York: Carroll & Graf Publishers, 2007.

David Yonke, *Sin, Shame, & Secrets: The Murder of a Nun, the Conviction of a Priest, and Cover-up in the Catholic Church,* New York: The Continuum International Publishing Group Ltd, 2006.

Documentary Films

Amy Berg, *Deliver Us From Evil,* 2006

Jason Berry, *Vows of Silence,* 2008

Mary Healy-Jamiel, *Holy Water-Gate: Abuse Cover-up in the Catholic Church,* 2005

Mary Raftery, *States of Fear,* 1999

SELECTED CHAPTER NOTES

Introduction

For the events surrounding the Italian conquest of Rome see:

- "Rome and Italy," *New York Times,* September 23, 1870, 1.
- "Rome is Now Completely Occupied by the Italian Troops," *New York Times,* September 24, 1870, 1.
- "Italian Unity," *New York Times,* October 4, 1870, 5.
- "War Letters," *New York Times,* October 5, 1870, 1.

For the creation of the modern Vatican state see:

- Arnaldo Cortesi, "Pope Becomes Ruler of a State Again," *New York Times,* June 8, 1929, 1.
- Arnaldo Cortesi, "Mussolini Explains New Vatican Status," *New*

York Times, May 14, 1929, 1.

- Arnaldo Cortesi, "Mussolini Reveals New Treaty Details," New York Times, March 15, 1929, 3.
- Arnaldo Cortesi, "4,000 Fascisti Cheer Mussolini's Praise of Vatican Accord," New York Times, March 11, 1929, 1.

For a thorough account of the Church's transition from a state power into a moral one see: Garry Wills, *Papal Sins: Structures of Deceit* (New York: Doubleday). Wills illuminates the story of the church from Pius IX through the current sexual abuse scandal with a fine sense of how the hierarchy interpreted history, theology, and modernity to build an unsustainable structure.

For *Humanae Vitae* see the original document at www.vatican.va

John Paul II's involvement with Eastern European freedom movements is documented throughout Carl Bernstein and Marco Politi's book *His Holiness* (New York: Penguin, 1997).

Figures on the cost of the sex abuse scandal as well as the number of priests prosecuted and imprisoned are based on running totals and author's accounting from Bishop

Accountability.org, a comprehensive archive of the scandal. See also: Robert Marquand, "Catholic Sexual Abuse Scandal Sharpens Rift Over What a Priest Should Be," *Christian Science Monitor;* online posted May 2, 2010.

For 1,400 Church closings, see: Stephanie Salter, "The Unfortunate Bottom Line . . . St. Ann's will Close" (Terre-Haute) *Tribune-Star,* September 4, 2011.

For Bishop Babini's comments see:

- **Tom Kingston, "Bishop 'Blames Jews' for Criticism of Catholic Church Record on Abuse," *The Guardian* April 11, 2011.**
- **Judy Mandelbaum, "Bishop Blames Jews for Child Molestation Scandal," Salon.com, April 12, 2010.**

"Santo subito" reported in Ian Fisher and Laurie Goodstein, "Pope Names U.S. Archbishop to Oversee Church Doctrine," *New York Times,* May 14, 2005, 1.

For Hans Hermann Groer, see:

- **Katrin Bennhold, "Future Pope's Complex Role in Abuse Case In Austria," *New York Times,* April 27, 2010, 4.**

- Rachel Donadio, "In Rare, Revealing Memo, Vatican Rebukes Cardinal," *New York Times,* June 29 2010, 4.
- Ross Douthat, "The Better Pope," *New York Times,* April 12, 2010, 25.

For the Pope's acknowledgement of the scandal and its effects, see:

- Rachel Donadio, "Pope Issues Forceful Statement on Sexual Abuse Crisis," *New York Times,* May 12, 2010, 4.
- Elisabetta Povoledo, "Before Crowd in St. Peter's Square, Pope Vows to Act in Abuse Crisis," *New York Times,* April 22, 2010. 7.
- Rachel Donadio, "From St. Peter's Square, Pope Pleads for Forgiveness Over Abuse and Vows Action," *New York Times,* June 12, 2010, 6.
- John F. Burns and Rachel Donadio, "Facing Protests in London, Pope Expresses Sorrow Over Child Abuse," *New York Times,* September 19, 2010, 18.

For the fallout from the abuse crisis in polls and in Europe see:

- "Pope Benedict Favorable Rating

Drops to 40 Percent in U.S. Gallup Poll," March 31, 2010.

- Dalia Sussman, "Poll: Catholic Church's Image at New Low," posted at ABC News.com, December 16, 2010.
- Robert Marquand, "Catholic Sex Abuse Scandal Raising Doubts for Young German Catholics," *Christian Science Monitor;* online posted April 26, 2010.
- "Critical Austrian Catholics Emboldened by Sex Abuse Scandal in Quest of Church Reform," Associated Press; posted online June 23, 2010.
- Juno McEnroe, "8,575 Log on to Renounce Religion Irish Examiner," Wednesday, March 31, 2010. http://www.irishexaminer.com/ireland/kfkfojsnaucw/rss2/#ixzz1LaFS7UDQ
- "Thou Shalt Not Defect: Baptism Is Forever," *The Irish Times* online, Saturday, October 16, 2010.

Megan Peterson's experience of clergy abuse was recounted by her in an interview with the author.

1. Clerical Culture

Pio Laghi's administration and personality, as well as conversations, drawn from interviews with Thomas Doyle. His personality, background and actions are also described throughout Jason Berry, *Lead Us Not Into Temptation: Catholic Priests and the Sexual Abuse of Children* (New York: Doubleday, 1992). See also: Eric Frattini and Dick Clusterpp, *The Entity: Five Centuries of Secret Vatican Espionage* (St. Martin's Press, 2008), 328–331. Also see: Laghi's obituary: Rachel Donadio, "Pio Laghi, Papal Envoy, Dies at 86," *New York Times,* January 14, 2000, B9.

For the assassination attempt on the Pope, see: George Weigel, *Witness to Hope: The Biography of Pope John Paul II* (New York: HarperCollins Publishers Inc., 1999), especially chapter twelve, "In the Eye of the Storm" and pages 423–425.

Doyle's experiences at the embassy and in the Lafayette case are from multiple sources, including author interviews and Berry's *Lead Us Not Into Temptation.*

Sources for the Gauthe case include Berry, *Lead Us Not Into Temptation;* interviews with Berry, Doyle, and attorney F. Raymond Mouton. See also:

- Berry's original reporting in the (Lafayette) *Times of Acadiana,* including: Jason Berry, "The Tragedy of Gilbert Gauthe," *Times of Acadiana,* May 30, 1985; "Fallen Priests," *Times of Acadiana,* June 13, 1985; and "Anatomy of a Cover-up," *Times of Acadiana,* January 30, 1986. Berry's reporting on Gauthe also appeared in the *National Catholic Reporter.*
- United Press International reported on Gauthe in "Jury awards $1.25 million in boy's molestation by priest," distributed by the wire service on February 7, 1986.
- The Gauthe case is also covered in Leon J. Podles, *Sacrilege: Sexual Abuse in the Catholic Church* (Baltimore, MD: Crossland Press, 2008), 80–88.

Michael Peterson's involvement in the early investigation of sexual abuse in the Catholic Church is recounted in Berry, *Lead Us Not Into Temptation* and in interviews that Berry, Doyle, and Mouton granted author.

For Michael Peterson's perspective on pedophilia and its cure see: Thomas C. Fox, "What They Knew in 1985: 17 Years Ago, a Report on Clergy Sex Abuse Warned U.S. Bishops of Trouble Ahead," *National Catholic*

Reporter, May 17, 2002.

For Pope Paul VI's consultation with Anna Terruwe, see her official biography at the Web site of Radboud University: http://www.ru.nl/snuf/english/facilities/dr-anna-terruwe/biography.

For Baars's address to American bishops, see: Conrad Baars, M.D. and Anna Terruwe, M.D., "The Role of the Church in the Causation, Treatment and Prevention of the Crisis in the Priesthood," November 1971, which is held at the online archive www.richardsipe.com.

The medical text that downplayed recurrence of pedophilia is J. W. Mohr, R. E. Turner, M. B. Jerry, *Pedophilia and Exhibitionism, A Handbook* (Toronto: University of Toronto Press, 1964).

For Humane Society report, see: "Child Abuse Potential is Present in All Segments of Society," Salinas (Ca.) *Journal,* October 10, 1971, 13.

David Finklehor, *Sexually Victimized Children* (New York: Free Press, 1979).

President Reagan's 1984 state of the union speech is available at: http://reagan2020.us/

speeches/state_of_the_union_1984.asp. See also: Steven Weisman, "President, Viewing State of the Union, Says 'We Cannot Turn Back'; Reagan Asks 2-Party Drive To Cut Deficits $100 Billion," *New York Times,* January 26, 1984, A1.

For McMartin case, see:

- **Edgar W. Butler, *Anatomy of the McMartin Child Molestation Case* (Latham, MD: University Press of America, 2001).**
- **Professor Douglas Linder of the University of Missouri Kansas City School of Law maintains an archive of McMartin preschool case documents at: http://law2.umkc.edu/ faculty/projects/ftrials/mcmartin/ mcmartin.html**

2. The Church Knows

Raymond Mouton's biography, his involvement in the church abuse scandal, and his work with Doyle and Peterson are based on author interviews with Mouton, Doyle, and Jason Berry, as well as on Berry's *Lead Us Not Into Temptation;* Michael Powell, "A Fall From Grace," *Washington Post,* August 4, 2002; Eamonn O'Neill, "What the Catholic Bishop Knew," *The Guardian,* April 3, 2010.

In 1961 the Vatican's Sacred Congregation for Religious banned from the priesthood "Those affected by the perverse inclination to homosexuality or pederasty . . ." in a document titled *Careful Selection and Training of Candidates for the States of Perfection and Sacred Ordination.*

Although widely discussed within the Church, the issue of gay men in the priesthood also received occasional public attention, as in:

- Michael Stephen, "On Homosexual Priests," *New York Times,* August 18, 1980, A23.
- Joseph Berger, "Religions Confront Issue of Homosexuality," *New York Times,* March 2, 1987, 1.
- A.W. Richard Sipe, *A Secret World: Sexuality and the Search for Celibacy* (New York: Brunner/Mazel Publishers, 1990), 105–108.
- See also: "Letter to the Bishops of the Catholic Church on the Pastoral Care of Homosexual Persons, Congregation for the Doctrine of the Faith," October 1, 1986: http://www.vatican.va/roman_curia/congregations/cfaith/documents/rc_con_cfaith_doc_ 19861001_homosexual-persons_en.html

For information on organizations promoting pedophilia, see:

- **Bernard Frits, *Paedophilia: A Factual Report* (Rotterdam: Enclave, 1985).**
- **"Dutch Priest Belonged to Pedophile Club," *Boston Globe,* May 20, 2011.**

3. Sexual Intellectuals

Jason Berry's childhood and personal life are based on interviews with author. Berry's encounters with "Chalice" are described here on the basis of interviews with Berry and his book, *Lead Us Not Into Temptation,* especially pp. 79–81, 82, 104, 135, and 167.

The work of Mouton and Doyle on their document is recounted on the basis of author interviews with the principals. It is also informed by Jason Berry and Gerald Renner, *Vows of Silence: The Abuse of Power in the Papacy of John Paul II* (New York: Free Press, 2004), especially chapter two, "Evidence of Things Unsaid."

For the state of scientific knowledge about pedophilia at the time Mouton and Peterson met, see: Ron Langevin and Reuben Lang, "Psychological Treatment of Pedophiles," *Behavioral Sciences and the Law,* Vol. 3, No. 4, 403–419.

Thomas Doyle, Raymond Mouton, and Michael Peterson, *The Problems of Sexual Molestation by Catholic Clergy* is available online at: www.bishopaccountability.org/reports/ 1985_06_09_Doyle_Manual/

The *National Catholic Reporter*'s coverage of the abuse scandal began June 7, 1985 with a package of articles preceded by an editor's note titled, "Priest Child Abuse Cases Victimizing Families; Bishops Lack Policy Response."

For additional information about Gilbert Gauthe's trials see:

- **"Suit May Go before Grand Jury,"** New Orleans *Times-Picayune,* September 6, 1984, A21.
- **"Court Appeal in Suit Against Priest,"** New Orleans *Times-Picayune* September 7, 1984, E21.
- **"Former Priest Pleads Innocent,"** New Orleans *Times-Picayune,* October 25, 1984, B2.
- **John Pope, "Sexual Abuse Case Trying Town,"** New Orleans *Times-Picayune,* November 4, 1984, 1.
- **John Pope, "Molestation Trial to Start for La. Priest,"** New Orleans *Times-Picayune,* October 14, 1985, 21.
- **"Bishop: Priest a Dr. Jekyll and Mr.**

Hyde," New Orleans *Times-Picayune*, January 26, 1985, 77.

- "Ex-priest Stands Trial in Sex Scandal," *San Diego Union*, October 16, 1985, 12.
- "Defrocked Priest Sentenced for Molesting 36 Children," *San Francisco Chronicle*, October 15, 1985, 20.
- Jon Nordheimer, "Abuse of Children By Priest Devastates Rural Communities," *Houston Chronicle*, June 23, 1985, 7.
- "Jury Awards Boy Molested by Priest $1 million," *Houston Chronicle*, February 8, 1986, 4.
- "Former Altar Boy Awarded $1.55 million," *Washington Post*, December 13, 1987, 18.

Time magazine's coverage of the Gauthe cases included "Religion: Painful Secrets," *Time*, July 1, 1985; and "Louisiana Prison for a Priest," *Time*, October 28, 1985.

The theological crackdown conducted by Pope John Paul II and then Cardinal Ratzinger's Congregation for the Doctrine of the Faith is described broadly in Thomas Fox, *The Pope's War*, (New York: Sterling Ethos, 2011), and the rationale for it is revealed in Joseph Cardinal Ratzinger and Vittorio Messori, *The Ratzinger Report*, (San Francisco:

Ignatius Press, 1985).

For Charles Curran's case, see:

- **Daniel Maguire, "Curran, Others Suffer in Vatican's Power Play," Minneapolis September 28, 1986, 21.**
- **Associated Press, "Group Terms Vatican Action 'Incomprehensible': Theologians Condemn Curran's Punishment,"** *Los Angeles Times,* **December 20, 1986, 2.**
- **Russell Chandler, "Hunthausen, Curran, Sweeney Among Targets Vatican Crackdowns Listed as Year's Top Religion Story,"** *Los Angeles Times,* **December 27, 1986, 4.**

For Doyle's meeting with canon lawyers, see: Jonathan Friendly, "Roman Catholic Church Discussing Priests Who Abuse Children," *New York Times,* May 4, 1986, A26.

For Michael Peterson's death, see: "Rev. Michael Peterson, Hospital Founder, Dies," *New York Times,* April 12, 1987, 42.

Doyle's appearance on *Hour Magazine* and subsequent meeting with Pio Laghi recounted in interviews.

The story of the bishop who assaulted a male

prostitute was eventually published. See: Carla K. Johnson and Kevin Taylor, "Late Bishop had Secret, Welsh Was Accused of Trying to Strangle Prostitute," *Spokesman-Review* (Spokane, WA), October 25, 2002.

Jeffrey Anderson's conversation with J. Minos Simon from author interview with Anderson.

4. Spiritual Betrayal

Much of the information in this chapter is from author interviews with Jeffrey Anderson, Julie Anderson, Thomas Krauel, and members of the Lyman family.

For Big Reggie's Danceland and other elements of the 1960s scene in the Twin Cities, see: Daniel Gabriel, "Dance Hall Days," *Minneapolis-St. Paul Magazine,* December 1994.

Philip Willkie and Rebecca Rand offered their recollections of events in interviews.

Bathhouse case is described in Tim Campbell, "Jury Acquits Bathhouse Workers," *The GLC Voice,* April 1981, 1.

The Lyman case is detailed in a multipart series by Robert Ehlert, published under the heading "Don't Tell Anybody . . . You'll Get in Trouble, and So Will I," in the Minneapolis

Star Tribune, December 1988.

Details of the Lyman case are also drawn from depositions and trial records of the Lyman family lawsuit against the Diocese of St. Paul, the Diocese of Winona, and Rev. Thomas Adamson.

Jeffrey Anderson's alcoholism and incidents related to it recalled in interviews with Anderson, Grant Hall, and Julie Anderson. For more on Jeffrey Anderson, see:

- **Terry Carter, "Collaring the Clergy: Jeffrey Anderson Goes Global with His Pursuit of Pedophiles,"** *American Bar Association Journal,* **June 18, 2007.**
- **Peter Slevin, "Career Fighting for the Underdog Led to Taking on the Church,"** *Washington Post,* **April 19, 2010, C1.**

5. The Catholic States of America

For Gauthe award, see: "Jury Awards Boy Molested by Priest $1 million," *Houston Chronicle,* February 8, 1986, 4.

In this chapter, all letters, documents, and testimony quoted are from the records of the lawsuit filed by the Lyman family against the Diocese of St. Paul, the Diocese of Winona, and Rev. Thomas Adamson.

Details of Anderson's work on the Lyman case from his personal records and interviews.

For estimate of U.S. Catholic Church revenues, see: Deborah Zabarenko, "After Scandal, Fiscal Troubles Deepen for U.S. Catholic Church," *Boston Globe,* December 29, 2004.

Rankings of top corporations from Fortune 500 list 2003.

6. A Weeping Priest
Thomas Adamson's deposition statements from official transcript.

Lyman family attitudes toward the lawsuit and Greg Lyman's condition from interviews with Greg Lyman.

Recollections of The Professionals case from interview with attorney Mark Condon. For more on the case, see: Dan Oberdorfer, "Judge Settles Case for Musicians," Minneapolis *Star Tribune,* July 2, 1986, 9B.

7. Five Brothers; Three Victims
Anderson's contacts with Jay Klein recalled by Klein and Anderson in interviews.

For John Ireland's settlement efforts in Minnesota, see: Evangela Henthorne *The Irish Catholic Colonization Association of the United States, 1879–1892,* (Champagne, IL: Twin City Printing Co., 1932).

James H. Moynihan, *The Life of Archbishop John Ireland* (New York: Harper and Brothers, 1953).

Further detail provided in deposition of Jay Klein, as well as depositions of Sr. Tierney Trueman and Sr. Micon Welsch.

Anecdotes from the Andersons' marriage from interviews with Julie Anderson.

8. The Angels Had to Cry
Jay Klein's dialogue with William Hull from official transcript of deposition.

"Vatican Boosts Signals for East Bloc Broadcasts," *Los Angeles Times,* December 2, 1986, 16.

For examples of the Vatican's political involvement, see:

- **Roberto Suro, "Vatican Wants Noriega Out, but Blames U.S." *St. Petersburg Times,* December 30, 1989, 1.**
- **Charles Hanley, "Cardinal Says**

Vatican Was Uneasy Over His Role in Philippine Revolt," *Boston Globe,* June 26, 1986, 6.

- Barry Newman, "Quiet Crusade: As Pope's Visit Nears, The Church in Poland Hews to Its Strategy; Essentially United, It Intends To Outlast Regime, Make Totalitarianism Less Total; Rulers' Offer to the Vatican," *Wall Street Journal,* June 1, 1987, 1.

Rembert Weakland's analysis of priests' sexuality offered in interview with author.

For the power of fundamentalist and orthodox faith, see: Laurence R. Iannaccone, "Why Strict Churches Are Strong," *American Journal of Sociology,* Vol. 99. No. 5, March 1994, 1180–1211.

For "Angels had to cry," see: Dennis J. McGrath and Martha Sawyer Allen, "Archbishop Roach Criticizes Barbara Carlson for Advocating Condoms as Christmas Gifts," Minneapolis *Star Tribune,* December 19, 1986, 03B.

Martha Sawyer Allen "Each Dawn, New Hope Archbishop Roach, 65, Finds it in His Faith," Minneapolis *Star Tribune,* December 25, 1986, 01A.

Anderson's conversation with attorney Hull based on Anderson's recollections.

The conversation between Greg Lyman and Anderson from interviews with both.

Phipps-Yonas' evaluation from interviews with Lyman and her report.

The second suit against Adamson and his employers see Virginia Rybin, Second Sexual Abuse Suit Charges Cover-up St. Paul *Pioneer Press Dispatch* Feb. 13, 1987 pg. 1.

and Virginia Rybin, Documents reveal Conflicts in When Church Knew of Abuses, *St. Paul Pioneer Press Dispatch,* Feb. 13, 1987 Pg. 5.

Further coverage in:

- **Kevin Diaz, "Bishop Says Church Erred in Handling of Sex Abuse Case," Minneapolis *Star Tribune,* February 16, 1987, 1.**
- **Clark Morphew, "Cover-up Denied on Priest's Sex Misconduct," *St. Paul Pioneer Press Dispatch,* February 16, 1987, 1.**

For Fulton Sheen on Freudianism see Robert Kugelman, *Psychology and Catholicism:*

Contested Boundaries (Cambridge: Cambridge University Press, 2011), 193.

The encounter between Tim Campbell and Jeffrey Anderson on the St. Paul skyway taken from interviews of both men.

Carl Cannon, "Catholic Church is Slow to Face Pedophilia Issue," *St. Paul Pioneer Press Dispatch,* January 10, 1988, 1.

9. "What Did the Priest Do to You, Greg?"
Greg Lyman's experience watching himself on *Geraldo* from interview with author.

Dialogue from *Geraldo* Transcript #303, Journal Graphics, November 14, 1988.

"Trash TV," *Newsweek,* November 14, 1988 (cover story).

Wendy Kaminer, *I'm Dysfunctional, You're Dysfunctional: The Recovery Movement and Other Self-Help Fashions* (New York: Addison Wesley, 1992).

William Luther's legislative efforts from interview with author.

10. The Measure of the Elephant
Barbara Blaine's experience related to author in multiple interviews.

Joseph Bernardin's life is described in Joseph Cardinal Bernardin, *The Gift of Peace* (Chicago: Loyola Press, 1997) and in Eugene Kennedy, *This Man Bernardin* (Chicago: Loyola Press, 1996).

Details of Blaine's experiences from Bill Frogameni, "Toledo Native Barbara Blaine Crusades against Sexual Abuse in the Catholic Church," *Toledo City Paper,* April 29, 2004.

Blaine also appears in Angela Bonavoglia, *Good Catholic Girls: How Women Are Leading the Fight to Change the Church* (New York: HarperOne, 2006); see chapter four "Sex, Priests and Girlhoods Lost."

Blaine's contacts with Jason Berry recalled by both in interviews.

Gary Olivero's death is recounted in a memorial issue of *Taking Sides, The Voice of St. Elizabeth Catholic Worker,* Chicago, 1989.

Life of Jeanne Miller recounted in interview with author. See also:

- **Hilary Stiles, *Assault on Innocence: For the First Time . . . The Untold Story of Pedophilia,* (Albuquerque, NM: B & K Publishers, Inc., 1987).**

- Jerry Thornton, "Group Works to Prevent Cleric Abuse," *Chicago Tribune,* November 4 1991, 3.

George Cornell, "Support Group Helps Victims of Clergy Sex Abuse Victims of Clergy Share Their Pain," *St. Petersburg* (FL) *Times,* November 7, 1992, 6E.

Michael Hirsley, "Silence Is Broken, Victims of Sexual Abuse by Clergy Seek Strength and Answers at Conference," *Chicago Tribune,* October 17, 1992, 5.

Lindsey Tanner, "Catholic Church Panel Probes Treatment of Pedophile Priests," *Las Vegas Review-Journal,* March 20, 1992, 14.

Accounts of Richard Sipe's life and background are based on interviews with author. See also his books, especially A. W. Richard Sipe, *A Secret World: Sexuality and the Search for Celibacy* (New York: Brunner/Mazel, Publishers, 1990). Also see early descriptions of his work in:

- Clark Morphew, "Church Must Re-examine Celibacy, Ex-priest Writes," *Austin American-Statesman,* November 11, 1989, E5.
- Martha Sawyer Allen, "For Some Ministers, Living by the Word Can

Be a Struggle," Minneapolis *Star Tribune,* April 23, 1991, 1.

For the case of Mt. Cashel in Newfoundland, see:

- John F. Burns, "Canadian Prelate Quits in Clerics' Sex Scandal," *New York Times,* July 20, 1990, 4.
- "Newfoundland Archbishop Offers to Quit for Ignoring Sex Scandal," *Chicago Tribune,* July 22, 1990, 20.
- Mary Williams Walsh, "Sex Scandal in Canadian Archdiocese Renews Debate on Celibacy, Doctrine, Catholicism," *Los Angeles Times,* July 21, 1990, 12.

For Greeley's criticism of Sipe, see: Andrew Greeley, "Some Married Men Aren't Faithful, but We Don't Say Marriage Is a Failure," *Los Angeles Times,* August 24, 1990, 7.

Bishop Quinn's address to the canon lawyers is reported in Jason Berry and Gerald Renner, *Vows of Silence: The Abuse of Power in the Papacy of John Paul II* (New York: Free Press, 2004), 68–70; and by Rod Dreher, "Mitered in the Mob?" *National Review,* March 28, 2002.

11. Willful Indifference

Origins of SNAP from author interviews with Blaine, Berry and early members of the organization.

For a comprehensive review of the issues around psychological trauma and the law, see: Daniel Brown, Alan W. Scheflin, & D. Corydon Hammond, *Memory: Trauma, Treatment, and the Law,* (New York, W.W. Norton & Company, Inc., 1998).

Portrayal of Frank Fitzpatrick's pursuit of James Porter is based on extensive contemporary reporting by Frank Bruni and Elinor Burkett, *A Gospel of Shame: Children, Sexual Abuse, and the Catholic Church* (New York: HarperCollins Publishers Inc., 2002). See also:

- Elizabeth Mehren, "Unlocking Painful Secrets from the Past," *Los Angeles Times,* June 7, 1992, 1.
- Tom Coakley, "Porter Pleads Guilty to Assaults as Priest Admits Molesting 28 Youths in 1960s," *Boston Globe,* October 5, 1993, 16. [City Edition]
- Linda Matchan and Stephen Kurkjian, "Porter Held in Minn. on Mass. Charges; Ex-priest Is Said to be Indicted in Abuse Cases," *Boston*

Globe, September 22, 1992, 1.

- **Chronology James Porter, Minneapolis *Star Tribune,* October 5 1993, 2B.**
- **Chuck Haga and Paul McEnroe, "Sins of the Father," Minneapolis *Star Tribune,* July 19, 1992, 1.**

For Cardinal Law's condemnation of *The Boston Globe,* see: Steve Marantz, "Law raps ex-priest coverage," *Boston Globe,* May 24, 1992, 23.

The case of Thomas Mrozka is told on the basis of the trial record, interviews with attorneys in the case, and extensive media coverage including:

- **Donna Halvorsen, "Adamson Testifies About Sex Offenses; Says Superiors Knew of Conduct," Minneapolis *Star Tribune,* November 6, 1990, 1.**
- **Donna Halvorsen, "Roach Acknowledges Mistakes with Adamson," Minneapolis *Star Tribune,* November 16, 1990, 1.**
- **Donna Halvorsen, "Two Catholic Dioceses Admit Responsibility for Sexual Abuse by Priest," Minneapolis *Star Tribune,* November 3, 1990, 1.**
- **Donna Halvorsen, "Priest's Victim Gets $3.5 Million; Church Says It**

Will Appeal Ruling," Minneapolis *Star Tribune*, December 8, 1990, 1.

Greg Lyman's arrest in Wisconsin described on the basis of interviews with Lyman and his wife.

12. An Attitude of Resistance

Prime Time Live report on James Porter aired on ABC, July 2, 1992.

SNAP conference in Boston reported on the basis of author interview with Blaine. See also: Elizabeth Stankiewicz, "Group Criticizes Church Response to Sex Offenders," *Boston Globe* July 26, 1992, 23.

Abbie Jones, "Irish Court Rules Permission of Teen Rape Victim to Travel for Abortion," *Chicago Tribune*, March 8, 1992, 1.

Kevin Cullen, "Beyond the Blarney Rosemary Mahoney Takes on the Irish Clergy," *Boston Globe*, October 15, 1993, 49.

George Cornell, "Sex Abuse by Priests Worries Bishops at a National Meeting," *Philadelphia Inquirer*, June 21, 1992, 4.

"Bishops Promise Swift Action in Cases of Abuse by Priests," June 21, 1992, pg. 6.

Details of Jason Berry's personal life from interviews.

Bernardin's relationship with Jeanne Miller reported on the basis of author interviews. See also:

- **"Support Group Helps Victims of Clergy Sex Abuse,"** *Los Angeles Times*, November 14, 1992, 12.
- **Michael Hirsley, "Bernardin Passes Up Opportunity,"** *Chicago Tribune*, October 16 1992, 2C7.

Comments at VOCALink-up conference quoted from copies of texts distributed at the conference and supplied to author by Jason Berry.

13. The Meaning of Memory
Barbara Blaine's experience at the bishops' conference based on interviews. See also:

Peter Steinfels, "Why Did God Make These Debates So Hard?" *New York Times*, November 22 1992, 6.

Chris Reidy, "Bishops Pledge Response in Abuse Cases," *Boston Globe*, November 20, 1992, 1.

"Bishops Urge Crackdown on Sexually Abusive Priests," *San Antonio Express-News*, November 20 1992, 8B.

George W. Cornell, "Bishops Vow to Pay Attention to Abuse Action Comes After Victims' Protests," *Orange County Register,* November 19, 1992, A01.

Bishop Murphy's recollection of his encounter with schoolchildren noted in Anna Quindlan, "Public & Private; Six for Women" *New York Times,* November 25, 1992, 21.

For more on Rita Milla, see: Patt Morrison, "Letters from L.A. Archdiocese Urged Him to Remain in Philippines," *Los Angeles Times,* March 28, 1991, 1.

Patt Morrison, "Ex-Priest Apologizes for Seducing Teen-Ager," *Los Angeles Times,* March 29, 1991, 3.

Susannah Rosenblatt, "A Victory for Victim of Abuse," *Los Angeles Times,* December 5, 2007, B3.

For David Clohessy, see: Virginia Young, "Memory Prompts Abuse Suit Against Priest," *St. Louis Post-Dispatch,* November 24, 1991, B1.

Kathryn Rogers Priest, "Accused of Abusing Altar Boy, Resigns His Post," *St. Louis Post-Dispatch,* September 29, 1993, 3B.

Frank Bruni, "Am I My Brother's Keeper?,"

New York Times Magazine, May 12, 2002, 42.

Jon Pareles, "Why Sinead O'Connor Hit a Nerve," *New York Times,* November 1, 1992, 27.

Jill Neimark, "The Diva of Disclosure, Memory Researcher Elizabeth Loftus," *Psychology Today,* Vol. 29, No. 1, January 1996, 48.

Richard Ofshe and Ethan Watters, *Making Monsters: False Memories, Psychotherapy, and Sexual Hysteria* (Berkeley: University of California Press, 1996).

E. F. Loftus and K. Ketcham, *The Myth of Repressed Memory* (New York: St. Martin's Press, 1994).

For review of Wakefield and Underwager, see: David L. Chadwick, "Accusations of Child Sexual Abuse," *Journal of the American Medical Association,* May 26, 1989.

Stephanie J. Dallam, "Crisis or Creation: A Systematic Examination of False Memory Claims." Published as a chapter in Charles L. Whitfield, Joyanna Silberg, and Paul Jay Fink, *Misinformation Concerning Child Sexual Abuse and Adult Survivors* (Philadelphia: Haworth Press, 2002).

For the satanic ritual abuse controversy, see: Frank Putnam and Kenneth Lanning, *Satanic, Occult, Ritualistic Crime: A Law Enforcement Perspective,* (Quantico: Behavioral Science Instruction and Research Unit, FBI Academy, 1989).

For legal concept of delayed discovery of harm in sexual abuse case, see: George J. Alexander and Alan W. Scheflin, *Law and Mental Disorder* (Durham: Carolina Academic Press, 1998), 239–241.

14. The Pendulum Swings

Thomas Doyle's struggle with alcoholism was related in interviews with author.

Jeffrey Anderson's conflicts with his wife described by both Anderson and his wife Julie in interviews.

Mark Chopko and Jeffrey Anderson, "Liability for Sexual Misconduct of the Clergy," *Tort Liability for Charitable, Religious and Nonprofit Institutions, American Bar Association,* Washington, D.C. 1992.

Story of the Bloomington road race collapse from interviews with the Andersons.

For case of Gerald O'Keefe see:

- **Jean Latz Griffin, " 'Memory' of Sex Abuse by Clergy Can be Cre-**

ated," *Orange County Register,* November 25, 1993, 31.

- **Chris Graves, "Psychiatrist Accused Again of Planting False Memories," Minneapolis *Star Tribune,* October 13, 1993, 5B.**

Martha Sawyer Allen, "Backlash Arises on Cases of Clergy Sex Abuse," Minneapolis *Star Tribune,* December 7, 1993, 12.

Richard John Neuhaus, "When Shepherds Go Astray," *First Things,* January 1993. http://www.firstthings.com/article/2008/04/when-shepherds-go-astray-50.

For "cases of scandal" see: Peter Steinfels, "Pope Endorses Bishops' Attempts To Rid Clergy of Child Molesters," *New York Times,* June 22, 1993, 1.

"Society Shares Blame for Scandals, Vatican Says," *Los Angeles Times,* June 26, 1993, 5.

15. Push Back
Joseph Bernardin's personal experiences during the period when he was accused of sexual abuse are drawn mainly from his memoir, Joseph Cardinal Bernardin, *The Gift of Peace* (Chicago: Loyola Press, 1997). See also:

- **Jack C. Doppelt, *Guilt by Allegation:***

Lessons from the Cardinal Bernardin Case (Chicago: Medill School of Journalism, 1994).

- Michael Hirsley and Jan Crawford, "I've Led a Chaste Life, Bernardin Says," *Chicago Tribune,* November 14, 1993, 1.
- "Chicago Prelate Is Accused of Sex Abuse and Denies It," *New York Times,* November 13, 1993, 12.
- Peter Steinfels, "Bishops Assail Press on Sex Charges," *New York Times,* November 16, 1993, 24.
- "Vatican Supports Accused Cardinal," *St. Petersburg Times,* November 14, 1993, 3.
- Michael Hirsley and Jan Crawford, "Bernardin Accuser Recants Sex Abuse Charge," *Chicago Tribune,* March 1, 1994, 1.

For Cardinal Sanchez's comment on sexual activity of priests see: Anson D. Shupe, *Spoils of the Kingdom: Clergy Misconduct And Religious Community* (Champaign, IL: University of Illinois), XXI.

Barbara Blaine's reaction to the Bernardin case from interview. See also:

- Michael Hirsley, "Bernardin Shows How to React," *Chicago Tribune,* No-

vember 19, 1993, 8.
- Steven J. Cook, "Bernardin lawsuit begs serious questions – Cardinal Joseph Bernardin; sex abuse accusations," *National Catholic Reporter,* December 3, 1993 (cover story).

Leon Jaroff, "Jeanne McDowell Repressed-Memory Therapy: Lies of the Mind," *Time,* November 29, 1993.

"Trial by Accusation," *Wall Street Journal,* December 1, 1993, 20.

Charles Krauthammer, "Defining Deviancy Up," AEI Bradley Lecture Series, September 13, 1993. http://www.aei.org/article/society-and-culture/ poverty/defining-deviancy-up/.

For Blackowiak case, see: Anne O'Connor, "Sex Abuse Victims Able to Sue After Time Lapse," Minneapolis *Star Tribune,* February 18, 1995, 2B.

"High Court Drops Suit Alleging Sex Abuse by School Counselor," Minneapolis *Star Tribune,* April 20, 1996, 3B.

Ember Reichgott Junge, "Recent Minnesota Supreme Court Ruling is Injustice to Victims of Sexual Abuse," Minneapolis *Star Tribune,*

May 24, 1996, 27.

16. Would a Bishop Lie?

Transcript of Homily by the Pope on the Great Lawn in Central Park, *New York Times,* October 8, 1995, 42.

Paul Baumann, "The Pope vs. the Culture of Death," *New York Times,* October 8, 1995, 4.13.

Philip Jenkins, "The Uses of Clerical Scandal," *First Things,* February 1995.

"John Paul II defends family life; lectures French on morality," *San Antonio Express-News,* September 21, 1996, 1.

For the story of Andrew Madden and Ivan Payne, author depended on interviews with Andrew Madden, his book *Altar Boy: A Story of Life After Abuse* (Ireland: Penguin, 2003), and contemporary news accounts. For examples, see:

- **Alan Murdoch, "Church gave sex claim priest pay-off money," *The Independent,* September 30,1995.**
- **"Sex abuse priest Ivan Payne to be released from jail," *Irish Times,* October 25, 2002.**

For the case of Brendan Smyth, see:

- Andy Pollack, "Clerical sex abuse guidelines to appear next week," *Irish Times,* January 1, 1996.
- "Report all child sex abuse suspicions to police, say bishops," *Irish Times,* January 31, 1996.
- Andy Pollack, "Garda sergeant relates circumstances of inquiry into clerical sex abuse claims," *Irish Times,* February 5, 1996.
- "Paedophile priest Brendan Smyth: A monster who targeted the vulnerable," *Belfast Telegraph,* March 15, 2010. http://www.belfasttelegraph.co.uk/news/local-national/paedophile-priest-brendan-smyth-a-monster-who-targeted-the-vulnerable-14720913.html#ixzz20YEGKPUT
- April Drew, "Child abuse monster Father Brendan Smyth ruined my life," IrishCentral.com, February 10, 2010.
- See also: http://www.irishcentral.com/news/Helen-McGonigle-My-years-of-abuse-at-the-hands-of-monster-Father-Brendan-Smyth-83985092.html#ixzz20YEjidTL.

Jon Pomfret, "Austrian Catholics seek reform; As many leave the church, movement asks for more compassionate policies," *Austin*

American Statesman, October 8, 1995, 21.

Jane Perlez, "New Austrian Cardinal Apologizes for Predecessor's Sex Crimes," *New York Times,* April 20,1998, 5.

For ad limina visits author relied on interviews with Archbishop Rembert Weakland. See also: Jason Berry and Gerald Renner, *Vows of Silence: The Abuse of Power in the Papacy of John Paul II,* (New York: Free Press, 2004), 96–97.

Thomas Doyle's transfers and posting from interviews.

Case of Rudy Kos from interviews with Demarest, as well as from court record of the case. See also:

- **Dan Michalski, "How Rudy Kos Happened," *D Magazine,* July 1, 1998.**
- **Brooks Egerton, "Judge in Kos Case Lets Emotions Out in Talk; Her Address after Final Arguments Called Unusual," *Dallas Morning News,* July 22, 1997.**
- **Ed Housewright and Brooks Egerton, "Kos Jury Awards $119 Million Diocese Found Grossly Negligent Sex Abuse Judgment Largest of Its Kind," *Dallas Morning News,* July 25, 1997.**

- Christine Wicker, "Parishioners Hope Church Learns Lesson," *Dallas Morning News,* July 25, 1997.
- Brooks Egerton and Ed Housewright "Kos Case Apparently Widening but Diocese Doubts Criminal Trial Likely," *Dallas Morning News,* July 26, 1997.
- "11 allege a conspiracy in Dallas sex abuse," *National Catholic Reporter,* June 20, 1997, 4.
- William F. Buckley Jr., "Buggery in Church," *National Review Online,* September 15, 1997.
- Michael Saul, "Kos Says He's Sorry for Crimes, Hopes for Forgiveness; Suspended Priest Contends Diocese Abandoned Him," *Dallas Morning News,* April 4, 1998.

17. Oliver O'Grady

Portrayal of the case of Oliver O'Grady based on court transcripts and video depositions, author interviews with attorneys and media reports. For examples of coverage, see:

- Amy Berg, *Deliver Us From Evil* (2006).
- Don Lattin, "$30 Million Awarded Men Molested By Priest," *San Francisco Chronicle,* July 17, 1998.

- Steve Lopez, "The Amazing Teflon Cardinal," *Los Angeles Times*, April 7, 2002.
- Ron Russell, "Mouth Wide Shut: Cardinal Roger Mahony's harboring of pedoriests didn't just start with the current Roman Catholic sex scandal. As his protection of a predator cleric in Stockton reveals, he's been at it for a long time," (Los Angeles) *New Times*, April 18, 2002.
- Don Lattin, "L.A. Cardinal's Roles Outrages Abuse Victims; Mahony lacks credibility to protect kids, critics say," *San Francisco Chronicle*, April 19, 2002.
- Elizabeth Bell, "Catholic Church goes on trial in alleged cover-up," *Stockton Record*, June 11, 1998.
- Elizabeth Bell, "Woman testifies that Catholic priest molested her," *Stockton Record*, June 12, 1998.
- Elizabeth Bell, "Cardinal testifies in molest trial," *Stockton Record*, June 15, 1998.
- Elizabeth Bell, "Ex-priest refuses to testify," *Stockton Record*, June 17, 1998.
- Elizabeth Bell, "Catholic official kept molestation suspicions quiet," *Stockton Record*, June 19, 1998.

- "Diocese allegedly told about priest," *Stockton Record,* June 24, 1998.
- Elizabeth Bell, "Accusers tell jurors of abuse at hands of Catholic priest," *Stockton Record,* June 26, 1998.
- Elizabeth Bell, "Attorneys seek $60M from Catholic Diocese," *Stockton Record,* July 10, 1998.

Jeffrey Anderson's recovery from alcoholism reported on the basis of interviews with him and with those who knew him in Alcoholics Anonymous.

For reference to Mahony's status as a candidate for the papacy, see: Mitchell Landsberg, "Roger Mahony leaves a mixed legacy," *Los Angeles Times,* February 23, 2011.

For "The devil really exists" see: James D. Davis, " '20/20' to Air Exorcism Rite," (Ft. Lauderdale) *Sun-Sentinel,* April 5, 1991.

"A Roman Catholic Bishop in Florida Resigns, Admitting He Molested 5 Boys" *New York Times,* June 3, 1998, 12.

"A Refreshingly Forthright Bishop," *St. Petersburg Times,* June 4, 1998, 18.

"Bishop's Brother Wonders How Secret Kept

So Long," *St. Petersburg Times,* June 8, 1998, 3B.

18. By Other Means
Portrayal of filmmaking based on transcript of film.

Events at St. John's School for the Deaf reported on the basis of court records, correspondence of Terrance Kohut, and author interviews with attorneys and participants in lawsuits.

For more on Fr. Ryan Erickson case, see:

- **Thomas H. Barland, *State of Wisconsin v. James E. Erickson,* Circuit Court Eau Claire, WS, July 8, 1999.**
- **Associated Press, "Police Await Results of Search of Dead Priest's Computer," *Grand Forks Herald,* June 15, 2005.**
- **Doug Stohlberg, "Double murder is now 10 years old," *Hudson Star-Observer,* February 5, 2012.**
- **Leon J. Podles, *The Rev. Ryan Erickson Case Study* (Baltimore: Crossland Foundation, 2008).**

For reporting on The Legionaries of Christ see: Jason Berry and Gerald Renner, *Vows of Silence: The Abuse of Power in the Papacy of*

John Paul II, (New York: Free Press, 2004) and Jason Berry, *Render Unto Rome: The Secret Life of Money in the Catholic Church* (New York: Crown Publishing Group, 2011).

Activities of Tom Doyle and Richard Sipe reported on the basis of interviews. See also:

- **Colleen Barry, "Priest jumped off fast track to speak for abuse victims,"** *San Antonio Express-News,* **April 21, 2002, 11.**
- **Jenna Russell, "Priest Lauded for 1985 Report on Abuse Urged the Church to Intervene But Was Rebuffed,"** *Boston Globe,* **January 26, 2003, 15.**

Alessandra Stanley, "Stop Squabbling, Pope Tells Austria's Divided Bishops as He Ends His Visit," *New York Times,* June 22, 1998, 10.

Alessandra Stanley, "Preview HYPERLINK "/nationalnewspremier/docvie w/430992679/137EAFF2C9A7B56FA5C/2?accountid= 8067" Pope in Austria to Heal a Troubled Church," *New York Times,* June 20, 1998, 4.

For the Irish abuse scandal author depended on interviews with principals in the crisis, including Colm O'Gorman, as well as contemporary media coverage. See also Mary Raftery, *States of Fear* (1999); *Report of the Commission to Inquire into Child Abuse,* government of Ireland, Dublin, May 29, 2009; the Web site Justice for Magdalenes, http://www.magdalenelaundries.com; and statement of Irish government, *Bertie Ahern Announces Government Measures Relating to Childhood Abuse,* Department of Education and Skills, May, 11, 1999.

For the "Celtic Tiger" see: David Lynch, "Foreign Cash Fuels Irish," *USA Today,* August 19, 199, B1.

For case of Sean Fortune, see: Colm O'Gorman, *Beyond Belief* (London: Hodder & Stoughton, 2010).

For Luciano Storero, see Laurie Goodstein, "Vatican Warned Bishops on Abuse Policy," *New York Times,* January 19, 2011, 10.

Address of John Paul II to the Bishops of Ireland on Their Ad Limina Visit, published by the Vatican, June 26, 1999.

Report of the Ferns Inquiry, Irish Department of Health, October 25, 2005.

Transcript of the BBC documentary *Suing*

the Pope can be viewed at: news.bbc.co.uk/2/ shared/spl/hi/programmes/ . . . /1879407.txt.

Aiden Doyle's story recorded in interview with author.

15. Paper Chase

The story of Michael Rezendes reported on the basis of interviews with him and Richard Sipe. See also: The Investigative Staff of *The Boston Globe, Betrayal: The Crisis in the Catholic Church* (Boston, Little, Brown, 2002).

The account of the scandal in Boston is based in large part of reporting of *The Boston Globe,* as well as on David France, *Our Fathers: The Secret Life of the Catholic Church in An Age of Scandal* (New York: Broadway Books, 2004). Other sources include author interviews with Roderick MacLeish who is profiled in David Lyons's "Sex, Greed, and God," *Forbes,* June 9, 2003. For more on MacLeish see also: Bella English, "The Hole in the Heart of a Star," *Boston Globe* April 18, 2010.

Melinda Hennenberger, "Vatican Weighs Reaction to Accusations of Molesting by Clergy," *New York Times,* March 3, 2002, 30.

Steve Wohlberg, "Sex, Shame and the Catholic Church," *Newsweek,* March 4, 2002 (cover story).

Cardinal Hoyos' letter is reported on the Reuters newswire website Tom Heneghan, in John Paul backed praise for hiding abuse, Apr 17, 2010 http:// www.reuters.com/article/ 2010/04/17/us-pope-abuse-cardinal-idUSTRE 63G1SH20100417

William Donohue's involvement in the abuse crisis and details of the Catholic League's development reported on the basis of author interview with Donahue, as well as Catholic League materials. See also:

- **Winnie Hu, "An Outspoken Church Defender,"** *New York Times,* **November 2, 1999, B5.**
- **Clyde Haberman, "A Soldier of Christ on the March,"** *New York Times,* **June 2, 1998, 1.**
- **Paul Vitello, "A 'Marine' for Catholics Sees a Time of Battle,"** *New York Times,* **May 14, 2009, 22.**
- **"William A. Donohue, president of the conservative Catholic League,"** *San Antonio Express-News,* **November 12, 1999, 25.**
- **Ann Rodgers-Melnick, "He's a Passionate Defender of Catholic Faith,"** **Pittsburgh** *Post-Gazette,* **May 7, 2000, 1.**

Olan Horne's recollection of being assaulted

from David France, *Our Fathers: The Secret Life of the Catholic Church in an Age of Scandal* (New York, Broadway Books, 2004), 332.

Founding and operation of BishopAccount ability.org from interviews with Terence McKiernan.

Mahony memos obtained from KFI-AM.

For examples of Steve Lopez's writings on Cardinal Mahony see:

- **"Half Measures Won't Stop Molesting by Priests,"** *Los Angeles Times,* **January 30, 2002, B1.**
- **"Simple Suggestions for Mahony,"** *Los Angeles Times,* **March 13, 2002, B1.**
- **"Church's Scandal Starts With Celibacy,"** *Los Angeles Times,* **March 27, 2002, B1.**
- **"Cardinals Look Out for No. 1 in Scandal,"** *Los Angeles Times,* **May 3, 2002, B1.**

Activities of SNAP officials Blaine and Isely from interviews with author and contemporary media accounts.

Bonnie Miller, "Survivor Group Gains Support Amid Priest Scandal," *Chicago Tribune,*

April 28, 2002.

Philip Jenkins, "Forum" (column) "The myth of the 'pedophile priest,' " Pittsburgh *Post-Gazette,* March 3, 2002.

Melina Henneberger, "Pope Says Shadow of Suspicion Has been Cast Across All Priests," *The New York Times,* March 22, 2002, 1.

Carl M. Cannon, "The Priest Scandal," *American Journalism Review,* May 2002.

"Major Sexual Abuse Cases Within The Church," *USA Today,* February 25, 2002, 3.

John Tagliabue, "Pope Accepts Polish Archbishop's Resignation," *The New York Times,* March 29, 2002, 12.

"Can The Catholic Church Save Itself?" *Time,* April 1, 2002 (cover story)

For Shupe on "no Protestant equivalents," see: Michael Paulson, "All faiths question handling of abuse debate," *The Boston Globe,* March 13, 2002, 1. Peggy Noonan, "The Pope Steps In," *Wall Street Journal,* April 19, 2002, 18.

20. Catholic Guilt
For events in the Boston scandal and the reactions/actions of Bernard Law, the author

relied on the reporting of *The Boston Globe,* as well as: The Investigative Staff of *The Boston Globe, Betrayal: The Crisis in the Catholic Church* (Boston: Little, Brown, 2002).

Other sources include interviews with many of those involved directly in events and materials such as:

- Edward Walsh, "Victims of Priests' Abuse Urge Church to Take Responsibility; Cardinals Hear Anguished Tales as Bishops Weigh Policy," *The Washington Post,* June 13, 2002, 24.
- Don Lattin, "Abuse victims meet with church leaders/Bishops asked to adopt tough policy at their historic session," *San Francisco Chronicle,* June 13, 2002, 1.
- A. John Sawyer and Patricia Rice, "Bishops Meeting On Sex Abuse Find They Are Now Main Target: Critics Say They're Like Enron, Too Compromised To Lead," *St. Louis Post-Dispatch,* June 13, 2002, 1.
- Monica Davey and David Heinzman, "Bishops reworking sex abuse policy; Defrock guilty, victims tell clerics," *Chicago Tribune,* June 13, 2002, 1.
- Alan Cooperman and Pamela Ferdinand, "Boston's Cardinal Resigns

Over Sex Abuse Scandal," *The Washington Post,* December 14, 2002, 1.

- Steve Bailey, *Philadelphia Inquirer,* June 12, 2002, 2.
- Frank Keating, "Trying to Restore a Faith," *The New York Times,* June 15, 2002, 17.

Efforts of Jeff Anderson, Raymond Boucher, and Laurence Drivon regarding statute window in California from interviews. See also:

- Daniel B. Wood and Jane Lampman, "L.A. Now The Flash Point On Priest Abuse," *The Christian Science Monitor,* December 31, 2002, 3.
- William Lobdell, "The State" (column) "Statute of Limitations Eased in Abuse Cases," *Los Angeles Times,* July 12, 2002, B8.

21. The Open Window

Patrick Wall's story drawn from interviews with author. His relationships with Manly and Sipe from interviews with all three.

John Manly, "Shield the Flock, Not the Wolf," *Los Angeles Times,* September 30, 2001, B15.

Details of the suits brought against Archdiocese of Los Angeles and Dioceses of Orange and San Diego counties drawn from court records, and interviews with attorneys and judges involved.

Carla Hall, "L.A. Archdiocese Enlists Services of Top PR Firm; Publicity: Sitrick & Co., advisor to Enron and other troubled clients, takes on priest scandal," *Los Angeles Times,* May 30, 2002, B1.

William Lobdell and Steve Hymon, "Victim Begins Vigil at Cathedral; Man plans an 8-day fast to protest Cardinal Mahony's handling of sex abuse cases," *Los Angeles Times,* April 14, 2003, B3.

Dialogue of Michael Hennigan and John Manly from deposition transcript.

Manly's pursuit of Oliver O'Grady depicted on the basis of interviews with Manly and Wall, as well as transcripts of O'Grady's depositions. Also see: Amy Berg, *Deliver Us From Evil,* 2006.

Francis D. Murphy, Helen Buckley, and Larain Joyce, *The Ferns Report,* presented to the Ferns Inquiry to the Minister for Health and Children (Dublin: Irish Government Publications, October 2005).

Information on Colm O'Gorman and One in

Four provided by O'Gorman.

21. A Reckoning

Details on the death of John Paul II drawn mainly from George Weigel, *The End and the Beginning: Pope John Paul II — The Victory of Freedom, the Last Years, the Legacy* (New York: Doubleday, 2010), specifically chapter nine, "The Last Encyclical: January–April 2005."

"The Way of the Cross, the 'filth' in the Church and the 'decay' of ideologies," March 25, 2005, 3. May be viewed online at: http://www.asianews.it /news-en/The-Way-of-the-Cross,-the-'filth'-in-the-Church-and-the-'decay'-of-ideologies-2867.html.

"Catholic Church's Costs Pass $1 Billion in Abuse Cases," *New York Times,* June 12, 2005, 33.

Marni McEntee, "Supporters of outspoken Ramstein priest question reasons for removal," *Stars and Stripes,* May 9, 2004.

The book Doyle, Sipe, and Wall produced is A. W. Richard Sipe, Thomas P. Doyle & Patrick J. Wall, *Sex, Priests, and Secret Codes: The Catholic Church's 2,000-Year Paper Trail of Sexual Abuse* (Los Angeles: Volt Press, 2006).

Fitzgerald letter is referenced in Laurie Goodstein, "Early Alarm for Church on Abusers in the Clergy," *New York Times,* April 3, 2009, 16. His letters may also be viewed online at: http://www.richardsipe.com/2009-09/Father .Gerald.Fitzgerald.pdf.

William Lobdell, "Missionary's Dark Legacy," *Los Angeles Times,* November 19, 2005, 1.

Chris Knap and Rachanee Srisavasdi, "Distant sex-abuse cases get local aid," *Orange County Register,* February 27, 2005, 1.

Associated Press, "Jesuit Order Settles Suit On Sex Abuse In Alaska," *New York Times,* November 19, 2007, 18.

Report to the People of God: Clergy Sexual Abuse, Archdiocese of Los Angeles, 1930–2003; can be seen online at: www.Bishop Accountability.org/usccb/natureandscope/dioceses/reports/losangelesca-rpt.pdf

John Jay College of Criminal Justice, *The Nature and Scope of the Problem of Sexual Abuse of Minors by Catholic Priests and Deacons in the United States,* United States Conference of Catholic Bishops, Washington 2004.

"Vindicates," from "Reports On Priestly

Sexual Abuse Welcomed," *Catalyst Online,* Catholic League Web site, April 22, 2004.

Judge Owen Kwong described his work on the settlement of abuse cases in interviews with author.

Christine Hanley and Richard Winton, "Clerics Take 2 Approaches to Clergy Scandal; Religion: Orange County's Bishop Brown tackles the molestation issue from the pulpit. L.A.'s Cardinal Mahony makes no statement," *Los Angeles Times,* March 25, 2002, B1.

Larry Stammer, William Lobdell, and Jean Guccione, "A Bishop's Bold Move; Tod D. Brown's role in settling O.C. abuse cases points out his contrasts with Cardinal Mahony," *Los Angeles Times,* December 5, 2004, B1.

Jean Guccione, "Orange Bishop to Apologize in Huge Abuse Settlement; A record-setting $100-million agreement in the Catholic Church's sex scandal also will make confidential files public," *Los Angeles Times,* January 4, 2005, B1.

Portrayal of Cardinal Mahony in his deposition based on deposition transcript.

David Pierson, "Man Arrested in Protest

During Mass at Cathedral; He handcuffs himself to a chair and later says Mahony's homily 'got me all fired up,' " *Los Angeles Times,* June 27, 2005, B3.

Gillian Flaccus, "L.A. Archdiocese Agrees to $600 Million Abuse Settlement; Sources Describe Deal, the Largest In Sex Scandal," *Washington Post,* July 15, 2007, 14.

Joe Mozingo and John Spano, "$660-million settlement in priest abuses; L.A. Archdiocese's payout to 508 claimants is the largest in the sex scandal that has rocked the Catholic Church," *Los Angeles Times,* July 15, 2007, 1.

23. Don't Trust Me
Anecdotes about Anderson based on interviews.

Report informed by documents filed in *John V. Doe v. Holy See,* U.S. District Court, Portland, and interviews with Jeffrey Lena, attorney for the Vatican, and Jeffrey Anderson. See also:

- **Julie Bolcer, "Supreme Court Rejects Vatican Appeal," Advocate .com, June 29, 2010.**
- **"Vatican lawyer responds to abuse accusations," Vaticanradio.com,**

August 12, 2011.

- **Denny Walsh, "Molestation Case/ Monetary Damages Sought Vatican Can Be Sued, Panel Rules Holy See May Be Liable For Acts Of Parish Priest,"** *Sacramento Bee,* **March 4, 2009, 4.**
- **Stacy Meichtry, "The Supreme Court: Vatican Bid To Dismiss Suit On Abuse Won't Get Review,"** *Wall Street Journal,* **June 29, 2010, A5.**

For William Donohue's views on Mark Silk, Jason Berry and others, visit the Web site of the Catholic League: www.catholicleague.org.

Finances of the Catholic League reported on the basis of public filings. Comparisons to other nonprofits based on data from Guide star.org, an independent source of information on nonprofit organizations.

Correspondence and documents in the case of Nicolas Aguilar Rivera from court filings.

John Spano, "Mexico Bars Lawyer After Suit; An American who said a cardinal protected an abusive priest is escorted to an airport," *Los Angeles Times,* October 15, 2006, B5.

Doug Irving, "Judge allows suit in U.S. against Mexican priest," *Orange County Reg-*

ister, March 2, 2011.

Information on Isely and Wisconsin cases provided by Isely and from court documents. See also: Jason Berry, "Activist's challenge to archdiocese began with Weakland," *National Catholic Reporter,* January 31, 2012.

Jane Lampman, "From Sex-Abuse Scandal, Cautious Hope Of Reform," *Christian Science Monitor,* March 8, 2002, 1.

Michael Paulson, "Farragher Priest Abuse Cases Focus On Adolescents," *Boston Globe,* March 17, 2002, 1.

Elizabeth Fernandez, "Men Blame Shattered Lives On Abuse In Youth By Priests/Victims Carry Burden Of Guilt, Betrayal," *San Francisco Chronicle,* April 16, 2002, 1.

John Keilman And Monica Davey, "Milwaukee Sets Archbishop Probe; Payoff To Accuser Under Scrutiny," *Chicago Tribune,* May 25, 2002, 1.

Richard Vara and Cynthia Lee, "Victims, Activists Criticize Policy On Abusive Priests," *Houston Chronicle,* November 11, 2002, 13.

Annie Correal, "Protesters Say Archbishop Mishandled Abuse Scandal," *New York Times,*

March 6, 2009, 22.

Nicole Winfield, "Vatican Defends Role In Wis. Abuse Case: Calls Criticism Of Decisions A Bid To Smear The Pope," *Boston Globe,* March 26, 2010, 10.

Laurie Goodstein and David Callender, "For Half a Century, Deaf Boys Raised Alarm on Priest's Abuse," *New York Times,* March 27, 2010, 1.

Laurie Goodstein, "Vatican Declined to Defrock U.S. Priest Who Abused Deaf Boys," *New York Times,* March 25, 2010, 1.

24. A Rolling Catastrophe

Jason Berry's experience with his daughter's death reported on the basis of interviews.

The Report of the Commission to Inquire into Child Abuse, Department of Health and Children, Dublin, May 2009.

For *The Irish Times* on Ryan Report: "The Savage Reality Of Our Darkest Days," *Irish Times,* May 5, 2009.

Nick Squires, "Pope Benedict scolds Ireland's bishops over sex abuse scandal," *Christian Science Monitor,* February 16, 2010, 14.

Elisabetta Povoledo and Alan Cowell, "Pope

Urges Irish Bishops To Confront Sex Abuse," *New York Times*, February 16, 2010, 7.

Gaia Pianigiani, "The Vatican: Pope Accepts Resignation of Irish Bishops," *New York Times*, May 6, 2010, 8.

Story of Terrance Kohut based on court filings. See also: Michael Stone, "Terry Kohut names Pope Benedict XVI in child sexual abuse lawsuit," Examiner.com, September 24, 2010.

Bill Hutchinson, "Abuse victim suing Pope Benedict, alleges cover-up in mid-1990s," New York *Daily News*, April 13, 2011.

Bill Hewitt, "Serving Rome: Lawyer Jeffrey Anderson Takes His Case to the Top, Suing the Vatican for Not Removing Predator Priests," *People*, April 22, 2002.

Erika Slife, "Chicago SNAP activists head to Europe to help priest sex abuse victims," *Chicago Tribune*, March 22, 2010. http://articles.chicagotribune.com/2010-03-22/news/ct-met-snap-europe-20100322_1_survivors-network-sexual-abuse-abuse-victims

For Jose Saraiva Martins's dirty laundry, see:

- **Philip Pullella, "Vatican says media**

in 'ignoble attempt' to smear pope," Reuters, March 25, 2010. http://www.reuters.com/article/2010/03/25/us-pope-abuse-idUS-TRE62O2X42010 0325

- **Rachel Donadio, "Don't blame pope, Vatican says; 'No knowledge' of pedophile's reassignment," _Boston Globe_, March 27, 2010, 4.**

Daniel J. Wakin and Rachel Donadio, "Vatican Priest Likens Criticism Over Abuse to Anti-Semitism," _New York Times_, April 3, 2010, 1.

Peggy Noonan, "Declarations: The Catholic Church's Catastrophe," _Wall Street Journal_, April 2, 2010, 13.

Jeffrey Lena's background from interview. See also: Jason Horowitz, "At Cross-Purposes; Jeffrey Lena: Sole practitioner in California is the voice of the Vatican in U.S. courts," _Washington Post_, April 19, 2010, C1.

Anderson and Lena's meeting with Kagan based on their recollections. Mosi Secret, "New York Archbishop May Face Deposition on Milwaukee Funds," _New York Times_, February 13, 2011, 23.

Stephen Castle and Nicholas Kulish, "Belgian

Police Raid Offices Of Church In Abuse Case," *New York Times,* June 25, 2010, 6.

Stacy Meichtry, "Vatican Criticizes Belgian Officials for Raid; Police Investigating Sex-Abuse Claims Question Top Bishops, Look Into Tombs," *Wall Street Journal,* June 26, 2010, 10.

Sarah Lyall, "Irish Rupture With Vatican Sets Off a Transformation," *New York Times,* September 17, 2011, 8.

Rachel Donadio, "Vatican recalls its envoy to Ireland over abuse report; Holy See plans a response amid firestorm," *Houston Chronicle,* July 26, 2011, 6.

David Zucchino, "Catholic official found guilty in child sex-abuse cover-up; Msgr. William J. Lynn of Philadelphia was accused of reassigning pedophile priests," *Los Angeles Times,* June 23, 2012, 4.

The documents filed in victim's charge of crimes against humanity against the Vatican at the International Criminal Court are available at CCRJustice.org. See also: Laurie Goodstein, "Abuse Victims Ask Court To Prosecute the Vatican," *New York Times,* September 14, 2011, 15.

Megan Peterson's case reported on the basis

of interviews and her complaint.

Mitchell Landsberg, "Society is blamed for priest sex abuse," *Los Angeles Times,* May 19, 2011, 10.

Laurie Goodstein, "Church Abuse Report Authors Defend Findings as Critics Weigh In," *New York Times,* May 19, 2011, 19.

Lisa Wangsness, "Authors defend report on clergy abuse," *Boston Globe,* May 19, 2011, 1.

Andy Newman, "Retired Cardinal Regrets '02 Apology on Abuse Cases," *New York Times,* February 8, 2012, 22.

Tim Townsend, "Group seeks to block clergy abuse order; Attorneys for victims say subpoena involving Kansas City priest could lead to disclosure of confidential information," *St. Louis Post-Dispatch,* December 31, 2011, 3.

Tim Townsend, "SNAP officials get subpoenas; They accuse Catholic officials of trying to hinder their efforts for abused," *St. Louis Post-Dispatch,* January 6, 2012, 2.

Jeffrey M. Jones, "Atheists, Muslims See Most Bias as Presidential Candidates; Two-thirds would vote for gay or lesbian," Gallup .com, June 21, 2012.

ABOUT THE AUTHOR

As part of a team of journalists from *Newsday*, **Michael D'Antonio** won the Pulitzer Prize for his reporting before writing many acclaimed books, including *Atomic Harvest* and *The State Boys Rebellion.* He has also written for *Esquire, The New York Times Magazine,* and *Sports Illustrated.*